The Construction Industry Handbook

The Construction Industry Handbook

SECOND EDITION

EDITED BY

R. A. Burgess, BArch ARIBA FIOB FIWSP
Professor of Construction, University of Salford

K. S. M. Crabtree
Information Officer, Department of Building, University of Manchester Institute of Science and Technology

P. J. Horrobin, MA ARIC
Visiting Lecturer, Department of Building, University of Manchester Institute of Science and Technology

Norman McKee, MIOB AInstInfSc
Honorary Secretary, North-West Building Productivity Committee

J. W. Simpson, BSc MSc MInstP
Senior Lecturer in Building, University of Manchester Institute of Science and Technology

Cahners Books division of Cahners Publishing Company, Inc.
89 Franklin Street, Boston, Massachussetts 02110

DEDICATION

To Ray Slater, who through a lifetime of service to the construction industry has inspired so much that is of lasting value. His dedicated work, both as a building scientist and a teacher, has been an example to all who have had the privilege of learning from him. This volume and all those published by MTP Construction owe much to the example he gave to one of his students.

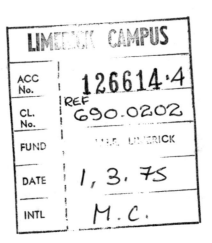
Copyright © 1973 by MTP

Published in Britain by MTP
Medical and Technical Publishing Company Limited

ISBN   0-8436-0119-1

Printed in Great Britain

Editorial

In the preface to the first edition of The Construction Industry Handbook, we commented that "We are conscious of breaking entirely new ground and we will welcome criticisms and suggestions as to how future editions may be improved." The fact that the first edition was entirely sold out within a comparatively short period of time and it also achieved a wide distribution throughout the world is some indication of the way that our aims for that edition were satisfactorily realised.

We did, however, welcome and appreciate the constructive and helpful suggestions that were offered by both correspondents and reviewers and we have endeavoured to follow their advice wherever appropriate. For example, as a result of one review, the Recent Developments and Reviews Sections have now been amalgamated in a much smaller section concentrating on a few subjects of major importance. In contrast, the information sections of the Handbook which were uniformly welcomed have been both extended and completely revised. In particular the Properties of Building Materials has been totally rewritten so as to match the new Master List for Materials issued by the CIB and the list of useful addresses has been greatly enlarged into a major new section entitled 'Information Sources in the Construction Industry.

Perhaps the most important changes in the structure of the Handbook are the inclusion of two completely new sections. The first, Building in the EEC reflects the urgent need to find out more about the construction industry in our neighbouring Common Market countries and the second provides a thorough and detailed analysis of our own construction industry. This new volume, therefore, is more than just a revision of the old and we trust that, like the first edition, it will find its way into all sectors of the industry as one of the key reference sources for members of all the construction professions.

Although the editors are no longer all members of the Department of Building of the University of Manchester Institute of Science and Technology, it is our pleasure to acknowledge all the help and co-operation that our colleagues and former colleagues in that Department have so willingly offered. We are grateful to them.

R.A. Burgess
K.S.M. Crabtree
P.J. Horrobin
Norman McKee
J.W. Simpson
June 1973

Contents

Part 1

Building in the EEC

Building in the EEC   1

Introduction   3
Belgium   5
France   15
West Germany   25
Italy   34
Netherlands   44
Conclusions   51
Bibliography   55

Analysis of the Construction Industry   61

P.J. Reynolds, BSc and P. Hesketh, BA,
*Department of Building, University of Manchester Institute
of Science and Technology*

Introduction   63
Review of the Industry   66
The Construction Industry and Quoted Companies   77
Quoted Company Accounts   81
Analysis of Company Accounts   94
Summary and Conclusions   100
Appendices
1. Construction Firms by Trade in 1970   105
2. Supplementary List of Quoted Companies with
   Substantial Construction Industry Interests   105

3. Companies Classifiable to Construction (SIC Definition) - Turnover and Average Number Employed   107

4. Construction Companies Ranked with respect to Turnover   112

5. Construction Companies chosen for more detailed Analysis of their Accounts   116

6. Construction Company Balance Sheets   117

7. Net Current Assets   120

8. Profit and Loss Accounts   123

9. Cash Flows   128

10. Liquidity Schedule   129

11. Fixed Asset Schedule   131

12. Tax Schedule   133

13. Financial Ratios   135

14. Balance Sheet Items as % of Capital Employed   136

15. Profit and Loss Gearing   138

16. Financial Gearing   139

17. 'Productivity' per Employee   140

18. Pre-Interest Margin   142

19. Capital Utilisation   144

Reviews and Developments

147

Development of the Industry   149
Norman McKee, MIOB, AInstInfSoc.

Smoke Control in Buildings   161
Eric W. Marchant, DipArch.(Nott'm), DBS
(L'pool), M.Arch.(L'pool), RIBA, ARIAS, MIFireE.

Building Measurement   189
W.M. Laing, FIOB

Clay Products   209
H.W.H. West, BSc, FGS, FICeram
*Head of the Heavy Clay Division and Officer-in-Charge of
the Mellor-Green Laboratories, British Ceramic Research Station*

Surveying   203
J.R. Smith, ARICS

Timber   207
P.R. Harman
Timber Research and Development Association

Part 2

The Metric System 217

SI Conversions 218

Properties of Building Materials

223

compiled by
H.J. Eldridge

*British Member of the CIB Commission on Properties of Building Materials.
British Member of the CIB Commission on Performance Concepts. Consultant
to the Building Research Station. Consultant to the Agrement Board.
Formerly Chief Experimental Officer, the Building Research Station.*

Introduction 225

The CIB Master List of Properties 233

Asbestos cement sheets 246

Asbestos insulating board 248

Asphalt 250

Bitumen felt 252

Blocks, concrete 254

Bricks, clay 258

Bricks, concrete 262

Bricks, flintlime 264

Bricks, sandlime 266

Cement, high alumina 268

Cement, portland 270

Fibre building boards 274

Floor finishes 276

Glass sheet 288

Limes 290

Metal, aluminium sheet 292

Metal, copper sheet 294

Metal, lead 296

Metal, stainless steel 298

Metal, steel sheet 300

Metal, zinc sheet 302

Plaster, gypsum 304

Plasterboard, gypsum 306

Plasterboard, cellular sheets, boards and slabs 308

Contents

Plastics, glass fibre reinforced sheets 314

Plastics, PVC sheet 316

Sealants 318

Stone, natural 320

Tile, clay roof 324

Tile, concrete roof 326

Timbers, hardwood 328

Timbers, resin-bonded wood chipboard 334

Timbers, softwood 336

Environmental Design Data

341

LIGHTING 343

Table 1 Colour properties of lamps for general lighting 344

Table 2 Recommended daylight factors 347

Table 3 Conversion of scalar illuminance to illuminance on horizontal plane for interior with light ceilings and walls 351

General Lighting Schedule 352

Table 4 Utilization factors 383

Table 5 Tabulated Lamp Data 391

HEATING

Table 1 Indoor service temperatures 395

Table 2 Typical values of thermal conductivity for building materials 396

Table 3 Outside surface resistance (R_{SO}) for 'sheltered', 'normal' (standard) and 'severe' exposures 399

Table 4 Inside surface resistance (Rsi) 399

Table 5 Standard thermal resistance of ventilated airspaces 400

Table 6 Standard thermal resistance of unventilated airspaces 400

Table 7 U values for external walls 401

Table 8 U values for roofs 402

Table 9 U values for typical windows 403

Table 10 U values for solid floors in contact with the earth with four exposed edges 403

Table 11 U values for solid floors in contact with the earth having two exposed edges at right angles 404

Table 12 Corrections to Tables 10 and 11 for edge insulated floors 404

Table 13   U values for suspended timber floors directly
                above ground   405

Table 14   U values for intermediate floors   405

SOUND INSULATION AND ACOUSTICS

Table 1   Single and double windows   407

Table 2   Partitions of single sheets or slabs   408

Table 3   Stud-framed partitions   409

Table 4   Single-leaf walls or partitions   409

Table 5   Double-leaf walls or partitions   410

Table 6   Concrete floors   411

Table 7   Wood joist floors   412

Table 8   Sound absorption coefficients   414

Information Sources in the Construction Industry

417

compiled by
Shirley Crabtree

Organisations in the United Kingdom   419

International Organisations   454

Index   459

Part 1

Building in the EEC

Analysis of the
Construction Industry

Reviews and
Developments

Building in the EEC

Now that the UK has become a full
member of the European Economic
Community the implications to the
construction industry have become a
matter of the utmost urgency. This
detailed analysis of each of our
neighbouring EEC members and their
respective construction industries
provides the background needed to
understand the problems and
opportunities presented by this vast
new market.

Introduction

This comprehensive review of Building in the EEC was undertaken by the Building Group of the City of Westminster Chamber of Commerce and we would like to thank them for their co-operation in allowing us to publish their report in this volume. The report was edited by Keith Grant and a full list of all the contributions is to be found on page 59.

The accession of the United Kingdom to the Treaty of Rome and thus to membership of the European Economic Community, is an event which has been accompanied by a crescendo of activity not only in the political sphere but also in the economic. Whatever may be the division of viewpoint in the country generally, there seems little doubt that industry and commerce whole-heartedly welcomes entry as affording a unique opportunity for the expansion of trade. Some of the evidence of this enthusiasm may be found in the number of conferences and missions which are currently being sponsored to study the problems and opportunities associated with entry.

Aims

The Building Group of the City of Westminster Chamber of Commerce decided in 1971 to promote a fact-finding mission to provide information to members and others on the prospects which face the British building industry. This decision was taken in the full knowledge that a certain amount of information was already available, and that further data would be forthcoming as time went by.

The Chamber mission was given the brief of examining and comparing conditions in the industries of the various EEC countries, of establishing the progress made in co-ordinating building regulations and practice between member states, of ascertaining the extent to which the general optimism surrounding Britain's entry was justified in the building industry, and finally of producing a report collating this information.

Methods

A lengthy questionnaire was drawn up, which aimed at obtaining factual information from all sections of the industry. These questions form the basis of each nation report. In addition, it was agreed that the mission should specifically try to obtain views on the effect that a number of years of national membership of the EEC had had on individual firms, and whether it was considered that Britain's entry would have any material influence on the building industry in the countries visited.

All questions were directed at people and firms within the EEC industry, and the answers received thus represent a first-hand account of existing conditions. The resulting report is not the final word on the EEC building industry - it is hoped rather that the broad picture provided will be of guidance to those considering investing time and money in the enlarged EEG.

The mission itself was sub-divided into four groups, each of which assigned a centre of investigation - Paris, Brussels, Dusseldorf and Milan. Some members of the Brussels Group diverted for 2 days to Amsterdam - the Netherlands report is accordingly shorter than the others. Each group consisted of a representative cross-section of the UK building industry which met and obtained views from its counterparts in the EEC during the period of 16th - 22nd April 1972. People and organisations met included:

Government departments	Architects
Chambers of Commerce	Engineers
Local authorities	Developers
Housing associations	Contractors

The following pages, containing the collective findings and conclusions of the mission, are the results of the members efforts.

Acknowledgement

It is evident that a complex operation such as that described can only be successful if supported by devoted and enthusiastic efforts by a number of people.

The Building Group Committee is happy to acknowledge with gratitude the assistance of the following:

Staff of the British Embassies in Brussels, Paris and Bonn

Staff of the British Consulates in Dusseldorf and Milan

Officials of EEC headquarters, Brussels

All Groups received a warm reception wherever they went and the Building Group Committee wish to place on record their deep appreciation of the assistance given to the Mission by so many diverse firms, official bodies and individuals in Europe.

Coverage in the professions and trades section was governed by the membership of each Group. Not all the Groups contained the full complement of professions, and one or two sections are accordingly not included.

Finally, the success of the Mission as a whole depended to a great extent on the enthusiasm of those participating. The Building Group Committee thanks all those members who took part for those efforts cheerfully given which played an essential part in what we hope is a worthwhile and useful result.

Belgium

Population: 9.7M Area: 12 000 sq. miles Capital: Brussels - 1M Chief cities: Antwerp - 675 000 Liège - 450 000 Ghent - 230 000 GNP: £11 000M Employment: 3.7M Cost of living index: 121.9 (1966 = 100)

INTRODUCTION

Belgium smallest of the EEC member countries apart from Luxembourg, has limited natural resources and relies heavily on small industry and export. The overall economy has been plagued by an extreme nationalities problem - 55% of the total population are Flemish Roman Catholics living in the prosperous north, while 33% are French-speaking Walloons in the comparatively depressed south. The great post-war industrial boom in the north, now reaching saturation point, left the south sorely lacking in investment, and nursing a grievance.

The government has recognised this but its regional aid programme, approved by the legislature in 1970, has unfortunately also foundered against the nationalities problem. To appear impartial, aid was to be distributed evenly throughout the country, but in April 1972 the EEC Commission decided that the programme was non-selective and that it should be re-allocated to the 28 most depressed of the country's 44 arrondissements.

However, Belgium has the invaluable advantage of good communications with the rest of Europe, and has been used by many countries as a commercial launching pad for EEC markets. Communications will be considerably improved by a network of motorways linking Ostend and Frankfurt through Brussels and Liège, and the Autoroute de Wallonie connecting Liège, Namur, Charleroi and Mons, all due for completion in 1973.

The national rate of growth is currently 3.9%, while the cost of living is increasing by 2 - 3%. A total of 414 000Mf was exported to the EEC in 1971 - a rise of around 18% from 1969. The building industry is at present passing through a slack period, but may well pick up with the increase in industrial investment, not only in the Golden Triangle of Brussels Antwerp and Liège, but also, after the 1970 economic expansion Act, in the hitherto less prosperous regions of the south.

THE PLANNING PROCESS

1. Political structure

The central government, a constitutional monarchy, consists of a two-chamber legislature - Senate and Chamber of Deputies - based in Brussels, with executive power vested in the Cabinet.

Belgium is divided into 9 provinces, and Brussels is split into 19 separate and autonomous planning units - called villes.

The government is empowered to make extensive regional plans, and collaborates with groups of municipalities to formulate sector plans. Each municipality in turn then makes detailed development plans for its own area.

2. Tax and sources of government finance

Corporation tax is levied at 47%. VAT has been operating for two years, but does not appear to have increased the cost of living. Selected rates are:

6% food and essentials
14% building
18% town planning

For building projects VAT is added to the fee account and paid by client and architect.

A major source of finance for the provinces is obtained from real estate income tax, levied by the central government and returned in major part to the provinces, for frequent use in local authority schemes.

Where a development project is of national interest, the central government would oversee it, with the Ministry of Works carrying out the development. If it is of regional importance only, the government would participate to a financial maximum of 60%.

3. Building laws and regulations

These operate basically as in the U.K, though there is a special regulation applying to the World Trade Development Area in Brussels. The regulations are administered by each individual local authority, and no agreement has been achieved over standardisation throughout the country. However, the Group was informed that a draft set of standard bye-laws was being considered this August.

The local authority administers building control, but does not assume any responsibility for defects. Under the Civil Code, the architect and builder are jointly responsible, and the law also requires the project to be certified by a registered architect.

Article 1792 of the Code requires constructors - architect and builder - to undertake a 10 year liability - dècannalle responsabilité. This covers any defects in the structure, even when due to faults in the subsoil. However, article 2270 which discharges the constructors after the 10 year period refers to liability for major works. This has not been defined by legislation and remains open to interpretation in law.

Consulting engineers and design bureaux carrying out architectural functions also qualify for the dècennalle responsabilité when linked directly to the client by contractual relationship. Otherwise they are subject to general third-party liability for accidents caused by themselves or by persons or equipment for which they have responsibility.

A few Belgian companies grant insurance for professional indemnity for architects and consulting engineers on third-party and 10 year liability. An annual premium is calculated on a basis of fees and specialities of the insured party, as well as the required amount of guarantees.

A policy is granted subject to control of the building works exercised by an independent firm, and covers defects during and after completion of the works. An all-risks on worksite policy is also available and includes cover for a maintenance period of two years after completion of the works.

4. Building approval	All development plans must be prepared by a registered architect. No structural calculations are required, though general details of drainage must be indicated. Signed by the client and architect, plans are submitted to the local or provincial authority.

For larger scale projects, development plans go before a College of Elders before submission to the Provincial Council. There may then be a public inquiry, the results of which are considered by a consultative commission before the plans are returned to the municipality for final approval. Permit fees are charged and these vary between authorities.

DEVELOPMENT, INVESTMENT AND FINANCE

5. Land tenure and development

The municipalities are empowered by Royal Decree to acquire large areas of land, which are at present being made available for leases of 27, 49 and 99 years.

The City of Brussels appears to have wide powers of compulsory purchase. There is no overall development plan and land is readily made available to developers. Demolition can begin as soon as 6 months after, and even the value of the land is often argued after construction has commenced.

6. Housing

Belgium is one of the few West European countries without a housing problem. There is currently a surplus - 400 000 units a year are constructed, mainly for owner-occupation.

7. Investment

Major commercial development is carried out for investment, outright disposal and owner-occupier. Nearly 20 UK developers are already operating in Brussels, but speculative development is realtively uncommon because most industrial property is owner occupied. However lease-hold occupation is now becoming common in industrial and commercial building. Office buildings are often let to one tenant on a floor by floor basis. Tenancy agreements are of 3, 6 or 9 years duration.

8. Finance

The government is prepared to participate financially in development schemes through the National Investment Corporation. A number of incentives are provided for the establishment of industry in depressed regions:

5% rebate on loan interest

tax incentives

grants based on 50% of fixed assets

Normally finance is available from banks and insurance companies. The length of loan available on the leaseback system is 50 - 75 years. In Brussels 20 - 27 year mortgage loans are available at around 7.75% interest, with a return of 10% when the property is let.

9. Average costs per m²

Municipal housing	10 000 - 11 000F
Private housing	15 000F
Offices: with a/c	13 000F
4 star with a/c	12 000F
2 star no a/c	9 500F
Factories	3 500F
Hotels	800 000F per room

PROFESSIONS AND TRADES

10. Division of work

The titles of both architect and engineer are protected by law. The former retains pole position in the design process, being obliged to sign drawings before building approval is given. There is no quantity surveying profession as is known in the UK, and specifications are prepared by the architect. Package deals are common, provided either by a contractor or by a technical bureau. The latter, which may be a limited company, provides the client with a package consultancy plus a fixed price contract.

11. Contract procedure

There is no one standard form of contract, though most contracts follow the standard conditions either of the Federation of Societies of Belgian Architects or of the Cahier de Charges de l'Etat. Government departments use Ministry of Works contracts. Standard escalation clauses are generally accepted.

12. Establishing a practice

It is only necessary to obtain a professional card to set up office in Belgium, but all drawings must be signed by a Belgian architect. Otherwise, there is no legal or taxation obstacles, though work permits are required for payroll staff.

Opportunities for collaboration with Belgian firms exist, and French, Dutch, German and UK firms have already done so.

Architect

Belgian architects are all university trained - the first two years are spent in general groundwork, the final two in specialisation. To establish a practice, they must be resident in a particular area and registered with the Order of Architects. UK architects can apply for registration, but the process may take 2 or 3 years. The Order is a statutory body, with an elected architect as president. There is also a Federation des Architectes Belges - FAB.

As well as preparing all drawings, the architects prepare specifications and schedules of quantities, and agree final accounts. They are responsible for a 10 year guarantee, but are not obliged to insure. They may not form limited companies.

Fee scales are laid down by the Order of Architects, on a sliding scale as in UK. VAT is added to the fee account and paid by the client and architect. Sums paid to the Tax Authority are based on monthly accounts, which are adjusted every 3 months.

A draughtsman may earn 127F per hour plus social security grossing 161F. Overtime is paid at 50% for the first 2 hours, then at 100% including week-end work.

The present practice in Belgium that architects must sign drawings means that it is not possible for a UK architect to set up an independent practice. It is therefore advisable to go in for joint ventures as a prelude to permanent partnership if project opportunities remain fruitful.

Consulting Engineer

The title is protected by law and may only be used by persons with the necessary university qualifications. The term Ingénieur Civil is used to denote a qualified engineer in any, or all of the engineering disciplines. Thus an

Ingénieur-Conseil in Belgium is usually an Ingénieur Civil, even if his field is mechanical or electrical work.

The official body for consulting engineers, represented on the Fédération Internationale des Ingénieurs-Conseils is La Chambre des Ingénieurs-Conseils de Belgique - CICB. The Chambre works from a modest budget of $10 000, and has a membership of 125 individuals from 144 consulting firms, forming a total of 250 employees. These firms divide themselves into 75 civil engineering, 14 mechanical and electrical, and 25 other specialisations.

There are 4 types of percentage fee, but fees may also, when the work can be defined accurately, be based on a previously agreed lump sum, which can be varied in proportion to the general price index. The lump sum system appears to be the most favoured. New fee scales are at present being negotiated with the Government.

Under the Civil Code, engineers are responsible for a 10 year liability for major defects. Though not obligatory, most insure against this, often with UK underwriters.

Consulting engineers may operate as limited liability companies. Usually a Société de Personnes à Responsabilité Limitée - SPRL - is formed, though some of the large firms operate as Societes Anonymes. Some of these larger firms are said to be influenced or even controlled by commercial interests, and their professional impartiality may be open to doubt.

In Belgium as in UK the consultant may be anything from a one-man firm to a large organisation with a staff of many hundreds. They operate either as independent advisors, employed directly by a client, or in collaboration with an architect or other professional. Large firms acting as project leaders include architects on their staff to conform with the Belgian law which requires an architect to be employed on all building work.

Some of the larger Bureaux d'Etudes carry out consulting engineering work, an extension of the purely detailing functions of other Bureaux common in France and also found in Belgium.

Generally, the consulting engineer as an independent professional does not seem to have developed to the extent of his UK counterpart. This may be because of a marked reluctance on the part of Belgian clients to employ professional experts. Their opinion appears to be that the architect should be able to carry out all design, and the employment of other specialists merely adds to the cost. This attidue is showing signs of change with the growing number of foreign developers coming to Belgium.

Quantity Surveyor

Future prospects for the establishment of the independent quantity surveyor in Belgium are slim. There are a limited number of UK firms successfully established, mainly in Brussels, for a number of years. Most of their work, however, is carried out for UK clients - either architects, developers, or industrialists. Belgian surveyors do exist - geometrearpenteurs - but they are usually merely technicians in architects' offices.

Where Belgian architects have worked with UK quantity surveyors they have apparently been impressed with their expertise and have often advised clients to employ a surveyor in future - unfortunately mostly without success.

The function and the benefits of this profession are little understood by the reluctant foreign client. He finds it difficult to accept that he must pay additional fees for a service which is at present being provided by the architect, at no additional cost.

Major building contractors are aware of the services available, but are unconvinced of the benefits of including a quantity surveyor in the building team, largely stemming from a lack of confidence in independent professionals.

When asked to submit a tender based on bills of quantities prepared by the architect, they frequently re-measure the work from the drawings and in effect prepare their own independent bill, basing their tender figure on this document.

It is doubtful if entry of the UK into the Common Market will enhance prospects for the quantity surveyor in Belgium. In the long term, prospects are perhaps not quite so bleak. An intensive programme of educating and informing overseas clients, performed by the professional bodies and individual practices, may convince them of the services and benefits of using independent quantity surveyors.

Developer

A superficial look at Belgium and Brussels in particular might lead the UK developer to the opinion that this is the place to commence continental operations, with the relative simplicity of corporate finance, favourable taxation and planning procedure. However, this lack of obstacles has led to virtual saturation in Brussels and Antwerp in both office and shop development, and accordingly rentals are low when compared to the high quality of buildings under construction.

First class hotels are plentiful and the motel business is now rapidly expanding, though there appears to be divergence of opinion over what the latter should offer. The optimum looks to be units of 100 beds with 4 star restaurant, heated pools, saunas, coupled with conference hall facilities.

In the industrial sector the government as in UK provides grants for schemes in new development areas. The grant is paid directly to the company to occupy the building, and the location of these areas makes the hazards of normal speculation even greater.

In Brussels most industrial development is taking place near the airport with US, German, and UK manufacturers occupying the choice positions. The Belgian equivalent of the UK Town and Country Planning Act is still in embryo stage and so land for building is not difficult to obtain. So far only ribbon development along the main highway to the Brussels airport has taken place.

Undoubtedly in industrial warehouse development UK expertise in estate layout is currently lacking, and though there is no obvious demand for units there is every indication that further expansion will take place, stemming mainly from UK entry to the Common Market, and the movement of German firms from their homeland where labour and handling costs are rising unabated.

Residential development is something of an enigma for house prices are high in the Brussels area, and there is every indication of a shortage yet it is difficult to find any encouraging signs that such development is profitable, and in fact some of the biggest casualties in the construction industry have come in this field.

The Belgians are demanding in their standards of housing yet they do not enjoy as favourable mortgage facilities as in UK, and the developer has to be financially sound to finance the scheme as well as possibly assisting in the monetary side of its disposal.

The Brussels market is certainly ripe for a modern version of Dolphin Square, and as the city enjoys such an excellent network of roads, the suburbs look ready for expansion. Any venture would require extensive market research and the watchword must be "tread warily".

Success is possible in Belgium for the UK developer, but quick and easy killings are not, for the population is small, relatively static and inward looking. However, the country enjoys excellent communication with its EEC neighbours.

Contractor

All building contractos belong to a confederation of 16 national federations looking after the various interests of construction disciplines - general contractors, road contractors, plumbers. A levy of about 0.2% is made on each contractor.

The vast majority of contractor organisations are small and privately owned - 85% employ less than 30 men. All contractors are classified by their turnover capacities and their specialities, and must obtain a renewable licence permitting them to tender for certain classes of work. There are 8 such categories of contractor.

Most work is obtained on a competitive basis. It is normal practice for the main contractor to appoint his own sub-contractor, but nominated sub-contractors are looked upon with disfavour by main contractors. Sub-contractors for heating and ventilating, air conditioning or plumbing are frequently Italian. Generally, there seems to be a reluctance amongst Belgian contractors to permit the use of specialist engineers.

The principle of plant hire does not seem to have caught on in Belgium. This industry might well develop when the EEC construction industry is more operative.

Belgian contractors have extremely good relations with the unions, of which there are 3 - Catholic, Socialist and Liberal - claiming 90% of the work force. The only national strikes in the industry since the war were in 1957 and 1968. Wage agreements are negotiated by a joint committee of the unions and the confederation. They are of 2 year duration, incorporating automatic escalation clauses based on the government index. They also include bad weather and sickness pay, pensions, and 4 weeks leave. Although basic wages - 87F per hour - are about the same level as in the UK, fringe benefits such as social security add up to 80% to the contractor's wage bill. Due perhaps to the limited number of trade unions, there appear to be no demarcation disputes, and little militancy.

Since 1965 the confederation has insisted on training young workers to attract more to the contracting industry. This training scheme is directed in conjunction with the unions, and is jointly funded. Foreign labour in Belgium has come from Spain, Portugal, Greece, Turkey and Eastern Europe, though in proportionately fewer numbers than are accepted in other EEC countries.

There has been a tendency for some contractors to form ad hoc partnerships with foreign firms for work abroad, but not to any great extent. All EEC construction firms are theoretically able to compete for overseas work through the European Development Fund, though there is some scepticism in Belgium as to the possibility of penetrating this market. Equally, the Belgian contracting market is difficult to penetrate due to the authorised lists of approved contractors which could be used discriminatorily against foreign companies.

CONCLUSIONS AND SUMMARY

The Brussels Group found that Belgian construction as a whole has only benefited from membership of the EEC from effectively providing the Capital of the Communicty and attracting foreign investment for property development, and also for the construction of industrial plants in the Golden Triangle.

The export of construction materials has been aided by EEC membership through the elimination of tariff barriers. Steel production is high, and heating, sanitary, and aluminium products are strong exports. 75% of Belgian flat glass is exported, of which 40% goes to the EEC markets.

In Belgium the university degree is accepted as the main criterion for professional competence. The architect and engineer are protected professions, but the relevant institutions do not generally have the same authority and standing as those in the UK.

Professional practices hoping to set up in Belgium in the future would be advised to form partnerships with local firms. This is largely because of the rule that national architects must sign all drawings before approval is granted for construction. British architects are thus debarred from setting up in totally independent practice under present procedures.

Responsibilities of professional and construction firms are the same in Belgium as in France, governed by the Napoleonic Code with its 10 year liability.

The Group felt that construction companies as well as professional firms should form consortia or partnerships with Belgian companies when commencing operations in Belgium. Where British companies have attempted to operate on their own, they have not generally been successful.

Very detailed discussions were conducted on value added tax with construction companies, who were generally very happy with its operation so far. At the time of its introduction in 1971 there was a moratorium of three months on accounts which contributed to smoothing its passage.

The Community has not had the expected effect of speeding the rationalisation of regulations and procedures. Such regulations as do exist in Belgium are modest compared with those in the UK, yet are confused due to a lack of common standard. The only regulation to have been tightened up in the last few years has been that controlling fire precautions, following a recent bad fire in Brussels. British insurance companies have a very strong influence on fire regulations because Belgian cover is often taken in the UK. The municipality of Brussels has its own regulations which are more stringent than the rest of the country.

The decline of the great coal mining industry has contributed to present generous government incentives for foreign investment, especially in development areas. Development in Brussels, particularly office building, is fast reaching saturation point. Developers are literally queuing up for much prized sites on Avenue des Arts and Avenue Louise and the extent of the incentives leaves less and less margin for profit. Yet the location of the EEC capital with its excellent communications to the rest of Europe continues to tempt foreign investors. Hypermarket development however, has temporarily reached an impasse with all permits stopped, because the authorities are not satisfied with present standards.

Development is now picking up in Wallonia with heavy industry along the canals, and lighter enterprises by the new motorways. Local industrial estates have been opened and thousands of new jobs have been created. The Ministry of Economic Affairs estimates that Liege was second only to Antwerp in the amount of industrial investment it attracted in 1971.

The construction industry could clearly benefit from an upsurge of industrial investment in which UK developers and building teams could participate. The Belgians met by the Group were without exception devoted Europeans, and very anxious that the UK should join the Community.

In fact, the Group found that many people with whom it had meetings had seen a considerable number of people from the UK over the past 12 months, and were beginning to wonder when the talking was going to stop, and action was going to take place.

BIBLIOGRAPHY AND REFERENCES

Available from the City of Westminster Chamber of Commerce

1. **Brussels office survey 1971** - report on changes in office accommodation over past few years and future trends. Jones Lang Wootton SA.

2. **Marq & Roba** - booklet on firm of heating and ventilating consulting engineers. 219-221, Boulevard Leopold II, Bruxelles 8.

3. **Promotion of foreign investments in Belgium** - booklet explaining provisions on investment following law on economic expansion 1970. Ministry of Economic Affairs.

4. **Régions de reconversion et de développement économiques** - map of redevelopment areas. L'Administration de l'Urbanisme et de l'Aménagement du Territoire.

Publications

5. **Belgium** - *Times* special report. May 31 1972.

6. **List of specifications and codes for exporters of building materials and components to Belgium** - Technical digest 2507B series 1 issue 1. Technical Help to Exporters.

7. **Je fais bâtir** - paperback with legal information on housebuilding in Belgium as well as France. L. Charles. Diffedit, Paris. 1967.

8. **Hints to businessmen - Belgium** - Department of Trade and Industry. 1971.

Regular Publications

9. **Centre Scientifique et Technique de la Construction, Revue Mensuelle** - journal of Construction Centre. Monthly.

10. **A-Z Immobilier et Commercial Bureau Gerard SPRL** - real estate advertising. Rue d'Arenburg 44   1000 Bruxelles.

11. **Technique des travaux**. 196 rue Grétry, Liège. Twice yearly.

Addresses

12. **British Embassy,** Britannia House, rue Joseph, 11 28 B-1040 Brussels.

13. **British Chamber of Commerce in Belgium,** Britannia House, 30 rue Joseph 11 28, Brussels 4.

14. **Ministry of Economic Affairs, foreign investment service.** Square de Meeus 23, 1040 Bruxelles. Tel: 126 690.

15. **Société Nationale d'Investissement, SNI** - National Investment Corporation. 30, Boulevard du Régent, 1000 Bruxelles.

16. **Fédération Royales des Sociétés d'Architectes de Belgique** - FAB. Rue Ernest Allard 21, 1000 Bruxelles.

17. **Ordre des Architectes.** Rue de Livourne 160, 1050 Bruxelles.

18. **Société Centrale d'Architecture de Belgique** - SCAB. Rue Ravenstein 3, 1000 Bruxelles.

19. **Fédération des Géomètres-Experts Indépendents** - Sanderur Straat 12, 200 Antwerpen.

20. **Union Belge des Géomètres-Experts Immobiliers** - UBG. Rue du Nord 76, 1000 Bruxelles.

21. **Fédération Royale des Associations Belges d'Ingénieurs** - FABI. Square Marie-Louise 49, 1040 Bruxelles.
    Affiliated professional groups of engineers, regionally based in Mons Liege, Anvers, Brabant Charleroi and Hasselt-Campine.

22. **Koninklijke Vlaamse Ingenieursvereniging** - KVIV. Jan van Rijswijcklaan 59, Antwerpen.

23. **Société Royale Belge des Ingénieurs et des Industriels.** Rue Ravenstein 3, 1000 Bruxelles.

24. **Union Nationales des Ingénieurs Techniciens** - UNIT. Boulevard de la Grande Ceinture 9, 1070 Bruxelles.

25. **Chambres des Ingénieurs-Conseils de Belgique** - CICB. Rue Rzvenstein 3, 1000 Bruxelles.

26. **Confédération Nationale de la Construction** - CNC. Rue de l'Etuve 12, 1000 Bruxelles.

27. **Fédération Nationale Belge du Bâtiment et des Travaux Publics.** Rue de l'Etuve 12, 1000 Bruxelles.

France

Population: 50M Area 213 000 sq. miles Capital: Paris - 2.5M Chief cities: Marseilles - 890.000 Lyons- 530 000 Toulouse - 380 000 GNP: £61 000M Employment: 20M. Cost of living index: 106.5 (1970 = 100)

INTRODUCTION

France has without doubt played the most prominent role politically in the EEC to date, Jean Monnet and Robert Schuman were the architects of the Community, and General de Gaulle was strongly instrumental during the 60s in shaping its policy. In 1971, Georges Pompidou paved the way for UK entry.

Firm political leadership has until recently been accompanied by a strong economy with a high rate of expansion and monetary stability. However, the strikes of 1968 paralysed the country and the threat of further trade union activity has in part influenced an increase of about 20% in Government spending on public works recently.

GNP has been expanding at a rate of 5.8% a year, and the population of Paris has quadrupled in the last 30 years - two factors which have opened the door to extensive development and a steep rise in land values in this region. UK developers have not been slow to recognise this and have imported the concept of the package deal, especially attractive in industrial estate development; The majority of residential development has taken place in the East of Paris, with office building in the West. The government has now imposed an almost total ban on new office development on central and western parts, in an attempt to restore the balance. This should speed decentralisation to the provinces, where Lille, Lyons and Marseilles are attracting developers' attention.

The construction industry contributes approximately 10% of the GNP, and accounts for 12% of the active labour force. About 55% of building in France can be classified as public work and 33% is government sponsored. In civil engineering, 80% is public sector and 20% private. Overall, 12% is public sector - hospitals, schools - 43% private housing 15% transport industries 30% repairs and maintenance.

According to the UN statistical yearbook, the industry has an output around twice that of the UK.

THE PLANNING PROCESS

1. Political structure

France is a Republic with executive powers vested in the President. The legislature consists of a national assembly and senate. The country is divided into 95 départements, all containing numerous communes or local authorities. The main government agency for building is the Bâtiment de France, within the Ministry of Cultural Affairs. It designates areas of natural beauty and is responsible for the upkeep of public buildings and monuments. There is a local architectural service at département level, and also regional offices at Bordeaux, Lyons, Montpelier and Rennes.

Regional planning is controlled by La Délégation a L'Aménagement du Territoire et a l'Action Régionale - DATAR - which reports directly to the office of the prime minister.

Development areas are the responsibility of the Ministre de l'Equipement. There are about 650 development plans covering the country, based as in the UK on surveys, land use, and zoning and communications. Plot ratios have been adopted, generally 1:1 in rural areas and 3:1 in large towns.

2. Tax and sources of government finance

Corporation tax is levied at 50%. All commercial and industrial activities are further subject to licence tax, collected for the disposal of the local communes. The rate varies between types of business and different communes, but generally consists of a proportional rate - accommodating rental value of premises, value of production plant, number of workers - and a fixed sum. Each branch of factory of a firm is assessed separately. Firms setting up in development areas may be exempt for 5 years.

Two real estate taxes, contributions foncieres et mobilieres - property tax and residential tax - are assessed on the rental value of buildings and land, and collected for the benefit of local authorities.

All industrial and commercial firms employing more than 10 wage-earners are also required to invest in housing projects. This sum, equal to 1% of total annual payroll, must be paid one year after each operating period.

All sales, either by a manufacturer, wholesaler or retailer, are subject to value added tax. The tax is multi-stage, but not cumulative, and is payable by the vendor in respect of the value he adds to the product. Initially, tax is assessed on the total sale receipts, including any commission, brokerage, interest, discounts, or transport charges borne by the vendor, and any tax included in the sale price. Certain deductions may be claimed:

1. the amount of tax on added value included in the purchase price of components or material used, or for finished products the amount of VAT included in the purchase price.

2. the amount of VAT included in the cost of assets - eg plant. No deduction may be claimed for tax included in the cost of construction or repairs to non-industrial or non-commercial buildings or to tourist vehicles or movable property not used in the manufacturing or sale of goods.

3. the amount of VAT included in the cost of services purchased by the business.

Taxpayers are required to file monthly or quarterly returns with the local Inspector of Taxes showing the amount of taxable sales during the preceding month or quarter and the amount of tax due.

The standard rate is 23%, which applies amongst others to goods transport and work on immovable property. An intermediate rate of 17.6% applies to certain works in connection with immovable property and building works on residential accommodation.

3. Building law and regulations

Building design and construction is controlled by law under articles 1792 and 2270 of the Code Napoléon for structural stability and weather tightness. These require the architect, and since 1967 the structural engineer and building developer, to give a 10 year guarantee against major defects. For very serious defects, liability may extend to 30 years.

The 10 year liability - décenalle responsabilité - is covered by professional indemnity insurance. About 80 insurance firms operate in the construction market.

There are no national regulations or local bye-laws as in the UK. Instead there are standards - Normes Francaises - published by AFNOR, the equivalent of the British Standards Institute. There are also DTU - Documents Techniques Unifiés - which are published as separate sets of codes covering reinforced concrete, structural steelwork, snow and wind loading. They are produced by committees containing representatives from professional and manufacturers' associations, the bureaux de contrôle, and the French Standards Association, under the chairmanship of the Centre Scientifique et Techniques du Bâtiment - CSTB.

4. Building approval

Planning permission is obtained by the architect on submission of plans and forms to the local authority. However, a government planning official is permanently employed in provincial council offices, responsible for scrutinising all applications. Disputes are referred to arbitration before the local Prefecture tribunal. No outline permission is given, but a full permit is granted subject to details being submitted. A simple decision is given within 2 months, but important projects may take up to 6 months.

5. Bureaux de Contrôle

Insurance companies require control to be exercised before giving professional cover. Only the larger projects are vetted in this way - about 3.0% of the total value of building work in France.

Control is arranged with a bureau de contrôle, an independent organisation which undertakes supervision of the project from start to finish. It also carries out a system of investigation of all major accidents in France and abroad, and some have compiled a computerised memory bank of over 15,000 cases.

The choice of bureau lies with the architect or developer. The bureau carries out the following functions:
1 checks all drawings and details produced by architect, engineer and bureau d'étude
2 site inspection to ensure plans are being followed
3 checks on soil investigation, surveys and foundations
4 checks on super-structures and all finishes
5 checks all mechanical and electrical services

There are 3 main organisations in France: Socotec, which specialises in building and civil engineering and inspects 75% of all new building work - Bureau Veritas, which specialises in mechanical and heavy engineering, but also inspects about 20% of new building and civil engineering work - and CEP, which is the newest Bureau and is responsible for 5%.

The Group visited Socotec, a Société Anonyme owned by the engineers within the firm. It has a staff of 1750, with branch offices in almost every departement, and contributes highly qualified specialists to the committees which formulate the DTUs. The firm draws its revenue from fees which range from 0.4 - 1% of the total costs of the works including tax, and which are paid by the building promoteur.

DEVELOPMENT, INVESTMENT AND FINANCE

6. Land tenure and development

Three important groups affect development projects in France. These are the Catholic Church, the largest landowners; the Communist Party, which controls the Paris banlieu where most city development is being carried out; and the Protestant banks, with a tradition for financial involvement in building.

New town corporations have been formed, which carry out town development but do not have the legal power of a local authority. The state provides finance as long term loans to enable the corporation to purchase land and roads, and effect landscaping. 5 new town projects are around the Paris region. The corporation visited by the Group at Evry New Town consisted of 7 Ministry officials and 7 local representatives.

7. Housing

France is not afflicted as Holland with a housing shortage, and 350 000 new units are constructed a year, but there is a lack of medium range apartments around Paris.

There are building developers which find land, design and erect houses, and then sell to a promoteur who in turn sells to the buyer, assisting in financial arrangements through the Credit Foncier - a state-assisted mortgage system available for new properties. 25% of the housing market is dependent on state aid.

8. Investment

Major commercial development has been largely carried out for owner occupation. Speculative development as operates in the UK is rare, despite the presence of a number of UK developers. Restrictions on office development in Paris have been introduced in the form of licences - agréments - and development tax - redevance - of around $400F/m^2$.

9. Finance

There are government subsidies for industrial development in selected areas. Otherwise, most large-scale building projects are financed by banks - private and state - which dictate the organisation of the building team. They choose the architect for basic design and the bureau d'étude for detailed design. Some have formed their own bureaux.

10. Average costs per m^2

Land around Paris   100F
Construction   800 - 850F
External services   18 000F house
Selling price: double total cost, including VAT at 17.56%.

PROFESSIONS AND TRADES

11. Division of work

The architect's role in France is limited effectively to that of a 1st stage designer and his functions have been extensively assumed by the bureaux d'études, which have grown from detailing offices to organisations capable of all aspects of the design process. Quantity surveyors, or métreurs-verificateurs, exist but their work is more often performed by architects or engineers.

| 12. Contract procedures | There is little standardisation, though a standard form of contract exists for private work, published by the Association Francais de Normalisation. A number of different forms are used by the various government departments. |

Contract documents can include a standard form - cahiers des conditions et charges generales; national codes of practice - prescriptions techniques particulières; specifications - cahier des prescriptions techniques particulières; special conditions of contract - cahier des charges particulieres; drawings - série de plans; bill of quantities - devis quantitatif et estiminatif; and form of tender - soumission. The lump sum contract is the most popular, based on drawings and specifications only.

For public projects, contracts are binding under common law with strictly defined mitigating circumstances. Assignment of work - dévolution des travaux - is called for on competitive tendering - adjudication - where complete specifications are provided and the lowest bidder wins; call for tenders - appel d'offres - where the lowest bid does not necessarily win; open competition - concours - where only the end requirements are stipulated; and directly negotiated contracts - marche de gré à gré.

Ministry contracts are normally let on the appel d'offre, but considerable negotiation takes place with approved contractors and competitive groupements consisting of architect, engineer and contractor. Public tenders generally are covered by the Code de Marché Public.

For private projects the dévolution des travaux is determined by the client. The contract is binding in civil law and is based on the common intentions of both parties to the contract. Litigation is thus easily arrived at, and is resolved if not by amicable settlement or arbitration, in the Tribunaux Judiciaires.

| 13. Establishing a practice | There appear to be no regulations preventing UK architects or consulting engineers from operating in France, but success would clearly be more probable in association with a French firm. |

Architect

Traditionally, French architects have been educated in the Ecoles des Beaux Arts, where entry requirements have lain more in skilled draughtmanship than mathematical ability, and the value of their diploma has accordingly declined. The Ecole Centrale des Arts et Manufactures is of higher standing and produces engineers as well as architects.

The Ministry of Cultural Affairs is at present engaged in reforming architectural education, and in establishing new schools in Paris and in the provinces.

Registered architects belong to the Ordre des Architectes. The Ordre has a recommended scale of fees, but these are almost always a basis for negotiation, and rarely accepted at the full value, which theoretically amounts to 6% of the total project cost. This is because the architect rarely carries out the same amount of work as his UK counterpart. Detail drawings are carried out mostly by the bureau d'études. The architect takes on average 3.4% for basic design, while the Bureau takes 2.6% for turning out working drawings and specifications.

It is obligatory for architects to insure under the code of professional duties adopted as a condition of membership of the Ordre des Architectes. They insure through the Ordre with Mutuel Francais des Architectes for a basic policy cover of 2M NF against negligence. For potentially higher claims the architect, engineer and contractor may take out a complementary group policy for the project.

The near future should prove crucial to architects in France, with the continuing debate on reform of the profession.

Bureau d'Etude

The comparatively small part played by architects in detailing after preliminary design has led to the growth of the bureaux. Some prepare architectural working drawings, specifications and schedules, whilst others perform the functions of civil, mechanical and electrical consultants. Others may specialise in reinforced concrete or M & E services design, but may also offer the preparation of structural quantities and the supervision of structural contracts. The functions of engineers, site engineers, clerk of works and quantity surveyor are also performed.

One bureau visited by the Group carries out feasibility studies, cost estimates, engineering design, site supervision, but does not offer architectural services. The Bureau often works in association with a number of architectural practices and is thus in a position to offer a total design and supervisory service to developers.

Another Bureau with offices in Nantes and Marseilles carries out architectural detail design work, structural design - including reinforcement drawings - and some of the functions of the quantity surveyor in providing cost estimates, preparing bill of quantities, and negotiating variations in cost.

Consulting engineer

Training in the grands écoles has been geared for work in public service. Thus the best-known school for engineers is the Ecole des Ponts et Chausées, which is attached to the Ministry of Public Works and Transport. The Ecoles Polytechniques were established as highly selective military schools in the Napoleonic era, and have since contributed to the unique educational system in France. Products of the Polytechniques form an elitist old-boy network with considerable influence in policy-making circles, and are open to criticism for being over-conservative. Civil engineers are generally produced by the Ecole des Ponts et Chaussées, the Ecole des Mines, and the Ecole des Travaux Publics, and the universities tend towards the pure sciences.

The FIDIC-associated body for consulting engineers is the Chambre des Ingénieurs-Conseils de France, with a membership of 760, consisting of 120 structural engineers, 300 civil, 150 industrial, and 190 planning and services. The CICF has various sub-associations which cover branches of engineering, such as SICOFEG, the civil engineering body.

One third of member firms are one-man organisations, a further 300 comprise 2-5 employees, and only 3 have between 60 and 120.

Recommended fee scales are fixed between 2-3% of total cost. The fee may be based on a single lump sum for the basic scheme plus a percentage fee for the working drawings and details, or a percentage fee for the whole project. This fee may also be based on a total cost of the works, a cost based on the number of Mm^3 of concrete in the project, or on the superficial floor area.

The fee percentage is further varied according to changes in construction cost indices, the location of works, and the complexity of construction, but an examination of the scales obtained from the CICF shows no basic difference to those in UK, apart from those for complex structures, which are considerably higher. It should be remembered that site supervision on large projects is affected by bureaux de contrôle, which take between 0.5 and 1%.

Engineers often find insurance hard to obtain, and frequently arrange cover through Lloyds, Northern Insurance, or a Swiss company.

At present the CICF is in the process of restructuring, and is also alerting the Government on the possible serious consequences of excessive intervention of State technical institutions into consulting engineering work.

Quantity Surveyor

This discipline does not exist in its own right in France, though most of the functions are performed at various stages by the ingénieur-géomètre or the géomètre-expert foncier.

The difficulty of introducing a further discipline might be resisted due to the inevitable increase in professional fees, not least by contractors who produce their own independent quantified assessments.

Contractor

The Fédération de Bâtiment - National Federation of Contractors - collaborates closely with the Ministère de l'Equipement - Ministry of Housing - and controls the majority of the contracting industry. It is roughly made up of:

1   200 enterprises with an average of 1000 employees
     each, totalling around 180 000 workers.
2   1 000 firms with an average of 200 employees.
3   approximately 4 000 firms with diverse employees.
4   28 000 firms with a handful of workers in each.

Members of the Fédération are graded according to experience and financial standing, and classified for certain types of contract. An organisation called Organisation Professionelle de Qualification et de Classification du Batiment - OPQCB - also grades contractors, and there is a special classification for electrical work - QUALIFELEC.

About 50% of tenders are negotiated. Competitive tendering, covered by the Code de Marché Public, is generally on price only. Included in the contractor's tender is the 1% fee for the Bureau de contrôle work, which is paid by the promoteur, or building owner. Tendering is on the increase in Council housing, schools and laboratories, and now accounts for about 25% of the total.

The main difference between contracting organisations in France and the UK is that French building contracts are directed by a Maitre d'Ouvrage or client's representative. Sometimes the contractor is responsible for procuring working drawings, which are sometimes obtained from a Bureau d'Etude, or else by a similar department within his own organisation. Basic insurance policy is similar to that of the architect, and is arranged through the Fédération with a special bureau of the insurance market, construction section, which fixes tariffs, accepts risks, and handles claims.

CONCLUSIONS AND SUMMARY

Generally, the Group found that very little impact had been felt in the construction industry from entry into the Common Market.

The professions, especially, have experienced little or no EEC competition, and have equally not been active in the other 5 member countries. The architectural profession appears to be in a state of utter confusion for its function is being limited to one of artist/designer work by the advent of the bureaux d'études. One architect visited by the Group stated that the position was scandalous. Only 27% of the work in France is carried out by architects as such.

Engineers in France can operate in various ways. They can form limited companies or may be professional firms as in UK. Quantity surveying does not appear in any clearly defined form, apart from UK firms in association with developers.

The operation of bureaux de controle of which there are 3 major firms, is unique. Insurance companies will not accept liability in covering professionals unless the bureaux have checked all drawings, ensured that plans are being implemented, and reported back to them. Much of this work would normally be carried out by **building in**spectors and district surveyors.

The inter-relationship between the professions was one of the most interesting aspects of the industry encountered by the Group. A distinct trend towards the all-in package deal was detected, often at the expense of the architect. Projects are often awarded on competitions, or concours, which are in effect invitations to submit a design, construct the project, and provide finance.

The bureau d'études are able to undertake this sort of project more readily than most architects who, as has been mentioned earlier, do not have adequate detailing facilities. The bureaux also have the advantage of financial backing from the large banks. The Group was informed of one bank which allocates 50% of its construction finance to public authority schemes and specifies a bureau for the work, thus effectively playing a role as a government agency.

The Group found that there is under development generally in the industrial field, certainly giving opportunities for outside participation. Similarly there is a great need for commercial and office development, and also for civil engineering work.

The property market is likely to be more profitable than in the UK and there are already established many development groups with UK professional teams often linking up with French professionals. One large development group from UK is already carrying out a £10M housing scheme south of Paris, and two very large office block complexes.

The Group was particularly impressed by its visit to the new town of Evry, outside Paris. This development, one of five similar undertakings around Paris, commenced in 1965. Much organisation and pre-planning had gone into the venture, which was ensuring good progress on construction. The land itself was fortunately in almost single ownership, and the development corporation was not obliged to exercise much power of compulsory purchase. All roads and services are being built in advance of building, and a central strip had even been reserved for future modes of transportation.

The construction industry as a whole in France is larger than that in UK. In 1969 it was responsible for over £5,000M of new works and £1,200M of civil engineering work.

Construction permits for residential units remained static at 42Mm² pa between 1964-8 - commercial development increased by 70% in the same period, and public works - hospitals and schools - increased by 120%. Meanwhile building permits for dwellings totalled on average 540,000 between January 1964 and December 1970.

One area where EEC membership has had slightly more effect has been in the supply of building materials and components, but the effect has been marginal if taken in the context of industry in general, in spite of the elimination of tariffs.

The sheer size of output of the French construction industry plus the widening market for property development schemes should ensure increasing scope for UK penetration for those patient enough to accept local rules and regulations.

BIBLIOGRAPHY AND REFERENCES

Available from the City of Westminster Chamber of Commerce

1. **Notes des honoraires** - fee scales for architects, Ordre des Architectes. 1969.

2. **Conditions syndicales d'études de béton armé et gros oeuvre** - consulting engineer fee scales for reinforced concrete and major works. Chambre des Ingenieurs-Conseils de France, Syndicat des Ingénieurs-Conseils de France en Génie Civil

Publications

3. **Hints to businessmen - France.** Department of Trade and Industry.

4. **Annuaire Statistique de la France.** Institut National de la Statistique et des Etudes Economiques, 24 Quai Branly, Paris 7. Annually.

5. **The French Construction Industry.** R & D paper. Ministry of Public Building and Works 1967.

6. **The French Building Industry.** RICS Information Series 1962.

7. **Public administration in France** - F. Ridley and J. Blondel. Routledge and Kegan Paul 1969.

8. **Règles administratives d'édification des locaux d'habitation, industriels et commercaux - textes et commentaires.** Le Moniteur des Travaux Publics et du Bâtiment 1969.

9. **Les nouvelles formules de demande des permis de construire.** Le Moniteur 1970.

10. **Je fais batir** - L Charles. Paris: Diffedit. 1967.

11. **Documents Techniques Unifies** - French standards and codes. Centre Scientifique et Technique du Bâtiment, Paris.

12. **La responsabilité décennale des architectes et entrepreneurs** - P Peter. Paris: Dunod. 1969.

Regular publications

13. **Ingénierie.** Monthly magazine for consulting engineers in France. 21, allee de clichy, 93 Le Raincy France.

14. **L'Information Immobilière** Publication advertising real estate for sale. 11 quai Anatole France, Paris 7è. Monthly.

Addresses

British Embassy. 35 Rue du Faubourg St. Honoré, Paris 8.

British Chamber of Commerce in France. 6 rue Halèry Place de l'Opéra, Paris 9.

15. **AFNOR** - French standards institute. Tour Europe, CEDEX 7, 92 Paris - La Défense.

16. **Centre scientifique du bâtiment - CSTB.** 4 Avenue du Recteur - Poincaré, Paris 16.

17. **Confédération Générale des Architectes Francais - CGAF,** 16 place de la Madeleine, 75 Paris 8.

18. **Conseils Superior de l'Ordre des Architectes.** 10 rue du Portalis, 75 Paris 8.

19. **Société des Architectes Diplômés par le Gouvernement - SADG -** education, research, building information and documentation. 100 rue du Cherche-Midi, 75 Paris 8.

20. **Ordre des Géomètres-Experts -** order of surveyors. 40 avenue Hoche, 75 Paris 8.

21. **Fédération des Association et Sociétés Francaises d'Ingénieurs Diplômés - FASFID.** 19 rue Blanche, 75 Paris 9.

22. **Société des Ingénieurs Civils de France.** 19 rue Blanche, 75 Paris 8.

23. **Chambre des Ingénieurs-Conseils de France - CICF.** 108 rue Saint-Honore, 75 Paris 1.

24. **Syndicat National des Ingénieurs des Travaux Publics, de l'Etat, des Ponts et Chaussées, et des Mines.** 63 rue Rivoli, Paris 1.

25. **Chambre Syndicale des Sociétés d'Etudes et de Conseils - SYNTEC.** 2, rue Oratoire, Paris 1.

26. **Societe des Ingenieurs-Conseils de France en Genie Civil - SICOFEG.** 108 rue Saint-Honore, 75 Paris 1.

27. **Chambre Syndicale des Bureaux d'Etudes Techniques de France.** 9 rue du Mont Thabor, Paris 1.

28. **Syndicat National des Ingénieurs et Techniciens Agréés.** 108 rue St Honore, Paris 1.

29. **Fédération Nationale du Bâtiment.** 33 avenue Kleber, 75 Paris 16.

West Germany

Population: 58.8M Area: 95 000 sq. miles Capital: Bonn - 138 000 Chief cities: Hamburg - 1.9M Munich - 1.3M Cologne - 850 000 GNP: £78 000M Employment: 22.5M Cost of living index: 123 (1962 = 100)

INTRODUCTION

West Germany has been a showpiece of economic prosperity, with growth consistently high, apart from a minor recession in 1966-7, and the Deutschmark remains one of the strongest currencies in the world. However, the country has recently been hit by inflation, the worst for 20 years. Industrialists have had to cater for sharp increases in wages - average rises of over 16% in 1970 - and have accordingly raised prices, in an attempt to keep profit margins up.

However, the export market continues to be strong, contributing to a greater availability of jobs than numbers of unemployed - at present around 0.7% - despite the presence of a foreign labour force of over 2M.

Pollution is becoming a problem with heavy industrialisation along the Rhine, and approximately half the population living in its catchment area. A Lander Committee for a Clean Rhine has been set up with funds of around DM10 000, and large industrial concerns in Dusseldorf and Cologne have spent large sums of money on filtration plants. The Minister of the Interior has recently suggested a role for consulting engineers in conservation of the environment.

The construction industry is currently turning over about DM100 000 annually Forecasts for annual growth in various sectors are: Housing - 500 000 units; Commercial - +5%; Roads - +10%. These figures apply to West Germany for the next ten years.

THE PLANNING PROCESS

1. Political structure

Germany is a Republic with a Federal government in Bonn, led by a chancellor elected by the Bundestag, the chief legislative organ which is in turn elected by universal suffrage. The country is divided into 11 regions, or Lander, each with its own parliament and each represented in the Federal government through the Bundesrat.

The central government has legal responsibility for regional and town planning, land tenure and compulsory acquisition, and building regulations. It frames overall legislation for public works such as roads, railways and airports, but otherwise the Lander parliaments legislate for planning which is enforced by town or country authorities in their region. These local authorities prepare detailed plans for their areas alone, though these must conform with the broad dictates of the Lander legislation.

25

2. Tax and sources of government finance

Revenue for local authorities comes, as in the UK, from general taxation. A business tax is also levied, amounting to 0.5% of the estimated construction costs on planning applications. The Federal government provides finance for local authority utility buildings. VAT on construction activities is 11%, payable separately on building materials and on labour, and has effectively raised overall building costs by 2%.

3. Building laws and regulations

General land use and development, land values and acquisition are covered by Federal building law. Particular laws and regulations governing building and civil engineering are issued by the Lander, usually in book form. Despite variations between Lander, a common standard - the Bauordnungen - exists.

The system is administered by building authorities, which are agencies of the Lander, not the municipality. Site inspection is carried out by the authorities' own officials or by independent structural consultants, called Prufungenieurs.

The technical basis for building control is provided by German Industrial Norms - DIN. These cover not only materials and dimensions, but also methods of construction, thus corresponding to British Standards and Codes of Practice. The norms are published by the German standards organisation - DNA - which is partly financed by the government, partly by contributions from industrial associations, and partly from the sales of its publications. Its norms are adopted uniformly throughout the country, unlike building regulations which vary between Lander.

The complex machinery of paid-for inspection and approval by the building authorities has resulted in their virtual assumption of responsibility on building sites.

4. Building approval

All planning applications are taken to the appropriate city council. Appeal against refusal is first considered by the council, and if necessary then by the district and Lander authorities.

DEVELOPMENT, INVESTMENT AND FINANCE

5. Land tenure and development

Land is generally held freehold, in smallish plots, apart from in some rural areas. In urban districts, it is usually held by private individual owners, though recent legislation on compulsory purchase rights for slum clearance schemes is giving more land ownership to the local authorities.

6. Housing

500 000 units per year are constructed, mainly for private ownership. Forms of housing association exist which provide subsidised units, the nearest equivalent being council housing in the UK. These were individual companies carrying out the entire development of housing projects. Units are then let to various owners on a subsidised basis, supported by the Federal state, the regional and local authority. Rentals in these properties appear to be approximately 33% of the market rate.

7. Investment

Major commercial development schemes are generally carried out for investment Few companies buy and sell property, largely due to the adverse effect of the business tax. There did not appear to be any major speculative developments as found in the UK, probably because of the acute land shortage, and the high price of land. The Group was also unable to find evidence of property companies - though there was one speculative housing development in Cologne put together by what could be termed a property company - or of the system of estate agency.

Leasehold occupation is not common. Leases in operation have been of 99 years duration, though this is slowly being reduced to 75 years and even less. The normal period for rent review is 5 years.

8. Finance

Development incentives are provided by the Federal government, particularly for those areas bordering East Germany, Bavaria, and for West Berlin. They mainly consist of tax deductions, but can also be based on a premium for the number of people employed.

Sources of finance generally available to prospective developers are very much as in UK - insurance companies, savings banks, commercial banks and mortgage companies. The length of loan is normally up to 30 years. The maximum period for rack rent leases is 10 to 20 years, with a 5 year review period based on the cost of living index.

The Group was advised that returns from investment funds range from 8-10%, whilst returns from a life insurance company range from 5-9%. The leaseback system of raising finance exists, but is restricted by taxation. Generally, financial institutions are now becoming more aware of property as a means of investment.

9. Average costs per m³

Local authority 4-storey flats	100DM
Private development 4-storey flats	220DM
Private enterprise small house	250DM
Schools	240-250DM
Office blocks up to 8-storey	250-350DM

PROFESSIONS AND TRADES

10. Division of work

In theory any person can be engaged in planning and development of land, but the work is most frequently carried out by architects and engineers. As with all other professions, the practice of architecture and engineering is laid down in law by the Lander parliaments.

Quantity surveyors as elsewhere in the EEC do not exist as a separate profession, and the costing function is often carried out by architects and project managers.

Town planners exist but there is no equivalent to the UK Royal Town Planning Institute. Their work appears to be an amalgamation of architecture and engineering, and also includes process planning for industry. They are frequently retained by Lander and municipalities.

Design and construct schemes are increasing in Germany. Small professional firms are combatting this by forming consortia to provide a competitive range of professional services. There is also a growth of small general contractors/ planning firms which are undertaking project management, previously the province of the architect.

11. Contract procedure

There are many types of building contract in use. Guidance on contract procedure is given by the Verdingungsordnung fur Bauleistung - VOB - which is similar to the RIBA standard form of contract. For almost all projects a Leistungsverzeichnis - bill of quantities - is prepared by the architect, and by the contractor for design/construct schemes.

There are four parties to the average contract - the client, architect, engineer and contractor. The principal contract is signed by the architect on behalf of the client and contractor. The principal rules of the VOB are that all tenders should be made public; the client must not negotiate prices and tenders; the tenderers are not allowed to agree on prices.

These rules are generally adhered to for public works projects, but for other work the contract is increasingly being prepared project by project.

The standard rules are further being modified in that contractors are publicly invited to apply; tender figures are not made public; and prices and tenders are negotiated. The average costs of tendering in Germany were recently estimated at 1½% of contract value.

12. Establishing a practice

For UK professional firms wishing to establish in Germany there appear to be no restrictions or legal difficulties associated with registration. There may, however, be some problems in recognition of UK qualifications and the extent of professional liability. A work permit is still required, usually issued for a 12 month period.

There has not been much evidence of an inter-relationship between professions in the EEC, even though it is easier for foreign firms to practise in Germany than in other EEC countries.

Architect

The title of architect is not protected as in the UK, but legislation now under consideration will make the signing of drawings by architects compulsory.

There are four types of architect in Germany:

1   Dipl - Ingenieur Architect - university trained with emphasis on structures. 5 - 6 years training including one year in practice.
2   Architect HFBK - university trained with emphasis on design and fine arts. 5 - 6 years training, one year in practice. 2 years in practice after obtaining degree. Same status as Dipl-Ing
3   Ingenieur - technical college education of about 4 years, followed by 6 - 7 years in practice
4   Self-taught - 8 years in practice, accepted only if standard of work is satisfactory.

All practising architects must register with Lander, apart from West Berlin, which have formed Regional Architects Chambers - Architekten Kammern. All the above categories of architect qualify for registration. There is also a Bund Deutscher Architekten, a society to which only well-known architects can belong, by invitation.

The architect has many responsibilities, often exceeding those of his UK counterpart. He signs the principal contract on behalf of the client and the contractor, and also produces approximate estimates, exercises cost control during the contract period, and agrees final accounts with the contractor.

Pre-planning or feasibility studies are not normally undertaken by the architect, though he frequently compiles a brief, prepares design drawings, obtains planning and bye-law approval, and then prepares detailed production drawings. On receiving tenders, which are usually obtained competitively from about 10 firms for private carcass work, the architect checks the lowest, negotiates where necessary and then enters into and signs a contract on behalf of the client and contractor. He then goes out to tender for sub-contracting work for the finishing trades.

A separate contract with the client defines the architect's responsibility for negligence of all parties on the project. By law the architect is required to take out a professional indemnity policy. Retention is usually 10% and defects liability period is up to 12 months, with a guarantee period varying between 2 and 5 years.

Consulting engineer

The title of engineer is not as yet protected in law, though the German Association of Consulting Engineers - Verband Unabhangig Beratender Ingenieurfirmen - has drafted a bill to the Federal government requesting a professional charter protecting the title not only of independent consulting engineers but also of limited companies practising this discipline. Structural and M & E engineers are not represented by separate professional institutes.

Generally the function of the consulting engineer is similar to that in the UK. However, the VBI is not satisfied on his role in the so-called right to submit construction projects, in relation to that of the architect. This right covers which person may sign, draft and submit construction data such as plans and calculations, and both professions are claiming it. A working party has been set up by the Lander which has prepared a draft entitling any qualified person in the disciplines of architecture, building and civil engineering to submit building projects.

Another discipline of engineering, unique to Germany, is that of the proof engineer - Prufingenieur. Employed by the Lander or municipality, he checks all calculations and structural provisions and has the authority to require compliance with his alterations. In fact, he could veto a whole structure if it did not meet with his requirements.

Fee scales exist, published in book form, but are at present in the process of revision. The Federal government has passed a bill providing for a set of regulations for architects' as well as engineers' fee scales. These regulate fees for the provision of advice to clients, planning and execution of building projects and technical installations, work on invitations to tender and awarding of building contracts, as well as preparation, planning and execution of town planning and transport schemes. At present engineers call for competitive tenders for their sectors of the project, under the overall co-ordination of the architect. The VBI, asked to participate in the drafting of these regulations, is emphasising that consulting engineers are increasingly involved in project management.

Consulting engineers may form limited companies, but problems are being experienced as to the extent of liability. Increasingly they are forming societies, consortia and planning groups, but existing company forms are inadequate for these purposes because reasonable liability provisions and taxation cannot be obtained. The Federal government has now introduced a partnership bill which limits the liability of these consortia to DM50,000.

Quantity surveyor

The work of the quantity surveyor in Germany, in the absence of an independent profession, is carried out by technicians in the other professional practices.

The Group found that present sophisticated techniques being employed in the UK had not filtered through to Germany. Accurate cost planning and cost control are sorely needed - evidence was found of cost errors between initial estimate and tender as high as 10%. The establishment of an independent profession could also have some effect on the recently exposed bid fixing.

Some of the professional bodies and members of the architectural profession met by the Group were aware of the benefits of the independent quantity surveyor, though some resistance on the part of contractors was encountered. The most likely means of obtaining work in this country would be in conjunction with a UK developer, or with a professional consortium.

However, the chances of success in Germany are probably less than in France and Holland, due to the lack of sufficient major private development. If the quantity surveyor could really demonstrate his value, the predominant national characteristics of precision and order would probably speed development of the practice.

Developer

The speculative developer barely exists in Germany. UK developers are understood to be starting a project in Hamburg, but there is no evidence that this will become regular practice.

The Group did however meet the director of a social housing company in Cologne, which designs and constructs the German equivalent of UK council housing.

The difficulties facing the developer lie mainly in the assembly of land. There are virtually no large holdings in the cities and towns, and the municipalities are very reluctant to use such compulsory purchase powers as exist. Under a recent law, central area land may be assembled by the municipality in partnership with private developers, but there are as yet no examples of this in operation.

Contractor

There are about 8 very large contractors with turnovers between £50M - £200M per year, and most firms in general are public companies. The nominal growth rate of the industry quoted was 15%, but taking inflation into account the actual rate in nearer 5% - 6%.

The main contractor is usually responsible for foundations and structure, and the architect may appoint a Bautrager - project manager contractor to co-ordinate site activity. Sub-contractors are rarely nominated, and the sub-letting of specialist services by services contractors is not known.

Work is usually obtained on competitive tender, either open in which case the award need not go to the lowest bidder, or selected and the lowest bidder must be given the award. The fixed price tender for M & E work does not exist, though a lump sum is used for periods up to 10 months, after which variation clauses are incorporated to cover the increased costs of labour and materials.

An unusual feature of German contracting is the joint venture, an ad hoc consortium formed by major contractors for large jobs. Reasons given to the Group for this arrangement were that it reduces the number of competitors in open tenders, spreads the risk, maintains work flow in large firms, and allows local politics to be accommodated by including the small local firm.

There is a single union to cover all building operations, industrially-based rather than trades. Agreements are reviewed annually, and rates are normally geared to the cost of living index though in some areas the basic rates are exceeded because of the shortage, particularly, of skilled workers. Labour is scarce in cities and industrial development areas are very much dependent on foreign inflow. Sources in S.Italy and Spain had dried up by the late 1960's and are now located in Turkey and Greece.

The basic rate of pay for building operatives is almost double that of the UK, and rising some 15% - 20% per year. Carpenters, masons and concreters receive DM 6.70 an hour, and social costs - health insurance, pensions - add 60% to these basic rates. Overtime is paid at time plus 25%, though Sunday workers receive time plus 50%.

German contractors carry out less work abroad than other EEC contractors, and minimal work in the EEC itself. A few foreign contractors have worked in Germany, usually on specialised projects, such as the Rhine and Moselle barrage scheme where German, French and Luxembourg contractors have all been working.

A problem for foreign contractors is that they must bring their own labour with them, because of the German labour shortage. However, Yugoslav and E European contractors are undertaking work in Germany, attracted by the Deutschmark currency.

CONCLUSIONS AND SUMMARY

The Group found that entry into the EEC had not markedly affected the building industry in Germany, apart from the introduction of certain building materials manufactured in other member countries. As these must still comply with German standards and codes of practice, even this activity is still limited.

It is unlikely that enlargement of the EEC will in itself improve prospects of increasing business. German contractors have undertaken little work outside their national boundaries, and little interest has been shown by other EEC countries for work in Germany. There may be an opening for the competitive UK general contractor, as these are still in their infancy in this country. Most people spoken to by the Group confirmed that it is hoped that the inward looking attitude will change with British entry.

Setting up a practice for UK professional firms would be relatively simple once the usual problems of understanding building law and regulations, obtaining registration, language barriers, and establishing business contacts have been overcome. Commissions would, however, be hard to come by because of enormous local competition, and the German practice of obtaining work by winning competitions.

Architects in Germany appear to perform more work than their UK counterparts. They carry out planning, drawings, production drawings, applications, as well as many of the functions of the quantity surveyor in taking out quantities and going out to tender, UK architects may not be attracted to carrying out this kind of work for a lower fee scale than they obtain in their own country.

The Group was also told that there are difficulties for an architect registered with one regional architects' chamber to practise in the area of another. However, British architects are not precluded from joining the chambers.

The best way of making inroads in Germany would probably be in association with a UK developer or with a German professional firm. British property companies will succeed if present rules on site acquisition, taxation and exchange rates are relaxed, though at present UK financial expertise in this form of development has yet to make any impact.

The planning framework with responsibilities for construction vested in the 11 Lander, has affected development projects. After many years of strong central government, the policy now is to decentralise with the result that much planning and development is initiated locally, and by the Lander. Land ownership is largely fragmented, and it is very difficult to obtain sites large enough to carry out large scale property development schemes for investment.

The Group felt it unlikely that English or foreign capital will be attracted for development purposes for the reason stated above. The Eurodollar market does not appear very active, and the leaseback system is on the decline. However, financial institutions are becoming aware of property as an investment, and there has been an increasing use of property bonds.

On the positive side, the government is encouraging construction of hospitals, schools and kindergarten, managed by the Lander and local authorities, and providing incentives in development areas for industrial projects. The latter consist of interest reductions of government loans, and tax reductions for people working in these areas.

The building industry is faring quite well in construction of houses, apartments and offices, but there is considerable slack in the civil engineering sector. Overall trends in growth forecast at 4.4% a year in private work, and 8.2% a year in the public sector. However, the Group was told that these government forecasts are somewhat high.

A cross-section of the industry, including architects, engineers, contractors, housing associations and local authorities involved in planning and building regulations were interviewed by the Group, providing a general picture of cautious optimism for future prospects.

The Group felt that at least another 8 - 10 years will pass before the EEC will affect the building industry to any significant extent, mainly because other issues will take precedence in the general welfare of the Community. There does exist, however, definite interest in Germany in collaboration in Third World countries, perhaps with British firms.

A joint commission of this sort in the developing world could well lead to a continuing association in Germany itself, and in fact has already done so. A bilingual firm would have added advantage in establishing itself in this way.

BIBLIOGRAPHY AND REFERENCES

Available from the City of Westminster Chamber of Commerce

1. **Bundesgesetzblatt** - equivalent to UK Town & Country Planning Act. In German.

2. **Deutscher Stadtetag** - booklet giving aims and work of society for preservation of historic buildings.

3. **Bund Deutscher Architekten** - booklet setting out rules and aims of German Order of Architects. In German.

4. **GOA - Verordnung uber die Gebuhren fur Architekten** - booklet setting out fee scales and regulations of Bund Deutscher Architekten. In German.

5. **Verband Beratender Ingenieur** - rules and aims of German Association of consulting engineers. Available in English.

6. **Einheits-Architektenvertrag** - uniform type of contract for mainly private work. In German.

7. **Allgemeine Vertragsbedingungen fur Nachunternehmer** - standard form of sub-contract.

8. **Verdingungsordnung fur Bauleistungen** - standard guide to building contracts. 1965.

9. **Bau-Tarifvertrage, Gewerbliche Arbeitnehmer** - building labour costs.

Publications

10. **This is the German Market.** Axel Springer.

11. **Hints to businessmen - W Germany,** Department of Trade and Industry.

12. **Federal Republic of Germany: a Survey for Businessmen.** London Chamber of Commerce, 1970.

13. **Bundesverband der Deutschen Industrie - BDI - Deutschland Liefert -** Federation of German Industries annual directory. Available from 33 Bruton St., London W1.

14. **Statistisches Jahrbuch fur die Bundesrepublik Deutschland.** Statisches Bundesamt, Wiesbaden.

15. **Deutscher Normenausschuss** - index of DIN standards, and building standards, Beith-Vertrieb, Berlin, 1969. Available in English.

16. **Bauaufsichtliche Zulassungen** - Bub/Reuter/Wagner Erich Schmidt. Collection of general approvals for construction materials. 1967.

17. **Building control in West Germany** - E Cibula. BRS current paper.

18. **Bundesbaugesetz und Durchfuhrungsverordunungen des Bundes -** Federal building law and implementation. Deutsches Volksheimstattenwerk, Cologne, 1969.

Regular Publications

19. **Deutsche Bauzeitung** - architectural journal Deutsche Verlags-Anstalt GmbH Stuttgart. Monthly.

20. **Consulting** - journal for consulting engineers. Vogel Verlag 8700 Wurzburg, Max-Planck-Strasse 7/9. Monthly.

Addresses

British Embassy. Friedrich-Ebert Allee 77, 5300 Bonn

British Trade Council in W Germany e V. Address as above.

21. **Bund Deutscher Architekten - BDA.** 53 Bonn. Ippendorfer Allee 14b.

22. **Bundesarchitektenkammer** - regional chambers of architects. Headquarters: 65 Mainz, Grosse Bleiche 31/33.

23. **Verband Deutscher Vermessungsingenieurs - VDV** - association for quantity surveyors, 56 Wuppertal-Barmen, Brahmsstrasse 4.

24. **Verein Deutscher Ingenieure - VDI.** 4 Dusseldorf 1, Graf-Recke-Strasse 84.

25. **Verein Beratender Ingenieure - VBI.** 43 Essen, Herkulesstrasse 3-5, Postfach 919.

26. **Verband Unabhangig Beratender Ingenieurfirmen - VUBI.** 53 Bonn, Wolkenburgstrasse 1, Postfach 603.

27. **Hauptverband der Deutschen Bauindustrie.** 6 Frankfurt/Main, Friedrich-Ebert-Anlage 38.

Italy

Population: 53M Area: 110 000 sq. miles Capital: Rome - 2.6M Chief cities: Milan - 1.7M Naples: 1.25M Turin: 1.2M GNP: £38 000M Employment: 19M Cost of living index: 113 (1970 = 100)

INTRODUCTION

In the European context, Italy stands out as an EEC member which while grappling with the same problems as the others, has certain additional difficulties which are entirely unique, stemming principally from its historical background.

The unification of Italy as a nation took place just over 100 years ago, superseding the old system of city states each with its own political and administrative organisation. No form of government since then appears to have succeeded in establishing an effective national bureaucratic structure. As a result, with a few honourable exceptions, it is now virtually impossible to obtain speedy action in any sector by following established procedures. This has led to widespread disillusion and frustration amongst Italians in all walks of life, and undoubtedly the building industry is a casualty of this.

After the 1939-45 War, the Italians re-established a democratic form of government, largely dominated by Christian Democrats, and embarked on what came to be called the Italian economic miracle. During this period, which lasted into the early 1960s, the building industry expanded fast in certain clearly defined sectors. These included the very impressive road-building programme, hydro-electric schemes, port development, factory building, office and private residential construction.

Based on hardworking and relatively lowly paid employees and high calibre engineering and administrative staff, Italian contractors made their presence felt in large international tenders in Africa, S America and elsewhere. Engineers like Nervi, Morandi, and architects like Gio Ponti, ensured international respect for Italian professional standards.

However, activity in the building industry is now at a low level and has been for the past 3 years. The industry as a whole is working at 30% capacity and no improvement is expected during 1972, though the public sector may improve in 1973, as a result of imminent government investment in major infrastructure projects.

THE PLANNING PROCESS

1. Political structure

Italy is a Republic with a presidential head of state, elected by two legislative houses - the Chamber of Deputies, elected by universal suffrage, and the Senate, consisting of regional representatives.

The country itself is divided into 19 regions, and further subdivided into provinces, and finally into Comuni - or local authorities.

Planning of transport facilities, communications, port installations, and utilities such as electricity generation and distribution are the responsibility of Ministries in Rome. Frequently these responsibilities are delegated to para-governmental public corporations known as Enti. Chief of these is IRI, an industrial agency with extensive powers and financial controls on organisations and industries throught the country.

The comune prepares and administers its own development plan and is the authority most directly responsible for approving private construction.

2. Tax and sources of government revenue

Revenue is derived from various sources, but with the eventual introduction of VAT in 1973, the basic structure of taxation will be changed.

A levy on all wage packets is at present collected by a government agency - GESCAL - and the funds are used for the construction of low-cost housing.

3. Building laws and regulations

The comuni are responsible for the institution and implementation of construction regulations both in building and civil engineering. Construction codes are applied locally and may differ between Comuni. The architect's or engineer's department is responsible for applying the regulations.

4. Building approval

The procedure is similar to that in the UK. Application for planning approval is addressed to the appropriate architect's department of the local authority, together with fully detailed drawings because basic outline planning approval is not given. The architect's department is responsible for ensuring adherence to local building regulations.

In certain protected areas, as in parts of the Italian Riviera, additional statutory bodies such as the Italian equivalent of the Fine Arts Commission may sometimes be required to sanction a proposed development. Certain private organisations such as Italia Nostra have become quite powerful in intervening in private and public development, considerably helped by the upsurge in concern over conservation of the environment.

DEVELOPMENT, INVESTMENT AND FINANCE

5. Land tenure and development

Land is almost universally held on a freehold basis. Large estates still exist in agricultural areas quite close to major cities such as Milan. Within city boundaries, land ownership is more fragmented. Leasehold occupation is common in industrial, commercial and residential premises, and leases tend to be of short duration, frequently renewed.

The Comuni have recently been given wide powers of expropriation for popular housing projects. Estate agents exist, but are not nearly so numerous as in UK. Some are extremely well organised with in-house computer-controlled information retrieval systems. There appears to be no widespread demand for the services of independent land and property valuers.

6. Housing

There are no new town developments in the public sector, but a reform law was passed in 1971 on popular housing. Responsibility for construction of housing is delegated to autonomous publicly owned institutes, organised on a provincial basis, which work in association with the Comuni.

7. Investment   Major commercial development schemes are carried out for investment or outright disposal. Property companies and wealthy individuals are active in this market. Comprehensive city centre developments are very rare, but most other types of building development - commercial offices, residential zones, industrial estates - are carried out.

8. Finance   Government incentives are heavily weighted in favour of designated areas of the South, Sicily, and Sardinia, where loans are available from the Cassa per il Mezzogiorno - Fund for the South. The Cassa was set up after the war to encourage investment in industry, tourism, and infrastructure projects in depressed regions.

No exchange controls are at present applied to capital brought in from overseas for approved purposes. Foreign sources of capital are generally welcome, but investors may be inhibited so far by the uncertain political and economic situation.

The banks are the main source of finance to prospective developers. A lending market derived from insurance or pension funds does not appear to be available. Finance from a bank would normally consist of a straight loan on a mortgage basis, or of overdraft facilities against adequate securities. Leaseback arrangements are beginning to appear in Italy, and gaining acceptance.

9. Average costs per m³

Local authority medium use flats	18 000 - 20 000 lire
Speculative office blocks	30 000 - 40 000 lire
Hotels	30 000 - 40 000 lire

PROFESSIONS AND TRADES

10. Division of work   The main professions engaged in the planning and development of land are architects and engineers. Both are strictly controlled by their respective Orders on conduct and fee scales. The Orders are instituted on a provincial basis. Quantity surveying as an independent profession is non-existent in Italy.

Design and contract schemes are very common in Italy and Italian contractors have undertaken this type of work extensively overseas. There is little evidence of an independent building services profession. A large firm of architects might carry a services department, but in general the trade itself provides designs and specifications.

11. Contract procedure   There are various standard forms of contract in use in Italy, and different Ministries use their own particular versions. The Collegio degli Ingegneri di Milano - Order of Engineers of Milan - issues the regularly up-dated standard forms for general work and for specialist sub-contracting. These are also extensively used for private work.

12. Establishing a practice   Given the strict provisions on registration regulating the practice of architecture and engineering, a UK firm would need to associate closely with a local firm, depending on that firm to sign drawings and thereby undertake professional responsibility. Work permits are required for any expatriate staff based in Italy. Taxation is exceedingly complex, and a tax expert should be consulted.

There was no evidence encountered by the Group of bi-national practices established by any of the professions directly as a result of EEC membership. International co-operation through joint enterprises or associations occurs occasionally, often where specialist expertise is required.

There is however a good opportunity for UK consultants working with Italian firms in the Third World, where both have expertise to contribute. These opportunities may increase with the enlargement of the EEC, and with trade agreements with associated African nations.

Architect

Professional qualification is dependent on obtaining a university degree. After approximately 7 years academic study and little specialisation, the graduate enters his profession fully qualified to take responsibility for design and signing drawings - without any practical experience.

The architect produces approximate estimates. Cost control as exercised in the UK is unknown, and depends on the competence of the architect. Besides signing drawings and generally performing the functions of his UK counterpart, he may also be appointed to supervise construction, though this is by no means automatic. More often this is undertaken by a Direttore del Lavoro - Director of Works - who must be professionally qualified and take responsibility for the satisfactory execution of the work.

Fee scales are regulated by government decrees or laws issued periodically and set out in a handbook available from the Order of Architects - Ingegneri Architetti: Tariffa Professionale. This handbook also sets out regulations on professional conduct.

By law all those associated with a project are held liable for defects or failures until responsibility is proved. If fatalities occur, imprisonment may follow. Professional indemnity cover is difficult to obtain.

Consulting engineer

The profession is strictly controlled in ethics and fee scales by Ministerial decrees also set out in the above handbook and administered by regionally organised Orders. The Associazione Ingegneri Consulenti Italiani - AICI - was recently formed in 1966, as Italy's representative on FIDIC, and already has 154 members, the vast majority of which practise in structural, civil, and transportation engineering, and town planning.

Qualification is achieved as with architects through university education, and newly qualified graduates similarly take design responsibility without previous practical experience.

Most consulting engineering firms are very small organisations, frequently composed of a number of partners who teach at universities during the day, and carry out commissions for clients during their spare time or vacation periods. This system of doubling-up helps resolve the problems of low-paid lecturers and fee scales which are certainly lower than UK levels.

There are a few large firms in Italy controlled with one or two exceptions by state organisations - Enti - or else by large industrial concerns such as FIAT. A comparatively large firm built up on personal reputation only is rarely found.

With building activity low at present, opportunities for UK firms are limited. In future these will most likely lie in association with suitable Italian firms who are in need of support - either in finance or technical expertise, or in back-up staff. A UK firm acting as consultant to a UK client for factory building or commercial development would be advised to associate with a firm of Italian consultants.

Quantity Surveyor

As in other EEC countries this profession does not exist in Italy. The function of preparing budget estimates, specifications, and contract documents is variously carried out by the architect or engineer or an employee in the design office known as a works officer, or geometra. Cost planning and financial control as practised in the UK seems unknown.

There could be unlimited opportunities for the quantity surveying profession in Italy if only the client and the construction industry in general can be convinced of the positive advantages. Change of heart is only likely following considerable efforts by quantity surveyors wishing to practice in Italy over an extended period. The low level of construction activity at present complicates the problem, and the best opportunity probably lies in working with a UK architect or engineer acting for a UK client.

Developer

Commercial estate agency seems considerably under-developed in Italy. Though there is an association of estate agents - Consiglio Nazionale di Agenti Immobiliari - registration is not mandatory. There are few agents practising, and if one is seeking to purchase property for a client, it is always difficult to know whom to contact. Opportunities could exist for the general practice surveyor in estate agency, investment in real estate and planning development.

By law insurance companies are required to invest a certain percentage of capital in real property and presumably are advised on an in-house basis. There is however very little advice for a potential investor in real estate in Italy, although there are indications that funds are becoming more interested in property as a means of investment. This dichotomy will become more acute with the increasing of foreign investors, particularly from the UK.

UK developers in the past have tended to ignore Italy due to its political climate. The series of coalition governments may have been unable to effect radical reform - particularly in taxation and planning - but the main obstacle has been the absence of locally available development finance. Property finance is still largely obtained via short/medium term mortgage arrangements based on the security of the mortgagor, rather than the bricks and mortar.

There is however a growing awareness of the possibilities of leasing systems as a means of finance, not only in property, but also in commerce generally. These leaseback systems will prove a great asset for industry wishing to establish in Italy, and should provide impetus to development.

At present Comune planning powers are limited to negative control rather than actively sponsoring commercial redevelopment schemes, or urban renewal. However, they can expropriate land for housing, highway and public services, and recent laws have been passed permitting expropriation of land for housing at a price based on a formula related to its agricultural value. This will result in very cheap land being available for housing in City centres. The measure has been taken to provide more low cost housing - casa populare - in an attempt to provide the continuing population drift from the South with accommodation.

The population problem, most marked in the industrial north, has resulted in some Comuni in Milan and Turin setting up ad hoc bodies in conjunction with the government sponsored body IRI to deal with housing.

The UK professional with experience of similar problems and of planned development and urban renewal in City centres could well find a place for his expertise in Italy.

Contractor

For official work contractors are required to qualify by size and type of contract, which then enables them to tender for any contract in their category. The Ministry of Public Works holds lists of approved contractors, thus making it difficult for foreign firms to make in-roads.

Tenders are usually submitted on a fixed price basis - for public works the contract must be awarded to the lowest. It is common for as many as 30-40 contractors to tender for a contract worth £1M. Negotiated contracts are reasonably common in the private sector.

Procedure for private concessionaires of public bodies such as ANAS permits the averaging out of prices to avoid unreasonably low bids. The successful bidder is then excluded from the following tenders.

The unions are oganised on religious or political lines. Conditions of employment tend to vary between one province and another, but there is a current trend towards standardisation. Further details on this, rates of pay and security payments are contained in monthly bulletins issued by each province. Wage agreements are normally negotiated for two year periods. Tradesman are permitted to carry out more than one craft, and there is no restriction on their transfer between provinces.

It is clear that Italy's membership of the Common Market has not resulted in her native contractors carrying out significantly greater amounts of work in other EEC countries, though they are generally active overseas. The Group felt that UK entry to the Common Market will not per se increase opportunities in EEC markets.

Those that exist may be facilitated due to freer movement of labour and money across frontiers, but greater standardisation of contract procedures, regulations, methods of construction and wage rates will need to be achieved before any significant improvement is attained. Responsibility for motivating these provisions clearly lies with governments.

Opportunities for the next few years are likely to be confined to selling some particular expertise, or to entering into joint venture arrangements where financial management skills or other skills can be grafted onto local roots.

CONCLUSIONS AND SUMMARY

The Italian post-war miracle may have produced, amongst others, engineers and architects of the calibre of Nervi and Gio Ponti, but successive governments have almost entirely ignored certain sectors of construction - hospitals and medical centres, schools, universities and popular housing - crucial to the welfare of the nation. Failures in these highly emotive areas have had political repercussions in the last few years, causing a polarisation towards extreme political solutions and making it difficult to form moderate centre governments with real power to take effective action.

In this context it can be clearly seen that the average Italian is mostly concerned with the political and economic problems on his own doorstep and tends to regard the European connection as somewhat irrelevant at present.

The Mission found this a consistent theme throughout discussions with representatives of the Italian building industry, whether on the professional or contracting side.

Certainly, there was unlimited goodwill regarding UK entry, and more than a pious hope that the innate British sense of order and organisation, administration, and ability in committee work would provide positive assistance to the various EEC commissions charged with Europeanising the activities of building industries in the member nations.

The Milan Group interviewed a representative cross-section of architects, engineers, property agents, contractors, local authority planners and a professional body. No instances of association, joint venture or any other form of collaboration with other EEC firms was discovered. The Group was told repeatedly that there was little added incentive for such association through EEC membership, and that this was more likely as a result of personal acquaintance through academic or professional conferences. By implication the Italian building industry did not expect a flurry of activity in Anglo-Italian groups after UK entry.

The Italian building industry is currently at its lowest ebb virtually since the war. Some very large and important firms are extremely short of work, and there appears to be no immediate prospect of an improvement. Although the last government passed new laws on the expropriation of land for popular housing, contractors do not regard this sector as particularly attractive to them.

It is therefore hardly likely that a powerful incursion of UK firms would be welcome unless accompanied by external finance or clients. It is also clear that British firms with the best chance of securing work in Italy are those with a specialisation not available in Italy, or where a broad expansion of investment might be expected. The Group had insufficient time to identify sectors, and advises any interested UK firm to carry out detailed investigation.

The urgent need for improved welfare facilities indicates a probable increase in public authority initiative on the construction of new hospitals, schools, and housing. Italian architects are interested in UK experience in this sector. Similarly, there is considerable respect for British experimentation in the development of new towns. Thus in the medium to long term, association between planners, architects and engineers of the two countries could be fruitful.

There is a developing interest in system building as a possible aid to speedy construction of schools and housing. Italian consultants and contractors are interested in discussing the use of these systems, though UK experience and disillusion with the efficacy of system building indicates that caution is advisable before entering into agreements in Italy.

Research and development facilities are generally lacking. State organisations spend very little and private companies hardly at all. This is an area where influence from Brussels headquarters may be brought to bear.

There is an acute awareness of the latent dangers of pollution. The plight of Venice has brought the problem widespread attention, and the country has probably the most severe laws of any EEC member in dealing with offenders.

Therefore, positive opportunities await any firm dealing with pollution control, whether in general consultancy or in design and manufacture of specialist plant. British pioneering work over many years in public health sectors - sewage treatment, water purification - should prove valuable credentials.

The Group found few likely opportunities for the manufacturers of building products in general. Local competition would be extremely strong, and there are no particular items which Britain could successfully export.

British contractors may find work through associating with Italian firms to bid for larger or more specialised contracts than the latter might be capable of alone. They will also be able to tender for state contracts, under liberalisation measures passed by the EEC Commission.

Professional firms should carefully investigate responsibility on building contracts. Italian law is severe on the individual where negligence or carelessness is suspected, and if there has been loss of life designers and contractors alike are imprisoned pending investigations.

It is interesting to note in the context of these severe precautions in the event of structural failure, that requirements for professional qualification are nowhere near as stringent as in the UK. Architects and engineers emerge from university able to assume design responsibility without any practical training under their belts.

Property developers may identify many attractive projects in many parts of Italy - including the South - but should investigate carefully the often complex and slow moving bureaucratic processes preceding commencement of construction. Many financially attractive propositions have turned sour as a result of interminable delays in securing approvals.

Finally, it can be said that Italy may eventually offer British firms more potential in most sectors of the building industry, once the present problems of sluggish activity and ponderous administration have been overcome. Harmonisation of professional qualifications and training, forms of building contract, regulations and codes of practice will all eventually assist UK firms. However, a large measure of patience will be essential.

The reform of regional, provincial and local government, giving responsibility to the regions for roads, waterways, tourism and markets, is hoped to speed up the decision-making process. Five of these regions, including Sicily and Sardinia, are specially designated because of local economic factors, and certainly need firm government. However, the Group found much scepticism about the reform in that it would merely add to the nation's bureaucratic problems.

BIBLIOGRAPHY AND REFERENCES

Available from the City of Westminster Chamber of Commerce

1. **Bollettino mensile** - monthly building cost indices. Società Generale Immobiliare, Roma. February 1972.

2. **Costi orari della mano d'opera edile per tutti i comuni della provincia di Milano** - building labour costs in Milan. Associazione imprese ed affini della provincia di Milano.

3. **Il Giornale dell 'Ingegnere** - engineering newspaper. Corso Venezia 16, Milano.

4. **Ingegneri Architetti: tariffa professionale** - government regulations on establishment of practice and fee scales for architects and engineers. L di Pirola, Milano, 1972.

5. **L'Ingegnere nei primi cento anni dell 'unita d'Italia** - history of 100 years of engineering in Italy. Convegno Nazionale degli Ingegneri Italiani. 2 vols.

6. **Listino dei prezzi delle opere edili in Milano** - unit building costs in Milan. Camera di Commercio Industria Artigianto e Agricoltura di Milano, via Meravigli 9b.

7. **Norme per il collaudo degli impianti di riscaldamento e di condizionamento** - standards for testing heating and ventilating plant in Milan. Collegio degli Ingegneri di Milano.

8. **Prospetto degli elementi della retribuzione, dei condipendenti dalle imprese edili ed affini della provincia di Milano** - basic social security contributions for workers and employers in building industry in Milan. Associazione imprese edili ed affini della provincia di Milano.

Publications

9. **Hints to businessmen** - Italy, Department of Trade and Industry, 1971.

10. **New regional development machinery in Italy** - article in OECD Observer, December 1970.

Regular Publications

11. **Annuario Statistico Italiano** - annual digest of statistics, Istituto Centrale di Statistico via Cesare Balbo 16, 00 100 Roma.

12. **Italian Economic Survey.** Association of Italian Joint Stock Companies, Piazza Venezia 11, 00187 Roma. Bi-monthly.

13. **Kompass: Register of Italian Industry and Commerce.** Etas-Kompass Edizioni per L'Informazione Economica SpA, 6 via Mantegna, Milano, or from Kompass Register Ltd, RAC House, Landsdowne Rd, Croydon CR9 2HE.

14. **L'Architectura** - architectural journal. Etas, via Andrea Mantegna 6, 20154 Milano. Monthly.

15. **Proprieta Fondiaria** - real estate advertising paper. Via Ravizza 4, 28100 Novara.

Addresses

British Embassy. Villa Wolkonsky, via Conte Rosso 25, 1-00185 Roma.

British Chamber of Commerce for Italy. via Tarchetti 1/3, 20121 Milano.

16. **Azienda Nazionale Autonoma delle Strade - ANAS.** National road corporation. Via Monzambano 10, 00185 Roma.

17. **Confederazione Generale del l'Industria Italiano - Confindustria.** Piazza Venezia 11, Roma.

18. **Confederazione Generale Italiana del Commercio - Confcommercio.** Piazza GG Belli 2, Roma.

19. **Istituto Centrale di Statistica - ISTAT.** Via Balbo 16, Roma.

20. **Istituto per Ricostruzione Industriale - IRI.** Industrial redevelopment corporation. Via Vittoria Veneto, 00187 Roma.

21. **Istituto Nazionale di Architettura** - Palazzo Taverna, via Monte Giordano 36, Roma.

22. **Consiglio Nazionale Ingegneri e Architetti Italiani - ANIA.** Piazza Sallustio 24, 00187 Roma.

23. **Consiglio Nazionale degli Ingegneri.** Via Bertoloni 31, 00197 Roma.

24. **Associazione Ingegneri Consulenti Italiani - AICI.** Via Settembre 3, 10121 Torino.

25. **Consiglio Nazionale dei Geometri** - national council of surveyors. Via Barberini 68, Roma.

26. **Associazione Nazionale Costruttori Edili - ANCE** - national association of building contractors. Via Guattoni 16, 00161 Roma.

27. **Associazione Imprese Edili ed Affini della Provincia di Milano** - association of building contractors in Milan. Via S Maurilio 21, Milano 20123.

Netherlands

Population: 13M Area: 16,000 sq. miles Capital: Amsterdam - 850 000 Chief cities: Rotterdam - 700 000 Den Haag - 570 000 Utrecht - 280 000 GNP: £13 000 Employment: Cost of living index: 142.1 (1964 = 100)

INTRODUCTION

The Dutch have grasped perhaps more than any other member country the benefits of an enlarged Common Market, and have consistently welcomed UK entry. 60% of their exports are sold in the EEC, 30% of which to West Germany on whom the economy greatly depends, though they are looking to the UK as a favourable added market.

The economy is at present facing inflation. Unemployment is at 1.5% and slowly rising, prices rose 5.5% in the first half of 1971, wages rose 12.5% in 1970, and the balance of payments is showing a deficit of around 2,000M guilders. This inflation rate, the highest in Europe, is accompanied by the highest rising rate of taxation.

This is despite an immense industrial conurbation boasting Europoort - the world's leading port, and one of Europe's largest petrochemical and oil-refining centres, the giant companies Royal Dutch Shell, Philips, Unilever; and a very strong transportation industry - Dutch carriers handle over 50% of Rhine transport and almost 33% of Western Europe road transport.

However, this industrialisation of the Ranstadt - an area based on Amsterdam, Rotterdam and Den Haag containing 50% of the population - has left the Government with the familiar European problem of regional neglect, a chronic housing shortage, and growing pollution.

The construction industry has felt the backlash of economic inflation, and the patterns of industrial development. The Government is anxious to pursue a policy of environmental control and construction is being actively discouraged, apart from the housing sector. Meanwhile, building costs continue to rise at over 10% per year.

THE PLANNING PROCESS

1. Political structure

The country consists of 11 provinces, with the seat of Government in Den Haag - a constitutional monarchy with executive power vested in a cabinet led by the prime minister. There are two houses of legislature - the Lower Chamber, elected by universal suffrage and holding ultimate legislative power, and the Upper Chamber.

The Ministry of Transport and Waterworks is responsible for public works schemes, and the Ministry of Housing and Physical Planning exercises wide

planning control and directs policy, through its power to issue building licences. Locally, the municipality is responsible for general planning control
within its area, leasing land for commercial and industrial development.

2. Tax and sources of government finance

Value added tax, known as BTW, was introduced to Holland in 1969. 14%
is added to all building work, and this includes professional fees and land
costs. When BTW was introduced, the rate was 12%, and the immediate effect
was to increase contract cost by some 6%.

3. Building law and regulations

Though by law the Government is empowered to frame national building
regulations, local government in fact has taken the initiative and the Association of Netherlands Municipalities has drafted standard national building
regulations which may be extensively amended by each local authority.

Municipal building inspectorates check building applications, inspect work
in progress, and charge a fee for their services. Testing and approval of materials and construction systems is carried out by KOMO, a branch of the
Association of Netherland Municipalities, and the Ratiobouw, a branch of the
Bouwcentrum, or Building Centre, which issues certificates — Kenmarkblad —
mainly for housing projects.

4. Building approval

Every development scheme requires a permit to be obtained from the municipality. Only one permit is issued following advice from four government
departments:

1. Town Planning Department
2. Building Police - covering building and safety regulations
3. Fire Officer
4. Beauty Council - conservation body on which 3 prominent architects sit

A permit from the municipality takes 12 to 18 months to be granted, and
there is no appeal from an unfavourable decision.

DEVELOPMENT, INVESTMENT AND FINANCE

5. Land tenure

The municipalities and the Government own large areas of land, much of
which is acquired from land reclamation, bomb damage and slum clearance.
This land is normally leased in perpetuity, with five-yearly rent reviews. Apart
from this, land is generally held freehold - including Chief Rents - though
leasehold occupation is also common. Land available for building is not sur-
prisingly limited in the Netherlands, and with a population growth expected to
double in 25 years, there is likely to be pressure for development of
agricultural land.

6. Housing

There is a serious housing shortage with 375 000 unfit houses in Holland,
increasing at a rate of 25 000 a year.

The Government is committed to building at least 1% of the national population
in housing units each year - 130,000. Housing associations do exist, in part
subsidised by the Government, which are bringing sophisticated industrialised
building methods and techniques to ease the overall problem. 50% of housing
construction is public, 30% subsidised, and the remainder is private.

7. Investment

Major commercial development appears to have been carried out for owner
occupation. Because land is mostly held freehold, owners are reluctant to sell

and prefer to develop independently. However, private developers are prominent in commercial projects, including 6 major UK companies, and the pattern is changing.

8. Finance

There are no government incentives, but land for industrial development is occasionally provided by the municipality at low ground rents. Government policy is aimed more at restricting development by licence control apart from in approved areas. In addition to this Green Belt policy, there are proposals for a levy on all development in the following areas - the Golden Triangle, or Ranstadt, of Amsterdam, Rotterdam, Utrecht and Den Haag.

Sources of finance to developers are the banks, insurance companies and pension funds, but these funds can be subject to Government pressure to invest in residential property - through refusal of building licences for other purposes. There have been mixed developments of residential and offices, but these are not popular with investors or municipalities. Insurance companies have tended to invest in real estate, buying up land and providing funds for development which provides a social service, such as housing.

9. Average costs per m³

Offices with air conditioning	250-380g
Subsidised housing	120-150g
Better class housing	150-180g
Hotels: 5 star	72 000g/bedroom

THE PROFESSIONS

10. Division of work

Though professional status is generally held in high regard, building may be designed by other than registered professionals. In effect, the Beauty Council sets high standards which tend to prevent this. Quantity surveyors are unknown, largely because most projects are quoted on a lump sum, with a list of prices for alterations to specifications. The contractor is responsible for calculating quantities.

Package deals are known, but not to the same extent as in other EEC countries.

11. Contract procedures

These normally conform to standard clauses prescribed by Government bodies called the Uniforme Administrative Voorschriften - UAV. Construction data prepared by the architect before tender is not very detailed and tenders are generally lump sum. Contractor estimating costs are paid by the client.

Public tendering is open and can include up to 50 tenderers. For competitive tendering the firms invited to tender are published. Tenders are usually called for on the basis of a firm price, subject to a rise and fall clause, of which the first 6-12 months are fixed. On commercial development a fixed price is usually negotiated for the entire contract period. For investment projects, negotiated tenders are normally accepted to avoid delays and a surcharge added to tenders by contractors to cover tendering costs.

12. Establishing a practice

The Group found no obvious obstacles to establishing a professional practice in Holland.

There appears to be no co-operation between professions of EEC countries, though a dialogue is taking place at Officer level on local government problems, particularly in town planning.

Architect

The architect is not protected, though there are registered architects, many of whom are members of the Bond Van Nederlandse Architecter - BNA - a similar body to the RIBA. Education is through university, technical college, sandwich courses and evening school.

Generally the architect produces approximate estimates, and agrees final accounts, in addition to furnishing designs.

Architectural draughtmen receive 700 guilders a month net, architectural assistants 1000 guilders. Social security and pensions add 45% to these basic wage costs.

There are opportunities for foreign architects to practice in Holland - unlike other EEC countires it is not necessary to register. However, it would be preferable to form an association with a local firm which is a member of the Institute - the BNA. This is mainly to overcome the problems associated with the strict planning regulations, and the operation of the Beauty Council which considers all planning applications.

It is felt by the Group that the best opportunities would lie in a UK architect working with a UK developer, particularly as local architects have less experience in the economics of commercial development.

Consulting engineer

There is a Dutch Association of consulting engineers - Orde van Nederlandse Raadgevende Ingenieurs, ONRI, though not all practising engineers are members. There are 157 members from 78 firms, the vast majority of which are structural engineers - other disciplines being town and regional planning, heating and ventilating, and electrical engineering. The other body for engineers if the Royal Institute of Engineers.

Firms are permitted to operate as limited liability companies, and 41 of the 78 member firms of ONRI do so. The liability is limited to a proportion of the fee.

Activity in the profession is at present centring on publicising the role and identity of the consulting engineer and improving his image.

Opportunity does exist for M & E engineers in Holland, and the group felt that they probably stand a better chance of obtaining direct commissions than either architects or quantity surveyors.

The method of working is similar to the UK for standards and regulations, and fee scales are also similar.

Quantity surveyor

Independent quantity surveyors are seldom found in Holland, apart from UK firms employed by other UK professional. Some time must pass before the building industry and the architectural profession becomes acclimatised to the use of their services.

However, the increased use of negotiated tenders in various forms must provide an excellent chance for the UK quantity surveyor to demonstrate his skill in cost control. Clients, architects, engineers and contractors are all showing interest at present in computer-aided information systems and integrated management systems determining fixing of budgets, and cost control during construction.

Contractor

All contractors are members of the association - NIVAG - or federation - NABU. About 4 have annual turnovers of £50M - £100M, and between 10-12 of £15M. All are general contractors with large planning departments.

The general tendering system is for the project to be quoted on a lump sum basis with a schedule of rates or prices for variation. As a result, contractors are geared to turnkey projects.

The contractors' association requires each tenderer to add up to 10% to the tender figure to cover tendering costs. An unsuccessful contractor in a design/construct tender would receive 0.6% from the successful contractor, while a tenderer on a construct scheme only would receive 0.2%. This procedure applies equally to the sub-contractor, with higher percentages to cover design costs. The overall effect can be to add over 10% to the building cost.

Specialist sub-contractors are occasionally nominated, but the main contractor generally prefers to maintain complete control of construction, including all sub-contractors. Where sub-contractors are nominated, a special planning engineer is appointed to co-ordinate the programme for the architect, contractor and the sub-contractor. Services sub-contractors do sub-let certain particularly specialised work such as sprinkler installations.

The contractors liability is limited to the contract value.

There are 3 unions, following a political pattern for construction workers, and there are no demarcation problems. Building rates have tended to follow labour rates in manufacturing industries where negotiations are based on productivity agreements. Increases are negotiated on a yearly basis between the unions and the contractors.

Basic labour rates on a 42 hour week are 9 guilders/hr including social security. Social security adds 45% to the wage rate making the wage bill to the contractor 15 guilders/hr. Production bonuses are operated as in UK but overtime is not common. At staff level, redundancy payments are made principally by the Government and up to 80% of salaries for a period of up to 12 months. Wage costs are now rising at a rate of 15% a year. Strikes are rare.

With the exception of the housing market, where there is still a serious shortage, the building and civil engineering industry seems currently depressed and competition is keen.

Directives recently under consideration by the EEC on the law of establishment of services and public tendering will to a limited extent assist contractors moving into third countries. The existing regulation on free mobility of labour has been especially taken advantage of by Dutch contractors who in 1967 carried out more work in the EEC than any other.

Bearing in mind the experience gained by other EEC countractors, the best way for a UK contractor to establish in Holland, would be through association with a local firm, especially if he has some expertise to offer. The association could be for one particular venture, or permanent, from which to base further expansion.

CONCLUSIONS AND SUMMARY

Entry into the Common Market appears to have had little direct benefit on the Dutch construction industry. Growth in the industry is at present low and dependent on an upsurge in the economy and a return to confidence by the investor. There are prospects that the Government will impose further restrictions on building in the shape of legislation for a levy of up to 100% on building development and this could seriously affect the industry.

The Dutch are well-disposed to the British and association at all levels should be straightforward. English is widely spoken and there are definite opportunities for specialised skills and expertise. In M & E work collaboration would be beneficial, as standard and methods are similar to the UK.

Tendering procedure is subject to much criticism, with the result that many private developers are relying on negotiated tenders. There are development and investment opportunities, where the quantity surveyor could make a useful contribution, particularly in the Golden Triangle of Rotterdam, Amsterdam and Utrecht. However, planning problems in Amsterdam tend to restrict implementation. Land acquisition is difficult.

The first indications that developers are going to experience serious difficulties have come with the government's plans to severely restrict office and factory building in the Ranstadt. Central government permits are already required for any development in this area, and the proposals are for additional taxation on commercial companies undertaking construction, based on the total investment involved for any project which has received planning permission. Holland's fears of over-industrialisation may thus prove a deterrent to investment.

The Government has certain problem areas of high unemployment, resulting from the closure of coal mines, but with the lack of incentives it is doubtful if these offer good development opportunities.

The future for prospective developers in Holland should hold much interest. The country's high population density and fast growing economy is ensuring considerable development in urban renewal and office building, but the Government's pursuance of a stringent conservationist policy means that projects will clearly have to be fought for.

BIBLIOGRAPHY AND REFERENCES

Publications

1. **The Netherlands.** *Times* special report. October 1971.

2. **Building regulations in the Netherlands** - FE Samson. Rotterdam; Bouwcentrum. 1967.

3. **Housing in the Netherlands.** Ministry of Housing and Physical Planning, Den Haag, 1966.

Regular Publications

4. **De Raadgevende - Ingenieur** - consulting engineering journal. Ungerplein 2, Rotterdam 4.

5. **Makelaarsweekblad.** Real estate advertising. Rokin 24, Amsterdam.

Addresses

British Embassy. Large Voorhout 10, Den Haag.

Netherlands - British Chamber of Commerce. Raamweg 45, Postbus 2804 Den Haag.

6. **Bouwcentrum** - building centre. Rotterdam.

7. **Stichting Ratiobouw.** Foundation for Rationalised Building, Rotterdam.

8. **Bond Van Nederlandse Architecten.** Keizersgracht 321 Amsterdam.

9. **Nederlandse Landmeetkundige Federatie** - federation of surveyors. Betje Wolffstraat 65 Zwolle.

10. **Koninklijk Instituut van Ingenieurs.** Prinsesses gracht 23 Den Haag.

11. **Orde van Nederlandse Raadgevende Ingenieurs - ONRI** - Order of consulting engineers. Javastraat 44, Den Haag.

12. **Vereniging van Nederlandse Aannemers met Belangen in het Buitenland - NABU** - Netherlands Association of International Contractors. Raamweg 44, Den Haag.

13. **Nederlandse Instituut van Aannemers Grootbedrijf - NIVAG -** Netherlands Institute of Major Contractors. Raamweg 44 Den Haag.

14. **Vereniging van Systeembouwers** - system builders association. Groot Hertoginnelaan 3, Den Haag.

Conclusions

The preceding pages provide a broad picture of the structure and activity of the building industry in each of the 5 EEC member countries visited by the Mission.

After more than 10 years existence of the Community it is quite evident that little headway has yet been made in harmonising and standardising training and educational systems, professional ethics and standards, planning and control methods, contract procedures, or sources of funding projects.

This is hardly surprising in view of the monumental task which still faces the Commission in Brussels of turning the broad concept of an economic community into a reality - a task which has demanded amongst other things the need to allocate priorities in the process of harmonisation. Inevitably, the construction industry has been relegated to a relatively low position in the list. It could perhaps be argued than an industry which in 1965 constructed $600 000 000 worth of buildings, representing 9% of total EEC output, and employed around 7M workers might be worthy of early attention. However, as aid by Dr C Friz, a director of the EEC Commission, at the Brussels conference, there are difficulties in integrating an industry which is so closely connected with national policy and so often used by government as an instrument of economic or electoral manipulation. Members of the UK industry know only too well that when the economy fares badly, building activity is among the first casualties.

In addition, there are dangers in the harmonisation process of a levelling down of standards of training, education, professional practice and construction. This will not be easily avoided with an enlarged Community of 10 seeking common standards.

Commission measures

However, there are now increasing signs of Commission action, the most important of these being probably the July 1971 directive suppressing national restrictions on foreign contractors taking part in public tenders. Directives so far enacted which affect the construction industry are:

1. abolition of tariffs and quota restrictions, and general rules of competition - finally eliminated 1968.
2. rights of establishment and providing services, excluding public sector - 1964.
3. free movement of capital - 1961, but still not entirely free.

4. free movement of labour - 1968.
5. harmonisation of taxation - 1967 directive on VAT
6. harmonisation of social and working conditions - still
    far from realisation.

The Commission has also been engaged in formulating common objectives for the EEC construction industry. These have centred around the vital need for more research and development, and some sort of co-ordination in its application, for more activity in the social field - schools, hospitals and, as has been seen in the preceding reports, housing. A Commission publication - Industrie de la Construction, March 1971 - lists all the measures envisaged at community level.

EEC effect on building industry

Up to the present, the advent of the EEC has had virtually no impact in expanding national building industries. Mission members were not unduly surprised by this, but had nevertheless expected a greater degree of inter-penetration and crossing of frontiers than in fact was discovered. Even joint enterprises between firms of different nationalities were not easily found.

There are, however, a number of Italian contracting companies active in France where they appear to operate successfully. Dutch marine contractors have also found work in Italy, exploiting their specialist knowledge. It also appears that building product manufacturers close to national borders find no difficulty in exporting their products across these borders, within fairly limited geographical limits.

The rather negative overall findings of the Mission must, of course, be kept in perspective. The United States is a geographical and economic union like the EEC, but after nearly 200 years still exhibits considerable variety in its state laws. These laws also affect the construction industry and there is no uniformity of regulations nor complete freedom to work anywhere in the States without complying with local formalities. Seen in this light, the 10 year existence of the European Community seems a very short time in which to achieve the ultimate aim of complete liberalisation.

Study of the conclusions reached by the individual Groups indicates the extent of variation in regulations, procedures, attitudes and levels of activity, and there will have to be much hard bargaining and goodwill in achieving uniformity which does not represent a lowering of standards. There is an urgent need for improvement in building techniques - both in design and con-struction - and a raising of standards in education and training of all those responsible for the operation of the industry, whether in design management or execution.

No-one would claim that the established UK procedures for the execution of construction projects are flawless, and the Mission as a whole found that very similar problems exist in the EEC. To a large extent these stem from an in-creasing specialisation in building which results in a multiplication of individuals and firms concerned with a single project. Unless organisational skills exist to co-ordinate the activities of a multiplicity of experts, then severe difficulties can arise, often in the form of claims by the client against the building team. Insurance cover against these eventualities is by no means easy to obtain in the EEC, a factor which any British firm operating in the area should investigate carefully.

During the long debate on Britain's entry into the Common Market, the point was frequently made that the major benefits lay more in the political field than any other. However, there is no escaping the fact that lowering of tariff barriers will expand the export of British capital and consumer goods. Such reductions in border taxes affect the provision of services such as those in the building industry to a lesser degree, and therefore while opportunities for expansion certainly exist, they need more careful identification with a full understanding of the local problems involved.

The opportunities

In broad terms, the main opportunities seem to lie where expertise and know-how possessed by British firms is lacking in an EEC country. These include:
Property development and financing
Project management
Computer applications in building
Urban planning, traffic engineering
Quantity surveying
General surveying and property valuation
Building services consultancy
Pollution control
In addition, the Italians appear interested in system building as applied to schools and hospitals.

A number of British firms - particularly quantity surveyors - may gain access to Europe with British property developers. Others with specialist knowledge will be able to associate with European firms for joint operations. Direct appointment by a European client may be secured where a firm has a virtual monopoly of the specialisation required. It may also be possible to secure contracts from multi-national companies such as Shell, in establishing new plants in the EEC.

The international concern now evident for safeguarding the environment must imply an increasing expenditure in expertise, services and equipment, and un-doubtedly British skills in pollution control will be in demand in the EEC.

A further potential source of work could arise from the European Development Fund. This fund was established to finance projects in associate-member countries of the EEC, which have so far been located mainly in the ex French African colonies. French contractors have unsurprisingly benefitted most from the application of these funds, causing some concern in other member countries. With Britain's entry, it is likely that the application of the fund will extend to ex British colonies, and Britain will be expected to contribute financially. This would provide useful opportunities for British firms, particularly in association with firms from other member countries.

It could of course be said that most of the above - mentioned opportunities already exist, and the UK entry will not alter the situation very much. However, the psychological impetus of entry should not be under-estimated and will probably create attitudes on both sides conducive to positive results. Certainly, contacts made by the Mission showed universal enthusiasm for UK membership and the contribution the British construction industry could make.

At first glance it would appear that the way into Europe will be clearer for British exporters of building components, although examination of the perform-ance of all existing member countries indicates no great expansion of such exports. Certainly, opposition is very fierce, particulary where suggestions of 'dumping' are made. Manufacturers of certain items have undoubtedly made inroads into other markets, particularly Italian ceramic products in Belgium. Price and quality obviously are of equal importance in achieving success. Building component manufacturers should of course accordingly undertake thorough market research before launching any sales programme.

Apart from acquiring a thorough knowledge of legislation, regulations, and procedures, and undertaking market surveys, any British firm would need to employ personnel with an intimate knowledge of the language of the country where penetration is envisaged. English is not sufficient, nor in some countries is French.

In conclusion, the Chamber intends to maintain the various contacts made in the Mission, and will endeavour to provide assistance in investigating potential sources of business in the EEC with up-to-date information and help in approaching sources of information in the appropriate countries. The bibliography of useful references which follows is only representative of a vast amount of available information, and should not be considered exhaustive.

Bibliography

This section is a general bibliography of selected sources of information on the Common Market as a whole.

GENERAL

1. **Britain and Europe** - short version of Government White Paper, HMSO.
2. **Britain & EEC** - reprints from *Trade & Industry*. Department of Trade and Industry 1971.
3. **Fact sheets on Britain and Europe**. HMSO 1971.
4. **The United Kingdom and the European Communities**. HMSO 1971.
5. **Directory of the Commission of the European Communities.** Brussels September 1971.
6. **Barclays Bank Economic Intelligence Department reports on the EEC.** 1972.
7. **Factual Guide to the Common Market.** Midland Bank, 1972.
8. **The Common Market and the United Kingdom guide to the European Economic Community and the possible effects of British entry.** National Westminster Bank 1971.
9. **Decision on Europe; an explanation of the Common Market** - DH Hene. Jordan 1970.
10. **The economics of the Common Market** - D Swann. Penguin 1970.
11. **EEC facts & figures.** Barclays Bank 1972.
12. **European living costs compared.** Confederation of British Industry 1972.
13. **Europe.** *Financial Times* report in two parts December 1971.
14. **Europe and the Environment.** *Times* special report April 1972.
15. **Overture for Europe.** *Economist* special survey January 1972.

INDUSTRY

16. **Britain and Europe,** CBI 1967.
17. **Britain in Europe: a second industrial appraisal.** CBI supplement to above study 1970.
18. **Industry and Europe: an industrial view of some economic objectives and problems of an enlarged European Community** - Council of European Industrial Federations Integration Committee. CBI 1971.

19. **European Development Aid.** EEC pamphlet from European Community Information service.

20. **The free movement of persons and services in the EEC** - C Maestripieri, Lecture to Course on Common Market, Den Norske Advokatforening May 1971.

21. **Regional policy in Britain and the Six: the problems of development** - H Lind. Chatham House/PEP 1970.

22. **Transport policy of the European Communities** - N Despicht. Chatham House/PEP 1969.

REGULAR SOURCES OF INFORMATION

23. There are a number of publications issuing information on the Community. This is a selection:

    Bulletin of the European Communities. European Communities Commission. Available from HMSO. Monthly.

    Common Market News. CEDIF - Compagnie Européenne pour le Développement Industriel et Financier - 124 rue du Commerce 1040 Bruxelles. UK subscriptions: David Elliott and Associates, 17 Berners St, London W1P 4DN. 44 times a year.

    Community topics. European Communities Press and Information.

    European Community. European Communities Press and Information. Monthly.

    European Community Information. *Financial Times.* Monthly.

    Journal officiel des Communautes européennes. Available from HMSO. Several issues weekly.

    Rapport général sur l'activité des Communautés - EEC. Available from EEC. Yearly.

24. **EEC/EFTA Information Unit.** 1 Victoria St London SW1H OET. Tel: 01-222 7877.

25. **Export Credit Guarantee Department.** Aldermanbury House, Aldermanbury, London EC2. Tel: 01-606 6699.

26. **Press and Information directorate-general of EEC** - European Community Information Service. Headquarters: Rue de la Loi, 1040 Bruxelles. UK Office: 23 Chesham St London SW1. Tel: 01-235 4904.

The following is a selected list of published information on the EEC building industry in particular.

GENERAL

1. **Community regulations on construction** - DR Bruns-Wustefeld: The Common Market and Construction Conference October 1971.

2. **Construction Industry and the Common Market** - Department of the Environment study August 1971.

3. **Construction market in the Common Market and likely UK impact** - David Cochlin: The Common Market and Construction conference October 1971.

4. **Industrie de la construction - la recherche et l'innovation dan le bâtiment** - report of Industrial, Technological and Scientific directorate-general of EEC Commission, Brussels April 1971.

5. **Industrie de la construction - recensement des action en faveur des actions de la construction qui pourraient être envisagées a l'échelon communautaire** - report of Industrial Technological and Scientific directorate-general of EEC Commission, Brussels March 1971.

6. **The Roles of Authorities, Designers, and Builders in Western Europe** - GA Atkinson; Chartered Surveyors conference 1971.

REGULATIONS

7. **Building law in Western Europe: how responsibility for safety and good performance is shared** - GA Atkinson: Building Research Station current paper.

8. **The structure of building control: an international comparison** - E Cibula BRS current paper.

9. **Systems of building control** - E Cibula: BRS current paper.

BUILDING PRODUCTS

10. **Building products and the European Community** - National Building Agency 1972.

11. **The Common Market: how suppliers can establish and operate in Europe** - CG Tudor Pole. The Common Market and Construction conference October 1971.

12. **European Coal and Steel Community pricing: the British Steel Corporation approach.** Steel pricing in the Common Market. Pamphlets from BSC April 1972.

PROFESSIONS & TRADE

13. **Architects in the EEC** - JP du Crayencour, RIBAJ May 1971.

14. **Consulting engineers in Europe** - JJ Gandy. Civil Engineering and Public Works Review May 1972.

15. **Federation Internationale des Ingenieurs-Conseils** - reports from member associations. FIDIC.

16. **How clients and professionals do business in Europe** - Jean-Claude Pick. The Common Market and Construction conference October 1971.

17. **Chartered surveyors and the EEC.** RICS Handbook.

18. **Planning and property development in Europe** - Colin Hunt. Chartered surveyors' annual conference 1971.

19. **Property acquisition and planning bye-laws approvals procedure in Europe** - A Lindsay, Chartered surveyors' annual conference 1971.

20. **British and European property development.** *Times* special report April 1972.

21. **Contract procedures and techniques in Europe and Scandinavia** - Bjorn Bindslev. Chartered surveyors' annual conference October 1971.

22. **Europe, Britain and the engineer** - GA Wilson. ICE presidential address 1971.

23. **How to get contracting business in Europe** - H Spierenburg. The Common Market and Construction conference October 1971.

SOURCES OF INFORMATION

24. A number of technical journals have been running regular EEC information features, including: Building Design, Chartered Surveyor.

25. **Inter-professional liaison group for construction.** Members: ICE, RIBA and RICS.

26. **RICS Technical Information Service.** Monthly publication: Abstracts and Reviews.

27. **United Information Services.** Intelligence bulletin on new European building projects with building, engineering and ancillary services specifications. UIS, Rowland House, Hinton Rd, Bournemouth. Fortnightly.

28. **Technical Help to Exporters** - publication, *Technical Digest*. BSI, Maylands Avenue, Hemel Hempstead, Herts.

29. **Construction Industry Directorate of Department of Environment.** 2 Marsham St London SW1.

THE CONTRIBUTORS

Brussels group membership

Dr DF Strongitharm
group leader
Head of Department of Building
Polytechnic of Central London

AJ Bamford
Partner
George M Bramall & Partners
Architects and building surveyors

CB Brown
Partner
CB Brown & Partners
Consulting engineers

JK Hayes
Partner
Hayes & Hussey
Quantity surveyors

WKE Jones
Partner
Andrews Kent & Stone
Consulting engineers

PE Leach
Partner
Tripe & Wakeham
Architects

BE Reed
Projects manager
Hills Structures & Foundations Ltd.,
Property developers

S Zins
Principal
Stefan Zins Associates
Architects

Paris group membership

A George
group leader/Principal
Alfred George & Associates
Architects

RAF Allen
Senior civil engineer
Taylor Woodrow Construction Ltd.,
Building & Civil engineering contractors

JR Barbour
Partner
WV Zinn & Partners
Consulting Engineers

GT Branch
Partner
Burley Lane & Partners
Quantity surveyors

RH Crapnell
Partner
Raymond Spratley & Partners
Architects

C Pascall
Senior Partner
Clive Pascall and Peter Watson
Architects

CM Rice
Partner
Franklin & Andrews
Quantity surveyors

HWB Semple
Partner
Louis Adair Roche & Paddy Semple
Architects

VFH Smith
Partner
AE Beer & Partners
Consulting engineers

F Warren
Contracts manager
John Laing Construction Ltd
Building and civil engineering contractors

Milan group membership

AB Grant
group leader/ Senior partner
Alan Grant & Partners
Consulting engineers

RA Butterfield
Partner
George Corderoy & Co
Quantity surveyors

ADH Grimmett
Contracts manager
Taylor Woodrow Construction Ltd
Building and civil engineering contractors

DA Knight
Principal
Stanley Peach & Partners
Architects and surveyors

JC Douglas
Senior partner
WH McAlister & Partners
Architects

R Morrison
Partner
Banks, Wood & Partner
Quantity surveyors

RJT Pope
Partner
Tripe & Wakeham
Architects

HM Rayner
Partner
Drivers Jonas
Surveyors

SJ Shelton
Consultant
Revall Hayward & Partners
Consulting engineers

Dusseldorf/Bonn group membership

R Steane
group leader/Partner
Ian Fraser, Roberts, Steane & Partners
Architects

K Buffery
Partner
Robert Matthew, Johnson -
Marshall & Partners
Architects

RH Davies
Director
Robin Developments
Developers

FD Dromgoole
Quantity surveyor
John Laing Construction Ltd.,
Building and Civil Engineering Contractors

M Glicker
Partner
Hildebrand & Glicker
Architects and Surveyors

LH Gregory
Principal
Lionel H Gregory
Quantity surveyors

JL Harwood
Senior partner
Frank N Falkner & Partners
Quantity surveyors

JM Heggadon
Group marketing manager
John Mowlem & Co Ltd
Construction Group

PC Hennell
Director
Robin Developments
Developers

CT Lovick
Partner
Oscar Faber & Partners
Consulting engineers

HF Nelson
General manager - Architects Advisory Department
The Cement Marketing Co Ltd
Cement manufacturers

SH Pickett
Managing director
London Group of Project Consultants
Project consultants

LA Roche
Partner
Louis Adair Roche & Paddy Semple
Architects

EL Smalley
Partner
Sydney A Paine & Partners
Quantity surveyors

JAR Spratley
Partner
Raymond Spratley & Partners
Architects

KCW Van der Lee
Projects manager
Taylor Woodrow Construction Ltd
Building and Civil Engineering Contractors

DJ Wood
Associate partner
Davis Belfield & Everest
Quantity surveyor

Amsterdam group membership

HG Huckle
group leader/ Senior partner
HG Huckle & Partners
Architects and town planners

SH Birch
Partner
E Wingfield-Bowles & Partners
Consulting engineers

AR Brown
Divisional director
Matthew Hall Mechanical Services Ltd
Mechanical services engineers

MD Bruce
Partner
Banks, Wood & Partners
Quantity surveyors

JB Burdekin
Projects manager
Taylor Woodrow Construction Ltd
Building and civil engineering contractors

RP Hildebrand
Partner
Hildebrand & Glicker
Architects and surveyors

KSJ Speller
Senior partner
Harris Rourke & Simpson
Quantity surveyors and building cost consultants

Analysis of the Construction Industry

P.J. Reynolds, BSc and P.Hesketh, BA

Department of Building, University of Manchester Institute of Science and Technology.

The construction industry is such a diverse body that a satisfactory analysis of all the companies it embodies has never been easy. This new analysis is unusual in that it not only provides a clear view of the construction industry as a whole but also probes in great depth into the total operations of a select group of contracting companies. As a result, the information presented and the conclusions reached are likely to be of far-reaching consequence.

Introduction

STANDARD INDUSTRIAL CLASSIFICATION

The Standard Industrial Classification (SIC) defines *Construction* as erection of all types of structures, road building, pipe laying, etc. Such activities as property development, estate agency, design, etc., are not included within the Standard Industrial definition although they may be considered as part of the construction industry as a whole.

Construction   Construction is defined in Order XX of the Standard Industrial Classification as follows:-

> "Erecting and repairing buildings of all types. Constructing and repairing roads and bridges; erecting steel and reinforced concrete structures; other civil engineering work such as laying sewers, gas and water mains and electricity cables, erecting overhead lines and line supports and aerial masts, extracting coal from open cast workings, etc. The building and civil engineering establishments of government departments, local authorities and New Town Corporations and Commissions are included as well as on-site industrial building.

> Establishments specialising in demolition work or sections of construction work such as asphalting, electrical wiring, glooring, glazing, installation of heating and ventilating apparatus, painting, plastering, plumbing, roofing, the hiring of contractors plant and scaffolding is included. This Order includes construction work carried out by employees of gas, electricity and water undertakings."

The Standard Industrial Classification uses establishments as a basis for data collection, the establishments usually being firms, which are classified according to their major activity. If a firm is engaged in a number of activities which are not in the same *Order* in the Standard Industrial Classification, and information is available separately for the activities, then that part of the firm concerned with each separate activity is considered as an establishment, otherwise the predominant activity determines the classification. Indeed it is virtually impossible to present a clear picture, since data is collected by government offices related to establishments rather than companies; and in any case the wide spread of activities of many companies makes it impossible to align their operations with the definition of the Standard Industrial

Classification. The information which is required from each establishment includes such data as employment figures, expenses, turnover and capital formation.

This review is restricted to the consideration of construction as defined by the Standard Industrial Classification, and its prime aim is to examine financial aspects of quoted companies in the industry; in the course of this examination, some attention is given to companies which might not be included in a list of quoted construction companies compiled strictly to the rules of the Standard Industrial Classification. This is because one cannot always tell whether construction was the company's major activity and information is not available for their construction activities separately. It was felt that these companies could not be excluded completely from a consideration of the quoted construction companies since they contributed substantially to the output of this part of the construction industry.

Problems of Classification

As in any attempt to define a sector of the economy, there are many problems of classification. While for example plant hire is included, a firm like Bristol Plant must on this definition be excluded, since the major part of its activities is composed of plant sales. Similar problems arise with firms such as Truscon and Concrete which both manufacture precast units and are involved in contracting.

Even more complex is the situation presented by the diverse activities of such firms as Tarmac, Trafalgar House Investments and Woodhall Trust. The upshot is that the best that it is possible to do is to produce a list of companies which to the best of one's belief represents the quoted companies which would, on the basis of the major element of their turnover, be classified to *construction* as defined by the Standard Industrial Classification.

Changes in the Industry

There have been a number of changes within the construction industry during the past few years. The number of firms and the number of employees engaged in construction work has declined steadily and the changes in the output of the construction industry over the past five years have not followed the same pattern as that of the rest of industry as a whole. The number of public construction companies has increased substantially from that in 1948, when there were only 46 quoted companies operating in construction. There are now (1970), on a comparable basis, 139.

Accounts

The accounts of thirty of these quoted companies operating in construction during 1970 have been studied as a sample; the accounts of the *average* company have been calculated and are discussed in section 3 in relation to the accounts of the *average* company in other industries. This brings up to date some aspects of a study conducted by C.F. Carter in the early fifties in which he examined the accounts of the quoted construction companies operating in the period 1949 - 1953 and contrasted them with the *average* accounts of all industry.

The main problem with a study of this kind is that there are a large number of variations in accounting practice between the companies so there are dangers in making inter-company comparisons. There is also the danger that the average accounts of the thirty companies selected for closer examination may not exhibit the same characteristics as the individual companies. The results of the study of the average accounts should therefore be assessed with these reservations.

The Year Under Review

The fact that the operations of the year 1970 have to be examined instead of a more recent year is indicative of another problem - the time lag between the activity occurring and information about it coming available. Unfortunately a study of this nature takes some time to complete; also, companies often take a long time to produce their results, which in addition do not always relate to the calendar year, but to a financial year overlapping into the following year. *Thus for this review, begun in 1972, it was not possible to obtain complete information for a year later than 1970.*

Since then there have been some changes. In terms of the value of output of the industry there has been an increase in contemporary prices from £5079M for 1970 to £5561M for 1971, a rise of 10%. However, at constant prices, the increase was only 1.7%. In terms of value added, or the industry's contribution to the gross national product there has been a corresponding increase from £2683M for 1970 to £2894M for 1971 in contemporary prices or 8%, which again reduces to 1.7% at constant prices.

There will have been some changes too, in the numbers of quoted companies, in their turnover and in virtually all aspects of their finances. It is hoped that in the future it may be possible to re-schedule publication dates to reduce the time gap between the year reported on and actual publication; meanwhile we hope that this review at least brings into a convenient form data on the subject in a way that has not recently been attempted. To the best of our knowledge all the data used in this review is correct. Though, naturally, we cannot guarantee the accuracy of the information presented we can say that every effort has been made to substantiate data used and we trust that the whole presents, a fair and accurate picture of the construction industry.

1 Review of the Construction Industry

PROFILE AND STRUCTURE

Profile of the Industry

The construction industry consists of a large number of firms and a quantity of direct labour in the public sector engaged in a variety of activities. The firms range in size from the large public quoted companies engaged in multi million pound contracts to the self employed craftsman engaged in the repair and maintenance of housing. The majority of the work which is classified as construction is the building of new structures, e.g. houses, shops, offices, factories, power stations, docks, roads, bridges, etc., but also included with this industry is the repair and maintenance of these structures, open cast mining and the laying of services such as gas mains, drains and sewers, etc. (See the SIC definition quoted in the introduction).

The industry is a significant contributor to the economy of the United Kingdom, both in terms of output and employment. The value of all constructional work undertaken during 1970 was a little over £5000M. A substantial part of this represents of course the output from other industries that is purchased by firms in the construction industry and incorporated in the final product. The contribution of the industry itself to the Gross National Product (£43 100M in 1970) was £2710M or 6.3%. In 1969 this was 6.6%. For the two years 1969 and 1970 employees in the industry totalled 1 677 000 and 1 575 000. These figures represent 6.53% and 6.19% respectively of the total working population. Thus the relationship between these two percentages - contribution to GNP and proportion of the working population changed from a ratio of 1.010 to 1.018 (% of employees : % of GNP) from one year to the next, suggesting that productivity in the industry has improved over the period.

The Structure of the Industry

In 1948 there were approximately 130000 firms in the construction industry; by 1960 there were 90508 and by 1965 there were 83696. In 1970 the total number of firms was 73420. This decline in the number of firms is not easily explained, but can be attributed largely to a growth in productivity per operative, associated with an increased use of technical expertise and an increased investment in plant[1]. Inevitably it tended to be larger firms that were able to support these activities and hence, perhaps, the large reductions

[1] Investment in plant and equipment by the construction industry amounted to
1960 - £33M   1965 - £87M   1970 - £87M.

in the numbers of small firms. This is, however, a complex topic and it is not the purpose of the writers to deal with it in this review.

These 73420 firms which remained in 1970 can be classified in terms of their trade as follows:- General builders, 31546; Building and civil engineering contractors, 2201; Civil engineers, 1567; the other 38106 consist of a variety of firms specialising in a particular trade, e.g. joiners and carpenters, demolition contractors, scaffolding contractors, electrical contractors, etc. The two largest specialist groups are painters, 12258 and plumbers, 4572. (See Appendix 1 for complete list).

OUTPUT AND PERFORMANCE TRENDS

Trends and Changes   The percentage of the total work undertaken in each sector of the industry's market has changed very little between 1966 and 1970. The changes which have occurred are that the percentage undertaken by direct labour in the public sector has risen and the percentage of work undertaken in repair and maintenance and new work done by contractors has fallen slightly. Within the new work sector there has been a change of position, in that in 1966 more work was undertaken in the private sector than in the public, but in 1970 the reverse was true.

Table 1.1   **Value of output during 1970 in Great Britain (£ M).**

Work done by contractors

New Housing - Public		586		
Private		549		
			1135	
Other New Work - Public		1170		
Private Industrial	554			
Private Non-Industrial	466			
		1020		
			2190	
Total New Work			3325	
Repairs & Maintenance - Housing		395		
Non Housing - Public	238			
Private	230			
		468		
Total of All Work done by Contractors			863	4188
Work done by operatives directly employed by public sector				783
TOTAL WORK UNDERTAKEN				4971

Note: The total is less than the value of work done quoted in the introduction, since the value of work done in Northern Ireland is excluded.

Table 1.2   **Value of output in various sectors as % of total work undertaken.**

		1970		*1966*
Total new work		67%		68%
Public	(35%)		(33%)	
Private	(32%)		(35%)	
Repairs & maintenance		17%		18%
Work done by direct labour in Public Sector		16%		14%
		100		100

Figure 1.1   **Trends in output of new work by contractors in public and private sectors 1966 - 1970 at constant (1963) prices.**

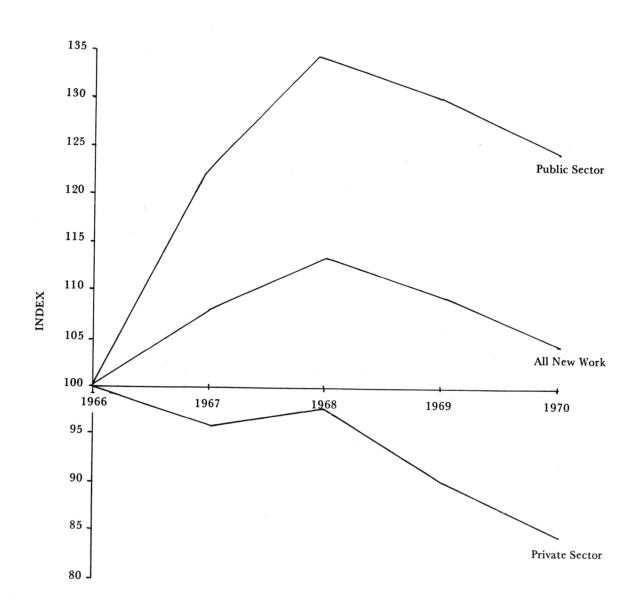

Table 1.3

Value of output by contractors of new work at constant (1963) prices.

£ Million	1966	1967	1968	1969	1970
Total New Work	2485	2589	2676	2600	2527
Public Sector	1193	1325	1401	1373	1335
Private Sector	1292	1264	1275	1227	1192

As can be seen from Figure 1.1 and Table 1.3 the output in the public sector has increased since 1966 but that in the private sector has decreased. A minor recovery is indicated in 1968 for the private sector but this was not sustained and the decline continued after 1968. Also during that year the total new work and the public sector new work reached a much higher level than the year before, thus implying a large growth in the output of the industry during that year. There seems to have been a steady decline in the total amount of new work undertaken since 1968 although by 1970 it had not fallen to the level of 1966.

Government Control

The amount of new work undertaken by contractors in both sectors can be regulated by action from Central Government. The activity in the public sector is directly influenced by the policies of Central and Local Government. A commonly used regulator of the economy is to alter the value of new orders for construction work in this sector. Any such action will have far reaching effects since the construction industry is basically a labour intensive industry. The activity of the private sector can also be regulated by Central Government by controlling the factors which affect investment, e.g. bank rate, company taxation, etc.

An example of control from Central Government was the recession in the public sector following the slow down of £500 million in public expenditure after devaluation between November 1967 and January 1968. As can be seen from Table 1.3 the effects of this reduction in expenditure did not manifest themselves until 1969 as a result of the fact that there is a long time lag between the authorisation of expenditure and the actual disbursement.

The recession pattern in the private sector may be a result of the changes in bank rate in the period 1966 - 1970. If a time lag of one year is assumed to allow for the effect described above, then the reduction in activity in 1967 could be explained by the increase in bank rate in 1966, the slight recovery in 1968 by the reduction of the bank rate between January 26th and November 18th 1967 and the following reduction in activity by increase in bank rate at the end of 1967 and its maintenance at a high level until April 1st 1971.

Other factors which will affect output in both sectors during any particular year are the weather conditions, employment situation and labour relations within the United Kingdom. Above all, expectations of the future economic climate strongly influence investment decisions: and since investment in new buildings and works represents half of the total fixed capital formation, the effect on these expectations of government policies can be crucial to the construction industry.

Performance

The performance of the industry over the last five years has not been particularly encouraging. In fact the output achieved in 1970 was only 1.2% higher than that of five years previous, measured at constant prices, although from 1966 to 1968 the output did grow considerably and in 1968 it was 6.1% higher than in 1966; but since then it has declined somewhat. This is shown in Figure 1.2 which contrasts the performance of construction with all manufacturing industries and all industry.

Figure 1.2 **Trends in output of construction and all manufacturing industries at constant prices (1963 - 100).**

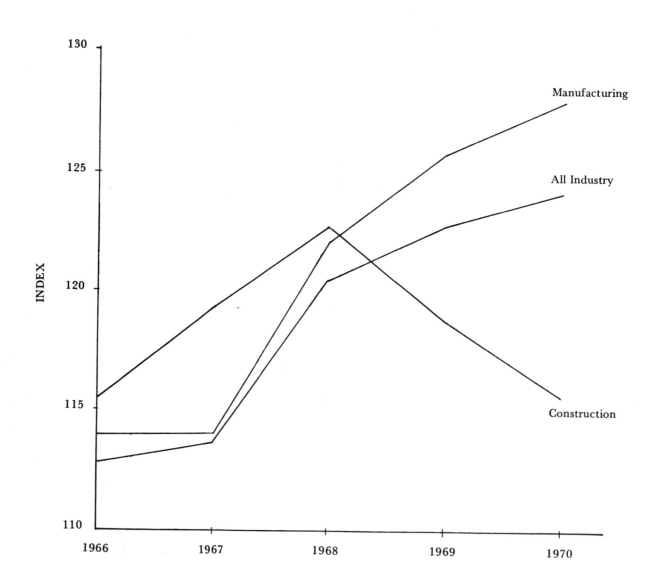

EMPLOYMENT IN THE CONSTRUCTION INDUSTRY

As can be seen from Table 1.4 the number of employees and operatives employed in the construction industry has decreased. This is probably due to the fact that the number of firms in the industry has reduced and that with increased efficiency, industrialisation and rationalisation which has occurred as the industry has developed the number of employees required has been reduced.

Table 1.4

Comparison of employment in construction and in all industry (thousands)

Employees in employment in the UK[1]	*1966*	*1967*	*1968*	*1969*[3]		*1970*
				a.	b.	
All industry	23 784	23 305	23 125	23 085		22 891
All Manufacturing Industry	11 852	11 455	11 254	11 250	11 266	11 086
Construction	1681	1590	1554	1491	1493	1367
Operatives employed in Construction [2]	1102	1059	1025	976		882

(Source - Dept. of Employment)

[1]   At mid June of each year.

[2]   Operatives (male and female) aged 15 and over employed by contractors. Administrative, technical, clerical workers and self employed operatives are excluded. Average number through year.

[3]   Numbers for 1969 (a) are classified according to Standard Industrial Classification (1958) and are not fully comparable with 1969 b. which are classified according to Standard Industrial Classification (1968).

Table 1.5

Percentage of employees in construction to those in all industry and in all manufacturing industry.

	1966	*1967*	*1968*	*1969*[1]	*1970*
Construction as % of all industry	7.1	6.8	6.7	6.5	6.0
Construction as % of all Manufacturing Ind.	14.2	13.9	13.8	13.3	12.3
Operatives as % of total employed in Construction	65.7	66.5	66.0	65.3	64.4

[1]   Numbers of employees are those classified according to the Standard Industrial Classification (1968).

Table 1.5 shows that the reduction in the labour force in the construction industry has been faster than that in both all industry and in all manufacturing industry. This is probably due to the labour intensive nature of the construction industry. Table 1.5 also shows that the proportion of operatives to total employees in employment in construction has been gradually decreasing, with the exception of 1967. This decrease in the proportion of operatives may be explained in two ways: firstly the major part of the increase in efficiency and rationalisation has occurred on site so reducing the number of operatives required; and secondly, with the development of the self-employed labour only sub-contractor, there has been a change in the average of the statistics. (Directly employed operatives are classified as operatives but some self-employed personnel may be excluded from the figures).

Table 1.6

Employment of operatives by contractors in the various sectors of the construction industry (Thousands)

	Number		*As % of Total*	
	1966	*1970*	*1966*	*1970*
Total	1102	882		100
Total New Work	790	630	72	72
Public Sector Total	375	328	34	37
New Housing	157	127	14	14
Other Work	218	201	20	23
Private Sector Total	415	302	38	35
New Housing	154	93	14	11
Industrial	129	106	12	12
Non Industrial	132	103	12	12
Repair & Maintenance	312	252	28	28

The distribution of operatives employed by contractors in 1966 and 1970 is shown in Table 1.6. It will be noticed that the reduction in the proportion of operatives employed on new housing in the private sector between 1966 and 1970 was greater than in any other type of work. Table 1.6 also shows that the percentage of operatives engaged in repair and maintenance in 1970 was the same as that in 1966. The fact that the private housing sector lost proportionally more operatives than any other may be explained with reference to the reduction in activity in that sector in relation to the reduction in the construction industry as a whole. It may also be that the particular conditions within that sector, i.e. type of operatives and type and method of work enabled a faster and more widespread development of labour - only subcontracting than in any other sector.

ACTIVITY WITHIN SECTORS OF CONSTRUCTION INDUSTRY

The Public Sector

As can be seen from Table 1.7 the major activity within the public sector is that of new housing. From 1966 to 1970 the only types of work to have a reduction in shares of output were housing, health and the work undertaken for public corporations, e.g. gas, coal mining, electricity, rail and air transport. The largest increase in its share of the orders was achieved by the offices, garages, factories and shops section with harbours, water and sewage second and roads third.

Figure 1.3   **Trends in type of work obtained by contractors in the public sector at contemporary prices.**

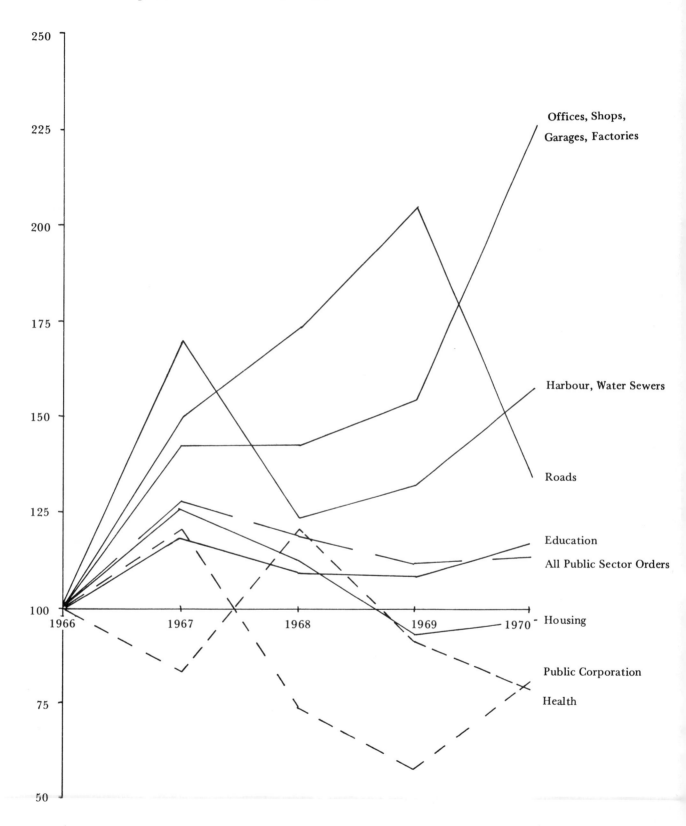

(Note that the index of the cost of new construction rose by 18% over this period.)

Table 1.7   **Value of new orders obtained by contractors in the public sector at contemporary prices.**

	£ million		% share	
	1966	1970	1966	1970
Housing	564	543	37.5	31.6
Roads	162	219	10.8	12.7
Education	196	227	13.0	13.2
Harbours, Water & Sewerage	122	193	8.1	11.2
Health	118	97	7.9	5.7
Offices, Factories, Garages and Shops	60	136	4.0	7.9
Public Corporations	182	151	12.1	8.8
Miscellaneous	99	153	6.6	8.9
TOTALS	1503	1719	100.0	100.0

The trends in type of work obtained by contractors in the public sector from 1966 onwards is shown in Figure 1.3. No type of work in this period has increased in value every year. The nearest to continuous growth was produced by the section including offices, shops, garages and factories where growth in orders occurred in every year but one. This section also had the largest rate of growth in any one year. The only types of work which have declined from 1969 to 1970 are roads and health. It must be emphasized, however, that in the public sector, variations in the value of orders are to be expected as a result of the size of contracts involved: for example, a couple of large hospital contracts would alone explain the difference between the figures for *health* for the two years 1966 and 1970.

The Private Sector   As can be seen from Table 1.8 housing in the private sector is the major type of work as it is in the public sector. In the private sector housing constitutes a larger percentage of the total output in that section than it does in the public sector. The types of work which had a reduction in orders from 1966 to 1970 were housing, garages and schools and colleges. The largest increase in its share of the total orders was achieved by the industrial section with offices second and entertainment third.

The trends in new orders for types of work in the private sector obtained by contractors is shown in Figure 1.4. In the period shown only one type of work had continuous growth, that was new industrial work. All other types of work showed a decline at some time during the period although from 1969 to 1970 all types of work showed some growth in new orders except the work done for schools and colleges. The new orders in this type of work were the same in 1969 and 1970. It also seems that 1966 was an exceptional year for this type of work, which is in any case of minor importance. The largest rate of growth in any one year was achieved by new orders for entertainment work.

Figure 1.4 **Trends in type of work obtained by contractors in the private sector at contemporary prices.**

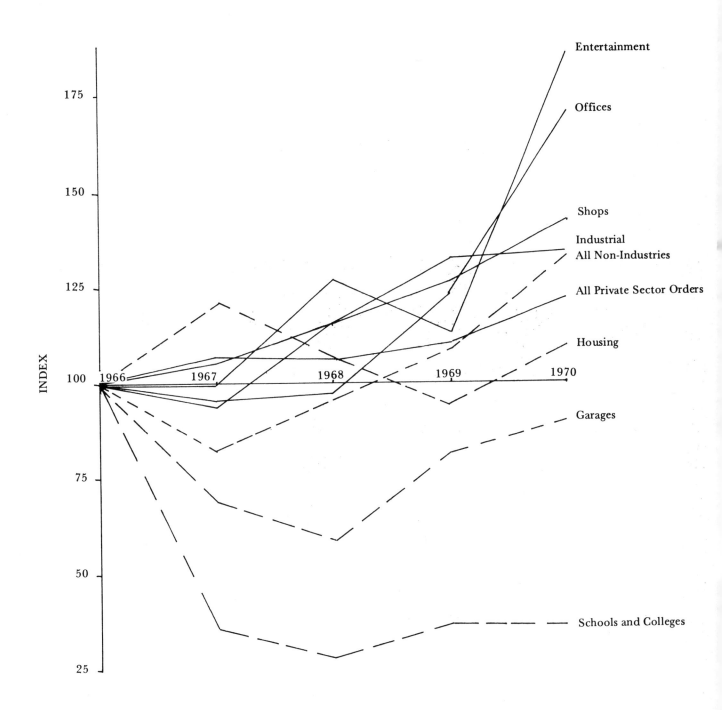

(As was noted in the Section dealing with the public sector, account must be taken in interpreting this graph of the fact that the index of the cost of new construction rose by 18% over this period.)

Table 1.8 **Value of new orders obtained by contractors in the private sector by type of work at contemporary prices.**

	£ million		% Share	
	1966	*1970*	*1966*	*1970*
Housing	590	630	42.9	37.8
Industrial	427	565	31.1	33.9
Offices	85	146	6.2	8.8
Shops	84	118	6.1	7.1
Entertainment	63	117	4.6·	7.0
Garages	29	25	2.1	1.5
Schools & Colleges	14	5	1.0	.3
Miscellaneous	83	60	6.0	3.6
Total Non-Industrial	358	471	26.0	28.3
TOTALS	1375	1666	100.0	100.0

2 The Construction Industry and Quoted Companies

THE QUOTED COMPANIES

Categories and numbers

The quoted companies referred to in this chapter are broadly those which may be classified to the construction industry for all or part of their activities according to the Standard Industrial Classification and have shares quoted on United Kingdom Stock Exchanges. Also included in this group are three public companies which are not quoted on any United Kingdom Stock Exchange but are classified as public companies by some technical qualification, (such as more than fifty share holders in the company) and are added for completeness. There may be a few quoted companies which although they might not be classified as part of the construction industry by the Standard Industrial Classification do contribute substantially to the output of construction work by quoted companies. The difficulties of classification were commented on in the introduction.

In 1948 there were forty-six quoted public companies operating in the construction industry. This represented only 0.035% of the total number of 'firms' operating in construction. By 1970 the number of quoted companies as reckoned above had increased to 139, representing 0.19% of the total number of firms operating in construction.

The constituents of the quoted company group, as classified above, are somewhat complex in structure and varied in their activities. There are the well known names of building and civil engineering contractors like Wimpey, Laing, Costain, etc., and there are the not so well known names of holding companies like Marchwiel, the holding company of Alfred McAlpine. There are also the companies like Trafalgar House Investments which consists of several contractors in a single group. Also included are some specialist contractors such as Heating and Ventilating Contractors, Plasterers and Plant Hire Companies. A list of these companies showing turnover and the average number of employees is given in Appendix 3.

Structure

The structure of the companies, especially the larger groups, is very complex. Within any one of the larger companies there may be a number of smaller companies operating and the variety of activities within the group may be quite extensive, with activities ranging from general building and civil engineering to materials manufacture, property development, trade specialisations and open cast coal mining.

The vast majority of the companies in this list are, however, builders, civil engineers and estate developers. The small number of specialist firms can be attributed to the fact that in general site work of such specialists tends to be a subsidiary activity to their main operations - for example many firms with an interest in heating and ventilating engineering are basically in engineering, producing goods which they sometimes instal themselves, but frequently supply to a contractor who performs this service.

The remainder of this section is devoted to consideration of the companies which are included in Appendix 3. These are the firms broadly classifiable to 'construction' as defined by the Standard Industrial Classification. This group consists of 139 companies, 134 of which are quoted on United Kingdom Stock Exchanges, the other five being unquoted public companies. Accounts were not readily available for one of the quoted companies, whose quotation had been suspended. This company is not included in the following analysis.

Output

In 1948 the 46 quoted construction companies accounted for about 8 - 10% of the total output of private construction firms. By 1953 the 49 construction companies quoted during that year account for approximately 12% of the output of private firms. In 1970 the total turnover of the construction companies, as defined above was £2275M, 54% of the total value of work undertaken by all firms in the construction industry. This, of course, is not the percentage share of all construction work undertaken by quoted building contractors but it does suggest that the quoted companies share of the work has increased substantially from its 1953 level.

There are three main reasons why the turnover of the construction companies mentioned above does not express the value of construction work undertaken by those contractors. The first is that the turnover of the companies is the sum of the turnover of all the activities undertaken by that company and in some cases construction activities contribute only little more than half of the total turnover of the company. Secondly, even when construction is the major activity, a substantial part may be done abroad. Thirdly the turnover of a company includes the work undertaken by sub-contractors. This work will also be included in the turnover of the sub-contractor, so if turnover is used as the value of work undertaken some work may be included twice. But notwithstanding these provisos, there has clearly been a large increase in the share of work going to firms which come within this category.

The turnover of the companies in the construction group is shown in Appendix 3. The range of turnover is very large, the largest being £225 million by George Wimpey & Co., Ltd., and the smallest being £56 000 by Lane Fox & Co., Ltd.

As can be seen from Table 2.1, the largest number of companies within any range is shown by the range £1M - below £3M. In fact 67.4% of the firms have a turnover of below £10 million.

Table 2.2 shows that 49.4% of the total turnover of all the quoted construction companies is attributable to the 11 companies which fall within the top two turnover ranges. Although two thirds of the firms fall in the range below £10 million turnover they only contribute 16.3% of the total turnover.

Table 2.1   **Distribution of companies with respect to turnover.**

Turnover range £m	No. of companies	% Share
100 and above	4	2.9
50 - below 100	8	5.8
30 - below 50	8	5.8
20 - below 30	13	9.4
10 - below 20	13	9.4
5 - below 10	25	18.1
3 - below 5	25	18.1
1 - below 3	32	23.2
less than 1	10	7.3
TOTALS	138	100.0

Table 2.2   **Distribution of turnover in ranges**

Turnover range £m	Total turnover of Cos.£m	% Share
100 and above	595	26.2
50 - below 100	556	24.5
30 - below 50	280	12.3
20 - below 30	319	14.0
10 - below 20	167	7.3
5 - below 10	183	8.0
3 - below 5	102	4.5
1 - below 3	66	2.9
Less than 1	7	.3
TOTALS	2275	100.0

Employment

The average number of employees in employment in the quoted construction companies in 1970 was 312 000. This figure represented about 23% of the total number of employees in employment in the construction industry in the United Kingdom. (The 54 companies in the largest size category by numbers employed, over 1200, made up 272 000 of the total i.e. 20% of all employees). This does not mean that 23% of the employees employed in construction were employed by the quoted companies since a proportion of the employees employed by the public companies were not involved in construction, in fact in a few of the companies the construction employees may only have represented a minor part of the total employees employed by that company. The figure quoted above for the average number of employees in quoted construction companies is not completely accurate since figures for eight of the 138 companies in the group were not available. However these were all small companies, measured by turnover (under £3M). The average number of employees employed by each company is shown in Appendix 3. The largest number employed was 32 000 (in the UK only) by George Wimpey & Co. Ltd., and the smallest was 81 by John Finlan Ltd.

Table 2.3

Distribution of construction firms with respect to average no. of employees in 1970.

Average number of employees	Number of firms		% Share	
	Quoted Construction companies	All firms	Quoted Construction companies	All firms
1200 and over	54	78	41.5	0.1
600 - 1199	28	132	21.6	0.2
300 - 599	29	233	22.3	0.3
115 - 299	16	820	12.3	1.1
Less than 115	3	72 157	2.3	98.3
TOTALS	130	73 420	100.0	100.0

Table 2.3 contrasts the number of public building contractors employing particular numbers of employees with the total number of construction firms employing that number of employees. It shows that two fifths of the quoted construction companies employed 1200 or more employees whereas only 1.7% of all construction firms employed 115 or more employees. In fact, of the 78 firms which employed 1200 or more employees two thirds were from the quoted companies.

It is of course rather dangerous to make comparisons between data collected from published accounts and that published by the Department of the Environment. In many instances the basic facts are not revealed in sufficient detail in published accounts and the task of investigating the many variations in accounting practice and the large number of queries resulting from these variations and from the other factors which affect the published accounts would be beyond the scope of this review.

The Largest Company

There are a number of ways in which companies can be ranked. Common practise has been to rank them with respect to one of the four following items - turnover, average number of employees, value of fixed assets and net assets or capital employed. The value of the first two of these items, i.e. turnover, and number employed is shown in Appendix 3 for the quoted construction companies.

The rank with respect to turnover is shown in Appendix 4. George Wimpey & Co., Ltd., was ranked number one. Using other criteria would produce different rankings, and too much attention should not be paid to the positions in this table of companies that have widely different interests.

3 Quoted Company Accounts

INTRODUCTION

This chapter contrasts the average accounts of a sample of thirty quoted companies in the construction industry, as defined in the previous chapter, with the average accounts for 737 quoted manufacturing companies and 1045 quoted manufacturing and distribution companies. The thirty companies were chosen from the list of 139 firms given in Appendix 3. Table 3.1 shows how these thirty companies were distributed amongst all the other construction companies with respect to turnover in 1970.

Table 3.1

Distribution of 30 Chosen Companies amongst other Building Firms

Turnover Range £m	No. of Companies within Range	No. of Companies chosen
100 and above	4	2
50 - less than 100	8	2
30 - less than 50	8	3
20 - less than 30	13	3
10 - less than 20	13	3
5 - less than 10	25	6
3 - less than 5	25	5
1 - less than 3	32	5
less than 1	10	1
	138	30

A list of these 30 companies is shown in Appendix 5, and their accounts are shown in Appendix 6; in Appendix 7 there is a breakdown of net current assets; and in Appendix 8 their profit and loss accounts.

The companies and their accounts are grouped 1 - 9, each group corresponding to the turnover ranges in Table 3.1 thus making comparisons of companies of similar size (i.e. turnover) a little easier. Care was taken, as far as possible, to exclude from the list of 30 companies chosen for more detailed study, companies with a large non-construction content in their turnover and within each group to choose companies which represented the other companies in that group with respect to turnover.

The Balance Sheets   Table 3.2 shows a summary of the balance sheets of the construction companies, manufacturing companies and manufacturing and distribution companies for the accounting year ending in 1970. Averages for each type are given together with the percentage of capital employed that is represented by each balance sheet item. The last two columns show the averages for construction companies.as a percentage of the averages for the manufacturing companies and of the averages for manufacturing and distribution.

The average value of capital employed was £8 017 000 for the building contractors but within these 30 companies the range of capital employed was very large. The largest being by Wimpey's - £67 577 000 and the smallest by Edward Jones - £278 000. Table 3.2 shows that the *average* building contractor employs about one third of the capital of the average companies in the other two industries.

The items which require discussion fall into two categories: sources of funds, which includes shareholders capital, loans and bank overdrafts, etc., and employment of funds which includes investment, debtors, stock and work in progress, etc. These are discussed in some detail in the following paragraphs.

SOURCES OF FUNDS

Shareholders   Table 3.2 shows that the ratio of equity interest to capital employed was
Interest   lower for construction than for the other two categories. Also, the ratios of preference share capital and minority interest were relatively much lower in construction than in the other industries.

Deferred Liabilities   This balance sheet item includes such things as deferred corporation tax, tax equalisation provisions, etc. These items are proportionately much higher in the case of the construction companies than for the other industries shown in Table 3.2. They provide a fluctuating source of funds which in the case of the construction companies constitutes about 3.6% of the capital employed. It is difficult to envisage why this disparity should exist.

Long Term Loans   The amount of long term loans relative to the capital employed was only
and Bank Overdrafts   slightly less for the construction companies than for the other companies although the bank overdraft was very much higher - in fact the percentage of the capital employed attributable to the bank overdraft for the construction companies was approximately twice that for the other industries. Although the average bank overdraft was very high, four of the thirty construction companies had no overdraft at all shown in their balance sheets for 1970.

Bank Overdrafts   As can be seen from Table 3.3 the majority of the construction companies had a bank overdraft of between 10 and 39.9% of their capital employed. The reliance of the construction companies on a large bank overdraft is probably related to the nature of their work. The work consists of contracts of various lengths with the money required for each contract fluctuating during the contract period, thus there are almost continuous fluctuations in the amount of cash required during any year. Short term borrowing via a bank overdraft seems to be the most convenient way of coping with this situation.

Table 3.2 **Balance Sheet Summary 1970**

Average of Companies £(000)

	(1) Bldg. Contr.	(2) % of Capital Employed	(3) Mfg.	(4) % of Capital Employed	(5) Mfg. & Distr.	(6) % of Capital Employed	(1) as % of (3)	(1) as % of (5)
Ordinary Cap.	1498	19	6042	24	5177	25	25	29
Cap. & Rev. Reserves	2714	34	9215	37	7941	38	29	34
Equity Int.	4212	52	15 257	61	13 118	62	28	32
Pref. Cap.	89	1	488	2	424	2	18	21
Minority Int.	148	2	884	4	709	3	17	21
Deferred Liab.	291	4	452	2	402	2	64	72
Debentures & Loan Stock	166	2	4957	20	4078	19	3	4
Loans & Mortgages	1288	16					26	31
Bank loan & Overdraft	1823	23	2745	11	2384	11	66	77
TOTAL CAPITAL EMPLOYED	8017	100	24 783	100	21 115	100	32	38
Fixed Assets (net)	3285	41	12 960	52	11 575	54	25	28
Investments	926	12	1818	7	1447	7	51	64
Stock & work in progress	4421	55	8452	34	7146	34	52	62
Trade & other debtors	3289	41	8450	34	7181	34	39	46
Cash & cash equivalent	302	4	1123	5	990	5	27	31
Others	948	12	16		26		5930	3650
TOTAL CURRENT ASSETS	8960	112	18 041	73	15 343	73	50	58
Trade & Other Creditors	4536	57	7260	29	6504	31	63	70
Current tax	481	6	1563	6	1403	7	31	34
Gross Dividends	178	2	539	2	502	2	33	35
Others	69	1						
TOTAL CURRENT LIABILITIES	5264	66	9362	38	8409	40	56	63
Net Current Assets	3696	46	8679	35	6934	33	43	53
Other Assets	110	1	1326	5	1159	5	8	9
EMPLOYMENT OF CAPITAL	8017	100	24 783	100	21 115	100	32	38

Table 3.3 **Distribution of Construction Companies by Overdraft Characteristics.**

Overdraft on 1970 Balance Sheet as % of Capital Employed	*No. of companies*	*% Share*
Zero	4	13.3
0.1 - 9.9	6	20.0
10.0 - 19.9	7	23.4
20.0 - 39.9	10	33.3
40.0 & above	3	10.0
	30	100.0

Although the explanation given above may explain why the construction companies, generally, have large overdrafts, the overdraft shown on the balance sheet of any particular company may not accurately represent the state of the company's bank balance throughout the year. The balance sheet of course gives the amounts attributable to each item at a particular point in time and the financial year end date and the accounting practice of the company may affect the amount set against any item.

The bank overdraft is particularly susceptible to these factors - it will depend upon the time of year, the day of the month and the accounting practice of the firm. In the autumn, when trading during the previous months has been high, the bank overdraft is likely to be high but in the spring, after a relatively slack period through the winter, it is likely to be lower. Also the less vigorous trading during the winter may allow an opportunity to settle outstanding accounts.

There is also the complication that a large sum may have to be paid in taxation at the beginning of the year. The company policy with respect to payments made to sub-contractors and suppliers will affect the bank balance at any particular time. It may be the company policy to pay all outstanding bills at the end of each month or possibly to only pay the bills a few days after having received payment from their clients, so the state of the bank balance will depend upon whether the company has just received payment from its clients and whether it has made payments to sub-contractors and suppliers before or after the accounting date. There is also a tendency in some companies to make a special effort to settle accounts immediately before the accounting date so strengthening the apparent financial position of the company.

Although the factors mentioned above will affect the state of the bank balance of any particular company as shown on the balance sheet it is unlikely that they will substantially affect the average construction company whose balance sheet is shown in Table 3.2.

Indeed, the whole picture of sources of funds revealed by the table may indicate something much more than the bare recital of the facts suggests. It may be that the pattern of heavy reliance on bank lending reflects as much the difficulty of obtaining more permanent finance in a motonously risky industry as much as it does conscious decisions to utilise the cheapest form of finance available to companies. On the basis of this evidence it is probable that many companies in construction have reached a position in which it is not possible to extend bank borrowing without increasing equity participation.

EMPLOYMENT OF FUNDS

Debtors and Creditors

Table 3.2 shows that for construction both these items are very large in relation to capital employed, compared with the other industries, and that the construction companies are generally net receivers of credit, i.e. creditors larger than debtors', whereas the other industries are generally net givers of credit. Although the 'average' construction company was a receiver of credit not all of the 30 companies studied were so. In fact 21 were receivers of credit and 9 were givers of credit.

Table 3.4

Distribution of Construction Companies by Net Credit

	No. of companies	*% Share*
Much received (more than 10% of capital employed)	17	57
Little received	4	13
Little given	3	10
Much given (more than 10% of capital employed)	6	20
	30	100

Table 3.4 shows that over half of the construction companies were large receivers of credit, i.e. creditors less debtors was more than 10% of capital employed. This table relates to net credit but a study of the accounts of the construction companies shows that for most of the companies both the creditor and debtor items tend to be large in relation to capital employed. A simple explanation of these large creditor and debtor items is that construction operations take a long time and settlement of the final accounts are subject to long delays so the contractor who is waiting for money from his client will tend to keep his creditors (sub-contractors, suppliers, etc.) waiting.

The peculiar distribution shown in table 3.4 may be explained by the variation in accounting practices already mentioned in relation to payment of creditors, but there are a number of other variations in accounting practice which will have a large effect upon the value set against the debtor and creditor items in the balance sheet. These variations are largely concerned with the allocation of the retention money in the accounts once the building has been handed over, i.e. during the defects liability period and later. The value of the retention is only about 2 - 3% of the contract sum but the defects liability period is usually 6 months and there may be some delay in settling the final account, so with a number of contracts in this state the allocation of this money in the balance sheet becomes quite important. (See page 188 'Studies in Company Finance' by Tew and Henderson, published by the National Institute for Economic and Social Research).

A straightforward way of dealing with the retention is to include it in work in progress until it is due for payment and then transfer it to debtors until paid. It seems that some companies transfer the retention to debtors at practical completion of the works so inflating the debtors item and two of the 30 construction companies studied apparently included all work in progress in the debtors item. Other companies it seems leave the work in progress item full of a large number of tail ends of substantially complete contracts and empty them occasionally into the debtors item. Inflation of the creditor item may be due to the companies including in this item retentions payable to sub-contractors before they are due for payment. Overseas contracts will also tend to inflate the debtor and creditor items since delays in settlement of accounts can be considerable.

Working Capital

To try to overcome some of the problems mentioned above it is useful to consider the item 'working capital', i.e. stocks and work in progress plus debtors minus creditors. For the construction companies this item represented 39% of capital employed, for the manufacturing companies it again represented 39% and for the manufacturing and distribution companies it represented 37% of capital employed. Table 3.5 shows that this item is much more stable than net credit for the construction companies, but this can also be affected by accounting practice. The most vulnerable items in this case are stocks and creditors. It seems that some of the companies treat as 'stock' items some of their plant especially loose tools and small portable plant, although others treat these as fixed assets. More importantly some companies also include land for development as stock. The creditor item may be affected by including hire purchase liabilities and current tax liabilities in with the other creditors.

Table 3.5

Distribution of Construction Companies by Working Capital

Working Capital as a % of Capital Employed	No. of Companies	% Share
Less than 10	1	3.3
10 - 29	5	16.7
30 - 49	16	53.3
50 - 69	7	23.4
70 & above	1	3.3
	30	100.0

Stocks and Work in Progress

Table 3.2 shows that the stock and work in progress item in the construction companies balance sheet was much larger in relation to the capital employed than it was for the other industries. As mentioned in the previous section the items included in 'stock and work in progress' depend greatly upon the accounting practice of the company. A further complication in the consideration of the stock and work in progress items is that some companies show amounts for stock items and work in progress items separately in the balance sheet, while others just show an amount which represents both items. Two of the companies of the 30 studied showed stock as a separate item but included all work in progress in the debtors item.

The stock and work in progress of the *average* construction company was 55% of the capital employed. Table 3.6 shows for the 30 construction companies the large variation in stocks and work in progress as a percentage of capital employed. The variations were due, in part, to the difference in activities of the companies, e.g. any company involved in property development will have relatively large fixed assets if it returns developments as investment, and these will constitute a large proportion of the net assets, so the stock and work in progress item as a percentage of the net assets will be relatively small even though the stocks and work in progress may represent a large proportion of the capital employed in construction as opposed to that employed in property development and investment. In contrast, land for development will probably be included as stock and inflate this figure. The variations in accounting practice already mentioned will also contribute to variations in the stock and work in progress as a percentage of capital employed for the construction companies.

Table 3.6

Distribution of Construction Companies by Stock and Work in Progress

Stock & Work in Progress as a % of Capital Employed	*No. of Companies*	*% Share*
1 - 19	4	13.3
20 - 39	5	16.7
40 - 59	6	20.0
60 - 79	3	10.0
80 - 100	9	30.0
above 100	3	10.0
	30	100.0

Investments

Table 3.2 shows that investment, related to capital employed, is higher in the construction companies than in the other companies. As already mentioned, some of the companies were involved in property development as well as investment in other companies. There were also a few companies involved in share dealing. Of the 30 construction companies studied only 18 had any sum set against investment in their balance sheets. With this item, as with the last two, there are variations in accounting practice which can affect this particular sum. The main difficulty is to define what is investment; some companies will only have investment in associated companies under the general heading of investment whereas others will have investment in other quoted or unquoted companies, Government securities, etc. In particular the popular device of creating companies which exist to own particular property developments, and in which the construction company has a minority holding, has an important role here.

Other Items

The relatively large value of other current assets and gross dividends and other current liabilities is also shown in Table 3.2. The other current assets includes items such as land for development, development property, tax certificates and loans, etc. and the other current liabilities includes hire purchase instalments, interest due, etc. Thirteen of the construction companies show amounts set against land for development and/or development property, this being the main contributor to the other current assets. The high value of other current liabilities is probably due to the practice of buying plant on hire purchase.

THE PROFIT AND LOSS ACCOUNT

A summary of the profit and loss accounts for the 30 construction companies, the 737 manufacturing and the 1045 manufacturing and distribution companies, studied in the last section, is shown in Table 3.7.

Table 3.7   **Profit & Loss Account Summary 1970**

	(1) Bldg. Constr.	(2) % of Capital Employed	(3) Mfg.	(4) % of Capital Employed	(5) Mfg. & Distr.	(6) % of Capital Employed	(1) as % of (3)	(1) as % of (5)
Trading Profit	1905	24	3567	14	3180	15	53	60
Plant Hire/ Rental	(462)	6	(116)	-	(119)	1	398	388
Depreciation etc.	(497)	6	(1165)	5	(979)	5	43	51
Operating Profit	946	12	2286	9	2082	10	41	45
Other Income	134	2	574	2	471	2	23	28
Pre-Interest Profit	1080	13	2860	12	2553	12	38	42
Loan Int. etc.	(244)	3	(316)	1	(260)	1	77	94
Net Profit Before Tax	836	10	2544	10	2293	11	33	36
Total Tax	(367)	5	(947)	4	(852)	4	39	43
Net Profit After Tax	469	6	1597	6	1441	7	29	33
Preference & other provisions	(18)	-	(31)	-	(27)	–	58	67
Ordinary Dividend[1]	(212)	3	(840)	3	(767)	4	25	28
Retained Profit	239	3	726	3	647	3	33	37

[1] Includes Minority Interest Dividend.

Averages for each type are given, together with the percentage of capital employed that is represented by each item. The last two columns show the items for the construction companies as a percentage of those for the manufacturing companies, and as a percentage of those for the manufacturing and distribution companies. Table 3.7 shows that the average trading profit of the construction companies was a little over half of that for the other industries but the average net profit after tax was a little under a third of that for the other industries with a capital employed by the construction companies of about one third of that employed by the other industries. The table also shows that the amount set against plant hire/rental for the construction companies was relatively much higher than for the other industries although this item is largely meaningless, and not all companies report it as a separate item.

The loan interest was also relatively higher for construction but other income, i.e. income not from trading activities was slightly lower. It can also be seen that the construction companies had a tendency to retain within the company a larger proportion of the profits than was distributed to the shareholders, but the other industries distributed a larger proportion of their profits to the shareholders than was retained in the company.

Depreciation

The amounts set against depreciation as a percentage of trading profit were 26% for construction, 32% for manufacturing and 31% for manufacturing and distribution. The lower value of depreciation for construction may be explained by the fact that the construction process is basically labour intensive compared with the other industries so there was less plant used to produce the profit than in the other industries. The tendency of the construction companies to hire plant rather than buy it could also explain why the amount set against depreciation is less for this industry than in the others.

Loan Interest and Other Income

The relatively high loan interest for the construction companies is probably due to the very large bank overdrafts which these companies have compared with the other industries. The relatively low amount (in relation to pre-tax profit) set against other income for the construction companies is not so easily explained since the amount of investment stated on the balance sheet as a percentage of the capital employed is relatively high. It may be that the construction companies receive a much lower return on their investment than the other companies or that the average accounting system of the other two categories does not classify investment and other income in the same way.

Equally it may be that a proportion of the investment of the public construction companies is in property building companies which offer scope of capital gains rather than dividend income. Thus the return on investment as shown in the item 'other income' in the profit and loss account may be negligible. The main difference in accounting practice is concerned with the classification of income in the summarised accounts, e.g. income from associated companies can appear in the accounts as 'other income' or in the investment item in the balance sheet. It is interesting to note that the *total tax* as a percentage of the *net profit before tax* paid by the *average* construction company was 43.9% but for both the other industries it was only 37.2% - reflecting the benefits of investment incentives to what are more capital intensive areas of industry than construction.

Cash Flow and Liquidity

The average cash flows for the three industries under consideration are shown in Table 3.8. All three industries had a positive cash flow and in fact of the 30 construction companies studied only one had a negative cash flow. The cash flows of all the construction companies are shown in Appendix 9.

Table 3.8   **Cash Flow for 1970.**

Average of Companies £(000)

	(1) Bldg. Constr	(2) % of Capital Employed	(3) Mfg.	(4) % of Capital Employed	(5) Mfg. & Distr.	(6) % of Capital Employed	(1) as % of (2)	(1) as % of (3)
Profit after Preference Div.	451	6	1566	6	1414	7	29	32
Depreciation	497	6	1165	5	979	5	43	51
Gross Cash Flow	948	12	2731	11	2393	11	35	40
Less Ordinary Dividend	212	3	840	3	767	4	25	28
Net Cash Flow	736	9	1891	8	1626	8	39	45

The average ratio of gross cash flow to ordinary dividend for the construction companies was 4.47; for the manufacturing companies it was 3.25 and for the manufacturing and distribution companies it was 3.12. The tendency in construction companies seems to be to retain the money in the company. Perhaps because it is difficult to raise new funds by rights issues, perhaps also because owing to the way in which the return and investment incentives operate, construction companies are hard-pressed for cash.

Table 3.9 shows the liquid position of the average companies of the three industrial groups. All of them had a negative liquid position but the construction companies had a much larger negative liquid position in relation to the capital employed than the other companies. The 'net cash position' highlights the difference between the industries since for the construction

Table 3.9   **Liquidity Schedule 1970 £(000).**

	Averages of Companies		
	Constr.	*Mfg.*	*Mfg. & Distr.*
Cash & Cash Equivalent	302	1123	990
Less - Overdraft	1823	2745	2384
Net Cash Position	(1521)	(1622)	(1394)
Less - [1]Quick Liabilities	728	2102	1905
Liquid Position	(2249)	(3724)	(3299)

[1] Quick Liabilities = Current liabilities less creditors.

companies it is shown at a value between those given for the other industries but they only had a capital employed of about one third of that employed by the other companies. This is due to the high bank overdrafts which the construction companies had, the reasons for which have already been mentioned.

Of the thirty construction companies studied seven had a positive 'net cash position' and one had a positive liquid position. The Liquidity Schedules for these companies are shown in Appendix 10.

COMPARISON WITH THE QUOTED COMPANIES OF 1953.

All the information relating to the period from 1949 - 1953 was extracted from Chapter 12, the volume edited by Tew and Henderson already quoted. The accounts studied were those of the 44 'continuing' quoted construction companies in the period 1949 - 53 and those of 2549 quoted companies in all industry which were in existence throughout the period.

The Balance Sheet   Table 3.10 shows the 'average' balance sheet for the building companies and for companies in all industry for 1953. It also shows the balance sheet items for building as a percentage of those for all industry. A comparison of this table with Table 3.2. - the balance sheet summary for 1970, reveals a number of changes in the companies. The changes in the source of funds are shown in Table 3.11 which contrasts the changes in the construction industry with that in other industry.

The tendency in both construction and the other industries has been to reduce the proportion of shre capital and increase the proportion of borrowed finance. This was probably due to changes in the tax laws which have made increases in share capital less attractive to companies. Broadly

Table 3.10 **Balance Sheet Summary 1953.**

Average per Company £(000)

	Building	% of Capital Employed	All Industries	% of Capital Employed	(1) as % of (3)
Ordinary Capital	265	21	616	23	43
Capital & Revenue Reserves	473	37	1150	43	41
Equity Interest	738	58	1766	66	42
Preference Capital	143	11	308	12	46
Minority Interest) Deferred Liabilities)	138	11	273	10	51
Debentures & Loan Stock) Loans & Mortgages)	136	11	226	8	60
Bank Loan & Overdraft	123	10	106	4	115
TOTAL CAPITAL EMPLOYED	1278	100	2679	100	48
Fixed Assets (net)	518	41	1326	50	39
Investments	-	-	-	-	-
Stock & Work in progress	729	57	1007	38	72
Trade & other debtors	597	47	623	23	96
Cash & cash equivalent	254	20	503	19	51
TOTAL CURRENT ASSETS	1580	124	2133	80	74
Trade & other Creditors	643	50	478	18	135
Current Tax) Gross Dividends) Others)	177	14	302	11	59
TOTAL CURRENT LIABILITIES	820	64	780	29	105
Net Current Assets	760	60	1353	51	56
Other Assets	-	-	-	-	-
EMPLOYMENT OF CAPITAL	1278	100	2679	100	48

Table 3.11 **Sources of Finance as a Percentage of Capital Employed.**

	Construction		All Industry	Mfg. & Distr.
	1953	*1970*	*1953*	*1970*
Equity Interest	57.7	52.5	65.9	62.1
Preference Capital	11.2	1.1	11.5	2.0
Minority Interest & Deferred Liabilities	10.8	5.5	10.2	5.3
Debentures and Loans etc.	10.6	18.1	8.4	19.3
Bank Overdraft	9.7	22.8	4.0	11.3

speaking the reduction in preference capital has been balanced by the increase in long term loans and the reduction in equity and minority interest is balanced by the increase in bank overdraft. In construction there has been a tendency to larger bank overdrafts at the expense of the long term loans whereas in the other industries the reverse was true. This difference between construction and the other industries is probably due to the fluctuating nature of the finance required for construction work.

There seems to have been some change in the pattern of employment of funds between 1953 and 1970. The 'stocks and work in progress' item was still relatively large for construction compared to other industries. Both the debtor and creditor items were still relatively high and the average company of the other industries was a giver of credit. The only major change was in the distribution of companies by 'net credit' (Table 3.12).

Looking at 'working capital' however (stocks, work in progress plus debtors, less creditors) there is a real change as far as construction companies are concerned. In 1953 this composite item amounted to 54% of capital employed; by 1970 it was 39%. The construction industry companies were granting less credit to their clients, and at the same time extracting more from their suppliers and subcontractors. A similar trend could be observed in the other categories of industries, but of smaller proportion.

Table 3.12   **Distribution of Companies by 'Net Credit'.**

	Construction Companies	
	1953 % Share	1970 % Share
Much Received - (more than 10% of Capital employed)	32	57
Little Received	2	13
Little Given	11	10
Much Given (more than 10% of Capital employed)	55	20
	100	100

The Profit and Loss Account

Table 3.13 shows the profit and loss account of the construction companies and the companies from all industry. It shows an average of the items per company per year from the accounts between 1949 and 1953. It also shows the items relating to the building companies as a percentage of those relating to the companies from all industry.

There are some items which have changed substantially between 1953 and 1970. Depreciation and appropriation of profit show shifts of emphasis. Table 3.13 shows that the building industry depreciation is very high in relation to capital employed compared with the other industries. In the 1949-53 accounts depreciation was 29% of trading profit less plant hire changes for the building companies, whereas it was only 14-15% for the other companies. In the accounts for 1970 depreciation was 32% of trading profit less plant hire charges for the construction companies, 34% for manufacturing and 32% for manufacturing and distribution. It would seem that the other industries have become much more capital intensive over the period 1949 to 1970 or that they have altered their accounting practice and were writing off their machinery etc. in a much shorter time in 1970 than they did in 1949, or more probably that they have done both.

Table 3.13   **Profit and Loss Account Summary 1949 - 1953 £(000)**

Averages per company per year

	(1) Building	(2) % of Capital Employed	(3) All Industry	(4) % of Capital Employed	(1) as a % of (3)
Trading Profit[1]	238	19	423	16	56
Depreciation etc.	(74)	6	(69)	3	107
Operating Profit	164	13	354	13	46
Other Income	5	-	18	1	28
Pre-interest Profit	169	13	372	14	45
Fixed interest payments) Preference dividend)	(8)	1	(14)	1	57
Taxation	(107)	8	(206)	8	52
Ordinary Dividend[2]	20	2	52	2	38
Retained Profit	34	3	100	4	34

[1] Plant hire charges already deducted

[2] includes minority interest.

The introduction of Investment Grants in 1966 probably caused some distortion in presentation of accounts but the treatment of these within the accounts varies from company to company.

The other change which has taken place is that between 1949 and 1970 the other industries altered the proportion of profits retained in the company and in fact reduced them, until by 1970 more profits were distributed to the shareholders than were retained in the company. To a lesser extent the same trend is observable in construction. This change was probably a direct result of the Finance Act 1965 which altered the taxation of company profits and dividends. In effect the alteration meant that for the shareholders to receive the same amount of money after tax more of the profits had to be allocated to them.

4 Analysis of Company Accounts

CONSTRUCTION COMPANY ACCOUNTS

The company accounts studied are those of the thirty construction companies chosen in Chapter 3. The accounts are shown in Appendix 6 - Balance Sheets, Appendix 7 - Breakdown of net current assets, and Appendix 8 - Profit and loss account. Appendices 11 and 12 are the Fixed Asset schedule and Tax schedule respectively and Appendices 13 to 19 show the relationship between particular items in the accounts of the companies. Appendices 9 and 10 give cash flow and the liquidity schedule already discussed. A detailed study of the information set out in Appendices 6 to 19 with a view to inter-company comparisons and determining a general pattern of behaviour for the construction companies is far beyond the scope of this review. However some comments are added on a few of the items shown in the appendices.

Fixed Assets

Appendix 11 shows a breakdown of the fixed assets of the companies and a number of ratios of the items which made up the fixed assets in 1970. A number of the companies did not supply sufficient information in their published accounts to make the analysis complete. The ratios of property and plant and equipment to net fixed assets was fairly constant for the companies although a few of the companies did show a very high proportion of property.

All of the companies, except one, which supplied information concerning the amounts of leasehold and freehold property owned by the company had larger amounts of freehold property than leasehold, but the ratio of leasehold to freehold property was far from constant. There also seemed to be a wide variation in the classification of items of plant and equipment.

Taxation

Appendix 12 shows a breakdown of the taxation paid by the companies for the accounting year studied. Corporation Tax of course was the major constituent in all cases although with Richard Costain Ltd. overseas tax was only a little less than the corporation tax for that company. W.J. Simms Sons & Cooke Ltd. were not liable to pay any tax since their accounts showed a loss during that year.

Financial Ratios

Appendix 13 shows for each of the companies a number of 'financial ratios'. The ratio of debtors to creditors was far from constant; the possible reasons for this have already been discussed. Quick liabilities include all current liabilities except creditors, as these are considered as a constant form of finance. The ratios of cash to quick liabilities and cash to overdraft are also far from constant although the majority of the companies had a small amount of cash at hand in relation to their quick liabilities and overdraft. All of the companies showed current assets larger than current liabilities and all except two showed current assets larger than current liabilities plus overdraft.

The last ratio shown, i.e. Current Assets less stocks and work in progress over current liabilities plus overdraft is another ratio which is not constant for all the companies, probably because of the variation already mentioned regarding the stock and work in progress item. For any particular company these ratios may be most useful when compared with ratios of the items from previous years accounts or with previous months accounts.

Balance Sheet Items
Appendix 14 shows the balance sheet items as a percentage of the capital employed by all the companies. There seemed to be no obvious general pattern of behaviour for the companies although there were similarities between some of them but not necessarily between those within a particular turnover group. Much of this variability is related to the non construction activities of many of the companies.

Profit and Loss Gearing
Appendix 15 shows the profit and loss gearing of the companies, i.e. profit and loss items as a percentage of trading profit. A detailed examination of this has not been made.

Financial Gearing
Appendix 16 shows the financial gearing, i.e. the percentage return on the various measures of investment in the companies and the interest as a percentage of the loans. The net return on equity interest, i.e. the ordinary dividend as a percentage of the equity interest, presents an interesting pattern in that it tends to be higher for the smaller companies than it does for the larger. No doubt to some extent this stems from the dividend policy that market and other forces compel directors to pursue. However, the same pattern is discernible for gross return on equity interest (i.e. earnings for equity as a percentage of equity interest). Here there seems to be a sag in the middle of the size range of firms, suggesting that the close supervision available to small firms is weakened in the middle range of firms which have not been able to take advantage of the specialisms and techniques that the largest firms emply. Perhaps too it reflects on the competitiveness of the market in which they operate. More will be said on this subject later.

Productivity per Employee
Appendix 17 shows the *productivity per employee* and the remuneration of the employees in the companies. The figures shown for productivity per employee do not show the true position as no account was taken of work done and profit made by sub-contractors, etc. Also some of the activities undertaken by the companies were not concerned with construction and may have had different labour/turnover characteristics. The figure used for turnover was that given in the published accounts of the companies and as explained previously this does not show the true position of the companies turnover with respect to its employees, etc. A number of the companies only give employment figures for the United Kingdom but the turnover, profit, etc. were those for the whole company. The only company to show a loss in the accounts had the smallest turnover per employee but the relationship between turnover and trading profit per employee was far from constant for the other companies.

95

**Management
Ratios**

Appendix 18 shows the *pre-interest margins* for the companies and
Appendix 19 shows the capital utilisation, i.e. the capital employed as a
percentage of turnover. Both these sets of tables use the turnover shown
in the accounts of the companies which as previously explained does not
show the complete position with respect to the work carried out.

The costs and margins shown in Appendix 18 seem to have a fairly wide
spread, perhaps not wider than one would expect given the spread of
activities of the various companies. It could be that this is a revealing
indication of what more uniform data and more detailed knowledge of
activities could tell us.

The number of times capital employed was turned over ranged from 0.8 to
7.4 times with the majority of companies turning over their capital employed
between 2.0 and 4.5 times, with the average 3.6 times. The relationship
between the number of times the capital employed was turned over and the
profit margins was far from constant for the companies.

However the Table 4.1 shows that both turnover of capital employed and
Net Current assets (which is closely akin to *working capital)* do follow a
pattern related to size groups of firms. The figures should be compared with
those in Table 4.2 which measure profitability, and with the comments
thereon.

Table 4.1

The number of items p.a. capital employed and net assets are
turned over by 30 companies in the sample.

Group	Turnover £ m	Unweighted average of times capital employed is turned over p.a.	Unweighted average of times net current assets are turned over p.a.
1	Over 100	3.4	9.2
2	50 to less than 100	3.5	5.3
3	30 to less than 50	5.1	10.4
4	20 to less than 30	4.4	8.5
5	10 to less than 20	4.5	8.6
6	5 to less than 10	3.6	5.1
7	3 to less than 5	3.2	5.5
8	1 to less than 3	2.4	4.2
9	Less than 1	3.1	7.1
	Average for sample	3.6	6.0

**Ratios and Com-
parisons with
Other Industries**

Table 4.2, below, illustrates some important ratios for each size group of
firms.

This confirms and enlarges on the comments made in Section 4.6 above,
dealing with financial gearing. Particularly important is the narrowing of
profit margins on sales for companies in the £10-50m turnover range, that
is reflected in the return on funds invested in these companies. The sample
as a whole shows 4.0% margin on turnover and 13.5% on capital employed.
This compares with figures of 11.5% and 12.1% on capital employed for
'manufacturing industry' and 'manufacturing and distribution' respectively.

Table 4.2   **Profit measures of Construction Companies in the Sample**

Group	Turnover range £ m	Unweighted average of pre interest profit as % of turnover	Unweighted average of pre interest profit as % of capital employed
1	100 and above	4.3	10.7
2	50 to less than 100	4.9	13.9
3	30 to less than 50	2.8	10.2
4	20 to less than 30	3.8	15.3
5	10 to less than 20	2.3	8.0
6	5 to less than 10	3.9	4.9
7	3 to less than 5	6.7	19.8
8	1 to less than 3	10.6	21.4
9	Less than 1	8.7	27.3
	Sample average	4.6	13.8

INFORMATION SOURCES AND PROBLEMS

Section 1

Section 1 reviewed the Construction Industry with particular reference to its structure, employment and output both of the industry as a whole and the various sectors within it. Most of the information set out in this chapter was obtained from four publications -

1. Annual Bulletin of Construction Statistics
2. Monthly Bulletin of Construction Statistics
3. The Monthly Digest of Statistics
4. Studies in Company Finance

(See Bibliography for further details of these publications).

Section 2

Compared with Chapter 1 the information contained in Chapter 2 was considerably less straightforward to collate. The main problem was to compile the list of quoted construction companies shown in Appendix 3. A number of sources of information was studied, none of which had a complete list of the public construction companies. The sources used were:-

1. *The Financial Times* list of shares quoted on the Stock Exchange. This list of Construction Companies and Building Materials companies was far from complete and without obtaining information about the activities of each firm it was almost impossible to determine whether a company was a materials manufacturer or a building company.

2. *Construction and Building Materials Review* included a list of the top fifty companies and the top one hundred public companies with respect to turnover. Once again there was the problem of determining whether a company was a materials manufacturer or a building company.

3.   *Guide to Key British Enterprises* includes a section which dealt with construction companies solely but there is no differentiation between private, public and quoted companies. To determine whether a company was public or not one had to consult the paragraph devoted to that company, within the main part of the text of the Guide. A further problem with this publication in compiling this review is that the list is incomplete.

4.   *Savory, Milln's Building Book* has a list of public Construction companies which was found to be fairly complete although a little out of date. The companies were grouped by their main activity. Once again there was no differentiation between quoted and unquoted companies.

5.   *Daily Statistics (Card) Service* by The Exchange Telegraph Co. Ltd. The index of companies for this service classifies companies according to their activities so one company may occur in the index a number of times. The original index was compiled in 1967 and there have been a number of supplements to it which give additions and deletions to the main index. Construction activities are divided into two groups - Section 17, General Building etc. and Section 35, Constructional Engineers, Bridge Builders, etc. The companies within the service are all quoted on U.K. Stock Exchanges.

6.   *Moodies Cards* . Similar comments to those made about the service of Exchange Telegraph Co. Ltd. apply to the indexing of this service.

7.   *Stock Exchange Year Book 1972* . The industry classification of this publication again had for our purpose similar disadvantages.

(see Bibliography for further details of these publications).

The list shown in Appendix 3 was derived from the above combined sources. A basic list of companies was compiled from the Exchange Telegraph index and Supplements and additions and deletions were made to it from the other sources.

The Exchange Telegraph Statistics Cards, (*Extel Cards)* were obtained for each of the companies in the list of Construction companies and their turnover, and the average number employed were recorded. These are shown in Appendix 3 and the companies were then ranked with respect to turnover (see Appendix 4). The Extel Service used was found to be incomplete in that for a number of companies only share price information, yield ratios etc. were available and not information on their accounts. Information was obtained about these companies from the *Moodies Card Service.*

Originally there were 139 companies in the list of construction companies but owing to difficulty in tracing data on one company the analysis was restricted to 138. Five of these companies were unquoted.

The other information shown in Section 2 was obtained from the same sources as those used for Section 1.

Sections 3 & 4   In Section 3 the comparison of the *average* accounts of 30 building contractors with the *average* accounts of 737 quoted manufacturing companies and 1045 quoted manufacturing and distribution companies was made using the accounts obtained from the Extel Card Service which are shown in the Appendices in a reasonably standard form. The sum of the accounts of the 737 manufacturing companies and the 1045 manufacturing and distribution companies were obtained from *Financial Statistics No. 115* published by the Central Statistical Office.

The information referred to in Section 4 is contained in Appendices 11 - 19 and is mostly ratios of items in the accounts of the 30 building contractors obtained from the Extel Card Service.

5 Summary and Conclusions

Summary

This review was divided into four sections, the first being a review of the construction industry as a whole with particular reference to the structure, output and employment of the industry. Section 2 was concerned with the public companies engaged in construction. Section 3 was a comparison of the *average* accounts of some public construction companies with those of other industries in 1970 and with the *average* accounts of public construction companies in the period 1949 - 53. Section 4, the final part of the study, provided a brief analysis of the accounts of 30 public construction companies, of which details are provided in the appendices.

Section 1 shows that there are a large number of firms in the construction industry and that most of these are small firms specialising in a particular trade. The number of firms engaged in construction work has steadily declined over a number of years and so has the number of employees and the number of operatives employed by construction firms. The output of the industry, as a whole, reached a peak in 1968 and has declined since. The output pattern of the public sector work from 1966 - 70 was the same as that of all construction work but the private sector has declined in output over 4 of these 5 years; there was a slight recovery during 1968.

In the public sector the only type of work which did not show a decline in any of the years between 1966 and 1970 was offices, shops, garages and factories. In the private sector the industrial work was the only type of work not to show a decline during that same period.

Section 2 shows the large increase in the number of quoted companies engaged in construction work. Lists of the companies engaged in construction work during 1970 is shown in Appendices 2 and 3. The section is mainly concerned with those companies that could broadly be classified to construction by reference to the Standard Industrial Classification. There were 137 of these during 1970 and figures for turnover, and the average number of employees for each of the firms are shown in Appendix 3. The companies are ranked with respect to turnover in Appendix 4. The largest 11 companies, with respect to turnover, were responsible for half of the turnover of the group of 135 companies. The quoted building contractors were mostly 'large' companies, in fact only ten of them had a turnover of less than one million pounds during 1970 and two fifths of the companies employed more than 1200 employees whereas only 1.7% of all the firms engaged in construction employed more than 115 employees.

In Section 3 thirty of these companies were selected to represent the construction industry's quoted companies. Their accounts for 1970 are shown in Appendices 6, 7 and 8 and a list of the companies is shown in Appendix 5. The *average* accounts of these 30 companies are compared with the *average* accounts of 737 manufacturing companies and 1045 manufacturing and distribution companies in this chapter. Comparison of the balance sheets revealed that the construction companies employed about one third of the capital employed by the companies in industry generally. The main difference in the sources of funds was that the construction companies had much higher overdrafts, this being probably owing to the nature of the work. The main differences in the employment of funds were to do with the *stocks and work in progress* items and the *debtor* and *creditor* items. All of these were large and the construction companies, on average, were receivers of credit whereas the other companies were givers of credit although there seemed to be no standard pattern of accounts within the construction companies. It was suggested that there were a large number of variations in accounting practice within the construction companies so a standard pattern of accounts was unlikely to be found.

Comparison of the profit and loss accounts of the industries revealed a number of variations between the companies in these industries. It was found that the construction companies had a higher trading profit relative to capital employed than the other companies but that there was much less difference in the net profit after tax relative to the capital employed. Plant hire may explain the low depreciation provisions relative to the trading profit although this may indicate that the activities of the construction companies are more labour intensive than those of the other industries. The high loan interest charges were a result of the high bank overdrafts of construction companies. The liquidity schedule shown in the Section indicates that the construction companies were in a more illiquid state relative to capital employed than was industry generally.

Section 3 also includes a comparison of the accounts of the construction companies and the other companies for 1970 with those of the period 1949 - 53. The main differences are, a change in the sources of funds (i.e. a tendency to raise more capital by borrowing rather than the issue of more shares) and a change in the appropriation of profit (i.e. less was retained within the companies in 1970 than in 1953). This was probably due to changes in taxation resulting from the Finance Act 1965, and a change in the depreciation item in the accounts. In 1953 depreciation was relatively much higher in the construction companies than in the other industries but in 1970 it was slightly lower.

The information referred to in Section 4 is contained in Appendices 11 - 19. It consists of a large number of ratios of items from the accounts of each of the 30 construction companies. It is an attempt to determine whether there is a standard pattern of accounts for the construction companies which is imposed upon them by the nature of the work they are engaged in, but to complete it would require more information than is obtainable from published data. However some tentative conclusions are suggested.

Conclusions

Taking an unweighted average of pre tax margins gives a value of 4.6% of turnover for 1970. In the same year capital employed averages 34.5% of turnover. If one deducts a nominal 40% of the pre tax margin for tax, i.e.

1.8%, this leaves 2.8% of turnover as net profit after tax available to shareholders. Preference dividends are negligible - broadly speaking the 2.8% is split equally between the dividend in ordinary shares and retentions, each taking about 1.4% of turnover.

In relation to capital employed, this represents a growth of 4%. This is inadequate to keep pace with inflation. It is a problem that is not unique to construction: industry generally faces a similar problem. What is different is that construction benefits much less than does manufacturing industry from investment incentives, which, from one viewpoint can be regarded as a balancing item to compensate for the inflation that our tax system refuses to recognize. It benefits less because its investment is in working capital rather than in fixed assets.

It is true that to some degree the construction industry can finance this by taking more credit from its suppliers and subcontractors and by utilising relatively cheap finance in the form of bank overdrafts. This review throws some light on what has already happened in this direction, and also indicates what may be a dilemma in which some firms may find themselves in the future if they exhaust their borrowing potential and at the same time find difficulties in the way of raising additional share capital in a risk industry.

BIBLIOGRAPHY

Studies in Company Finance,(Chapter 12 - Quoted Companies in the Building Industry - C.F. Carter) Edited by: Henderson & Tew (National Institute for Economic and Social Reform).

Understanding Company Financial Statements, R.H. Parker (Pelican).

Monthly Bulletin of Construction Statistics, Statistics Construction Division, (Dept. of the Environment - HMSO).

Annual Bulletin of Construction Statistics, Statistics Construction Division, (Dept. of the Environment - HMSO).

Financial Statistics No. 115, Central Statistical Office, (HMSO).

Monthly Digest of Statistics No. 310, Central Statistical Office, (HMSO).

Construction and Building Materials Review 1971, (Gower Economic Publication).

Guide to Key British Enterprises, (Dun & Bradstreet Ltd.).

Savory, Milln's Building Book, 1969 - 70, (E.B. Savory & Milln & Co. Ltd.).

Daily Statistics (Card) Service, (The Exchange Telegraph Co. Ltd.).

Moodies Cards, (Moodies Services Ltd.).

Moodie News Sheets, (Moodies Services Ltd.).

Technical and Managerial Manpower in the Construction Industry, S.M. Nazem (PhD Thesis: UMIST).

Working Capital in the Building Industry, S.M. Nazem and P. Hesketh, (Report submitted to the Dept. of the Environment).

Appendices

1. Construction Firms by Trade in 1970.

2. Supplementary List of Quoted Companies with Substantial Construction Industry interests.

3. Companies Classifiable to Construction (SIC Definition) - Turnover and Average Number Employed.

4. Construction Companies Ranked with respect to Turnover.

5. Construction Companies chosen for more detailed Analysis of their Accounts.

6. Construction Company Balance Sheets.

7. Net Current Assets.

8. Profit and Loss Accounts.

9. Cash Flows.

10. Liquidity Schedule.

11. Fixed Asset Schedule.

12. Tax Schedule.

13. Financial Ratios.

14. Balance Sheet Items as % of Capital Employed.

15. Profit and Loss Gearing.

16. Financial Gearing.

17. 'Productivity' per Employee.

18. Pre-Interest Margins.

19. Capital Utilisation.

Appendix 1

Construction firms by trade in 1970

Company type	*Number*
General Builders	31 546
Building & Civil Engineering Contractors	2 201
Civil Engineers	1 567
Plumbers	6 718
Joiners & Carpenters	4 572
Painters	12 258
Roofers	1 349
Plasterers	2 615
Glaziers	281
Demolition Contractors	284
Scaffolding Specialists	96
Reinforced Concrete Specialists	240
Heating & Ventilating Engineers	2 211
Electrical Contractors	4 095
Asphalt & Tar Sprayers	303
Plant Hirers	1 475
Flooring Contractors	438
Constructional Engineers	363
Insulating Specialists	84
Suspended Ceiling Specialists	76
Floor & Wall Tiling Specialists	298
Miscellaneous	350
	73 420

Appendix 2

Supplementary List of Quoted Companies with substantial construction industry interests

Road Surfacing, Quarry Products, Road Building Materials

Amey Group Ltd.
Anglo-American Asphalt Co. Ltd.
Atlas Stone Ltd.
Breedon & Cloud Hill Lane Works Ltd.
British Dredging Co. Ltd.
Cawoods Holdings Ltd.
Consolidated Gold Fields Ltd. (Building Activities)
Dunning & Son Ltd.
English China Clays Ltd.
Hoveringham Gravels Ltd.
Limmer Holdings Ltd.
Man-Abell Holdings Ltd.
Marshalls (Halifax) Ltd.
Ready Mixed Concrete Ltd.
Redland Ltd.
Val De Travers Asphalte Ltd.
Vectis Stone Ltd.

Structural Engineers, Construction Engineers, Bridge Builders

A.C.E. Machinery Ltd.
Avonmouth Engineering Corporation Ltd.
Babcock & Wilcox Ltd.
Blackwood Hodge Ltd.
John Booth & Sons Ltd.
Braithwaite & Co. Engineers Ltd.
British Steel Construction (Birmingham) Ltd.
Clarke, Chapman & Co. Ltd.
Cocksedge (Holdings) Ltd.
Construction Holdings Ltd.
Dorman, Long & Co. Ltd.
Grampian Holdings Ltd.
Guest, Keen and Nettlefolds Ltd.
Head Wrightson & Co. Ltd.
P. & W. Maclellan Ltd.
McIntyre & Sons Ltd.
McNeill Group (N.I.) Ltd.
Richards (Leicester) Ltd.
Sears Engineering Ltd.
Wm. Neill & Son (St. Helens) Ltd.
Smith & Pearson Ltd.
William Tawse Ltd.
Teesside Bridge & Engineering Ltd.
Wade Charles & Co. Ltd.
Thomas W. Ward Ltd.
Westwood Dawes & Co. Ltd.
Whessoe Ltd.
Winn Industries Ltd.

*Specialist Contractors - Heating, Plumbing, Electricity, Air
Conditioning & Refrigeration and Sanitary Engineering etc.*

Alwyn Holdings Ltd.
Brightside Engineering Holdings Ltd.
Carrier Engineering Co. Ltd.
Christy Bros. Ltd.
T. Clark & Co. Ltd.
Clark & Fenn (Holdings) Ltd.
Crown House Ltd.
The Deritend Stamping Co. Ltd.
Doxford & Sunderland Ltd.
Econa Ltd.
Gaskell & Chambers (Holdings) Ltd.
Kitson's Insulations Ltd.
John Mollett Ltd.
Talbex Ltd.
Tattersall (Holdings) Ltd.
Tranmer Group Ltd.
Watshanis Ltd.
Westdock Group Ltd.

Shop Fitters

> Courtney Pope (Holdings) Ltd.
> Harris & Sheldon Corporation Ltd.
> Russell Brothers (Paddington) Ltd.
> C.D.O. Sage Ltd.
> A.J. Wait (Holdings) Ltd.

Reinforced Concrete Engineers, Precast Concrete Structures, System Built Structures

> Austin-Hall Group Ltd.
> Banbury Buildings Holdings Ltd.
> J. Brockhouse & Co. Ltd.
> E.C. Cases Ltd.
> Eleco Holdings Ltd.
> Hahn Holdings Ltd.
> Hall Engineering (Holdings) Ltd.
> Vic Hallam Ltd.
> Hardun Bux Holdings Ltd.
> Kenkast Ltd.
> The Lafarge Organisation Ltd.
> Marley Ltd.
> Mixcrete Holdings Ltd.
> Stephenson Developments (Holdings) Ltd.
> Weir Group Ltd.

Appendix 3

Companies Classifiable to Construction (SIC definition) for accounting year 1970 unless otherwise stated

Company		Turnover £ 000	Average No. Employed
Aberdeen Construction Group Ltd.		28 389	6 220
Norman C. Ashton Ltd.		1 420	244
Ashworth and Stewart (Holdings) Ltd.		1 386	NK
Octavius Atkinson and Sons Ltd.		1 480	356
Bacal Construction Ltd.		11 800	1 656
Ben Bailey Construction Ltd.		699	141
Bardolin Ltd.		10 223	723
Bath and Portland Group Ltd.		33 520	5 521 UK
Beechwood Construction Ltd.	1971	2 045	287
Benfield and Luxley Ltd.		940	264
Burns-Anderson Ltd.		4 322	411
Bett Bros. Ltd.		8 873	1 642
Henry Boot & Sons Ltd.		9 734	1 875
Alfred Booth & Co. Ltd.	unquoted	15 645	2 893
Bovis Holdings Ltd.		97 800	11 740
Brown & Jackson Ltd.		3 192	664
Bryant Holdings Ltd.		34 000	4 268
Burnett and Hallamshire Holdings Ltd.		11 957	608

Company		Turnover £ 000	Average No. Employed
David Charles Ltd.		11 003	992
Comben & Wakeling Ltd.	(15 months)	8 818	540
Concrete Ltd.		24 481	4 934
Constable, Hart & Co. Ltd.		4 835	764
Richard Costam Ltd.		108 000	7 918 UK
H. Cox & Sons (Plant Hire) Ltd.		1 013	195
Crest Homes Ltd.		5 044	487
Cronch Group Ltd.		6 100	665
Daleholme Holdings Ltd.		2 738	428
Dares Estates Ltd.		4 270	444
Dean Smith Holdings Ltd.		1 469	133
G. Dew & Co. Ltd.		4 271	710
Robert M. Douglas (Contractors) Ltd.		22 006	3 621
Drake & Cubitt Holdings Ltd.		67 015	13 580
Drury Holdings Ltd.		15 970	1 990
Earlsgate Holdings Ltd.		3 230	665
Ellis (Kensington) Ltd.		5 913	1 556
F.C. Construction (Holdings) Ltd.		2 375	448
F.P.A. Construction Group Ltd.		9 119	1 783
Leonard Fairclough Ltd.		23 352	2 944
Five Oaks Investments Ltd.		832	55
John Finlan Ltd.		1 994	81
E. Fletcher Builders Ltd.	1971	6 142	780
Fram Group Ltd.		33 128	5 191
W. & C. French Ltd.		45 600	6 102
Galliford Brindley Ltd.		8 882	1 695
M.J. Gleeson (Contractors) Ltd.	1971	27 273	3 043
W. & J. Glossop Ltd.		3 678	684
Eldon R. Gorst & Son Ltd.		786	NK
Greaves Organisation Ltd.		5 756	349
Greensitt & Barrett Ltd.		1 624	251
H.A.T. Group Ltd.		12 623	2 603
Haden Carrier Ltd.		50 556	6 762 UK
Matthew Hall & Co. Ltd.		33 424	4 465 UK
Hall-Thermotank Ltd.		25 800	4 252 UK
James Hamson Holdings Ltd.		6 302	1 250
Hart Builders (Edinburgh) Ltd.		1 980	382
Harvey Plant Holdings Ltd.		4 343	493
Hawkins Developments Ltd.		7 487	710
Hewden-Stuart Plant Ltd.		3 611	810
Higgs & Hill Ltd.		30 000	2 710
W.A. Hills & Sons Ltd.		2 187	402

Company		Turnover £ 000	Average No. Employed
Hoskins & Horton Ltd.		2 910	523
Howard Shuttering (Holdings) Ltd.		783	235
John Howard & Co. Ltd.	unquoted	11 579	2 489
Howards of Mitcham Holdings Ltd.	*Information not readily available*		
I.D.C. Group Ltd.		9 707	1 282
Ernest Ireland Ltd.		5 254	719
H.C. Janes Ltd.		7 114	931
J. Jarvis & Sons Ltd.		9 592	1 183
E.E. Jeavons & Co. Ltd.		3 094	891
Tudor Jenkins & Co. Ltd.		2 477	393
Edward Jones (Contractors) Ltd.		872	110
Kay Bevan Ltd.		2 968	150
J.L. Kier & Co. Ltd.		21 120	2 770
B.B. Kirk & Co. Ltd.		1 208	163
John Laing & Son Ltd.		113 000	14 900
Lane Fox & Co. Ltd.		56	NK
F.J.C. Lilley Ltd.		4 856	924
London & Northern Securities Ltd.		69 755	10 626
Y.J. Lovell (Holdings) Ltd.		19 621	3 253
Sir Robert McAlpine and Sons Ltd.	unquoted	66 000	10 941
McIntyre & Sons Ltd.		496	NK
John McLean & Sons Ltd.		6 072	565
McManus Group Holdings Ltd.		1 768	NK
Marchwiel Holdings Ltd.		56 118	7 505
Mears Bros. Holdings Ltd.		11 136	1 449
Melville, Dundas & Whitson Ltd.		7 000	905
Stanley Miller Holdings Ltd.		4 335	906
Mitchell Construction Holdings Ltd.		30 300	3 277
Modern Engineers of Bristol (Holdings) Ltd.		3 735	449
A. Monk & Co. Ltd.		27 200	4 679
William Moss & Sons Ltd.	unquoted	12 817	2 276
John Mowlem & Co. Ltd.		39 890	4 700
A. & G. Mucklow Group Ltd.		2 216	188
Norris Warming (Holdings) Ltd.		4 872	884
Northern Developments Holdings Ltd.		4 383	239
North Midland Construction Co. Ltd.		1 646	NK
Norwest Holst Construction Ltd.		29 845	5 655
Page Johnson Builders Ltd.		5 045	253
Sir Lindsay Parkinson & Co. Ltd.		26 200	3 350 UK
C.H. Pearce & Sons (Contractors) Ltd.		1 559	335
Pochins Ltd.		4 193	656

Company		Turnover £ 000	Average No. Employed
William Press & Son Ltd.		51 796	12 285
Rawlings Brothers Ltd.		2 300	325
Reed & Mallik Ltd.		4 282	700
Reynards (Excavators) Ltd.		834	155
Richards & Wallington Industries Ltd.		10 460	2 253
Rowlinson Construction Group Ltd.		2 374	379
S.G.B. Group Ltd.		21 691	4 328
James Scott Engineering Group Ltd.		20 600	4 077
Scottish Homes Investment Co. Ltd.		8 387	1 596
Shellabear Price (Holdings) Ltd.		3 421	503
W.J. Simms Sons & Cooke Ltd.		9 709	2 118
William Sindall Ltd.		5 250	910
J. Smart & Co. (Contractors) Ltd.		4 303	932
Southern Construction (Holdings) Ltd.		2 738	353
G.W. Sparrow & Sons Ltd.		2 467	460
Staffordshire Public Works Co. Ltd.		2 960	598
Streeters of Godalming Ltd.		2 634	333
Stuarts Granolithic Co. Ltd.	unquoted	1 331	270
O.C. Summers (Holdings) Ltd.		5 533	1 340
A.E. Symes Ltd.		4 233	821
Taylor Woodrow Ltd.		97 000	11 050
Tilbury Contracting Group Ltd.		12 583	1 895
Truscon Ltd.		8 051	1 108
Turriff Construction Corp. Ltd.		21 091	4 106
Thomas Vale & Sons Ltd.		1 339	271
Varney (Holdings) Ltd.		3 793	562
Alfred Walker & Son Ltd.		1 454	NK
Arthur Wardle Group Ltd.		2 959	337
Thomas Warrington & Sons Ltd.		3 814	760
Way Holdings Ltd.		1 497	585
Joseph Webb & Co. Ltd.		975	NK
Whatlings Ltd.		7 647	1 302
William Whittingham (Holdings) Ltd.		2 995	528
C.S. Wiggins & Sons Ltd.		3 617	597
Wilson (Connolly) Holdings Ltd.		4 200	546
George Wimpey & Co. Ltd.		225 000	32 000 UK
Wood Hall Trust Ltd.		149 139	2 760
Young, Austen & Young Ltd.		4 981	1 102

**Supplementary list of companies classifiable to construction
(SIC definition) that have obtained a quotation since 1970**

	Quote month/yr	*Turnover £ 000*	*Employees*
Derek Crouch (Contractors) Ltd.	10/71	10 533	NK
Fairview Estates Ltd.	5/71		
Federated Land and Building Co. Ltd.	5/72	4 561	NK
Galliford Estates Ltd.	4/71	2 673	NK
Greensquare Properties Ltd.	6/72	584	19
Gough Cooper Ltd.	4/72	5 274	404
Joviel Properties Ltd.	6/72	1 916	NK
M.P. Kent	10/71		
Lawdon Ltd.	7/71	1 426	NK
Orme Developments Ltd.	11/71	1 514	NK

Note - in some instances figures quoted in this list refer to a year subsequent to 1970.

Addenda

1. Constable Hart & Co. Ltd. is, since September 1971, a wholly owned subsidiary of Thomas Roberts (Westminster) Ltd.

2. Crest Homes Ltd. is, since March 1972, a subsidiary of Crest Securities.

3. Daleholme Holdings was acquired by Northern Developments in 1972.

4. Earlesgate Holdings Ltd. is now Wight Construction Holdings.

5. Eldon R. Gorst & Son Ltd. was acquired by Christian Salveson (a public unquoted company) in September 1971.

6. Lane Fox & Co. Ltd. is a subsidiary of Donshire Investment Development Ltd.

7. Orme Developments acquired Tudor Jenkins & Co. Ltd. in February 1972 and Norman C. Ashton in June 1972.

8. Page Johnson Builders became a subsidiary of Bovis Ltd. in December 1971.

9. Rawlings Bros. Ltd. is a subsidiary of D. & W. Murray Ltd.

10. Way Holdings Ltd. became a subsidiary of Dulciner Investments in May 1972.

Appendix 4   **Construction companies ranked with respect to Turnover**[*]

Rank No. with respect to Turnover	Company	£(1000)	Average no. employees
1	George Wimpey & Co.Ltd.	225 000	32 000 UK
2	Wood Hall Trust Ltd.	149 139	2 760
3	John Laing & Son Ltd.	113 000	14 900
4	Richard Costain Ltd.	108 000	7 918 UK
5	Bovis Holdings Ltd.	97 800	11 740
6	Taylor Woodrow Ltd.	97 000	11 050
7.	London & Northern Securities Ltd.	69 755	10 626
8	Drake & Cubitt Holdings Ltd.	67 015	13 580
9 unquoted	Sir Robert McAlpine & Sons Ltd.	66 000	10 941
10	Marchwiel Holdings Ltd.	56 118	7 505
11	William Press & Son Ltd.	51 796	12 285
12	Haden Carrier Ltd.	50 556	6 762 UK
13	W. & C. French Ltd.	45 600	6 102
14	John Mowlem & Co. Ltd.	39 890	4 700
15	Bryant Holdings Ltd.	34 000	4 268
16	Bath and Portland Group Ltd.	33 520	5 521 UK
17	Mathew Hall & Co. Ltd.	33 424	4 465 UK
18	Fram Group Ltd.	33 128	5 191
19	Mitchell Construction Holdings Ltd.	30 300	3 277
20	Higgs & Hill Ltd.	30 000	2 710
21	Norwest Holst Construction Ltd.	29 845	5 653
22	Aberdeen Construction Group Ltd.	28 389	6 220
23 (1971)	J. Gleeson (Contractors) Ltd.	27 273	3 043
24	A. Monk & Co. Ltd.	27 200	4 679
25	Sir Lindsay Parkinson & Co. Ltd.	26 200	3 350 UK
26	Hall - Thermotank Ltd.	25 800	4 252 UK
27	Concrete Ltd.	24 481	4 934
28	Leonard Fairclough Ltd.	23 352	2 944
29	Robert M.Douglas (Contractors) Ltd.	22 006	3 621
30	S.G.B. Group Ltd.	21 691	4 328
31	J.L. Kier & Co. Ltd.	21 120	2 770
32	Turriff Construction Corp. Ltd.	21 091	4 106
33	James Scott Engineering Group Ltd.	20 600	4 077
34	Y.J. Lovell (Holdings) Ltd.	19 621	3 253
35	Drury Holdings Ltd.	15 970	1 990
36 unquoted	Alfred Booth & Co. Ltd.	15 645	2 893
37 unquoted	William Moss & Sons Ltd.	12 817	2 276

[*] These are the companies listed in appendix 3 as classifiable to construction

Rank No. with respect to turnover	Company	£(1000)	Average no. employees
38	H.A.T. Group Ltd.	12 623	2 603
39	Tilbury Contracting Group Ltd.	12 583	1 895
40	Burnett & Hallamshire Holdings Ltd.	11 957	608
41	Bacal Construction Ltd.	11 800	1 656
42 unquoted	John Howard & Co. Ltd.	11 579	2 489
43	Mears Bros. Holdings Ltd.	11 136	1 449
44	David Charles Ltd.	11 003	992
45	Richards & Wallington Industries Ltd.	10 460	2 253
46	Bardolm Ltd.	10 223	723
47	Henry Boot & Sons Ltd.	9 734	1 875
48	W.J. Simms Sons & Cooke Ltd.	9 709	2 118
49	I.D.C. Group Ltd.	9 707	1 282
50	J. Jarvis & Sons Ltd.	9 592	1 183
51	F.P.A. Construction Group Ltd.	9 119	1 783
52	Galliford Brindley Ltd.	8 882	1 695
53	Bett Bros. Ltd.	8 873	1 642
54 (15 months)	Comben & Wakeling Ltd.	8 818	540
55	Scottish Homes Investment Co. Ltd.	8 387	1 596
56	Truscon Ltd.	8 051	1 108
57	Whatlings Ltd.	7 647	1 302
58	Hawkins Developments Ltd.	7 487	710
59	H.C. Jones Ltd.	7 114	931
60	Melville, Dundas & Whitson Ltd.	7 000	905
61	James Hamson Holdings Ltd.	6 302	1 250
62 (1971)	E. Fletcher Builders Ltd.	6 142	780
63	Crouch Group Ltd.	6 100	665
64	John McLean & Sons Ltd.	6 072	565
65	Ellis (Kensington) Ltd.	5 913	1 556
66	Greaves Organisation Ltd.	5 756	349
67	O.C. Summers (Holdings) Ltd.	5 533	1 340
68	Ernest Ireland Ltd.	5 254	719
69	William Sundall Ltd.	5 250	910
70	Page Johnson Builders Ltd.	5 045	253
71	Crest Homes Ltd.	5 044	487
72	Young, Austen & Young Ltd.	4 981	1 102
73	Norris Warming (Holdings) Ltd.	4 872	884
74	F.J.C. Lilley Ltd.	4 856	924
75	Constable, Hart & Co. Ltd.	4 835	764

Rank No. with respect to turnover		Company	£(1000)	Average no. employees
76		Northern Development (Holdings) Ltd.	4 383	239
77		Harvey Plant Holdings Ltd.	4 343	493
78		Stanley Miller Holdings Ltd.	4 335	906
79		Burns - Anderson Ltd.	4 322	411
80		J. Smart & Co. (Contractors) Ltd.	4 303	932
81		Reed & Mallik Ltd.	4 282	700
82		G. Dew & Co. Ltd.	4 271	710
83		Dares Estates Ltd.	4 270	444
84		A.E. Symes Ltd.	4233	821
85		Wilson (Connolly) Holdings Ltd.	4 200	546
86		Pochins Ltd.	4 193	656
87		Thomas Warrington & Sons Ltd.	3 814	760
88		Varney (Holdings) Ltd.	3 793	562
89		Modern Engineers of Bristol (Holdings) Ltd.	3 735	449
90		W. & J. Glossop Ltd.	3 678	684
91		C.S. Wiggins & Sons Ltd.	3 617	597
92		Hewden-Stuart Plant Ltd.	3 611	810
93		Shellabear Price (Holdings) Ltd.	3 421	503
94		Earlsgate Holdings Ltd.	3 230	665
95		Brown & Jackson Ltd.	3 192	664
96		E.E. Jeavons & Co. Ltd.	3 094	891
97		William Whittingham (Holdings) Ltd.	2 995	528
98		Kay Bevan Ltd.	2 968	150
99		Staffordshire Public Works Co.Ltd.	2 960	598
100		Arthur Wardle Group Ltd.	2 959	337
101		Hoskins & Horton Ltd.	2 910	523
102		Daleholme Holdings Ltd.	2 738	428
103		Southern Construction (Holdings) Ltd.	2 738	353
104		Streeters of Godalming Ltd.	2 634	333
105		Tudor Jenkins & Co. Ltd.	2 477	393
106		G.W. Sparrow & Sons Ltd.	2 467	460
107		F.C. Construction (Holdings) Ltd.	2 375	448
108		Rowlinson Construction Group Ltd.	2 374	379
109		Rawlings Brothers Ltd.	2 300	325
110		A. & J. Mucklow Group Ltd.	2 216	188
111		W. A. Hills & Sons Ltd.	2 187	402
112	(1971)	Beechwood Construction Ltd.	2 045	287
113		John Finlan Ltd.	1 994	81
114		Hart Builders (Edinburgh) Ltd.	1 980	382
115		McManus Group Holdings Ltd.	1 768	NK

Rank No. with respect to turnover		Company	£(1000)	Average no. employees
116		North Midland Construction Co.Ltd.	1 646	NK
117		Greensitt & Barrett Ltd.	1 624	251
118		C.H. Pearce & Sons (Contractors) Ltd.	1 559	335
119		Way Holdings Ltd.	1 497	585
120		Octavius Atkinson & Sons Ltd.	1 480	356
121		Dean Smith Holdings Ltd.	1 469	133
122		Alfred Walker & Son Ltd.	1 454	NK
123		Norman C. Ashton Ltd.	1 420	244
124		Ashworth & Stewart (Holdings) Ltd.	1 386	NK
125		Thomas Vale & Sons Ltd.	1 339	271
126	unquoted	Stuarts Granolithic Co. Ltd	1 331	270
127		B.B. Kirk & Co. Ltd.	1 208	163
128		H. Cox& Sons (Plant Hire) Ltd.	1 013	195
129		Joseph Webb & Co. Ltd.	975	NK
130		Benfield & Loxley Ltd.	940	264
131		Reynards (Excavations) Ltd.	834	155
132		Five Oaks Investments Ltd.	832	55
133		Eldon R. Gorst & Son Ltd.	786	NK
134		Howard Shuttering (Holdings).Ltd.	783	235
135		Edward Jones (Contractors) Ltd.	872	110
136		Ben Bailey Construction Ltd.	699	141
137		McIntyre & Sons Ltd.	486	NK
138		Lane Fox & Co. Ltd.	56	NK

Appendix 5   **Construction companies chosen for more detailed analysis of their accounts**

	No.	*Company*
Group 1	1	George Wimpey & Co. Ltd.
	2	Richard Costain Ltd.
Group 2	3	Bovis Ltd.
	4	Marchwiel Ltd.
Group 3	5	W. & C. French Ltd.
	6	John Mowlem & Co. Ltd.
	7	Higgs & Hill Ltd.
Group 4	8	Norwest Holst Ltd.
	9	M.J. Gleeson (Contractors) Ltd.
	10	Robert M. Douglas (Contractors) Ltd.
Group 5	11	Y.J. Lovell (Holdings) Ltd.
	12	William Moss & Sons Ltd.
	13	Mears Bros. Holdings Ltd.
Group 6	14	W.J. Simms, Sons & Cooke Ltd.
	15	J. Jarvis & Sons Ltd.
	16	F.P.A. Construction Group Ltd.
	17	Whatlings Ltd.
	18	E.Fletcher Builders Ltd.
	19	William Sindall Ltd.
Group 7	20	Stanley Miller Holdings Ltd.
	21	G. Dew & Co. Ltd.
	22	A.E. Symes Ltd.
	23	W. & J. Glossop Ltd.
	24	Brown & Jackson Ltd.
Group 8	25	Kay Bevan Ltd.
	26	The Arthur Wardle Group Ltd.
	27	Southern Constructions (Holdings) Ltd.
	28	Beechwood Construction Ltd.
	29	B.B. Kirk & Co. Ltd.
Group 9	30	Edward Jones (Contractors) Ltd.

Appendix 6   Balance Sheets £m.

Company Number Date of Accounts	1 Dec. 31 1970	2 Dec. 31 1970	3 Dec. 31 1970	4 Oct. 31 1970	5 Mar. 31 1970	6 Dec. 31 1970
Ordinary Capital	16.000	1.811	3.830	2.000	2.965	1.728
Capital Reserves	- -		4.182	1.580	0.413	2.570
Revenue Reserves	22.400	10.217	2.771	8.227	2.639	2.296
Equity Interest	38.400	12.028	10.783	11.807	6.017	6.594
Preference	- -	0.700	0.125	0.500	- -	0.030
Minority Interest	- -	0.535	3.519	0.233	- -	- -
Deferred Liabilities						
- Corporation Tax	- -	0.296	1.390	1.202	0.093	0.243
- Tax Equalisation	- -	- -	0.511	- -	0.636	- -
- Others	- -	- -	- -	- -	1.949	- -
Debentures and Loan St.	2.000	- -	- -	0.080	0.290	- -
Loans & Mortgages	8.482	10.148	11.919	- -	- -	0.426
Bank Overdraft	18.695	7.577	12.758	- -	2.754	1.182
CAPITAL EMPLOYED	67.577	31.284	41.005	13.822	11.739	8.475
Fixed Assets	23.725	17.483	12.703	5.388	7.770	2.203
Investments	18.480	1.424	0.571	3.132	0.348	0.320
Other Assets	- -	1.010	0.015	- -	0.521	- -
Net Current Assets	25.372	11.367	27.716	5.302	3.100	5.952
EMPLOYMENT OF CAPITAL	67.577	31.284	41.005	13.822	11.739	8.475

Company Number Date of Accounts	7 Dec.31 1970	8 Mar.31 1970	9 June30 1971	10 Mar.31 1970	11 Sep.30 1970	12 Dec.31 1970
Ordinary Capital	1.123	1.111	1.000	1.513	1.052	0.798
Capital Reserves	0.497	2.119	1.308	0.21	0.757	0.379
Revenue Reserves	0.948	1.946	1.849	2.907	0.752	0.613
Equity Interest	2.568	5.176	4.157	4.441	2.561	1.790
Preference	0.250	0.300	- -	- -	0.275	0.228
Minority Interest	0.074	0.045	- -	- -	0.019	0.015
Deferred Liabilities						
- Corporation Tax	- -	- -	- -	- -	0.007	- -
- Tax Equalisation	- -	0.043	0.182	- -	- -	- -
- Others	- -	- -	- -	- -	- -	- -
Debentures and Loan St.	1.000	- -	- -	- -	1.600	- -
Loans & Mortgages	- -	4.902	- -	- -	- -	- -
Bank Overdraft	0.548	1.917	0.254	0.015	1.166	0.263
CAPITAL EMPLOYED	4.440	12.383	4.593	4.456	5.628	2.296
Fixed Assets	2.211	4.753	4.161	1.972	1.894	1.461
Investments	0.020	0.759	- -	0.110	- -	0.005
Other Assets	0.363	- -	- -	- -	0.005	- -
Net Current Assets	1.846	6.871	0.432	2.374	3.729	0.830
EMPLOYMENT OF CAPITAL	4.440	12.383	4.593	4.456	5.628	2.296

Appendix 6   Balance Sheets (continued)

Company Number	13	14	15	16	17	18
Date of Accounts	Sep.30 1970	Dec.31 1970	Mar.31 1971	Dec.31 1970	Sep.30 1970	Mar.31 1971
Ordinary Capital	1.000	1.000	0.250	1.979	0.500	1.097
Capital Reserves		0.245	0.376	0.279	0.046	0.173
Revenue Reserves	0.383	0.376	0.428	0.003	0.421	1.558
Equity Interest	1.383	1.621	1.054	2.261	0.967	2.828
Preference	- -	- -	0.114	- -	- -	- -
Minority Interest	- -	- -	- -	- -	- -	- -
Deferred Liabilities						
- Corporation Tax	0.283	- -	0.101	0.024	0.022	0.372
- Tax Equalisation	0.101	- -	0.015	0.033	0.015	0.075
- Others	- -	- -	- -	- -	- -	- -
Debentures and Loan St.	- -	- -	- -	- -	- -	- -
Loans & Mortgages	0.221	- -	- -	- -	- -	0.900
Bank Overdraft	0.521	1.570	0.011	0.769	0.783	1.197
CAPITAL EMPLOYED	2.509	3.191	1.295	3.087	1.787	5.372
Fixed Assets	1.447	1.903	0.745	0.800	0.283	0.431
Investments	- -	- -	0.006	- -	- -	2.156
Other Assets	- -	0.034	- -	0.675	0.010	- -
Net Current Assets	1.062	1.254	0.544	1.612	1.494	2.785
EMPLOYMENT OF CAPITAL	2.509	3.191	1.295	3.087	1.787	5.372

Company Number	19	20	21	22	23	24
Date of Accounts	Dec.31 1970	Dec.31 1970	Oct.31 1970	Jan.31 1970	Jan.31 1971	Dec.31 1970
Ordinary Capital	0.250	0.400	0.750	0.400	0.576	0.400
Capital Reserves	0.046	0.100	- -	0.065	0.103	- -
Revenue Reserves	0.516	0.262	0.639	0.509	0.514	0.370
Equity Interest	0.812	0.762	1.389	0.974	1.193	0.770
Preference	- -	- -	- -	0.100	0.060	- -
Minority Interest	- -	- -	- -	- -	0.002	- -
Deferred Liabilities						
- Corporation Tax	0.027	0.059	0.170	0.095	- -	0.097
- Tax Equalisation	0.011	0.001	- -	- -	- -	0.006
- Others	- -	- -	- -	- -	- -	- -
Debentures and Loan St.	- -	- -	- -	- -	- -	- -
Loans & Mortgages	- -	0.175	- -	- -	- -	- -
Bank Overdraft	0.876	0.025	- -	0.510	0.075	0.024
CAPITAL EMPLOYED	1.726	1.022	1.559	1.679	1.330	0,897
Fixed Assets	0.870	0.452	0.683	0.402	0.572	0.291
Investments	0.018	0.002	- -	- -	0.040	- -
Other Assets	- -	0.185	0.202	0.007	0.53	0.177
Net Current Assets	0.838	0.383	0.856	1.270	0.665	0.429
EMPLOYMENT OF CAPITAL	1.726	1.022	1.559	1.679	1.330	0.897

Appendix 6   Balance Sheets (continued)

Company Number	25	26	27	28	29	30
Date of Accounts	Dec.31	Dec.31	Dec.31	Mar.31	Nov.2	Dec.31
	1970	1970	1970	1971	1970	1970
Ordinary Capital	0.450	0.354	0.200	0.150	0.100	0.144
Capital Reserves	0.675	0.256	0.040	0.163	- -	- -
Revenue Reserves	0.220	0.340	0.268	0.297	0.269	0.103
Equity Interest	1.345	0.950	0.508	0.610	0.369	0.247
Preference	- -	- -	- -	- -	- -	- -
Minority Interest	0.003	- -	- -	- -	- -	- -
Deferred Liabilities						
- Corporation Tax	0.064	0.151	0.092	0.124	0.023	0.028
- Tax Equalisation	0.006	0.095	0.021	0.043	0.007	0.003
- Others	- -	- -	- -	- -	- -	- -
Debentures and Loan St.	- -	- -	- -	- -	- -	- -
Loans & Mortgages	1.442	0.025	- -	- -	- -	- -
Bank Overdraft	0.699	0.280	- -	0.105	0.129	- -
CAPITAL EMPLOYED	3.559	1.501	0.621	0.882	0.528	0.278
Fixed Assets	2.903	0.128	0.319	0.445	0.106	0.042
Investments	- -	0.243	- -	- -	0.021	0.114
Other Assets	0.233	- -	- -	0.002	- -	- -
Net Current Assets·	0.423	1.130	0.302	0.435	0.401	0.122
EMPLOYMENT OF CAPITAL	3.559	1.501	0.621	0.882	0.528	0.278

Appendix 7   **Net Current Assets £m.**

Company Number Date of Accounts	1 Dec.31 1970	2 Dec.31 1970	3 Dec.31 1970	4 Oct.31 1970	5 Mar.31 1970	6 Dec.31 1970	7 Dec.31 1970	8 Mar.31 1970	9 June30 1971	10 Mar.31 1970
Stocks & Stores	55.886	--	3.505	1.072	--	5.706	0.677	--	--	1.314
Work in Progress	--	9.683	--	12.257	7.530	--	--	4.114	5.227	0.688
Land for Development	--	--	8.209	--	--	--	--	2.398	--	--
Development Property	--	--	4.185	--	--	--	--	--	--	0.064
Debtors	10.884	16.781	25.981	2.463	2.773	7.343	6.270	7.166	0.268	4.172
Cash & Equivalent	1.530	1.474	1.562	0.406	1.284	1.193	0.078	0.006	0.013	0.635
Life Assurance Policies	--	--	--	--	--	--	--	--	--	--
Investment Grants Rcble.	--	0.996	--	--	--	--	--	--	--	--
Investments & Loans	--	0.430	--	0.156	--	--	--	--	--	--
Tax Certificates	--	--	--	2.167	--	--	--	--	--	--
Others	--	1.107	--	0.311	0.945	--	--	--	0.272	--
CURRENT ASSETS	68.300	30.471	43.442	18.832	12.532	14.242	7.025	13.684	5.780	6.873
Creditors	34.850	18.371	13.960	11.605	8.419	7.721	4.648	5.726	4.824	3.762
Current Tax	6.638	0.139	1.021	1.524	0.687	0.291	0.334	0.787	0.344	0.455
Provisions for										
- Ordinary Dividends	1.440	--	--	0.401	--	0.276	0.179	0.278	0.180	0.282
- Preference Dividends	--	--	--	--	--	0.002	0.018	0.022	--	--
- Minority Interest Divs.	--	--	--	--	--	--	--	--	--	--
Gross Dividends	1.440	0.234	0.745	0.401	0.326	0.278	0.197	0.300	0.180	0.282
H.P. Instalments etc.	--	--	--	--	--	--	--	--	--	--
Others	--	0.360	--	--	--	--	--	--	--	--
CURRENT LIABILITIES	42.928	19.104	15.726	13.530	9.432	8.290	5.179	6.813	5.348	4.499
NET CURRENT ASSETS	25.372	11.367	27.716	5.302	3.100	5.952	1.846	6.871	0.432	2.374

Appendix 7 Net Current Assets (continued)

Company Number	11	12	13	14	15	16	17	18	19	20
Date of Accounts	Sep.30 1970	Dec.31 1970	Sep.30	Dec.31	Mar.31	Dec.31	Sep.30	Mar.31	Dec.31 1970	Dec.31 1970
Stocks & Stores	0.556		0.144		0.026		0.525		0.114	
Work in Progress	4.042	1.824	2.662	0.526	0.630	1.805	2.914	0.876	1.467	0.997
Land for Development	- -	- -	- -	- -	- -	0.996	- -	1.356	0.065	- -
Development Property	0.502	0.788	0.468.	- -	0.846	- -	- -	- -	- -	- -
Debtors	1.889	0.069	0.059	3.220	0.993	1.322	0.172	1.932	0.488	0.296
Cash & Equivalent	0.010	- -	- -	0.009	0.030	0.028	0.010	0.008	0.001	0.065
Life Assurance Policies	- -	- -	- -	- -	- -	- -	0.057	- -	- -	- -
Investment Grants Rcble.	0.021	- -	0.085	- -	- -	- -	- -	- -	- -	- -
Investments & Loans	- -	- -	- -	- -	- -	- -	- -	- -	- -	- -
Tax Certificates	- -	0.100	- -	- -	- -	- -	- -	- -	- -	- -
Others	0.037	- -	- -	- -	- -	- -	- -	1.041	0.082	- -
CURRENT ASSETS	7.057	2.681	3.518	3.755	2.525	4.151	3.678	5.313	2.217	1.358
Creditors	2.625	1.670	2.272	2.481	1.910	2.051	1.971	1.248	1.222	0.839
Current Tax	0.073	0.113	0.001	- -	0.021			0.311	0.082	0.119
Provisions for										
- Ordinary Dividends	0.105	- -	- -	- -	- -	- -	- -	- -	- -	- -
- Preference Dividends	0.020	- -	- -	- -	- -	- -	- -	- -	- -	- -
- Minority Interest Divs.	- -	- -	- -	- -	- -	- -	- -	- -	- -	- -
Gross Dividends	0.125	0.048	0.075	0.020	0.050	- -	0.037	- -	0.021	0.017
H.P. Instalments etc.	- -	- -	0.076	- -	- -	- -	- -	- -	0.054	- -
Others	0.505	0.020	0.032	- -	- -	0.488	0.176	0.969	- -	- -
CURRENT LIABILITIES	3.328	1.851	2.456	2.501	1.981	2.539	2.184	2.528	1.379	0.975
NET CURRENT ASSETS	3.729	0.830	1.062	1.254	0.544	1.612	1.494	2.785	0.838	0.383

Appendix 7   Net Current Assets (continued)

Company Number Date of Accounts	21 Oct.31 1970	22 Jan.31 1970	23 Jan.31 1971	24 Dec.31 1970	25 Dec.31 1970	26 Dec.31 1970	27 Dec.31 1970	28 Mar.31 1971	29 Nov. 2 1970	30 Dec.31 1970
Stocks & Stores	0.160	0.145	0.077	0.083	--	--	0.051	0.116	0.015	--
Work in Progress	0.626	0.632	0.371	0.714	0.700	0.590	0.494	0.400	0.352	0.227
Land for Development	--	0.421	--	0.067	--	0.642	--	--	--	0.039
Development Property	--	--	--	--	--	--	--	--	0.080	--
Debtors	0.214	0.633	0.645	0.137	0.409	0.482	0.053	0.175	0.240	0.026
Cash & Equivalent	0.134	0.047	0.053	--	0.180	0.010	0.138	0.001	0.001	0.035
Life Assurance Policies	--	--	--	--	--	--	--	0.017	--	--
Investment Grants Rcble.	--	--	--	--	--	--	0.009	0.045	--	--
Investments & Loans	0.350	--	--	--	0.001	--	0.050	--	--	--
Tax Certificates	0.140	--	--	--	--	--	0.025	--	--	--
Others	--	0.131	--	--	--	--	--	--	--	--
CURRENT ASSETS	1.624	2.009	1.146	1.002	1.290	1.724	0.820	0.754	0.688	0.327
Creditors	0.549	0.621	0.223	0.457	0.590	0.411	0.400	0.271	0.247	0.121
Current Tax	0.137	0.066	0.092	0.083	0.187	0.124	0.078	--	0.028	0.044
Provisions for										
- Ordinary Dividends	--	--	0.101	0.021	0.086	0.059	0.040	0.048	0.012	0.040
- Preference Dividends	--	--	0.003	--	--	--	--	--	--	--
- Minority Interest Divs.	--	--	0.016	--	0.004	--	--	--	--	--
Gross Dividends	0.082	0.052	0.120	0.021	0.090	0.059	0.040	0.048	0.012	0.040
H.P. Instalments etc.	--	--	--	--	--	--	--	--	--	--
Others	--	--	0.046	0.012	--	--	--	--	--	--
CURRENT LIABILITIES	0.768	0.739	0.481	0.573	0.867	0.594	0.518	0.319	0.287	0.205
NET CURRENT ASSETS	0.856	1.270	0.665	0.429	0.423	1.130	0.302	0.435	0.401	0.122

Appendix 8   Profit & Loss Accounts £m.

Company Number	1	2	3	4	5	6
Date of Accounts	Dec.31	Dec.31	Dec.31	Oct.31	Mar.31	Dec.31
	1970	1970	1970	1970	1970	1970
Turnover	225.000	108.000	97.800	56.118	43.600	39.890
Overseas Turnover						
& Exports	40.000	47.000	- -	NN	NN	8.923
Trading Profit	12.766	5.506	7.587	8.757	5.280	1.316
- Plant Hire & Rental			(2.355)	(4.724)	(1.879)	(0.676)
- Depreciation &						
Amortisation	(4.868)	(1.754)	(0.956)	(1.441)	(1.558)	(0.038)
- Directors Remuner-						
ation	(0.226)	(0.169)	(0.186)	(0.076)	(0.094)	(0.085)
Operating Profit	7.672	3.583	4.090	2.516	1.749	0.517
Investment Income	0.189	1.151	- -	0.012	- -	0.028
Net Rental & Property						
Income	0.375	0.596	0.611	0.024	- -	0.087
Dividends & Interest						
Receivable	- -	- -	0.093	0.197	0.011	- -
Pre-Interest Profit	8.236	5.330	4.794	2.749	1.760	0.632
- Debenture & Loan						
Interest	(0.396)	(0.437)		(0.005)	- -	- -
- Bank Charges & Interest	(1.747)	(1.014)	(1.453)	(0.005)	(0.609)	(Cr. 0.096)
- Mortgage Interest	- -	- -	- -	- -	- -	0.036
Net Profit Before Tax	6.093	3.879	3.341	2.739	1.151	0.692
- Total Tax	(2.657)	(1.535)	(1.347)	(1.215)	(0.487)	(0.309)
- Minority Interest						
Dividends	- -	(0.109)	(0.154)	(0.022)	- -	Cr. 0.014
- Other Liabilities	- -	(0.360)	- -	- -	- -	- -
- Preference Dividends	- -	(0.039)	(0.009)	(0.035)	- -	(0.001)
Profit Available for Ordinary	3.436	1.836	1.831	1.467	0.664	0.396
Earning %	21.5	102.0	49.7	73.3	22.4	22.9
Dividend %	9	22	20	20	11	16
Cost of Ordinary Dividend	1.440	0.396	0.736	0.400	0.325	0.277
RETAINED PROFIT	1.996	1.440	1.095	1.067	0.339	0.119
Items Excluded - Debts	- -	0.024	- -	- -	- -	- -
" " - Credits	- -	0.090	0.034	- -	- -	0.044

Appendix 8   Profit and Loss Accounts (continued)

Company Number	7	8	9	10	11	12
Date of Accounts	Dec.31 1970	Mar.31 1970	June30 1971	Mar.31 1970	Sep.30 1970	Dec.31 1970
Turnover	30.000	29.845	27.273	22.006	19.621	12.817
Overseas Turnover & Exports	3.000	- -	- -	- -	- -	- -
Trading Profit	1.301	3.207	2.071	1.896	0.935	0.598
- Plant Hire & Rental	(0.345)	(0.873)	(0.657)	(0.318)	(0.339)	(0.143)
- Depreciation & Amortisation	(0.273)	(1.100)	(0.581)	(0.658)	(0.081)	(0.180)
- Directors Remuner- ation	(0.082)	(0.085)	(0.058)	(0.024)	(0.047)	(0.092)
Operating Profit	0.601	1.149	0.775	0.896	0.468	0.183
Investment Income	- -	0.086	- -	0.011	- -	Dr. 0.015
Net Rental & Property Income	0.017	0.029	0.046	- -	- -	0.031
Dividends & Interest Receivable	0.026	- -	0.046	0.003	- -	0.018
Pre-Interest Profit	0.644	1.264	0.867	0.910	0.468	0.217
- Debenture & Loan Interest		(0.223)	- -	- -	(0.124)	- -
- Bank Charges & Interest	(0.078)	(0.172)	(0.012)	- -	(0.087)	(0.008)
- Mortgage Interest	- -	- -	- -	- -	- -	- -
Net Profit Before Tax	0.566	0.869	0.855	0.910	0.257	0.209
- Total Tax	(0.234)	(0.436)	(0.351)	(0.459)	(0.097)	(0.090)
- Minority Interest Dividends	(0.004)		- -	- -	- -	(0.004)
- Other Liabilities	- -	(0.039)	- -	- -	- -	(0.002)
- Preference Dividend	(0.018)	(0.022)	(0.001)	- -	(0.020)	(0.014)
Profit Available for Ordinary	0.310	0.372	0.503	0.451	0.140	0.099
Earning %	27.7	33.5	50.3	29.8	13.3	12.4
Dividend %	16	25	18	20	10	10
Cost of Ordinary Dividend	0.179	0.278	0.180	0.282	0.105	0.080
RETAINED PROFIT	0.131	0.094	0.323	0.169	0.035	0.019
Items Included - Debts	- -	0.058	- -	- -	- -	- -
" " - Credits	0.063	0.113	- -	0.057	- -	- -

Appendix 8   Profit and Loss Accounts (continued)

Company Number	13	14	15	16	17	18
Date of Accounts	Sep.30	Dec.31	Mar.31	Dec.31	Sep.30	Mar.31
	1970	1970	1971	1970	1970	1971
Turnover	11.136	9.709	9.592	9.119	7.647	6.142
Overseas Turnover & Exports	- -	- -	- -	- -	- -	- -
Trading Profit	0.938	L 0.248	0.502	0.693	0.631	1.263
- Plant Hire & Rental	(0.362)	(0.095)	(0.145)	(0.047)	(0.394)	(0.057)
- Depreciation & Amortisation	(0.192)	(0.157)	(0.059)	(0.160)	(0.056)	(0.142)
- Directors Remuneration	(0.062)	(0.064)	(0.060)	(0.018)	(0.040)	(0.032)
Operating Profit	0.322	L 0.564	0.238	0.468	0.141	1.032
Investment Income	- -	- -	- -	- -	- -	- -
Net Rental & Property Income	- -	0.012	- -	0.011	- -	- -
Dividends & Interest Receivable	0.002	- -	0.001	0.001	- -	- -
Pre-Interest Profit	0.324	L 0.552	0.239	0.480	0.141	1.032
- Debenture & Loan Interest	(0.027)	- -	- -	- -	- -	
- Bank Charges & Interest	(0.042)	(0.156)	(0.007)	(0.156)	(0.095)	(0.202)
- Mortgage Interest	- -	- -	- -	- -	- -	- -
Net Profit Before Tax	0.255	L 0.708	0.232	0.324	0.046	0.830
- Total Tax	(0.144)	- -	(0.103)	(0.142)	(0.024)	(0.328)
- Minority Interest Dividends	- -	- -	- -	- -	- -	- -
- Other Liabilities	- -	- -	- -	- -	- -	- -
- Preference Dividend	- -	- -	(0.008)	- -	- -	- -
Profit Available for Ordinary	0.111	L 0.708	0.121	0.182	0.022	0.502
Earning %	11.2	- -	48.5	9.2	4.4	45.7
Dividend %	12.5	2	30	- -	7.5	31.9
Cost of Ordinary Dividend	0.124	0.020	0.075	- -	0.038	0.350
RETAINED PROFIT	M 0.13	M 0.728	0.046	0.182	M 0.016	0.152
Items Excluded - Debts	- -	- -	- -	- -	- -	- -
" " - Credits	0.055	0.754	- -	0.029	- -	- -

Appendix 8   Profit and Loss Accounts (continued)

Company Number	19	20	21	22	23	24
Date of Accounts	Dec.31 1970	Dec.31 1970	Oct.31 1970	Jan.31 1970	Jan.31 1971	Dec.31 1970
Turnover	5.250	4.335	4.271	4.233	3.678	3.192
Overseas Turnover & Exports	- -	- -	- -	- -	- -	- -
Trading Profit	0.199	0.244	0.644	0.326	0.401	0.347
- Plant Hire & Rental	(0.047)	- -	(0.115)	- -	- -	(0.034)
- Depreciation & Amortisation	(0.050)	(0.079)	(0.099)	(0.046)	(0.090)	(0.042)
- Directors Remuneration	(0.026)	(0.031)	(0.051)	(0.046)	(0.051)	(0.031)
Operating Profit	0.076	0.134	0.379	0.234	0.260	0.240
Investment Income	- -	- -	- -	- -	0.003	- -
Net Rental & Property Income	0.068	- -	- -	- -	- -	- -
Dividends & Interest Receivable	- -	0.004	0.026	- -	- -	0.016
Pre-Interest Profit	0.144	0.138	0.405	0.234	0.263	0.256
- Debenture & Loan Interest	- -	(0.013)	- -	- -	- -	- -
- Bank Charges & Interest	(0.060)	- -	- -	(0.018)	(0.004)	- -
- Mortgage Interest	- -	- -	- -	- -	- -	- -
Net Profit Before Tax	0.084	0.125	0.405	0.216	0.259	0.256
- Total Tax	(0.027)	(0.057)	(0.170)	(0.103)	(0.092)	(0.107)
- Minority Interest Dividends	- -	- -	- -	- -	(0.016)	- -
- Other Liabilities	- -	- -	- -	- -	- -	- -
- Preference Dividends	- -	- -	- -	(0.007)	(0.003)	- -
Profit Available for Ordinary	0.057	0.068	0.235	0.106	0.148	0.149
Earning %	22.9	16.9	31.3	26.6	25.7	37.3
Dividend %	17.5	20	18	13	20	12.5
Cost of Ordinary Dividend	0.021	0.035[1]	0.121	0.052	0.115	0.021
RETAINED PROFIT	0.036	0.033	0.114	0.054	0.033	0.128
Items excluded - Debits	- -	- -	0.001	- -	- -	- -
" " - Credits	0.025	- -	- -	0.001	0.005	0.008

[1] - Actual cost £80 000 but £45 410 waivered.

Appendix 8   Profit and Loss Accounts (continued)

Company Number Date of Accounts	25 Dec.31 1970	26 Dec.31 1970	27 Dec.31 1970	28 Mar.31 1971	29 Nov.2 1970	30 Dec.31 1970
Turnover	2.968	2.959	2.738	2.045	1.208	0.872
Overseas Turnover & Exports	- -	- -	- -	- -	- -	- -
Trading Profit	0.311	0.389	0.422	0.465	0.141	0.094
- Plant Hire & Rental	- -	(0.033)	(0.126)	(0.026)	(0.038)	(0.005)
- Depreciation & Amortisation	(0.022)	(0.016)	(0.051)	(0.106)	(0.017)	(0.009)
- Directors Remuner- ation	(0.037)	(0.032)	(0.033)	(0.031)	(0.019)	(0.016)
Operating Profit	0.252	0.308	0.212	0.302	0.067	0.064
Investment Income	- -	- -	- -	- -	- -	- -
Net Rental & Property Income	0.159	0.025		- -	- -	- -
Dividends & Interest Receivable	- -	- -	0.008	- -	- -	0.012
Pre-Interest Profit	0.411	0.333	0.220	0.302	0.067	0.076
- Debenture & Loan Interest	(0.033)	(0.002)	- -	- -	- -	- -
- Bank Charges & Interest	(0.055)	(0.013)	- -	(0.008)	(0.013)	- -
- Mortgage Interest	(0.079)	- -	- -	- -	- -	- -
Net Profit Before Tax	0.244	0.318	0.220	0.294	0.054	0.076
- Total Tax	(0.105)	(0.138)	(0.092)	(0.119)	(0.024)	(0.029)
- Minority Interest Dividends	(0.007)	- -	- -	- -	- -	- -
– Other Liabilities	- -	- -	- -	- -.	- -	- -
- Preference Dividends	- -	- -	- -	- -	- -	- -
Profit Available for Ordinary	0.133	0.180	0.128	0.175	0.030	0.047
Earning %	29.5	50.9	63.8	116.4	30.0	32.8
Dividend %	28	25	25	55	30	27.5
Cost of Ordinary Dividend	0.086	0.089	0.050	0.066	0.030	0.040
RETAINED PROFIT	0.047	0.091	0.078	0.109	- -	0.007
Items excluded - Debits	0.003	- -	- -	- -	- -	- -
" " - Credits	0.007	0.009	0.006	- -	- -	0.003

L = Loss   M = Minus

Appendix 9   Cash Flows £m.

Company Number	1	2	3	4	5	6
Profit Available for Ordinary	3.436	1.836	1.831	1.467	0.664	0.396
Depreciation etc.	4.868	1.754	0.956	1.441	1.558	0.038
Gross Cash Flow	8.304	3.590	2.787	2.908	2.222	0.434
Ordinary Dividend	(1.440)	(0.396)	(0.736)	(0.400)	(0.325)	(0.277)
Net Cash Flow	6.864	3.194	2.051	2.508	1.897	0.157
Retentions	1.996	1.440	1.095	1.067	0.339	0.119
G.C.F./Ord. Div.	5.76	9.07	3.77	7.28	6.83	1.57

Company Number	7	8	9	10	11	12
Profit Available for Ordinary	0.310	0.372	0.503	0.451	0.140	0.099
Depreciation etc.	0.273	1.100	0.581	0.658	0.081	0.180
Gross Cash Flow	0.583	1.472	1.084	1.109	0.221	0.279
Ordinary Dividend	(0.179	(0.278)	(0.180)	(0.282)	(0.105)	(0.080)
Net Cash Flow	0.404	1.194	0.904	0.827	0.116	0.199
Retentions	0.131	0.094	0.323	0.169	0.035	0.019
G.C.F./Ord. Div.	3.26	5.30	6.02	3.93	2.10	3.49

Company Number	13	14	15	16	17	18
Profit Available for Ordinary	0.111	L0.708	0.121	0.182	0.022	0.502
Depreciation etc.	0.192	0.157	0.059	0.160	0.056	0.142
Gross Cash Flow	0.303	M 0.551	0.180	0.342	0.078	0.644
- Ordinary Dividend	(0.124)	(0.020)	(0.075)	- -	(0.038)	(0.350)
Net Cash Flow	0.179	M 0.571	0.105	0.342	0.040	0.294
Retentions	M 0.013	M 0.728	0.046	0.182	M 0.016	0.152
G.C.F./Ord. Div.	2.44	M 27.52	2.40	- -	2.05	1.84

Appendix 9 Cash Flows (continued)

Company Number	19	20	21	22	23	24
Profit Available for Ordinary	0.057	0.068	0.235	0.106	0.148	0.149
Depreciation etc.	0.050	0.079	0.099	0.046	0.090	0.042
Gross Cash Flow	0.107	0.147	0.334	0.152	0.238	0.191
- Ordinary Dividend	(0.021)	(0.035)	(0.121)	(0.052)	(0.115)	(0.021)
Net Cash Flow	**0.086**	**0.112**	0.213	0.100	0.123	0.170
Retentions	0.036	0.033	0.114	0.054	0.033	0.128
G.C.F./Ord. Div.	5.10	4.20	2.76	2.92	2.07	9.10

Company Number	25	26	27	28	29	30
Profit Available for Ordinary	0.133	0.180	0.128	0.175	0.030	0.047
Depreciation etc.	0.022	0.016	0.051	0.106	0.017	0.009
Gross Cash Flow	0.155	0.196	0.179	0.181	0.047	0.056
- Ordinary Dividend	(0.086)	(0.089)	(0.050)	(0.066)	(0.030)	(0.040)
Net Cash Flow	0.069	0.107	0.129	0.115	0.017	0.016
Retentions	0.047	0.091	0.078	0.009	- -	0.007
G.C.F./Ord. Div.	1.80	2.20	3.58	**2.74**	1.57	1.40

Appendix 10 Liquidity Schedule £m.

Company Number	1	2	3	4	5	6
Cash & Equivalent	1.530	1.474	1.562	0.406	1.284	1.193
- Overdraft	18.695	7.577	12.758	- -	2.754	1.182
Net Cash Position	(17.165)	(6.103)	(11.196)	0.406	(1.470)	0.011
- Quick Liabilities[1]	8.078	0.733	1.766	1.925	1.013	0.569
Liquid Position	(25.243)	(6.836)	(12.962)	(1.519)	(2.483)	(0.558)

Company Number	7	8	9	10	11	12
Cash & Equivalent	0.078	0.006	0.013	0.635	0.010	0.069
- Overdraft	0.548	1.917	0.254	0.015	1.166	0.263
Net Cash Position	(0.470)	(1.911)	(0.241)	0.620	(1.859)	(0.194)
- Quick Liabilities[1]	0.531	1.087	0.524	0.737	0.703	0.181
Liquid Position	(1.001)	(2.998)	(0.765)	(0.117)	(1.859)	(0.375)

Appendix 10   Liquidity Schedule (continued)

Company Number	13	14	15	16	17	18
Cash & Equivalent	0.059	0.009	0.030	0.028	0.010	0.008
- Overdraft	0.521	1.570	0.011	0.769	0.783	1.197
Net Cash Position	(0.462)	(1.561)	0.019	(0.741)	(0.773)	(1.189)
- Quick Liabilities[1]	0.184	0.020	0.071	0.488	0.213	1.280
Liquid Position	(0.646)	(1.581)	(0.052)	(1.229)	(0.986)	(2.469)

Company Number	19	20	21	22	23	24
Cash & Equivalent	0.001	0.065	0.134	0.047	0.053	- -
- Overdraft	0.876	0.025	- -	0.510	0.075	0.024
Net Cash Position	(0.875)	(0.040)	(0.134)	(0.463)	(0.022)	(0.024)
- Quick Liabilities[1]	0.157	0.136	0.219	0.118	0.258	0.116
Liquid Position	(1.032)	(0.096)	(0.085)	(0.581)	(0.280)	(0.140)

Company Number	25	26	27	28	29	30
Cash & Equivalent	0.180	0.010	0.138	0.001	0.001	0.035
- Overdraft	0.699	0.280	- -	0.105	0.129	- -
Net Cash Position	(0.519)	(0.270)	(0.138)	(0.104)	(0.128)	(0.035)
- Quick Liabilities[1]	0.277	0.183	0.118	0.048	0.040	0.084
Liquid Position	(0.796)	(0.453)	(0.020)	(0.152)	(0.168)	(0.049)

[1] Quick Liabilities - Current Liabilities less Creditors

Appendix 11   Fixed Asset Schedule £m.

Company Number	1	2	3	4	5	6
Freehold Property	9.166	6.248			1.742	1.333
Leasehold Property	1.876	4.043	7.049	1.307	0 488	0.832
Fixed Plant						0.038
Loose Plant & Tools				3.977	0.791	- -
Machinery	- -	- -	- -	- -		- -
Equipment	- -	7.192	5.654	0.104	- -	- -
Furniture, Fixtures & Fittings		- -	- -	- -	- -	- -
Vehicles	15.606	- -	- -	- -	4.749	- -
Others	- -	- -	- -	- -	- -	- -
	26.648	17.483	12.703	5.388	7.770	2.203
Less Investment Grants	2.923	- -	- -	- -	- -	- -
Net Fixed Assets	23.725	17.483	12.703	5.388	7.770	2.203
% of Net Fixed Assets						
Total Property	46.6	58.9	55.5	24.2	28.7	98.3
Freehold Property	38.7	35.7	NK	NK	22.4	60.5
Leasehold Property	7.9	23.2	NK	NK	6.3	37.8
Plant etc.	65.7	41.1	44.5	75.8	71.3	1.7
Leasehold as % of Freehold	20.5	64.8	NK	NK	28.0	62.3
Plant etc. as % of Property	141.2	69.8	80.2	312.9	248.5	2.8
Investment Grants as % of N.F.A.	12.3	- -	- -	- -	- -	- -

Company Number	7	8	9	10	11	12
Freehold Property	0.933	2.511		0.594	1.329	0.967
Leasehold Property	0.348	0.228	2.031	0.080	0.201	0.164
Fixed Plant	0.930					
Loose Plant & Tools	- -	1.929	1.937		0.329	
Machinery	- -	- -	- -	1.443	- -	
Equipment	- -	0.125	- -	0.058	- -	- -
Furniture, Fixtures & Fittings	- -	- -	- -	- -	- -	0.267
Vehicles	- -	0.536	0.193	- -	0.035	0.063
Others	- -	- -	- -	- -	- -	-
	2.211	5.329	4.161	2.175	1.894	1.461
Less Investment Grants	- -	0.576	- -	0.203	- -	- -
Net Fixed Assets	2.211	4.753	4.161	1.972	1.894	1.461
% of Net Fixed Assets						
Total Property	58.0	57.6	48.8	34.2	80.8	77.4
Freehold Property	42.3	52.8	NK	30.1	70.1	66.1
Leasehold Property	15.7	4.8	NK	4.1	10.7	11.3
Plant etc.	42.0	54.5	51.2	76.2	19.2	22.6
Leasehold as % of Freehold	37.3	9.1	NK	13.5	15.1	17.0
Plant etc. as % of Property	99.7	94.6	104.8	222.9	23.8	29.2
Investment Grants as % of N.F.A.	- -	12.1	- -	10.4	- -	- -

Appendix 11   Fixed Asset Schedule (continued)

Company Number	13	14	15	16	17	18
Freehold Property		1.234	0.291	0.347	0.090	0.154
Leasehold Property	0.330	0.078	0.012	0.007	- -	- -
Fixed Plant			0.007	0.430		
Loose Plant & Tools	1.117		0.265	0.049	0.080	
Machinery	- -	- -	- -	- -	- -	- -
Equipment	- -		- -	- -	- -	- -
Furniture, Fixtures & Fittings	- -	0.489	0.026	- -	0.017	- -
Vehicles	- -	0.102	0.163	- -	0.096	0.277
Others	- -	- -	- -	(0.033)	- -	- -
	1.447	1.903	0.764	0.800	0.283	0.431
Less Investment Grants	- -	- -	0.019	- -	- -	- -
Net Fixed Assets	1.447	1.903	0.745	0.800	0.283	0.431
% of Net Fixed Assets						
Total Property	22.8	69.0	40.6	44.2	31.8	35.2
Freehold Property	NK	64.8	39.0	43.3	31.8	35.2
Leasehold Property	NK	4.2	1.6	0.9	- -	- -
Plant etc.	77.2	31.0	61.9	55.8	68.2	64.8
Leasehold as % of Freehold	NK	6.3	4.1	2.2	- -	- -
Plant etc. as % of Property	338.5	45.0	152.2	126.1	214.5	182.0
Investment Grants as % of N.F.A.	- -	- -	2.5	- -	- -	- -

Company Number	19	20	21	22	23	24
Freehold Property	0.398			0.272		0.123
Leasehold Property	0.134	0.240	0.198	- -	0.176	- -
Fixed Plant						
Loose Plant & Tools		0.212	0.485			0.024
Machinery	0.186	- -	- -	0.083	- -	0.083
Equipment	- -	- -	- -	- -	0.396	- -
Furniture, Fixtures & Fittings	0.019	- -	- -	0.017	- -	
Vehicles	0.039	- -	- -	0.030	- -	0.061
Others	0.094	- -	- -	- -	- -	- -
	0.870	0.452	0.683	0.402	0.572	0.291
Less Investment Grants	- -	- -	- -	- -	- -	- -
Net Fixed Assets	0.870	0.452	0.683	0.402	0.572	0.291
% of Net Fixed Assets						
Total Property	61.2	53.2	29.0	67.7	30.7	42.2
Freehold Property	45.8	NK	NK	67.7	NK	42.2
Leasehold Property	15.4	NK	NK	- -	NK	- -
Plant etc.	38.8	46.8	71.0	32.3	69.3	57.8
Leasehold as % of Freehold	33.6	NK	NK	- -	NK	- -
Plant etc. as % of Property	63.5	88.3	244.8	47.8	225.0	136.8
Investment Grants as % of N.F.A.	- -	- -	- -	- -	- -	- -

Appendix 11   Fixed Asset Schedule (continued)

Company Number	25	26	27	28	29	30
Freehold Property	1.268	0.095	0.130	0.108	0.006	0.013
Leasehold Property	0.560	0.006	- -	- -	0.039	- -
Fixed Plant						
Loose Plant & Tools	0.102			0.439	0.061	0.029
Machinery	- -	0.013	0.157	- -	- -	- -
Equipment	- -	- -	0.009	- -	- -	- -
Furniture, Fixtures						
& Fittings	- -	0.011	- -	- -	- -	- -
Vehicles	- -	0.033	0.023	- -	- -	- -
Others	0.973	- -	- -	- -	- -	- -
	2.903	0.158	0.319	0.547	0.106	0.042
Less Investment Grants	- -	0.030	- -	0.102	- -	- -
Net Fixed Assets	2.903	0.128	0.319	0.445	0.106	0.042
% of Net Fixed Assets						
Total Property	62.9	78.9	40.7	24.3	42.4	31.0
Freehold Property	43.7	74.2	40.7	24.3	5.7	31.0
Leasehold Property	19.2	4.7	- -	- -	36.7	- -
Plant etc.	37.1	44.5	59.3	98.7	57.6	69.0
Leasehold as % of Freehold	44.1	6.3	- -	- -	650.0	- -
Plant etc. as % of Property	58.8	56.4	145.4	406.5	135.5	223.0
Investment Grants as %						
of N.F.A.	- -	23.4	- -	23.0	- -	- -

Appendix 12   Tax Schedule £m.

Company Number	1	2	3	4	5	6
Total Tax	2.657	1.535	1.347	1.215	0.487	0.309
Tax as % of Pre-Tax Profit	43.6	39.6	40.3	44.4	42.2	44.6
Corporation Tax	2.251	0.664	1.297	1.201	0.373	0.234
Overseas Tax	0.546	0.601	- -	0.014	0.029	0.075
Other Tax & Equalisation	- -	0.560	0.221	- -	0.085	- -
Tax Relief, Reserves etc.						
Credit	0.140	0.290	0.171	- -	- -	- -

Company Number	7	8	9	10	11	12
Total Tax	0.234	0.436	0.351	0.459	0.097	0.090
Tax as % of Pre-Tax Profit	41.4	50.2	41.1	50.5	37.7	43.1
Corporation Tax	0.221	0.544	0.257	0.422	0.097	0.093
Overseas Tax	- -	0.009	- -	0.072	- -	- -
Other Tax & Equalisation	0.013	- -	0.094	- -	- -	- -
Tax Relief, Reserves etc.						
Credit	- -	0.117	- -	0.035	- -	0.003

Analysis of the Construction Industry

Appendix 12 Tax Schedule (continued)

Company Number	13	14	15	16	17	18
Total Tax	0.144	- -	0.103	0.142	0.024	0.328
Tax as % of Pre-Tax Profit	56.4	- -	44.4	43.8	52.2	39.5
Corporation Tax	0.134	- -	0.100	0.142	0.022	0.375
Overseas Tax	- -	- -	- -	- -	0.002	- -
Other Tax & Equalisation	0.010	- -	0.003	- -	- -	- -
Tax Relief, Reserves etc.						
Credit	- -	- -	- -	- -	- -	0.048

Company Number	19	20	21	22	23	24
Total Tax	0.027	0.057	0.170	0.103	0.092	0.107
Tax as % of Pre-Tax Profit	32.1	45.6	42.0	47.7	35.5	41.8
Corporation Tax	0.027	0.059	0.170	0.103	0.092	0.097
Overseas Tax	- -	- -	- -	- -	- -	- -
Other Tax & Equalisation	- -	- -	- -	- -	- -	0.010
Tax Relief, Reserves etc.						
Credit	- -	0.002	- -	- -	- -	- -

Company Number	25	26	27	28	29	30
Total Tax	0.105	0.138	0.092	0.119	0.024	0.029
Tax as % of Pre-Tax Profit	43.0	43.4	41.8	40.5	44.5	38.2
Corporation Tax	0.105	0.142	0.094	0.095	0.024	0.029
Overseas Tax	- -	- -	- -	- -	- -	- -
Other Tax & Equalisation	- -	- -	- -	0.024	- -	- -
Tax Relief, Reserves etc.						
Credit	- -	0.004	0.002	- -	- -	- -

Appendix 13   **Financial Ratios**

Company Number	1	2	3	4	5	6
Debtors/Creditors	0.31	0.91	al. 1.86[1]	0.21	0.33	0.95[1]
Cash/Quick Liabilities	0.19	2.01	0.88	0.21	1.27	2.10
Cash/Overdraft	0.08	0.19	0.12		0.47	1.01
Current Assets/Curr.Liabs.	1.59	1.60	2.76	1.39	1.33	1.72
Curr. Assets/Curr. Liabs. & OD	1.11	1.14	1.54	1.39	1.03	1.34
C.A.-St. & WIP/C.L. & OD	0.20	0.78	bl. 1.40[2]	0.41	0.41	0.80[2]

Company Number	7	8	9	10	11	12
Debtors/Creditors	1.35	1.25	0.06	1.11	0.72	0.47
Cash/Quick Liabilities	0.15	0.01	0.02	0.86	0.01	0.38
Cash/Overdraft	0.14	-	0.05	42.30	0.01	0.26
Current Assets/Curr. Liabs.	1.36	2.01	1.08	1.53	2.27	1.45
Curr. Assets/Curr. Liabs & OD	1.23	1.57	1.03	1.52	1.68	1.27
C.A.-St. & WIP/C.L. & OD	1.11	1.09	0.10	1.08	0.55	0.41[3]

Company Number	13	14	15	16	17	18
Debtors/Creditors	0.21	1.30	0.52	0.64	0.09	1.55
Cash/Quick Liabilities	0.32	0.45	0.42	0.06	0.05	0.01
Cash/Overdraft	0.11	0.01	2.73	0.04	0.01	0.01
Current Assets/Curr. Liabs.	1.43	1.50	1.28	1.64	1.68	2.10
Curr. Assets/Curr. Liabs & OD	1.18	0.92	1.26	1.25	1.24	1.43
C.A.-St. & WIP/C.L. & OD	0.24	0.79	0.94	0.71	0.08	1.16

Company Number	19	20	21	22	23	24
Debtors/Creditors	0.40	0.35	0.39	1.02	2.89	0.30
Cash/Quick Liabilities	0.01	0.48	0.61	0.40	2.06	- -
Cash/Overdraft	- -	2.60	-	0.09	0.71	- -
Current Assets/Curr. Liabs.	1.61	1.39	2.11	2.72	2.38	1.75
Curr. Assets/Curr. Liabs & OD	1.01	1.36	2.11	1.61	2.06	1.67
C.A.-St. & WIP/C.L. & OD	0.29	0.36	1.09	0.99	1.25	0.34

Company Number	25	25	26	27	28	30
Debtors/Creditors	0.69	1.17	0.13	0.65	0.97	0.21
Cash/Quick Liabilities	0.65	0.05	1.17	0.02	0.02	0.42
Cash/Overdraft	0.26	0.04	-	0.01	0.01	-
Current Assets/Curr. Liabs.	1.49	2.91	1.58	2.36	2.40	1.59
Curr. Assets/Curr. Liabs & OD	0.82	1.97	1.58	1.78	1.65	1.59
C.A.-St. & WIP/C.L. & OD	0.38	1.30	0.53	0.56	0.77	0.49

Key   C.A. - St. & WIP/C.L. & OD:– Current Assets less Stocks etc. & Work in Progress
Current Liabilities & Overdraft

[1] Debtors & Work in Progress/ Creditors,   [2] C.A. - St./C.L. & OD work in progress excluded

[3] C.A. - St. & WIP & Land/C.L. & OD

Appendix 14   Balance Sheet Items as % of Capital Employed

Company Number	1	2	3	4	5	6
CAPITAL EMPLOYED						
Ordinary Capital	23.7	5.8	9.3	15.4	25.2	20.4
Equity Interest	56.8	38.4	26.3	85.4	51.2	77.7
Preference	- -	2.2	0.3	3.6	- -	0.4
Minority Interest	- -	1.8	8.6	1.7	- -	- -
Deferred Liabilities	- -	1.0	4.6	8.7	22.8	2.9
Debentures & Loan St.	3.0	- -	- -	0.6	2.5	- -
Loans & Mortgages	12.6	32.4	29.1	- -	- -	5.0
Bank Overdraft	27.6	24.2	31.1	- -	23.5	14.0
EMPLOYMENT OF CAPITAL						
Net Fixed Assets	35.2	55.9	31.0	38.9	66.2	26.1
Investments	27.3	4.6	1.4	22.7	3.0	3.8
Other Assets	- -	3.2	- -	- -	4.4	- -
Net Current Assets	37.5	36.3	67.6	38.4	26.4	70.1

Company Number	7	8	9	10	11	12
CAPITAL EMPLOYED						
Ordinary Capital	25.3	8.9	21.8	34.0	18.7	34.8
Equity Interest	57.9	41.8	90.4	99.7	45.5	78.1
Preference	5.6	2.4	- -	- -	4.9	9.9
Minority Interest	1.7	0.4	- -	- -	0.3	0.6
Deferred Liabilities	- -	0.3	4.0	- -	0.1	- -
Debentures & Loan St.	22.5	- -	- -	- -	28.4	- -
Loans & Mortgages	- -	39.6	- -	- -	- -	- -
Bank Overdraft	12.3	15.5	5.6	0.3	20.8	11.4
EMPLOYMENT OF CAPITAL						
Net Fixed Assets	49.8	38.4	90.6	44.2	33.7	63.7
Investments	0.4	6.1	- -	2.5	- -	0.2
Other Assets	8.2	- -	- -	- -	0.1	- -
Net Current Assets	41.6	55.5	9.4	53.3	66.2	36.1

Company Number	13	14	15	16	17	18
CAPITAL EMPLOYED						
Ordinary Capital	39.8	31.4	19.3	64.1	27.9	20.4
Equity Interest	55.2	50.8	81.4	73.2	54.1	52.6
Preference	- -	- -	8.8	- -	- -	- -
Minority Interest	- -	- -	- -	- -	- -	- -
Deferred Liabilities	15.3	- -	8.9	1.8	2.1	8.3
Debentures & Loan St.	- -	- -	- -	- -	- -	- -
Loans & Mortgages	8.8	- -	- -	- -	- -	16.8
Bank Overdraft	20.7	49.2	0.9	25.0	43.0	22.3
EMPLOYMENT OF CAPITAL						
Net Fixed Assets	57.6	59.6	57.5	25.9	15.8	8.0
Investments	- -	- -	0.5	- -	- -	40.2
Other Assets	- -	1.1	- -	21.8	0.6	- -
Net Current Assets	42.4	39.3	42.0	52.3	83.6	51.8

Appendix 14   Balance Sheet Items as % of Capital Employed (continued)

Company Number	19	20	21	22	23	24
CAPITAL EMPLOYED						
Ordinary Capital	14.5	39.1	48.2	23.8	43.2	44.7
Equity Interest	47.1	74.5	89.1	58.1	89.7	85.8
Preference	- -	- -	- -	6.0	4.5	- -
Minority Interest	- -	- -	- -	- -	0.2	- -
Deferred Liabilities	2.2	5.9	10.9	5.7	- -	11.5
Debentures & Loan St.	- -	- -	- -	- -	- -	- -
Loans & Mortgages	- -	17.1	- -	- -	- -	- -
Bank Overdraft	50.7	2.5	- -	30.2	5.6	2.7
EMPLOYMENT OF CAPITAL						
Net Fixed Assets	50.4	44.2	43.8	24.0	43.0	32.4
Investments	1.0	0.2	- -	- -	3.0	- -
Other Assets	- -	18.1	1.3	0.4	4.0	19.8
Net Current Assets	48.6	37.5	54.9	75.6	50.0	47.8

Company Number	25	26	27	28	29	30
CAPITAL EMPLOYED						
Ordinary Capital	12.6	23.6	32.2	17.0	19.0	51.8
Equity Interest	37.8	63.3	81.8	69.2 ·	69.9	88.9
Preference	- -	- -	- -	- -	- -	- -
Minority Interest	0.1	- -	- -	- -	- -	- -
Deferred Liabilities	2.0	16.4	18.2	18.9	5.7	11.1
Debentures & Loan St.	- -	- -	- -	- -	- -	- -
Loans & Mortgages	40.5	1.7	- -	- -	- -	- -
Bank Overdraft	19.6	18.6	- -	11.9	24.4	- -
EMPLOYMENT OF CAPITAL						
Net Fixed Assets	81.7	8.5	51.4	50.5	20.1	15.1
Investments	- -	16.2	- -	- -	4.0	41.0
Other Assets	6.6	- -	- -	0.2	- -	- -
Net Current Assets	11.7	75.3	48.6	49.3	75.9	43.9

Appendix 15 **Profit & Loss Gearing (i.e. % of Trading Profit)**

Company Number	1	2	3	4	5	6
TRADING PROFIT	100.0	100.0	100.0	100.0	100.0	100.0
Plant Hire/Rental	- -	- -	31.1	54.0	35.6	51.4
Depreciation	38.1	31.9	12.6	16.5	29.5	2.9
Directors Remuneration	1.8	3.4	2.5	0.9	1.8	6.5
Interest	16.8	26.4	19.2	0.1	ł1.5	4.6[1]
Other Income	4.4	31.8	9.3	2.7	0.2	8.7
PRE-TAX PROFIT	47.7	70.1	43.9	31.2	21.8	52.5

Company Number	7	8	9	10	11	12
TRADING PROFIT	100.0	100.0	100.0	100.0	100.0	100.0
Plant Hire/Rental	26.5	27.2	31.8	16.8	36.3	23.9
Depreciation	21.0	34.3	28.1	34.7	8.8	30.1
Directors Remuneration	6.3	2.6	2.8	1.3	5.0	15.4
Interest	6.0	12.3	0.6	- -	22.6	1.3
Other Income	3.3	3.6	4.4	0.7	- -	5.7
PRE-TAX PROFIT	43.5	27.2	72.9	47.9	27.3	35.0

Company Number	13	14[2]	15[2]	16	17	18
TRADING PROFIT	100.0	100.0	100.0	100.0	100.0	100.0
Plant Hire/Rental	38.6	38.3	28.9	26.8	62.5	4.5
Depreciation	20.5	63.2	11.7	23.1	8.9	11.2
Directors Remuneration	6.6	25.8	11.9	2.6	6.3	2.5
Interest	7.4	63.0	1.4	22.5	15.1	16.0
Other Income	0.2	4.8	0.2	1.7	- -	- -
PRE-TAX PROFIT	27.1	285.3	46.3	46.7	7.2	65.8

Company Number	19	20	21	22	23	24
TRADING PROFIT	100.0	100.0	100.0	100.0	100.0	100.0
Plant Hire/Rental	23.6	- -	17.8	- -	- -	9.8
Depreciation	25.1	32.4	15.4	14.1	22.4	12.1
Directors Remuneration	13.1	12.7	7.9	14.1	12.7	8.9
Interest	30.1	5.3	- -	5.5	1.0	- -
Other Income	34.2	1.6	4.0	- -	0.7	4.6
PRE-TAX PROFIT	42.3	51.2	62.9	66.3	64.6	738

Appendix 15   Profit and Loss Gearing (continued)

Company Number	25	26	27	28	29	30
TRADING PROFIT	100.0	100.0	100.0	100.0	100.0	100.0
Plant Hire/Rental	- -	8.5	29.9	5.6	27.0	5.3
Depreciation	7.1	4.1	12.1	22.8	12.0	9.6
Directors Remuneration	11.9	8.2	7.8	6.7	13.5	17.0
Interest	53.7	3.9	- -	1.7	9.2	- -
Other Income	51.2	6.4	1.9	- -	- -	12.8
PRE-TAX PROFIT	78.5	81.7	52.1	63.2	38.3	80.9

[1] Credit
[2] Loss

Appendix 16   Financial Gearing

Company Number	1	2	3	4	5	6
Return on Capital Employed	9.0	12.4	8.1	19.8	9.8	8.2
Interest as % of Loans	7.3	8.2	5.9	1.3	20.0	3.7[1]
Gross Return on Minority Interest	- -	20.4	4.4	9.4	- -	- -
Preference/Profit after Tax	- -	2.1	0.5	2.3	- -	0.3
Gross Return on Equity Interest	8.9	15.2	17.0	12.4	11.0	6.0
Net Return on Equity Interest	3.7	3.3	6.8	3.4	5.4	4.2

Company Number	7	8	9	10	11	12
Return on Capital Employed	12.7	7.0	18.6	20.4	4.7	9.1
Interest as % of Loans	5.0	5.8	4.7	- -	7.6	3.0
Gross Return on Minority Interest	5.4	NK	- -	- -	- -	26.6
Preference/Profit after Tax	5.5	5.6	0.2	- -	12.5	12.4
Gross Return on Equity Interest	12.1	7.2	12.1	10.1	5.5	5.5
Net Return on Equity Interest	7.0	5.4	4.3	6.3	4.1	4.5

Company Number	13	14	15	16	17	18
Return on Capital Employed	10.2	(22.2)	17.9	10.5	2.6	15.5
Interest as % of Loans	9.3	9.9	63.6	20.3	12.1	9.6
Gross Return on Minority Interest	- -	- -	- -	- -	- -	- -
Preference/Profit after Tax	- -	- -	6.2	- -	- -	- -
Gross Return on Equity Interest	8.0	(4.4)	11.5	8.1	2.3	17.7
Net Return on Equity Interest	9.0	1.2	7.1	- -	3.9	12.4

Appendix 16   Financial Gearing (continued)

Company Number	19	20	21	22	23	24
Return on Capital Employed	4.9	12.2	26.0	12.9	19.5	28.5
Interest as % of Loans	6.8	6.5	- -	3.5	5.3	- -
Gross Return on Minority Interest	- -	- -	- -	- -	800.0	- -
Preference/Profit after Tax	- -	- -	- -	6.2	2.0	- -
Gross Return on Equity Interest	7.0	8.9	16.9	10.9	12.4	19.4
Net Return on Equity Interest	2.6	4.6	8.7	5.3	9.7'	2.7

Company Number	25	26	27	28	29	30
Return on Capital Employed	6.9	21.2	35.4	33.3	10.2	27.3
Interest as % of Loans	7.8	4.9	- -	7.6	10.1	- -
Gross Return on Minority Interest	233.5	- -	- -	- -	- -	- -
Preference/Profit after Tax	- -	- -	- -	- -	- -	- -
Gross Return on Equity Interest	9.9	18.9	25.2	28.7	8.1	19.0
Net Return on Equity Interest	6.4	9.4	9.9	10.8	8.1	16.2

[1] Credit

Appendix 17   'Productivity' per Employee £

Company Number	1	2	3	4	5	6
Turnover	7.030	13.650	8.320	7.475	7.150	7.260
Trading Profit	0.398	0.696	0.646	1.167	0.866	0.239
Pre-Tax Profit	0.190	0.490	0.284	0.365	0.189	0.126
Capital Employed	2.110	3.955	3.490	1.842	1.925	1.540
Net Fixed Assets	0.742	2.210	1.080	0.718	1.272	0.401
No. of Employees (Total)	32.000	7.918	11.740	7.505	6.102	4.700
Total Remuneration £m.	47.000	12.741	17.686	12.119	9.527	7.822
Remuneration per Employee	1.470	1.610	1.505	1.617	1.562	1.665

Company Number	7	8	9	10	11	12
Turnover	11.050	5.290	8.950	6.080	6.030	5.630
Trading Profit	0.480	0.568	0.679	0.524	0.287	0.263
Pre-Tax Profit	0.209	0.154	0.281	0.251	0.079	0.092
Capital Employed	1.638	2.190	1.508	1.230	1.728	1.010
Net Fixed Assets	0.815	0.840	1.364	0.544	0.582	0.642
No. of Employees (Total)	2.710	5.655	3.043	3.621	3.253	2.276
Total Remuneration £m.	4.360	8.692	6.014	4.824	4.098	3.088
Remuneration per Employee	1.608	1.536	1.975	1.331	1.260	1.360

Appendix 17   'Productivity' per Employee (continued)

Company Number	13	14	15	16	17	18
Turnover	7.690	4.580	8.100	5.120	5.870	7.870
Trading Profit	0.647	L 0.117	0.424	0.389	0.484	1.640
Pre-Tax Profit	0.176	L 0.334	0.196	0.182	0.032	1.064
Capital Employed	1.731	1.508	1.095	1.732	1.370	6.890
Net Fixed Assets	1.000	0.899	0.630	0.448	0.217	0.552
No. of Employees (Total)	1.449	2.118	1.183	1.783	1.302	0.780
Total Remuneration £m.	2.186	2.589	1.936	2.322	1.819	1.089
Remuneration per Employee	1.510	1.222	1.636	1.304	1.395	1.395

Company Number	19	20	21	22	23	24
Turnover	5.775	4.780	6.015	5.160	5.370	4.800
Trading Profit	0.219	0.269	0.907	0.397	0.587	0.523
Pre-Tax Profit	0.092	0.138	0.570	0.263	0.379	0.386
Capital Employed	1.898	1.129	2.193	2.049	1.945	1.352
Net Fixed Assets	0.956	0.500	0.962	0.490	0.836	0.438
No. of Employees (Total)	0.910	0.906	0.710	0.821	0.684	0.664
Total Remuneration £m.	1.330	1.096	1.230	1.066	0.939	0.812
Remuneration per Employee	1.462	1.210	1.734	1.300	1.371	1.222

Company Number	25	26	27	28	29	30
Turnover	19.150	8.780	7.750	7.125	7.400	7.920
Trading Profit	2.070	1.153	1.194	1.620	0.865	0.854
Pre-Tax Profit	1.625	0.944	0.623	1.024	0.331	0.691
Capital Employed	23.680	4.450	1.756	3.070	3.240	2.525
Net Fixed Assets	19.350	0.380	0.904	1.550	0.650	0.382
No. of Employees (Total)	0.150	0.337	0.353	0.287	0.163	0.110
Total Remuneration £m.	0.159	0.448	0.533	0.373	0.205	0.123
Remuneration per Employee	1.060	1.330	1.510	1.300	1.258	1.120

N.B. Ratios for companies 1, 2, 4 and 5, use U.K. employees only.

Appendix 18   **Pre-Interest Margins (all items as % of Turnover)**

Company Number	1	2	3	4	5	6
Wages	20.9[1]	11.8[1]	18.1	21.6[1]	21.8[1]	19.6
Plant Hire/Rental	- -	- -	2.4	8.4	4.3	1.7
Other Costs	73.5	83.3	74.3	62.9	66.3	77.3
Trading Margins	5.6	4.9	5.2	7.1	7.6	1.4
Depreciation	2.2	1.6	1.0	2.6	3.6	0.1
Operating Margin	3.4	3.3	4.2	4.5	4.0	1.3
Other Income	0.3	1.6	0.7	0.4	- -	0.3
Pre-Interest Margin	3.7	4.9	4.9	4.9	4.0	1.6
Pre-Tax Margin	2.7	3.6	3.4	4.9	2.6	1.7

Company Number	7	8	9	10	11	12
Wages	14.5	29.1	22.0	21.9	20.9	24.1
Plant Hire/Rental	1.2	2.9	2.4	1.4	1.7	1.1
Other Costs	81.4	60.5	70.7	69.6	74.6	72.0
Trading Margins	2.9	7.5	4.9	7.1	2.8	2.8
Depreciation	0.9	3.7	2.1	3.0	0.4	1.4
Operating Margin	2.0	3.8	2.8	4.1	2.4	1.4
Other Income	0.1	0.4	0.4	- -	- -	0.3
Pre-Interest Margin	2.1	4.2	3.2	4.1	2.4	1.7
Pre-Tax Margin	1.9	2.9	3.1	4.1	1.3	1.6

Company Number	13	14	15	16	17	18
Wages	19.6	26.7	20.2	25.4	23.8	17.8
Plant Hire/Rental	3.2	0.9	1.5	0.5	5.1	0.9
Other Costs	72.6	76.6	75.2	67.2	68.6	62.2
Trading Margins	4.6	(4.2)	3.1	6.9	2.5	19.1
Depreciation	1.7	1.6	0.6	1.8	0.7	2.3
Operating Margin	2.9	(5.8)	2.5	5.1	1.8	16.8
Other Income	- -	0.1	- -	0.2	- -	- -
Pre-Interest Margin	2.9	(5.7)	2.5	5.3	1.8	16.8
Pre-Tax Margin	2.3	(7.3)	2.4	3.6	0.6	13.5

Company Number	19	20	21	22	23	24
Wages	25.4	25.3	28.8	25.2	25.5	25.4
Plant Hire/Rental	0.9	- -	2.7	- -	- -	1.1
Other Costs	71.3	69.8	57.3	68.2	65.0	64.7
Trading Margins	2.4	4.9	11.2	6.6	9.5	8.8
Depreciation	1.0	1.8	2.3	1.1	2.4	1.3
Operating Margin	1.4	3.1	8.9	5.5	7.1	7.5
Other Income	1.4	0.1	0.6	- -	0.1	0.5
Pre-Interest Margin	2.8	3.2	9.5	5.5	7.2	8.0
Pre-Tax Margin	1.6	2.9	9.5	5.1	7.0	8.0

Appendix 18   Pre-Interest Margins (continued)

Company Number	25	26	27	28	29	30
Wages	5.4	15.1	19.5	18.2	17.0	14.1
Plant Hire/Rental	- -	1.1	4.6	1.3	3.1	0.6
Other Costs	85.4	72.9	66.3	60.6	73.0	77.0
Trading Margins	9.2	10.9	9.6	19.9	6.9	8.3
Depreciation	0.7	0.5	1.9	5.2	1.4	1.0
Operating Margin	8.5	10.4	7.7	14.7	5.5	7.3
Other Income	5.3	0.8	0.3	- -	- -	1.4
Pre-Interest Margin	13.8	11.2	**8.0**	**14.7**	**5.5**	**8.7**
Pre-Tax Margin	8.2	10.7	8.0	14.3	4.5	8.7

[1] Figure shown represents U.K. wages/Total turnover. The relevant ratios for U.K. wages/U.K. turnover for these companies are as follows:

    1. 25.4;   2. 20.9;   4. 22.7;   5. 23.0

Appendix 19   Capital Utilisation (Capital Employed as % of Turnover)

Company Number	1	2	3	4	5	6	7	8	9	10
Fixed Assets-Property	4.9	9.6	7.2	2.3	5.1	5.4	4.3	9.2	7.4	3.1
-Other	6.9	6.7	5.8	7.3	12.7	0.1	3.1	8.7	7.8	6.8
- Investment Grants	1.3	- -	- -	- -	- -	- -	- -	1.9	- -	0.9
Total Net Fixed Assets	10.5	16.3	13.0	9.6	17.8	5.5	7.4	16.0	15.2	9.0
Other Assets	- -	0.9	- -	- -	1.2	- -	1.2	- -	- -	- -
Stock & Work in Progress	24.9	9.0	3.6	23.7	17.3	14.3	2.3	13.8	19.2	9.1
Debtors	4.8	15.5	26.6[1]	4.4	6.4	18.4[1]	20.9	24.0	1.0	19.0
Cash	0.7	1.4	1.6	0.7	2.9	3.0	0.2	- -	- -	2.9
Others	- -	2.3	12.7	4.7	2.1	- -	- -	8.0	1.0	0.2
Current Assets	30.4	28.2	44.5	33.5	28.7	35.7	23.4	45.8	21.2	31.2
Creditors	15.5	17.0	14.3	20.6	19.3	19.4	15.5	19.2	17.7	17.1
Current Tax	3.0	0.1	1.0	2.7	1.6	0.7	1.1	2.6	1.3	2.1
Others	0.6	0.6	0.8	0.8	0.7	0.7	0.7	1.0	0.6	1.2
Current Liabilities	19.1	17.7	16.1	24.1	21.6	20.8	17.3	22.8	19.6	20.4
Net Current Assets	11.3	10.5	28.4	9.4	7.1	14.9	6.1	23.0	1.6	10.8
Operating Capital	21.8	27.7	41.4	19.0	26.1	20.4	14.7	39.0	16.8	19.8
Investments	8.2	1.3	0.6	5.6	0.8	0.8	0.1	2.5	- -	0.5
Total Capital Employed	30.0	29.0	42.0	24.6	26.9	21.2	14.8	41.5	16.8	20.3
No. of times Capital is turned over	3.3	3.5	2.4	4.1	3.7	4.7	6.8	2.4	5.9	4.9

[1] -Debtors includes Work in Progress

144

Appendix 19   Capital Utilisation (continued)

Company Number	11	12	13	14	15	16	17	18	19	20
Fixed Assets-Property	7.8	8.8	3.0	13.5	3.2	3.9	1.7	2.5	10.1	5.5
-Other	1.9	2.6	10.1	6.1	4.3	4.9	2.1	4.4	6.5	5.0
-Investment Grants	- -	-·	- -	- -	0.2	- -	- -	- -	- -	- -
Total Net Fixed Assets	9.7	11.4	13.1	19.6	7.3	8.8	3.8	6.9	16.6	10.5
Other Assets	- -		- -	0.4	- -	7.4	0.1	- -	- -	4.3
Stock & Work in Progress	23.4	14.2[2]	25.2	5.4	6.8	19.8	45.0	15.9	30.1	23.0
Debtors	9.6	6.2	4.2	33.2	10.3	14.5	2.2	32.4	9.3	6.8
Cash	0.1	0.5	0.5	0.1	0.3	0.3	0.1	0.1	- -	1.5
Others	2.9	- -	1.6	- -	8.9	10.9	0.8	38.3	2.8	- -
Current Assets	36.0	20.9	31.5	38.7	26.3	45.5	48.1	86.7	42.2	31.3
Creditors	13.4	13.0	20.4	25.6	19.9	22.5	25.8	20.3	23.3	19.3
Current Tax	0.4	0.8	- -	- -	0.2			5.1	1.6	2.7
Others	3.2	0.6	1.6	0.2	0.5	5.3	2.8	15.8	1.3	0.5
Current Liabilities	17.0	14.4	22.0	25.8	20.6	27.8	28.6	41.2	26.2	22.5
Net Current Assets	19.0	6.5	9.5	12.9	5.7	17.7	19.5	45.5	16.0	8.8
Operating Capital	28.7	17.9	22.6	32.9	13.0	33.9	23.4	52.4	32.6	23.6
Investments	- -	- -	- -	- -	0.1	- -	- -	35.1	0.3	- -
Total Capital Employed	28.7	17.9	22.6	32.9	13.1	33.9	23.4	87.5	32.9	23.6
No. of times Capital is turned over	3.5	5.6	4.4	3.0	7.3	2.9	4.3	1.1	3.0	4.2

[2]-Stock & Work in Progress includes Land for Development

Appendix 19   Capital Utilisation (continued)

Company Number	21	22	23	24	25	26	27	28	29	30
Fixed Assets-Property	4.6	6.4	4.8	3.9	61.6	3.4	4.7	5.3	3.7	1.5
-Other	11.4	3.1	10.8	5.2	36.3	1.9	7.0	21.5	5.1	3.3
- Investment Grants	- -	- -	- -	- -	- -	1.0	- -	5.0	- -	- -
Total Net Fixed Assets	16.0	9.5	15.6	9.1	97.9	4.3	11.7	21.8	8.8	4.8
Other Assets	0.5	0.1	1.3	5.5	7.9	- -	- -	0.1	- -	- -
Stock & Work in Progress	18.4	18.4	12.2	25.0	23.6	19.9	19.9	25.2	30.4	26.0
Debtors	5.0	15.0	17.5	4.3	13.8	16.3	1.9	8.6	19.9	3.0
Cash	3.1	1.1	1.5	- -	6.0	0.3	5.0	- -	0.1	4.0
Others	11.5	2.9	- -	2.1	- -	21.7	3.1	3.0	6.6	4.5
Current Assets	38.0	47.4	31.2	31.4	43.4	58.2	29.9	36.8	57.0	37.5
Creditors	12.8	14.7	6.1	14.3	19.9	13.9	14.6	13.2	20.4	13.0
Current Tax	3.2	1.6	2.5	2.6	6.3	4.2	2.8	- -	2.3	5.0
Others	2.0	1.1	4.5	1.0	3.0	1.9	1.5	2.4	1.1	4.6
Current Liabilities	18.0	17.4	13.1	17.9	29.2	20.0	18.9	15.6	23.8	23.5
Net Current Assets	20.0	30.0	18.1	13.5	14.2	38.2	11.0	21.2	33.2	14.0
Operating Capital	36.5	39.6	35.0	28.1	120.0	42.5	22.7	43.1	42.0	18.8
Investments	- -	- -	1.1	- -	- -	8.2	- -	- -	1.7	13.1
Total Capital Employed	36.5	39.6	36.1	28.1	120.0	50.7	22.7	43.1	43.7	31.9
No. of times Capital is turned over	2.7	2.5	2.8	3.6	0.8	2.0	4.4	2.3	2.3	3.1

Reviews
and Developments

Since the first edition of the
Construction Industry Handbook
was published only a few of the topics
originally included in the Recent
Developments Section have changed
sufficiently to warrant the inclusion
of a further article in this volume.
Consequently, the Recent Developments and the Reviews Sections have
been amalgamated to bring together
a selection of important articles on
topics ranging from Smoke Control in
Buildings to Site Surveying.

Development of the Industry

Norman McKee, MIOB, AInstInfSoc.

This article has in mind, those who have entered the building industry in more recent years and who may not be fully aware of the demands made on us by the industry in the last twenty-five years. It attempts to show what those demands were, in what degree they have been met and their effect on the development of the industry. There are references for those who wish to make a deeper study.

THE TASK BEFORE THE INDUSTRY.

The State of the Industry

This brief review commences by recalling the achievements of the industry in the two decades between the wars and comparing these with what was done in the two decades after the war.

In the earlier period, the industry can be said to have met many of the immediate needs. Despite the slump which reached its crisis in 1931, it had started intensive programmes of slum clearance and new house building. The post-war period began with the industry run down to a very low ebb. Labour, particularly in the crafts, was seriously depleted by both losses in the forces and dispersal to other industries. War damage repairs occupied much of the available labour and continued to do so for several years.

The building materials manufacturers were in a similar plight with regard to labour and through the run down of their processes and shortage of raw materials, they were unable to meet the demands made on them. Bricks, traditionally used in vast numbers, had almost ceased to be made and many works had been closed down. The licencing of what was agreed as essential work, started during the war, was continued after the war ended, to regulate the amount of building and repair work done and included strict control of the supply of materials, including timber, of which there was a shortage.

The immense amount of reconstruction and new construction to be done had to cover the needs of industry, commerce, housing, schools, hospitals and so on. Not only had war damage and its results to be dealt with, but there were the consequences of the war time "gap" in building (when only essential work was done) to be overcome. Add to this the additional work now required to meet both the higher standards expected in all structures and to satisfy the generally higher standards of living and working and the high priority that had to be given to the building of homes, and it can be seen that the task which faced the industry in 1946 was very much greater than that faced in 1918 when the damage to property was comparatively minimal.

The run-down state of the industry (1945) presented an opportunity which, though obvious with hindsight, was unfortunately missed at the time. When stocks were low and building was almost at a standstill, then was the time for the greater application of standardisation and for the introduction of modular sizes. But no action was taken and the development of modular co-ordination in Britain has been difficult and prolonged.

Official Reports

While many reports on the industry have appeared, two are selected for reference in this review. They were both called for in 1942 when the war·was still in progress. Each of the two anticipated the end of the war and the task before the industry; one deals with contracts and management and the other with housing.

'The Placing and Management of Building Contracts' (1) which became known as the *Simon Report* (taking its name from the Chairman of the committee which prepared it) looked at the demands which would be made on the industry and recommended efficient methods in the placing of contracts, examined the many kinds of contracts available and emphasised the need for close co-operation on the part of all concerned.

'House Construction' (2) considered materials and methods of construction suitable for houses and flats, covering alternative methods used previously and having regard for economy, speed of erection and recommendations for post-war practice.

It must be mentioned that these and many similar official reports have produced expert advice and sound recommendations. But few of them embody marketing incentives and perhaps as a result many matters which they have dealt with remain unheeded.

Housing

In addition to the new homes required to meet the increasing demands of an expanding population and the increased rates of household formation through marriage and higher standards of space and privacy, there was the replacement of unfit dwellings and the improvement of older ones. It was obvious therefore, and this has been set out in the report 'House Construction', (2) that the industry must use other methods than those known as traditional and new kinds of materials, to deal with the grave shortage of homes. Among the requirements of non-traditional methods speed of erection ranked high on the list. As a result the shell of some of the non-traditional houses could be erected in only four days. This speed was however illusory, for the finishing times, when these were traditional, i.e. wet trades, were no quicker in such houses and earlier occupation dates were seldom achieved. As time has advanced, however, many methods and materials originally *non-traditional*, have become in their turn *traditional* through regular use.

PREFABRICATION

Not all the non-traditional or as they became known, *alternative methods* of construction of homes were prefabricated: they may be listed under the following broad headings:-

1. Temporary Prefabs

2. Alternative methods (Systems)

3. Traditional, with partial prefabrication and the greater use of components

4. Industrialised building

1. Temporary Prefabs

Large numbers of these small compact buildings were made in sections and erected on prepared bases on selected sites, often war demolished areas. Their intended life was ten years to cover the period until permanent homes would replace them. Neither by architectural treatment or landscaping, were prefab areas made to look attractive.

They incorporated at least some of the amenities considered desirable and though criticised for lack of space inside, they helped to fill part of the need for homes. The over-estimate of capacity to catch up with new housing needs and so dispose of the prefabs, gave the word a derogatory connotation which their quality and durability did not deserve.

2. Alternative Methods (Systems)

In addition to examining alternative methods of house construction used in between 1918 and 1938, several of which again went into production (at least two of which are still being produced), new methods were developed by the Ministry of Works, in efforts to effect economies in labour and materials in short supply. Investigations included tests to prove suitability for a sixty year life and observations of time and costs of erection were recorded. The types included concrete cast in situ with a cavity, no-fines concrete cast in situ, precast concrete posts and panels, concrete slabbing and several others (3) (4).

Generally speaking their appearance was not considered attractive and they did not become fashionable, their use being mostly in the public sector. Building Societies, which play a large part in providing mortgages in the private sector, leaned on the side of orthodoxy, and very few alternative methods attracted their financial support.

3. Traditional with greater use of components

The investigation of the systems mentioned above proved that it was possible to save site man-hours but the cost savings were not so clear and often any saving of overall time was not apparent.

With the increase in brick production and the more general availability of other materials more and not less construction of houses was done on traditional lines. The private sector had little incentive or desire to adopt alternative methods which were not positively demonstrated to be more economical than traditional methods. But there was change in the greater use that was made of components and in many cases parts or sections of the structure were prefabricated and then built in. This development was made possible by the more general use of mechanical plant which enabled the heavier units to be off loaded and placed in position. Examples of prefabrication used in this way included roofs, floors and *heart units.* In the modernisation of older houses, complete units including bathrooms and kitchens have been supplied ready for installation.

151

4. Industrialised Building

Efforts to rationalise the form of structure have resulted in many complete systems geared to large schemes with an anticipated continuity of output. Where large sections are prefabricated, the plant may be set up on site or established in a factory. However a factory may be remote from the site and thus require long hauls to be made by rail or road. Success demands a continuity of orders to provide for amortization of the immense sums invested in setting up factories and plant.

Many systems were brought to this country from the Continent and others have been developed in Britain. Investment in establishing and developing them has been heavy. However, while many homes have been erected in Britain by these means output is now reduced to the degree where industrialised building may be said to be non-existant. Some dimensional co-ordination appeared in these systems, but such was the absence of interchangeability that with the decline of the systems little of the expenditure on them could be salvaged.

The number of homes built by alternative methods has remained in the minority compared with traditional and the housing shortage in public and private sectors still exists. Though in general terms the alternative systems have probably cost more, it can of course be pointed out that if homes had not been provided in this way the shortage would be correspondingly greater. Of the other factors affecting the shortage, the problem of shortage of available land and its restriction of use, is outside the industry's ambit.

In general again, few of the houses built can be said to be much better than those put up in the inter-war years with the exception, that is, of the amenities they now include.

THE NEED FOR MECHANISATION

Extent of Use of Mechanical Plant

Simultaneously with developments in methods and materials in construction in the early post-war years, and the need for economy and problems through shortage of suitable labour, it was necessary to develop mechanical plant to increase output.

Not only were men unwilling to carry out certain heavy, grimy and tedious tasks, but there were often large units to be off-loaded and placed; units up to that time not usual in house building and the smaller type of building operations. There was therefore a need for plant to be developed, especially for house building.

In civil engineering and in large building projects, cranes, excavators and similar plant had been in use from the days when steam provided the power. But to the immediate post-war period, small and lower medium sized building firms, who were to have a considerable share in the intense house building programme, had used very little mechanical plant. From the marketing standpoint, the manufacturers had little cause to develop machines for use in this direction.

Development By The Field Test Unit (FTU)

To meet the situation, the Chief Scientific Adviser's Division of the then Ministry of Works, set up the Field Test Unit near London. It was later transferred to the Building Research Establishment and became known as the Mechanical Engineering Division. The FTU encouraged the development of mechanisation and brought many machines to the prototype stage. Their site trials of plant, whether prototypes they had developed or of proprietory machines, formed a large part of their activities.

Among the work carried out by the FTU was the provision of aids in moving and placing concrete in foundations, and the handling of materials on site by such means as mobile goods hoists, power barrows, dumpers and the versatile *"Humper"*. A full scale investigation was made of the problem of handling bricks from source to site. One solution was the binding of bricks in packages held by steel binding straps and cages and other means to provide for safety when multiple packages were lifted to heights (6).

The Tower Crane

Perhaps the most spectacular item of plant in which the Building Research Establishment was involved was the organisation for use on site of a tower crane. This type of crane was first developed on the Continent and had been in widespread use in France and Germany for years before its introduction to Britain.

It is the most generally useful building crane, having been designed specially for such work. It has the ability to reach out over a wide area of the site according to the limit of the radius of the jib in a static position. If the crane is mounted on rails or crawler tracks the area is extended. With its permanently horizontal jib with traversing trolley, it enables loads to clear surrounding obstructions according to the height of the tower and place them at or near their point of use. It thus gives vertical and horizontal transfer of load.

In addition to the horizontal jib type, already referred to, there is the derricking jib crane and also that known as the climbing crane. This is supported by the structure and climbs on collars held in the floors. The supporting collars are transferred to higher floors as the building rises.

The advantages of the tower crane may be set out as follows:
(i)   Loads may be moved in one operation from production point, stack or delivery vehicle, to point of use and usually in range of the driver's vision. In many cases remote control is operable.

(ii)   The number of men required for off-loading and movement on site is reduced.

(iii)   Loads of considerable weight or size can be moved more efficiently and the crane can, if necessary, hold a unit in place for fixing until it is secured.

The disadvantages are that expensive foundations or well constructed and carefully maintained track are required. Above a limited height it must be tied to the building. In high winds a tower crane on rails may have to be guyed and permitted to weathervane. In such circumstances a portal crane or a hoist would probably continue working with other than loads of broad expanse. Climbing cranes have load limitations which tend to suit in-situ concrete work and their decline in use has followed the increasing use of precast components.

The Norwich Experiment

The Building Research Establishment purchased a rail mounted tower crane from Germany in 1951 (7). While it might be considered that only a marginal saving could be expected on two storey house construction, this crane, after experimental testing, was used at Norwich. Arrangements were made with the City Engineer for a pilot trial on the local authority housing scheme, in which the direct labour organization was to use the crane. This trial, on 14 houses, demonstrated that shells, foundations and roof could be built with a tower crane to a planned programme and savings could be effected. During this pilot run it was realized that the advantages of producing the shells rapidly would be partly lost unless finishing operations could be phased to match the rate of shell production - a similar situation to that referred to earlier.

By arrangement with the Norwich City Engineer it was decided to plan for and observe production through all stages on a production run of 32 houses. The results proved that with efficient organisation, a very significant number of man hours were saved together with saving of overall building time. This of course meant less on-costs and because the high degree of organisation covered not only the operations in which the crane was involved, but also the finishing and other work on site in which the crane had no lifting to do, savings were effected in these operations as well. The site work was traditional with certain items prefabricated on site, opportunities which the crane made possible.

Other trials at Manchester and elsewhere confirmed the Norwich results and it was shown that improved results were possible without the crane provided that a high degree of organisation was applied. It may be said, that in developing the use of what was then an unusual piece of equipment, focus was brought to bear on the need for more attention to site organisation than the industry, in part at least, had given to them. It was also noticeable that the use of tower cranes in Britain increased rapidly from about this time.

Portal Cranes

Where large units weighing several tons have to be handled in such work as industrialised building the portal crane has proved safe in use. Such a crane can straddle the building and so facilitate the placing of units. On the large Hulme 5 site in Manchester, two portal cranes were used each capable of lifting up to 10 tons (8).

Mixing and Placing Concrete

The use of concrete in large quantities is part of almost every building Development and its greater use has demanded more mechanisation in mixing and placing (9). As a result a new industry developed, which almost covers the country, to provide ready mixed concrete.

According to the complications occurring in the erection of a structure, it is not unusual to see several means of providing and delivering concrete to its required location on site. In a recent example, where the form of structure on a confined site presented many problems, five distinct methods of transporting and placing were needed!

ORGANISATION AND CONTROL

Control

Put in simple terms, control or regulation of operations is established by stating the quality and amount of work to be done in a given time, and then taking the necessary steps to see that the work is done as required and within the limits set out.

The methods of charting and recording progress, must readily indicate any tendency for operations to deviate from the intention in time for possible corrective efforts to be applied.

Gantt Bar Charts

Early attempts to programme building operations were carried out by means of this type of chart. It uses a horizontal time scale against which operations are blocked to indicate the period intended for each operation.

The hatching in or colouring of the blocks indicates the amount of work completed and an additional horizontal line records when the work was done. It should also indicate key dates relating to plant and materials deliveries. This type of chart is comparatively easy to use and is readily understood (10).

The Limited Use of Programming

It may be a surprise to some readers to know that large sections of the industry took a long time to appreciate not only the need to programme work effectively, but to see how inadequate were the efforts of those who failed to use proper methods. There were many even who averred that such methods could not be applied to building! Those concerned with the country's needs for higher productivity pointed out that railways, with highly complicated interconnections had to be programmed (by the use of time tables) and that those concerned in the industry must undertake similar responsibilities.

As a result of one of the recommendations in the *Simon Report* (1) and in an effort to get more efficient organisation on site, it became a condition of formal contracts that a programme schedule should be prepared. This usually took the form of a Gantt chart. It has been said many times that when architects visited sites and requested to see the chart, the site supervisor was liable to open a draw in the plan chest and exhibit, with obvious pride, an unmarked and unused chart!

Programming and the Use of Plant

Efforts in proving the effect of adequate control, showed , among other results, that the economic use of expensive plant, demanded a high degree of site organisation, in order to obtain justifiable results in time and cost (7). A higher degree of site organisation is now much more common. But the present state of the industry, demands that still more attention must be given to the application of adequate and proper management techniques (11).

Other Control Techniques

Three other control techniques have been selected for mention. Their introduction to the industry has been more recent than that of the planning and programming mentioned above.

(i)   Network Analysis introduced to the industry about twelve years ago, has made it possible to identify more easily those critical activities on which output depends. The series of interrelated networks show the dependency of one operation upon another and make it possible to recognise the critical sequences which must be followed, i.e. the *critical path*. Thus it is possible to pick out activities which require attention to secure completion in time if accumulating delays are to be avoided (12).

(ii)   The Line of Balance Method has provided an effective aid to control in large repetitive housing contracts. The National Building Agency has been largely responsible for its use in Britain (13).

(iii) Work Study is a systematic and analytical technique to provide reliable data and record existing methods of working in order to develop improvements (14).

The above techniques have tended to become the concern of specialists, often applied in support of an incentive bonus scheme. There are also other operational research techniques and procedures which could be applied to the industry if it was less fragmentary. Such as lineal programmes, bidding theory, value analysis and other techniques which have a place in general industry and are there for introduction to the building industry when the time is ripe.

SUPERVISION OF OPERATIONS

The Vital Link

The senior site supervisor in building has been described as the *Vital Link* in a chain of administration. On the one side is the management of the firm, and on the other the administration and control of the project he has to manage.

Civil engineering, where the term *agent* was originally used to describe the senior supervisor's post, recognised its importance and demands highly qualified men in the position. With many of the larger firms being engaged in both civil engineering and building work, the term came to be used in the building industry, though here the term *General Foreman* was often used for the man who carried out similar duties.

More recently the terms *Site Manager, Contract Manager* or *Project Manager* have become usual to describe the man in charge of the project. He may have one or more general foremen under him according to the supervision requirements and the extent of operations. These *links* may be extended on the management side of the chain in the larger firms, by *Contracts Managers* who are each responsible for a number of projects.

Leadership

Under the heading *Leadership* in the *Simon Report,* these observations were made and they are quoted here, because in many respects they are equally important today.

"Perhaps the most important single factor in securing good production is good management. It is now realised that the management of human beings, 'personnel management', is exceedingly difficult and a most important part of the whole problem of management. The selection and promotion of managers and agents down to the charge-hand, is of the utmost importance. The special qualities required for personnel management may be summed up as follows: the manager must have an active personal interest in human beings. He must have a strict sense of fairness and inspire confidence among the workers in his integrity. He must have the power not only to drive but also to praise and encourage judiciously. In our view the selection and education of personnel managers, is one of the aspects of the building industry in which there is most room for improvement". (1)

Training of Supervisors

While technical education in building has usually been thorough and of a high standard through much of the present century, the training of supervisors, (as with management training generally) has been a recent development. The administrative complexities which supervisors then had to deal with, had increased. Courses of study were devised to provide an adjunct to practical

experience. At the Brixton School of Building in 1947, *ad hoc* courses
for general foremen in building drew many applicants and other courses
were held in London and other parts of the country.

In 1954, the City and Guilds of London Institute set up a course
General Foremanship Studies in Relation to the Building Industry which
provided an examination and the award of a certificate to successful
candidates. The subjects covered were; elements of supervision and industrial
history, site administration and control, personnel administration and site
organisation and method. The recommended minimum was 240 hours of
study spread over a period of two years. This course never drew large numbers
of candidates and the last examination is being held in 1973.

To replace it, a new course has been introduced by the City and Guilds. The
title is *Construction Site Supervision,* course number 628. It is suitable for
foremen undertaking general responsibilities in respect of building site work.
It is also suitable for accompanying formal training in foremanship duties
and through the provision of project work, can with advantage be closely
integrated with such training.

Management Courses

To meet the needs of development of methods of management arising out
of the changes in the industry, short intensive courses have been held in
educational centres, dealing with management at various levels and providing
opportunities for participation in the practical application of the matters
being studied.

Starting in 1962, the Department of Building in the University of Manchester
Institute of Science and Technology, was early in the field. The Construction Industry Training Board (CITB), the Advisory Service for the Building
Industry, the National Federation of Building Trades Employers and other
organisations are involved in providing this kind of training, and the CITB,
at its Training Centre at Bircham Newton, Norfolk, has a wide programme
of residential courses.

These residential courses include Work Study, Supervisory Training and
training of Training Staff and it is here that plant operation courses are
held where operators are trained to use mechanical plant under actual site
conditions on what was previously an airfield.

ORGANISATION FOR BUILDING IN IMCLEMENT WEATHER

**An Outdoor
Industry**

Adverse weather conditions and lack of daylight place a heavy burden
on the organisation of construction work, the out of doors part being a
large proportion of the regular work of the industry. The question may be
asked why such a long period was allowed to elapse before the industry
gave attention to the problem in Britain. The labour force, most of which
was employed on an hourly basis, had always been without pay for time
lost when weather interrupted work and this method of payment must
have been one factor affecting the industry's attitude. Most building contracts included a clause dealing with weather conditions, the general effect
of which permitted extension of the agreed contract period if such
conditions interrupted the work; this may well have been another factor.

The introduction of the guaranteed week whereby a minimum number of
hours had to be paid, subject to the operatives making themselves available

for work, brought forward the need for means of continuing operations. But for a period there were a number of comparatively mild winters and the very uncertainty of the effect of weather conditions probably tended to delay positive action.

Research

Both the Ministry of Public Building and Works and the Building Research Establishment, (now both part of the Department of the Environment) were involved in the research and development of techniques to help the industry deal with the problem of continuous outdoor work. In addition a Winter Building Adviser was appointed by the Ministry (15).

Among the matters dealt with are:

(i) Methods of concreting and bricklaying during frost (16) (17).

(ii) Temporary shelter, protection of materials and enclosure of work under construction.

(iii) Site lighting.

(iv) Heating equipment.

(v) Protective clothing.

From the economic angle the problem is one of saving effort and cost and it appears surprising that this aspect of organisation has been one of the later developments to be more generally accepted.

CONCLUSION

Summary

This review has considered some of the developments in building during half a century. The matters do not cover the whole field of development and they are not intended to be a study in depth but the aim is to stimulate further study and the form of presentation and the references may be helpful. The *Simon Report* has been used because it has been proved sound in many of its observations, some of which can still be considered applicable.

The number of homes built by alternative methods remain in the minority as compared with traditional. In view however of the experience gained in developing alternative methods, which in their turn led to further developments of value to the industry, parts at least of the effort and cost involved may well have been justifiable expenditure.

Future Developments

There is still much development needed to increase the industry's productivity. That design and construction must be more closely knitted together has been obvious for too long. Efforts in this direction must include full consideration by the designer, of the methods and plant the builder is likely to use. The growth of more design teams, where all the consultants work together as a team is a hopeful indication of the possibilities that lie ahead.

Waste of materials, waste of manpower and waste and loss through accidents, are still a blot upon the industry. Better ways must be developed for motivating men. Surely there must be possibilities here when a considerable proportion of the labour force is in the industry simply because of a desire to see a tangible product resulting from its effort.

REFERENCES

1. Ministry of Works (1944) *The Placing and Management of Building Contracts* (London: HMSO)
2. Ministry of Works (1944) *Post War Building Studies No 1 House Construction* (London: HMSO)
3. Ministry of Works (1948) *National Building Studies Special Report No 4 New Methods of House Construction* (London: HMSO)
4. Ministry of Works (1949) *National Building Studies Special Report No 10 New Methods of House Construction - Second Report* (London: HMSO)
5. Eden J.F. (1966) *Current Papers Construction Series No 14: The Work of BRS on the development of mechanical plant for Buildings* (Building Research Station)
6. Francis C.A. *Bricks and Efficiency* (London: The National Federation of Clay Industries)
7. Broughton H.F. et al (1960) *Mobile Tower Cranes for two and three storey building, National Building Studies. Special Report No 13* (London: HMSO)
8. Vallings H.G. (1971) "Construction Plant" *The Construction Industry Handbook.* Ed. Burgess R.A. et al (Lancaster: MTP)
9. Mcintosh J.D. (1971) "Concrete Technology" *The Construction Industry Handbook* Ed Burgess R.A. et al (Lancaster: MTP)
10. Dept of the Environment (1972) *Advisory Leaflet No 14 Programming & Progressing* (London: HMSO)
11. Burgess R.A. (1971) "Construction Management" *The Construction Industry Handbook* Ed Burgess R.A. et al (Lancaster: MTP)
12. Reynaud C.B. (1967) *The Critical Path: Network Analysis applied to Building* (London: Godwin)
13. Lumsden P. (1968) *The Line of Balance Method* (Oxford: Pergamon Press Ltd)
14. International Labour Office (1952) *Introduction to Work Study* (ILO: Geneva)
15. Smith J.R. (1971) "Winter Building Techniques" *The Construction Industry Handbook* Ed Burgess R. A. et al (Lancaster: MTP)
16. Dept of the Environment Advisory Leaflet No 7 (1971) *Concreting in Cold Weather* (London: HMSO)
17. Dept of the Environment Advisory Leaflet No 8 (1972) *Bricklaying in Cold Weather* (London: HMSO)

Smoke Control in Buildings

Eric W. Marchant, DipArch. (Nott'm), DBS (L'pool),
MArch. (L'pool), RIBA, ARIAS, MIFireE.
The University of Edinburgh

INTRODUCTION

This section discusses some of the problems that are created when smoke (in a burning building) and people (the occupants or firefighters) are combined.

A wide interest is being developed in this topic because of the publicity given to the fact that plastics burn and in doing so produce combustion products which are dangerous to health and safety. This does not mean that the combustion products from conventional construction materials are not harmful but that their toxicity may be less severe.

One major difference between the fire behaviour of plastics materials and conventional construction materials is that with similar surface areas available for combustion the smoke and gases produced by plastics will be more toxic and have a greater opacity than the combustion products of conventional materials.

Some problems of escape route design are discussed as are methods of smoke control in buildings. A basic intention in smoke control techniques is to confine the smoke to the room where the fire starts, the room of origin, or in large spaces, as close to the fire source as possible. This intention is most important as some of the more toxic gases are colourless and/or odourless. If possible, none of the combustion products should be present in the protected escape routes. The design of escape routes is becoming more complex as buildings become bigger, and therefore, house more people. In some situations it is known that smoke and hot gases can travel at a faster rate than is possible for the escaping multitude.

Because of the serious effects of smoke some thought is being given to the development of a *smoke load* rating for building spaces which would include a toxicity index for the products of combustion of furnishings and fittings of the space in addition to the lining materials and the processes or activities to be carried out in the space. This will enable a realistic estimate to be made of the nature and quantity of smoke that would need to be controlled in a building fire.

SOME EFFECTS OF COMBUSTION PRODUCTS

The design of fire protection systems for buildings has, as a first priority, the protection of human life. This is made very difficult because the human body operates properly only over a short range of environmental limits. Outside these limits, one, or more, body components begin to malfunction. These malfunctions may have psychological or physiological origins but any malfunction could initiate a sequence of events which would culminate in the same result - death.

Temperature

To keep the human body functioning properly the temperature of the inner body should be kept at 37^0C (98.4^0F). As the effort required for work increases, more energy is released from the energy stores of the body and all excess heat must be removed from the body or its inner temperature will rise causing reduced muscle activity (1), heat stroke, collapse or death (2). The maximum inner body temperature at which the excess heat produced in the body can be liberated to its surroundings is 38^0C (101^0F).

The individual value of this maximum operating temperature depends on the ability of the body tissues to transmit heat but its dissipation is limited either by the humidity of the atmosphere or by the capacity of the body to perspire in dry conditions. Environmental temperature above 66^0C (approx 150^0F) can be tolerated for limited periods, the length of time depending upon the dryness of the air, the amount of protective clothing worn and the exertion required at the time. Above a temperature of 94^0C (approx 200^0F) human tolerance time is reduced greatly and at 120^0C (approx 250^0F) it is only 15 minutes and drops to 5 minutes at 145^0C (approx 250^0F). At 176^0C (approx 350^0F) irreversible injury occurs to the skin in less than one minute. These tolerance times compare unfavourably with temperatures in fires (3), (greater than 1000^0C (1832^0F) at full development) as a local temperature of 260^0C (500^0F) will be generated quickly during the first phase of development when tolerance time will depend on distance from the fire and on not being enveloped in hot gases.

Although higher temperatures can be tolerated for short times, a reasonable upper limit range would be $50-66^0$C ($120-150^0$F). This temperature range has an influence on the design of escape routes and refuges, as all such spaces must be kept at temperatures lower than 50^0C (120^0F) for them to function as safe places. The importance of temperature control on escape routes is reinforced by Fackler who stated (4) that: "when the main objective is the evacuation of occupants the principal danger is from the elevated temperature of the smoke. From different tests it appears that a human organism cannot survive for any length of time in a smoky atmosphere exceeding 60^0C (140^0F)."

Smoke

"Most of the people killed by fire in buildings have first of all failed to find an exit because of smoke, and have later been poisoned by carbon monoxide (gas) or suffocated by lack of oxygen" (5).

Generally, smokes are clouds of particles, each too small to be normally visible but in aggregate scatter light and are opaque to visible light producing similar conditions to those in fog. The particle size varies but an arbitrary definition of smoke is that the particle diameter is less than 1 micron and can be suspended in a gas. Above this dimension the particles become dust.

During combustion most carbonaceous materials and hydrocarbons produce smoke if burned incompletely. It is thought that unreacted carbon molecules agglomerate on leaving the combustion zone, forming long chains of carbon particles - soot (6). The chemical composition of smoke is regarded as less important than its density as it is this property which blocks vision. The presence of irritant gases accentuates this effect which causes a person to lose all sense of direction and the presence of smoke contributes to the obscuration of exits and exit ways. A possibility exists for some of the gases of combustion to condense on the carbon particles, as the gas temperature is reduced, and these particles would cause much discomfort if inhaled or deposited on the eyes.

The majority of smoke particles are too large to be inhaled into the lungs and the nose and mouth are an efficient filtering system. After the capacity of these filters has been exceeded the agglomerated particles are swallowed. The overall result is that the mucus membranes of the eyes, nose, throat and stomach become congested and inflamed, causing nausea and vomiting. Thus, the particulate fraction of combustion products has a serious effect on the gastrointestinal tract which can incapacitate escapees and firefighters. Some particles of smoke are small enough to enter the lungs but until more research is carried out on the smoke problem it is thought that smoke has little effect on the respiratory system. (7)

Table 1.   *Smoke Production by Different Building Boards*

Board	Density g/cm³	Thickness mm	Visibility m
Plasterboard	0.82	9.5	17.0
Wood-fibre insulating board	0.25	12.7	17.0
Phenolformaldehyde faced hardboard	1.30	4.0	5.2
Polyurethane foam sandwich	0.08	13.0	4.8
Birch plywood	0.69	6.4	4.3
Hardboard	0.86	3.7	4.1
Melamine faced hardboard	1.35	3.2	4.0
PVC-faced hardboard	1.03	5.7	3.0
Rigid pvc	1.56	1.6	2.8
Chipboard	0.64	12.7	2.7
Glass fibre reinforced polyester	1.80	3.3	1.5*

* approximate value

Reviews and Developments

Smoke Production

To compare the amount of smoke emitted from different constructional materials a test is being developed where an index of some smoke production is taken as the maximum opacity (density) achieved under test conditions. The following table (8) indicates the relative performance of some common building boards.

In the above table *Density* and *Thickness* are properties of the board and *Visibility* is taken as the comparative measure of smoke production and is related to the ability of the average eye to discern an illuminated exit sign at the distances indicated. As most of the materials give visibilities between 2m. and 5m. this may suggest a limiting distance for the spacing of escape route location signs.

The comparison given is for specimens which are burning with a flame; if materials are allowed to smoulder, under optimum conditions for pyrolysis, smoke production will be greater.

Recently, more experiments have been carried out (9) to establish the possible smoke density which would occur in pedestrian precincts (shopping malls). Four materials commonly found in shops were burned under well-ventilated conditions. Table 2 gives some of the results obtained in the tests.

Table 2.

Comparison of Smoke Production in Terms of Visibility

Material	Optical Density	Mass required to give 4.5m (15 ft) visibility		Equivalent volume of material		Mass of Fuel converted into smoke
		(kg)	(lb)	(cm³)	(ft³)	(per cent)
Wood	0.10	1.2	2.6	2500	0.09	3
Polyurethane Foam	0.13	0.91	2.0	22000	0.80	4
Foam Rubber	0.55	0.22	0.49	1100	0.04	18
Expanded Polystyrene	0.76	0.16	0.35	12000	0.43	25

The small quantities of materials given in columns 3 and 4 were sufficient to reduce visibility to 4.5 metres in a volume of 3m x 6m x 30m, i.e. 540 m³ (20,000 ft³). This emphasises the potential danger to building occupants in or near a fire area as much greater quantities of material would be available to burn soon after ignition in a real situation. The greater quantities of material would produce sufficient smoke to obscure vision totally in a very short time. From the final column it can be seen that two of the common plastics materials are extremely efficient smoke producers. This is due to the high temperatures usually associated with fire which initiate a chemical reaction releasing large amounts of carbon normally fixed in a benzene ring. These latter are a molecular feature of polystyrene and other synthetic polymers. The carbon, is produced much faster than it can be consumed by the fire - resulting in black smoke (10).

Other experiments (11) have shown that flame resistant plastics produce denser smokes than others. In normal situations additional ventilation to the fire space will reduce the opacity of the smoke but some plastics materials produce smoke at a greater rate with additional ventilation.

If the smoke load of a compartment is to be estimated a detailed survey of combustible contents and building surfaces should be made so that their chemical composition can be found and decomposition products predicted. This information combined with relevant test data would enable a fire surveyor to evaluate the possible smoke production potential of any occupied space.

As such small quantities of material are able to produce sufficient smoke to give total obscuration in large volumes, methods of controlling smoke flow are needed to protect the building occupant.

Gaseous Products of Combustion

The products of complete combustion, carbon dioxide and water, are simple compounds which do little harm, unless in massive concentrations. Unfortunately, very few combustion processes are complete and a variety of toxic or noxious compounds are formed. Some of the effects of particulate smoke have already been touched on and here some of the gaseous products of combustion are discussed.

A fire can generate quantities of gas, dangerous to human life, in times that are similar to the period between ignition and discovery (5). If the gases leak outside the compartment a very high ventilation rate is required to dilute them to a tolerable level. This is important in multi-occupancy buildings where any leakage would probably take place into an escape route. Therefore, some system of controlled ventilation has been recommended for multi-occupancy buildings (12) as very few doors can be expected to maintain a gas-tight seal and so confine combustion gases to a limited volume.

The generation of gases precedes that of smoke and in experiments with mice sluggishness of movement and a paralyzed condition are seen soon after ignition and before the density of smoke would obscure light significantly. These experiments indicate that very rapid evacuation from the fire area is necessary and, indirectly, that combustion gas detectors may be more instrumental in saving lives than smoke detectors.

All the common products of combustion are toxic and as further evidence for the need to control them some of their initial, and perhaps superficial, physiological effects are noted below.

Carbon Dioxide: This gas is always present in combustion products. An increase in the carbon dioxide concentration of an atmosphere affects the respiratory process particularly if accompanied by a decrease in oxygen concentration. In addition to the gradual increase in depth and frequency of breathing with increasing concentration of carbon dioxide, hearing, blood pressure and pulse rate are affected, the symptoms being headache, sweating and tremor. (13).

Since high concentrations of carbon dioxide increase the breathing rate, they also increase the rate of intake of other toxic gases that may be present, and therefore, increase the exposure hazard (14).

Oxygen: In fire conditions, especially in closed spaces, the oxygen content of the air will diminish as the fuel is oxidised. Oxygen depletion is not a serious problem as the amount of carbon dioxide produced by combustion will reach toxic levels long before the oxygen content is lowered to a dangerous concentration. In Table 3 it will be seen that the oxygen

165

content needs to fall below 15 per cent. before deleterious effects occur. These values could be important in the design of refuge ventilation systems.

Table 3   *Effects of Oxygen Concentration**

Oxygen content of inhaled air, per cent	Effects
21	Normal air
17	Safe limit for prolonged exposure
15	No immediate effects except sense of fatigue
10	Dizziness, shortness of breath; deeper and more rapid respiration; quickened pulse, especially on exertion.
7	Stupor sets in; memory and judgement are affected.
5	Minimal concentration compatible with life.
2-3	Death within a few minutes.

* Assuming normal people at normal atmospheric pressure

Carbon Monoxide: Carbon monoxide is present in all combustion products and is due to the process of combustion being incomplete as the gas can be *burnt* with excess oxygen to form carbon dioxide. However, in normal fires insufficient heat is produced to maintain the high temperatures required for the reaction and too little oxygen is available.

Carbon monoxide is toxic in very small concentrations but it appears that people accustomed to inhaling the gas e.g. tobacco smokers, have a greater resistance to its ill-effects. Carbon monoxide poisoning by exposure to small concentrations over a long period can often be more harmful than a brief exposure to a very high concentration. Heavy labour, especially at high ambient temperatures (i.e. people actively escaping from fire) will increase the effects of poisoning.

Carbon monoxide poisoning is characterised by the formation of carboxyhaemoglobin (CO-Hb) and carboxymyoglobin (CO-Mb) which replace the normal oxyhaemoglobin and oxymyoglobin of the blood's haemoproteins. Haemoglobin has 200 to 300 times the affinity for carbon monoxide as it has for oxygen, but the return to normal haemoglobin after moderate poisoning can be readily achieved by inhaling normal air (13). However, on prolonged exposure to low concentrations of carbon monoxide the oxygen level in the blood is reduced and the oxygen may dissociate less readily at the tissues than under normal conditions so that inadequate quantities of oxygen are being delivered to where it is needed throughout the body (3).

Table 4 (13) gives an indication of the effects on normal people at normal atmospheric pressure of different carbon monoxide concentrations.

The values given in Table 4 are in reasonable agreement with those given by Kishitani (15) for human beings. Kishitani also presents some information which compares the carboxyhaemoglobin (CO-Hb) content of blood for victims of carbon monoxide poisoning and victims of fires. In the poisoning cases (mainly due to the inhalation of town gas) 50 per cent. of the fatalities had a 90 per cent. CO-Hb level in the blood. The same CO-Hb concentration only accounted for 20 per cent. of the fire victims, the remainder having much lower concentrations. Table 5 (15) summarises the comparative results which indicate that many of the deaths in fires were not caused by carbon monoxide poisoning only.

Table 4   **Effects of Different Carbon Monoxide Concentrations***

Carbon Monoxide Content of Inhaled Air	Corresponding Carboxyhaemoglobin in blood			Effect
per cent	ppm	non-smoker per cent	smoker per cent	
0.0002	2	1	2-10	Normal conditions
0.0025	25	2-4	4-14	Slight impairment of vision
0.005(TLV)	50	8-10	10-20	Safe limit for prolonged exposure
0.01	100	15-20	15-27	No effects for 3 hours exposure but perceptible effects after 6 hours. Headache and nausea after 9 hours. Continuous exposure poisonous but not lethal
0.02	200	25-30	25-35	Possible mild frontal headache after 3 hours. Continuous exposure probably results in permanent blindness if not death.
0.04	400	40-45		Deep breathing; dimness of vision. Frontal headache after 1-2 hours; rear of headache after 2½ - 3½ hours. Probable coma after 5 hours. Continuous exposure means certain death.
0.08	800	60-65		Headache, dizziness and nausea in ¾ hour; collapse and possible unconciousness in 2 hours. Possible death in about 4 hours.
0.64	6400			Headache in 1 or 2 minutes. Danger of death in 10-15 minutes.
1.28	12800			Immediate effect; danger of death in 1-3 minutes.

* Assuming normal people at normal atmospheric pressure.

The production of smoke, carbon dioxide, carbon monoxide and oxygen depletion are major reactions which occur in all fires. Other gases, such as hydrogen cyanide, hydrogen sulphide, hydrochloric acid gas, are produced only by specific materials but their effects are not less fatal than the common combustion products. Therefore some of the effects of these gases will be considered but somewhat more briefly than the major products of combustion.

Table 5

Level of Carboxyhaemoglobin in Fatalities Due To Poisoning and Burning

CO-Hb (per cent)	Fatalities	
	Poisoning* (per cent)	Burning** (per cent)
10	-	6.2
20	1.3	9.0
30	-	7.2
40	3.0	10.2
50	4.7	13.2
60	11.2	18.0
70	22.3	13.2
80	49.4	20.4
90+	8.1	1.8

*   Total number of fatalities was 233.
**   Total number of fatalities was 167.

Ammonia: Ammonia is formed during the burning of combustible material containing nitrogen (14). As it is a common refrigerant its accidental release during a fire should be regarded as a potential toxic hazard. Little is known of the human reaction to ammonia, and other irritant gases, but they do cause excessive flow from the tear ducts which, in turn, causes a blurring of vision. The respiratory tract is affected also causing coughing and choking. For these reasons persons normally will not remain in an ammonia containing atmosphere long enough to suffer serious effects but the presence of irritant gases may increase an escapee's liability to panic, or irrational behaviour, in the fire situation.

Exposure to atmospheres containing 0.25 to 0.65 per cent ammonia for half an hour is sufficient to cause death or serious injury.

Hydrogen Cyanide: This gas is highly toxic but it is not likely to be produced in dangerous quantities in most fires. Hydrogen cyanide is produced by the action of water and acids on cyanides and may be a product of the incomplete combustion of wool, silk and plastics compounded from nitrogen containing chemicals. Concentrations of the gas as low as 0.01 per cent may be·lethal and a concentration of 0.3 per cent is rapidly fatal.

Hydrogen Sulphide: The incomplete combustion of organic sulphur containing materials, such as wool, meat and hair, yields this gas. Its distinctive *rotten egg* smell is not reliable as an indication of exposure as at concentrations of about 0.02 per cent the sense of smell is fatigued rapidly. On increasing concentration the gas becomes more lethal and at more than 0.07 per cent the gas is acutely poisonous affecting the nervous system then causing a rapid rate of respiration followed by respiratory paralysis.

Sulphur Dioxide: The complete oxidation of sulphur containing organic materials produce sulphur dioxide which is an irritant gas affecting the eyes and respiratory tract. Concentrations about 0.05 per cent. should be considered dangerous, even for short exposures. In addition it is important to note that the gas is colourless and 2.25 times heavier than air. This means that the gas could sink into the *clear air* space that is found near floor level, in partially smoke-filled spaces, through which escapees can crawl to safety.

Mixtures of hydrogen sulphide and sulphur dioxide are evolved by burning rubber and small quantities in inhaled air (0.05 per cent) can be lethal.

Nitrogen dioxide: Nitrogen dioxide (peroxide) is an extremely toxic gas which is formed during the decomposition and combustion of cellulose nitrate and in fires which involve ammonium nitrate and other inorganic nitrates. Fortunately the gas can be identified by its reddish-brown colour. The initial action of the gas on the human body is to anaesthetise the throat, so that its presence may not be recognised, and it should be noted that a concentration of only 0.0025 per cent may be injurious although the reaction will be delayed or may be acceptable for a few minutes. Concentrations between 0.02 and 0.07 per cent could prove rapidly fatal (14).

Hydrochloric Acid Gas: This gas is produced by polyvinyl chloride (pvc) plastics and the quantity of production varies with the amount of ventilation found in the fire space. If ventilation is restricted the evolution of hydrochloric acid gas may be delayed up to thirty minutes when compared to the time of carbon monoxide evolution from cellulosic materials. However, if the ventilation is unrestricted the evolution of hydrogen chloride will take place almost as quickly, and in similar quantities, to the production of carbon monoxide. This reaction will take place between 300 and 500° C. Other combustion products including phosgene and ammonia gas, are present but in quantities too small to have a significant effect on the overall toxicity of the gases contributed by the burning pvc.

A problem in the assessment of products of combustion, from any material, is the accurate prediction of its toxicity. Research has been carried out using animals (15, 16, 17) on some of the gases which exist in combustion products. Unfortunately it has not been possible to isolate all the gases present in smokes and then subject animals to all the gases singly and in combination. It has been shown, however, that the combination of two or three gases produce toxic effects that are at least additive (16) and some of the more lethal gases may well produce synergistic effects. The Fire Research Station is at present supervising some work on the toxic effects of plastics smokes where many of the gaseous components have been identified (18, 19, 20).

In the preceding notes some of the sources and the physiological reactions for gaseous products of combustion have been discussed. Many other gases could be present as dictated by the nature of the combustible materials and the type of burning. The combustion products of many traditional materials have been measured and evaluated but in recent years the use of synthetic plastics has been increasing both for constructional and furnishing materials. Therefore it is important that the basic molecular units for all new plastics should be understood so that their decomposition products can be evaluated for toxicity.

Investigations into the thermal decomposition products of polypropylene (21) and polyisobutylene (22) have shown that a large number of gaseous compounds are formed at low temperatures (300-400° C). Each of the products, even at very low concentrations, could be sufficiently toxic to cause serious damage to people even if the gaseous fraction had liquified because of distance from the heat source. However, as the authors point out (23) there is a lack of data on the concentrations of gases required for death to occur. They suggest also a toxicity index (23) for combustion products which includes a factor for the expected rate of burning as this is proportional to the rate of gas production.

ESCAPE ROUTE DESIGN

Basic precepts

In all buildings and building complexes it is necessary to provide a safe means of escape for the occupants in the event of fire. The success of any escape route design can be assessed using two basic precepts (24(a)):-

1.   Any given part of a premises should be capable of being evacuated within a shorter time than that which smoke and/or fire will take to spread into that part of the premises and constitute a danger to the occupants.

2.   All persons should be able to turn their backs on any smoke or fire that may be present in any compartment, or section, of a building and reach a place of safety by their own unaided efforts without being adversely affected by the fire or its combustion products.

The first precept suggests that the two major factors which are important to define are the possible speed of travel of the building occupants and the time available before smoke, gases and/or heat reach lethal concentrations.

The second precept indicates that the layout of escape routes within the spatial geometry of a building must be designed so that alternative routes to safety are available to the escapee. It is not always possible for the building occupant to effect escape unaided and the amount of assistance that a person will require depends on the mobility of the individual. This available degree of mobility requires careful assessment at the design stage of a building. A general relationship between the possible degree of mobility of building occupants and the size of building has suggested four approaches to design for life safety (25).

These have been given the following definitions:

1.   Escape. Occupants able to leave the building immediately.

2.   Slow Escape. Occupants leave the building more slowly and need intermediate places of refuge, from which escape is slow and orderly.

3.   Refuge. Occupants move to a protected area within the structure; here they may 'ride out' the fire or be evacuated over a period of time.

4.   Minimal Disruption. The place of safety, for the great majority of occupants, is at their normal locations. The fire is confined to the area of origin and those from this area find safety in other parts of the building.

However, a recent study (26(a)) has shown that people like to be active, both mentally and physically, during an emergency so that the inactivity implicit in providing refuges, or other fixed places of safety, within buildings may have a deleterious effect on the building occupants. But as time is the most important factor it may not be physically possible for even normal adults to escape from a tall building, say 40 stories high, to a place of safety in the open air before smoke and gases from the fire have spread into part of the escape route. (27)

In some situations it is possible for smoke to travel faster than escapees. Experiments (28) have shown that in 2½ minutes smoke from a small shop fire can spread along an adjacent mall for 70 m (230 ft) in both directions along the major axis of the mall. If the fire reaches flashover conditions the combustion products may travel 200 m (660 ft) in 2½ minutes. These distances are important as personal movement is calculated as 35 m (115 ft) in 2½ minutes.

This rate of travel is taken from current building regulations (29) but it is stated (30) that a rate of 12.5m / minute is acceptable for escape route capacity calculations, albeit an extremely slow shuffle which would obtain with a close column of people moving along a level corridor. There are many situations where such estimates are inappropriate. For some occupancy types an overall evacuation time is recommended. For example, 20 minutes is suggested for old persons homes (31). Although this is a reasonable overall time it requires very careful application as a polyurethane foam mattress will produce lethal products of combustion in less than 2 minutes after ignition.

It is apparent that no one technique can ensure the safety of people in all types of building and all possible techniques must be considered at the design stage of a building.

Once the line(s) of escape have been defined exit widths have to be calculated. This requires an estimate of the numbers of people than can be expected in each section of a building. In those occupancy types where numbers cannot be predicted with accuracy guidance is given in the form of occupancy load factors. Table 6 (32) gives some typical examples.

Table 6   *Occupancy load factors**

| Occupancy | Area per person | | | | | |
| | Canada | | USA | | Scotland | |
	m²	(ft²)	m²	(ft²)	m²	(ft²)
Assembly (no fixed seating)	0.75	(8)	0.65	(7)	0.46	(5)
Assembly (standing space)	0.37	(4)	0.28	(3)	0.46	(5)
Offices	9.29	(100)	9.29	(100)	5.10	(55)
Dormitories	4.64	(50)	11.15	(120)	4.64	(50)
Shops A†	2.79	(30)	2.79	(30)	1.39	(15)
Shops B†	5.57	(60)	5.57	(60)	1.86	(20)
Kitchens	9.29	(100)	-		9.29	(100)
Warehouses	27.87	(300)	9.29	(100)	27.87	(300)

* This table gives the allowable area per person, the number of people being simply calculated by dividing the building area by the occupancy load factor.

† Shops A refer to the ground floor and basement sales area in Canada and USA, but only basement areas in Scotland. Shops B refer to all floors excepting ground floor and basements in Canada and USA but includes the ground floor in Scotland.

Design of Openings

The next problem is to calculate the width of opening required for safe discharge of the occupants into a protected part of the route from their normal space of occupancy. Doors which are adequate for normal usage may be inadequate for emergency use. Pleschl (33) has shown that safe discharge cannot be achieved with openings less than 1.2 m (3.9 ft) wide.

This is because stable arches of people are formed across the opening creating a blockage. Any stoppage, or significant slowing of movement, is likely to create a panic situation as people continue to press towards the opening. During some experiments the people forming the arch were frequently held against the sides of the opening by an arm or leg and in all cases the people passing through the doorway stumbled or fell. Such actions could be very serious in a real situation. If the density of people is sufficiently large no continuous flow is possible due to the formation of dynamic arches across openings, the result being a pulsating flow.

When designing openings through which large numbers of people need to pass consideration should be given to the shape of the walls. Pleschl found that smoother flows, and a lesser frequency of arch formation, were created when the walls adjacent to the opening were curved. Figure 1 indicates the plan shapes of the openings. Although these studies are directly applicable to a corridor opening situation similar factors are involved when considering the discharge of people from a space into a corridor.

Similar conclusions are drawn by Hankin and Wright (34) in that the type of flow of people in corridors is influenced by the width of the corridor. At dimensions less than 1.2 m (4 ft) for the width of the corridor multiples of shoulder width dimensions are important for estimating the capacity of the corridor. At dimensions greater than 1.2 m the flow of people becomes directly proportional to corridor dimensions. This finding is incorporated in to existing building regulations.

Figure 1   **Plan shape of opening**

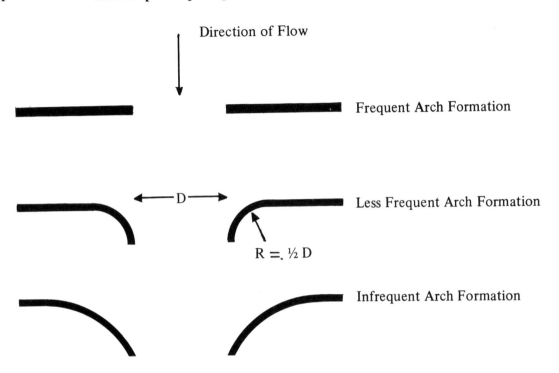

Rate of Movement on Escape Routes

The rate of movement of people along a corridor, assuming no restrictions, is dependent on the density of the crowd. A number of investigations (34, 35, 36) have measured this phenomenon and some information on traffic flow (37) indicates a similar effect, that is the greater the number of vehicles, or persons, using a length of road, or corridor, the slower their progress.

The speed of normal individuals along a level path is given as 1.7 m/sec (34) and 1.3 m/sec (36). When moving up or down stairs these values are modified to 0.8 m/sec and 0.65 m/sec respectively, the actual speed being modified further by angle of stairs - the steeper the stair the slower the speed. As the density of people using a route increases the rate of travel decreases (30, 34).

For a crowd situation, as found in cinemas, other places of entertainment, some factories and office blocks, the rate of movement has been measured at 0.1 m/sec on level footways and a faster speed of 0.5 m/sec (95 ft/min) on staircases. Some recent measurements of people in office blocks during fire drills gave sppeds of up to 0.8 m/sec (160 ft/min) on staircases. Although these speeds are much faster than the values given in various building regulations and design guides they suggest that the approach to life safety design proposed by Caravaty and Winslow (25) should be adopted.

So far the description of people movement has omitted two important aspects of escape route design. The first is the assumption that all escape routes are kept clear of obstructions and the second is that no smoke or gases are present in the escape route.

The primary obstructions to people flow are bends and corners. Whilst these are inevitable they may not be an important factor if the numbers of people on any escape route are dictated by the discharge capacity of exit doors as the restriction at a door opening will be greater than any restriction caused by a bend providing that no section of the route is narrower than the preceeding section. An increase in width for the same flow of people will enable a faster speed of movement as there will be less crowding.

A problem, not covered by specific regulations, is that of merging and crossing flows as it is assumed that all the occupants begin their escape at the same time. This is not always possible and it is discouraged by some current recommendations for 2-stage escape (24(b)). The two stages are: alert, or stand-by, followed by evacuation and is intended for people in large buildings who, initially, are not in direct danger from the fire. However, the situation can be envisaged when people on, say, the fifth floor of a building, escaping directly from a fire on that floor, may meet the people exiting from the first floor who may have been held back on *stand-by* until the order for complete evacuation was given. Escape route design must provide for such possibilities by making the common escape route proportionately wider so that the extra people can move parallel to the main flow. Any attempts at merging with or crossing the main flow will result in excessive time delays for the minor flow and a high probability of personal injury would exist.

Too often escape routes can be observed where physical obstructions have been placed. These may be tables and chairs, office machines, stored goods or even rubbish awaiting collection. Although no data is available on the reduced capacity of such routes some guidance may be given by road traffic data measured in one-way streets (37). Here the percentage reduction in capacity is 60 per cent. for roads 7.3 m (24 ft) wide and 33 per cent. for roads 14.6 m (48 ft) wide.

A 100 per cent. flow is taken as the value in roads where no waiting and no parking is allowed and no cross traffic exists. The reduced capacity is for all purpose streets, of the same widths, which allow parking, access to adjacent buildings and contain junctions. If such flow reductions are applicable to buildings the careful management of escape routes as *clear-ways* is essential.

The most important aspect of escape route design is the presence or absence of combustion products. The study by Wood (26) has shown that people are willing to travel through a smoky atmosphere but this willingness and the distance travelled vary in different situations. The probability of a person willing to move through smoke is greatest if that person is male, thinks the fire to be serious, is familiar with the building and the fire occurs at night time. It is shown also that the proportion of people willing to move through smoke was greater in the *home* environment than in the *work* environment. The distance that people are prepared to move through smoky atmospheres depends upon a number of factors, but those who knew than an emergency escape route existed, i.e. were familiar with the building, were prepared to move more than 14 m (45 ft) through smoke even if this distance was further than their range of visibility.

From the above discussion of escape route problems it is clear that more study on the possible behaviour of people in building fires is required with particular emphasis on the times that are required for people to react to and to take positive action in a fire situation. Such information would enable realistic data to be fed into escape route design techniques. Although the problems associated with people moving through smoke require solution, it is equally important to keep escape routes clear of combustion products for as long a time as possible after ignition of the fire so that escapees do not need to suffer the consequences of exposure to the potential smoke and toxic gas hazard present in most buildings.

SMOKE FLOW AND SMOKE CONTROL IN BUILDINGS

Most buildings consist of well defined spaces and for human safety three types of space are important to consider. Firstly, the single room. As any room may be the room of origin of fire, early detection and control of combustion products is necessary for the complete protection of the building and its occupants although escape may not be a problem through or from a single space.

Secondly, the long horizontal space. Although the rate of smoke travel is dependent on its rate of production, and may other factors, smoke flow along corridors and pedestrian malls presents a danger to escapees. In an ideal situation no smoke should be allowed to enter this type of space especially those designated as escape routes.

Thirdly, the long vertical space. This type includes lift shafts and staircases the latter being an important part of an escape route in buildings which are three or more floors in height.

The Single Room

In an infinite atmosphere which is originally at rest and isothermal a small heat source will generate a stream of hot gases. The nature of the flow will at first be laminar and have a constant cross-section but due to acceleration, caused by the heat source producing a gas less dense than the surrounding air, it will become turbulent at a height above the heat source. This height is dependent on the rate of heat production.

In ordinary (real) building fires the flow of gases from the fire is likely to be totally turbulent from a time soon after ignition so that entertainment of cold air is a continuous process. Although the quantity of entrained air is usually many times the original mass of gases emitted by the burning fuel the resultant mixture is still toxic and its flow needs to be controlled. The rising smoke and gas mixture will form a layer beneath the ceiling of the space and because it becomes a relatively stable layer it mixes with the cooler air beneath very slowly, if at all (38). As the fire continues the depth of hot smoky gases will increase until the space is completely filled with smoke (smoke logged). This situation is possible in normal buildings because of the air leakage which is accepted in present day construction and this leakage would be sufficient to provide a supply of oxygen to the *small* fire. As the pressure inside the compartment rises, due to the increase in temperature, hot gases and smoke will be pushed out of the space through the same air leakage cracks in the construction. At this stage sufficient fresh air could still reach the fire because of the vertical pressure differentials created in the compartment of origin; i.e.: smoke being pushed out of the space above a neutral pressure plane and fresh air being drawn in below that plane.

The Single Storey Building

Removing smoke from a space is a simple matter in a single-storey building (38, 39, 40) or in the topmost floors of multi-storey buildings. In these cases automatically operating vents can be installed in the roof which, in the event of fire, will open and provide an exit for the rising hot gases and smoke. Although such vents are prone to adverse wind conditions, and other problems of design and selection, their use in single-storey buildings is accepted as being advantageous for normal commercial and industrial premises. The satisfactory operation of vents is dependent on an adequate supply of fresh air into the fire space and this supply rate should be equal to or greater than, the mass flow rate of gases that can be emitted through the open vent area.

It is possible for the whole stream of hot gases, from a small fire, to flow directly through the vent if its area is greater than the diameter of the stream. For the evacuation of smoke it has been estimated (38) that about 90 per cent of the hot gases will pass straight through a vent having a diameter equal to one-third of the height of the building irrespective of the rate of heat generation. The effectiveness of this suggestion is limited because a small fire in a 6.0 m (20 ft) high space would require a vent directly over the fire greater than about 2m x 2m (7 ft x 7 ft) in area. Fires covering a larger floor area, even though burning slowly, would require very large vents for a 90 per cent smoke evacuation. The effectiveness of vents can be increased by the construction of screens which reduce the lateral spread of smoke by forming reservoirs.

Figure 2   **The principle of fire venting**

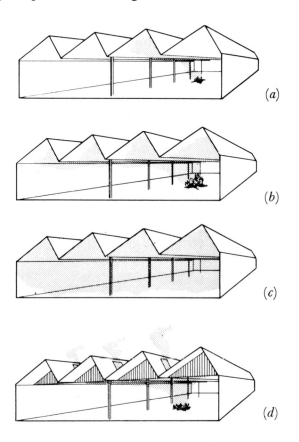

(a)

(b)

(c)

(d)

(a) Fire in unvented individed building. *(b)* Unrestricted smoke spread. *(c)* Ultimate smoke-logging. *(d)* Restriction of smoke spread by screens and vents.

The Partially Enclosed Space

An example of the partially enclosed space would be a hotel bedroom. Here, a common case is the room being bounded on four sides by solid construction, the fifth having a door opening onto a corridor and the sixth being an external wall containing a window. A small fire in such a space will depend for combustion air on the air leakage characteristics of the building's construction. (Assuming no air conditioning or mechanical ventilating systems).

The pressures developed in the room, due to temperature rise, will tend to push combustion products through the external wall and the door cracks. (Assuming that the other four surfaces are air tight). The smoke passing through the external wall (the cracks around windows etc.) will aid the identification of source but the external leakage may not be sufficient for complete pressure relief. The combustion products will also be pushed into the corridor through the door gaps, and any other spaces. This latter state is a danger as the corridor will be part of an escape route. Each volume of smoke reaching the escape route needs to be diluted by 100 volumes of clear air to keep the escape route tenable, and this, coupled with the fact that the volume of smoke produced is directly proportional to the absolute temperature in the fire compartment, makes effective smoke dilution by natural air movement very difficult to achieve. To control the flow of smoke so that none percolates into the corridor two methods are possible.

Firstly, to install emergency air extraction units in the external wall of the partially enclosed space. In the event of an emergency these units would produce a negative air pressure in the space. The power of the extract unit should be sufficient to extract all products of combustion during the period required for safe escape of all occupants, i.e. three to ten minutes. This would reduce the possibility of smoke percolating into the corridor and if the pressure reduction is sufficient, clean air would be drawn into the fire space from the escape route especially when the room/corridor door was opened for a few seconds to allow passage of escapees.

Secondly, air pressure could be increased in the corridor so that air would flow from the corridor into the fire compartment and then exhausted under pressure to the outside. Depending upon the pressure differences such a system would always contain smoke within the fire compartment and thus keep escape routes clear of smoke and gases. The two main types of horizontal space which people use are the conventional corridor in buildings, which may be part of an escape route, and the development of the corridor into the enclosed shopping street, the arcade or mall.

The Corridor

Until recently corridors in multi-occupancy, multi-storey buildings, such as blocks of flats, have been required to be built with areas of permanent ventilation so that any smoke reaching the corridor would be dispersed by the air movement always present in the common space. This provision of ventilation has led to many complaints from occupiers because of the corridor space always being cold and draughty. In addition experiments have shown (41) that natural ventilation cannot be relied upon to clear smoke from corridor sections of escape routes. It is possible for any overpressure, caused by wind, in the corridor or lobby to create a pressure differential across a door sufficient to aid the expulsion of smoke through the external wall of the fire compartment i.e: air flow would be from the ventilated corridor, through the occupied space and thence through the external wall. Unfortunately wind conditions at the time of fire cannot be predicted or be relied upon to control smoke in this way.

In general, if smoke is percolating from a fire compartment into a corridor it will flow in the same direction as the bulk flow of air in the corridor but some can flow *upstream*, i.e. against the bulk flow. This latter component of smoke usually travels as a layer flowing above and against the main air stream and only disappears when the velocity of the air stream exceeds a certain critical value. This critical value is proportional to the cube root of the heat release rate from the fire (42) and is especially applicable to the smoke movement from fires which occur in the corridor , or mall.

However, it is possible to make an estimate of the mass air flow rate required in a corridor to prevent back flow of smoke. For a room of area 4m x 4m containing combustible furniture and carpet (i.e. about 30 sq. m. of combustible surface) an air flow rate of 3-4 m/s is required to carry all the smoke, from a fully open door, in the direction of the air flow. If the air flow rate is only 1 m/s backflow will commence when the fire is only 0.75 sq. m (42). If the corridor is pressurised there may be no leakage of smoke from the fire compartment. This is because a mechanism of pressurisation is to create high velocities in the small gaps around the door and so prevent backflow of smoke through them.

Natural Systems of Smoke Control

Open corridor access to stairs and elevators (43, 44): Each corridor which provides access to stairs or elevators is permanently open to the outside and the building may be regarded as a number of superimposed storeys without linking shafts. The pressure difference will be high across the floors due to the absence of interconnected vertical shafts, but this will only affect the floor above the fire but holes in floors should be kept to a minimum. Service shafts, where necessary, would need to be fire and smoke sealed at every fifth floor, and two staircases, remote from one another, are an essential part of the method. This method of control is not likely to be popular for buildings higher than ten storeys or in places which suffer very cold winters and high winds.

Automatic airflow control (A.A.C.): A simple system of smoke control in escape routes has been developed by Wilkinson (45, 46) and has been proved effective, by experiment and actual fires, in blocks of flats up to nine storeys high. In principle, the A.A.C. system uses below-centre horizontally pivoted, outward opening windows as a major part of the required ventilation (a small area of permanent ventilation being retained to provide air changes). The windows are normally closed but smoke entering the corridor is sensed by smoke detectors which actuate the window mechanism. The window is spring loaded so that any positive wind pressure can be overcome and when open allows fresh air to enter at low level displacing the smoky air which flows out of the upper opening. The system appears to function independently of wind direction but some reliance is placed on the effectiveness of self-closing-fire-resistant doors which are installed in each opening to the common lobby.

Each floor of the building is able to operate independently and no problems of unexpected smoke flow have been experienced due to stack effect or other motive forces of air movement. The buildings where the system has been used have a large number of separate compartments so that the possible size of fire is limited and it is possible that the system could be used in other building types which have similar spatial requirements.

Mechanical Systems of Smoke Control

Smoke-free corridor: In many buildings which contain large numbers of people, especially where sleeping accommodation is provided, corridors are necessary for communication and they usually form the first stage of any escape route through the building. Therefore it is essential that such areas be kept free of smoke in the initial stages of fire development. The use of differential air pressures is considered to be of great value in buildings. Here the principle is that air pressures should be created above or below atmospheric pressure (positive or negative pressures) so that the pressure differential will contain smoke in the compartment of origin and/or exhaust the smoke to the atmosphere.

A simple system of individual intake fans for pressurising 60 metre (200 feet) lengths of corridor has been suggested by Leworthy (47). Here the fans would not normally operate but be connected to a smoke sensitive device for emergency operation. The fan would be installed to draw fresh air into a corridor thereby maintaining a supply of clean air and creating a positive pressure in the corridor. The power and capacity of the fan would be selected after evaluation of appropriate air leakage factors so that an adequate pressure difference can be developed between the corridor and the compartment on fire. To assist in the flow of smoke away from the escape route some smoke sensitive device should operate an automatic vent on the external surface of the affected compartment. Perhaps part of the window. Such a device would delay pressure increase due to the fire, thereby making any corridor pressurisation more effective.

The Mall

The enclosed shopping mall is a logical development in the provision of personal comfort conditions for shoppers as it protects them from the rigours of the weather. The shopping mall usually consists of a covered central area flanked by shops. The shops are commonly two storeys high and the upper entrances, for shoppers, are connected to the lower mall level by stairs, escalators or elevators, access being provided by wide balconies or a complete, but perforated, floor over the area of the mall. Although the common public space is normally rectangular it is difficult to predict the probable movement of smoke and hot gases in such spaces should any shop unit catch fire and studies have been made in this field only recently (48, 49, 50, 51, 52).

The problems of smoke movement in shopping malls are different to those in other building spaces. This is chiefly because of the large numbers of people (2-5000) who could be in the area of the mall at any one time. The appearance of smoke could initiate a very rapid panic reaction and the smoke would have unlimited access to people in the mall. Therefore, control over the direction of smoke movement must be sought. The provision of automatic smoke vents has been suggested so that removal of smoke from any affected area would be possible. This would be of doubtful value as the cool smoke at roof level would have little buoyancy and any adverse external air pressure regime would mix the smoke with the clear air at lower levels. However, certain combinations of venting systems may give adequate control over smoke flow.

Control of Smoke Flow in Shopping Malls (52)

There are two principal approaches to smoke control. The first is to take advantage of the natural buoyancy of the hot gases generated by the fire and the second is to impose flow paths on the air in the total shopping area by mechanical means. In both cases the object of the techniques is to keep smoke away from the mass of people in the mall. This means that no smoke should be lower than 3 metres from lower floor level and ideally no smoke should enter the mall from any adjacent shop fire.

Confinement of smoke to shop of origin: The preferred method of smoke control is to prevent smoke escaping from the shop of origin. The most obvious method is to fit a shop front (of a type which will remain in position during the fire) which is pierced only be self-closing fire doors. Unfortunately there is generally some leakage around fire doors and through joints in shop fronts and frequently ventilation openings are unavoidable. Smoke will then penetrate to the mall through these openings and this may be sufficient to cause smoke logging. To prevent smoke penetrating to the mall it is recommended that a pressure difference of from 2.5 - 5mm water gauge (opposing the pressure difference due to the hot gases) be maintained across the shop front; this allows for pressures of both the winds and the fire. The pressure difference may be developed by exhausting air from the shop or possibly by supplying air to the mall. The former method requires a much smaller air supply but the fans and ducting need to be able to withstand the hot gases. The latter method might be considered for closed malls, although the possible loss of pressure due to people escaping through doors leading from the malls and thus keeping them open must be taken into account. Vents would have to be provided at the rear of shops and in the event of fire it would probably be advantageous if all the vents except those in the shop on fire were closed, thus reducing the loss of pressurising air.

Whichever method is adopted it is essential that the doors and any ventilation openings to the mall of the shop on fire be closed (except to allow the passage of people escaping): preferably by automatic door closers and fire dampers. Failure of the shop front would of course lead to the rapid spread of smoke in the mall and thus the shop front should be fire resisting or have fire resisting back-up walls unless sprinklers are fitted, when the possibility of large fires is reduced.

Methods to maintain a layer of clear air near the floor: As stated earlier the formation of a layer of hot smoky gases beneath a ceiling can only be avoided if a very large vent can be placed directly above the fire. Because of the improbable nature of such a relationship the presence of a layer of hot gases is generally inevitable but this need not be an obstacle to escape providing that the layer of clear air beneath can be maintained at a sufficient height for people to move about *normally.*

Although the amount of mixing between the layers of smoke and clear air is small the greater the extent of the smoke layer the cooler its outer parts become and the greater the tendency for mixing. Thus the greater the spread of the layer of hot gases the more smoky will the air beneath become. It is therefore necessary to restrict the spread of the layer of hot gases by dividing the space beneath the ceiling into smoke reservoirs by screens extending down from the ceiling. Once smoke is collected in a reservoir it needs to be extracted from the building at a rate equal to the maximum rate at which the hot gases are likely to flow into it. This quantity is dictated by the quantity of smoke and gas generated by a fire and a flow rate can be calculated given a constant fire size. If a sprinkler system is installed in the building (all shops and in the mall) it is reasonable that a fire would be kept in check and the size of fire calculated from the spacing of sprinklers and expected fuel load and smoke load in the shops.

Screens designed to create smoke reservoirs could be part of the shop front and here the fascia will trap smoke in the shop. The smoke could be extracted through the ceiling or it could be allowed to spill into the mall and be extracted from the roof of the mall. The depth of the screens is tentatively suggested to be one-third of the height of the space and to be effective the height of the space should be at least 4 metres.

There is no reason why perforated, but fire-resisting, suspended ceilings should not be installed below the smoke reservoir screens although it would be unwise to have no screen projection below the suspended ceiling (52).

The extraction of smoke by natural ventilation has the advantages of simplicity, a limited number of mechanical devices and low cost. But problems such as adverse pressures caused by wind and inefficiency when the gases of combustion are at a low temperature still exist. Powered extract systems are, in theory, better because it should be possible to ensure the required flow whatever the temperature and pressure regimes. However, the volumes of air to be moved (approximately equivalent to 14 air changes per hour) would require a great amount of air handling plant in a shopping complex. If an air handling system was controlled centally for a complete shopping area it would be possible to design a sophisticated air flow control system so that the smoke is completely under control as soon as it is detected.

The Long Vertical Space

The prime mover of air in a tall building is the stack effect created by the temperature differences between outside and inside a building (53, 54, 55, 56, 57). This has the effect of allowing dense cold air, in winter, to flow into a building at the bottom and to displace warmer, less dense air. The pressures exerted by the gas (air) in the building give rise to air movement upwards through the building the greatest mass following the path which offers least resistance. The paths are usually the vertical transport elements of a building, i.e. stair and elevator shafts.

No building is completely sealed against air penetration so simple movement of gases is modified by building leakage, which is a measure of the amount of void contained in each division or barrier. Although the flow through the floors is small in comparison to the walls smoke will be able to flow to compartments above and below the fire floor because of the pressure differences created by the rise in temperature and the stack pressures. The flow pattern for any building can be modified by wind forces movement as it will change the pressure patterns on the outside of the building and cause air to flow horizontally throughout the building from windward to leeward.

Internally, the air flow pattern is modified also by air handling systems. In the event of a fire they can recirculate smoke throughout a building by the return and supply air systems. For this reason some standards require a shut-down of all major air handling systems as soon as excessive smoke or

181

heat is detected in the return air system. With the system off, vertical air ducts may still act as additional paths for smoke migration to upper floors (44).

When a fire occurs in a vertical shaft the air movement pattern is modified so that air flows into the shaft at low levels, and smoke will flow into the upper floors. The fire will induce downward flow in any other shafts in the building. Fire in a shaft can cause recirculation of smoke throughout a building (44) and a similar flow pattern can be expected if a floor area adjacent to a vertical shaft is involved in the fire. Therefore, air and smoke movement in a tall building can be extremely complex and a number of research workers have developed computer programs to predict probable smoke flow patterns in tall buildings(58, 59, 60).

Smoke Control in Tall Buildings

In this section an attempt is made to describe the principal features of some of the several current methods of smoke control for tall buildings. Those in the first part take advantage of the natural forces of air movement whilst those in the second part rely on mechanical equipment to guide air along predetermined paths.

Stairways

A common feature of all tall buildings is the stairway which is, basically, a continuous vertical shaft from the bottom to the top of the building, i.e. a large chimney. To use the stairway as an effective device for smoke control full advantage must be taken of the stack effect potential of the shaft. This means that adequate ventilation openings must be available at the bottom and the top of the shaft and it must be heated to a reasonable temperature, especially in winter, so that the pressure differentials across doors from a corridor and stair shaft are not excessive (43) for normal use. A brief summary of current British Legislation (61) suggests that the greatest value of a staircase is for smoke clearance by the fire-fighters after the occupants of the building have made their escape.

If ventilated smoke lobbies are placed between a corridor and the stair shaft, this would keep the staircase free of smoke in favourable weather conditions. Such an arrangement is given a variety of names: lobby approach staircase (61), protected vestibule access (43) and smokeproof tower (62), but in each case the vestibule must be provided with self-closing-fire-resisting doors. A similar arrangement for lifts would help to prevent smoke transport through the building but the lift shaft should also be ventilated at the bottom and the top. The protected vestibule access staircase could be a separate tower adjacent to the building but separated by a bridge at each floor level.

In many buildings escape to a safe place will entail the use of a staircase and in most cases these can be considered separately for smoke control purposes because of the requirements for smoke stop doors to be placed between corridors and staircases. It is commonplace for escape staircases in tall buildings to be one continuous vertical shaft. Whilst it is possible to introduce a positive air pressure into such a space (63, 64) it may be found more practicable to design the staircase as a series of separate shafts each about five storeys high. Each section sould have a pressurising fan unit, which could be operated continuously or in a fire emergency only. The pressure developed in each section could be related to the height of the building and the possible adverse pressure effects due to wind. This would be important in buildings higher than about fifteen storeys, and especially those in exposed locations and as the overall pressure differentials (stack and wind effects) in short sections will not be as great as those over the whole height of the building. Also short sections of staircase can be pressurised by small fans which may result in lower plant costs when compared to that required for pressurisation of a shaft the total height of a building (47).

Tests (65, 66) on a three storey staircase have shown that without pressurisation the escape area can become untenable in as little as ten minutes after ignition if normal smoke stop doors are used for smoke control. A continuous pressure differential of 0.7 mm (0.028 in.) of water is sufficient to prevent smoke penetrating smoke stop doors and a pressure of 1.4 mm (0.056 in.) of water may overcome deterioration in the performance of doors due to deformation under heat conditions. Continuous pressurisation of stairways and escape routes would present problems in buildings with air-conditioning systems because the air flow may be in the wrong direction. In such cases a system operating only under fire conditions *on demand* would be preferable, but then higher pressures would be required in order to clear the smoke that had already penetrated into the staircase enclosure. It has been shown that this can be achieved with a pressure of about 2 mm (0.08 in.) of water (65). If we want personnel to be able to move freely and evacuate the building under all conditions we believe it is necessary to have recourse to mechanical ventilation, particularly where external means of rescue are ruled out, and where tall buildings are involved (67).

The Vertically Divided Building

The main objective of this method is to enable occupants to reach a place of safety in a short time (less than 3 minutes) and is appropriate for multi-storey hospitals or other buildings where the occupants are not able to move quickly. The whole building is divided into two parts (Figure 3 (43)) with a ventilated linking lobby. The lobby would have permanent ventilation so that smoke from one side could not penetrate the adjacent building. In

Figure 3   **The vertically divided building – plan**

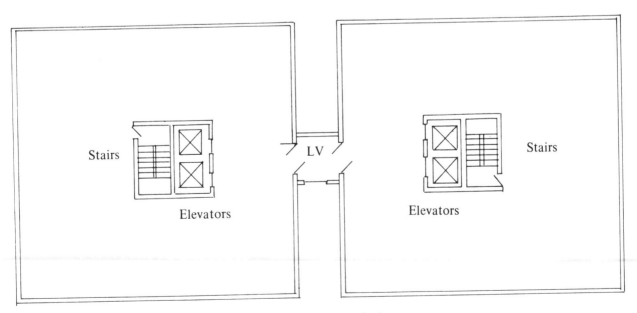

LV = Linking vestibule

this situation there would be no need to use stairs or elevators as all escapees would be able to take refuge in the adjacent building. The construction of the facing facades would need special attention to avoid fire spread by radiation.

CONCLUSION

All tall buildings present problems of life safety especially with regard to the movement of smoke and 'the use of a forced ventilation system seems to offer the best chance of maintaining smoke-free escape routes and to minimise contamination a (positive) pressure (system) rather than an exhaust system is to be preferred'.

'Among the possible measures than can be taken to combat the smoke and toxic gas hazard are to be found, at one extreme, the use of smoke stop doors and natural ventilation, which it has been shown will not alone solve the problem. At the other extremes, a completely sealed building, protected against the effects of weather conditions over which no control can be exerted, can provide safe conditions on escape routes and in other occupied zones of the building with quite modest ventilation pressures . . . . Somewhere between these two extremes must lie an acceptable compromise. Research has not yet shown where it lies . . (65)'.

REFERENCES

1. Barber H.H. (1951) (3rd Edition) "Physiology and Pharmacology for Pharmaceutical Students" p 95 (London: Bailliere, Tindall and Cox)
2. Van Straaten J.F. (1967) "Thermal Performance of Buildings" p 34 (London: Elsevier Publishing Company)
3. Philips Anne (1971) "Fire Effect on the Human Body" (p A-16) in *Fire Safety in High Buildings* (Washington, D.C.: General Services Administration)
4. Fackler J.B. (translation by L. Issen) (1967) "Fire and Smoke Invasion of Apartments" Symposium on Fire Test Methods - Restraint and Smoke 1966, ASTM, STP 422. p 218 (Philadelphia: ASTM)
5. Kawago K. (1968) "Structural Design and Fire Protection" *Build International*, 1, No 3, p 28.
6. Kirk R.E. and Othmer D.F. (Eds) (1969) "Kirk-Othmer Encyclopedia of Chemical Technology" 18, p 400 (Chichester: Interscience Publishers)
7. Thomas D.M. (1969) "Respiratory Problems of Fire Fighters" *International Association of Fire Chiefs (Newsletter)* Feb. 1969 (2), p 6.
8. Bowes P.C. and Field P. (1969) "The Assessment of Smoke Production by Building Materials in Fires - Part 2. Test Method Based on Smoke Accumulation in a Compartment" *Fire Research Note No 749* (Boreham Wood: Fire Research Station)
9. Heselden A.J.M. (1971) "Fire Problems of Pedestrian Precincts Part 1. The Smoke Production of Various Materials" *Fire Research Note No 856* (Boreham Wood: Fire Research Station)
10. Sumi K. and Tsuchiya Y. (1970) "Combustion Products of Organic Materials" *Fire Fighting in Canada, Vol 14, No 2* April, pp 6-10.
11. Gaskell J.R. and C.R. Veith (1968) "Smoke Opacity from Certain Woods and Plastics" *Fire Technology*, 4, part 3, pp 185-195.
12. Rasbash D.J. and Stark G.W.V. (1966) "The Generation of Carbon Monoxide by Fires in Compartments" *Fire Research Note No 614* (Boreham Wood: Fire Research Station)
13. Kent A.D. (1970) "Hazards From Products of Combustion and Oxygen Depletion in Occupied Spaces" *Occupational Health Review,* 21 (1-2), p 1-18.
14. Tryon G.H. (Editor (1969) "Fire Protection Handbook" (13th Edition) p 4-32 (Boston, Mass: National Fire Protection Association)

15. Kishitani K. (1971) "Study on Injurious Properties of Combustion Products of Building Materials at Initial Stage of Fire" *Journal of the Faculty of Engineering, University of Tokyo,* **XXXI**, (1) pp 1-35.

16. Pryor A.J.,Johnson D.E. and N.N. Jackson (1969) "Hazards of Smoke and Toxic Gases Produced in Urban Fires." Final Report of OCD Contract No DAHC 20-70-C-0212 Southwest Research Institute, Texas.

17. Autian J. (1970) "Toxicologic Aspects of Flammability and Combustion of Polymeric Materials" *Journal of Fire and Flammability,* **1** (July) p 239.

18. Woolley W.D. (1971) "Decomposition Products of PVC for Studies of Fires" *British Polymer J.* 3,July, p 186.

19. Woolley W.D. (1972) "Nitrogen-containing Products from the Thermal Decomposition of Flexible Polyurethane Foams" *British Polymer J.* 1972, **4**, p 27-43.

20. Woolley W.D. (1972) "Studies of the Dehydrochlorination of PVC in Nitrogen and Air" *Plastics and Polymers,* August 1972, p 203.

21. Tsuchiya Y. and K. Sumi (1969) "Thermal Decomposition Products of Polypropylene" *J. of Polymer Science.* **7**, July, pp 1599-1607.

22. Tsuchiya Y. and K. Sumi (1969) "Thermal Decomposition Products of Polyisobutylene" *J. of Polymer Science,* **7**, pp 813-826.

23. Tsuchiya Y. and K. Sumi (1972) "Evaluation of the Toxicity of Combustion Products" *J. of Fire and Flammability,* **3**, (1), Jan. p 46.

24. Home Office and Scottish Home and Health Department (1972) "Fire Precautions in Town Centre Redevelopment" *Fire Precautions Guide No 1* (a) p 13, (b) p 21. (London: HMSO)

25. Caravaty R.D. and W. F. Winslow (1970) "A New Approach to Fire Codes" *Architectural and Engineering News* (March) pp 22-25.

26. Wood P.G. (1972) " The Behaviour of People in Fires" *Joint Fire Research Organisation Contract No AT/1170/08/FRS p 92.*

27. Galbreath M. (1969) "Time Evacuation by Stairs in High Buildings" *Fire Fighting in Canada* (February).

28. Hinkley P.L. (1970) "A Preliminary Note on the Movement of Smoke in an Enclosed Shopping Mall" *Fire Research Note no 806.* (Boreham Wood: Fire Research Station)

29. The Building Standards (Scotland) (Consolidation) Regulations (1970) (London: HMSO)

30. Scottish Development Department (1972) "Explanatory Memorandum to Parts D and E of the Building Standards (Scotland) (Consolidation) Regulations 1971." (London: HMSO)

31 Scottish Home and Health Department (1965) "Fire Precautions in Old Persons Homes" *Fire Precautions Note No 3/1965* (Edinburgh: The Department)

32. Marchant E.W. (1972) "Escape Routes" in *A Complete Guide to Fire and Buildings* p 62 (Lancaster: MTP)

33. Pleschl I.A.S.Z. (1971) "Flow Capacity of Door Openings in Panic Situations" (In Dutch) *Bouw,* **26**, (2), pp 62-67.

34. Hankin B.D. and Wright R.A. (1958) "Passenger Flow in Subways" *Operational Research Q.* **9**, (2), p 81-88.

35. Weston J.G. and J. Marshall (1972) "The Capacity of Passageways for Uni-directional and for Crossing Flows of Pedestrians" (Department of Operational Research Memo M 258: The London Transport Executive)

36. Togawa K. (1955) "Study on Fire Escapes basing on the Observation of Multitude Currents" (Building Exits Code) *Report of the Building Research Institute No 14.* (Tokyo: Building Research Institute).

37. Ministry of Transport and the Scottish Development Department (1965) "Urban Traffic Engineering Techniques" (London: HMSO)

38. Thomas P.H. and Hinkley P.L (1964, 1965) "Design of Roof-Venting Systems for Single-storey Buildings" *Fire Research Technical Paper No 10* (London: HMSO)

39. Thomas P.H. Hinkley P.L., Theobald C.R. and Simms D.L. (1963, 1964) "Investigations into the Flow of Hot Gases in Roof Venting." *Fire Research Technical Paper No 7* (London: HMSO)

40. Langdon-Thomas G.J. and Hinkley P.L. (1965) "Fire Venting in Single-Storey Buildings" *Fire Note No 5* (London: HMSO)

41. Malhotra H.L. (1967) "Movement of Smoke on Escape Routes Pt 3. Effect of Permanent Openings in External Walls" *Fire Research Note No 653* (Boreham Wood: Fire Research Station).

42. Thomas P.H. (1968) (1970) "The Movement of Smoke in Horizontal Passages Against an Air Flow

   (1) *Fire Research Note No 723* (Boreham Wood: Fire Research Station).

   (2) *Institute of Fire Engineers Quarterly,* **30** (77) p 45-53.

43. Anon (1970) "Explanatory Paper on Control of Smoke Movement in High Buildings" (NRCC 11413) (Ottawa: National Research Council of Canada).

44. Tamura G.T. and McGuire J.H. (1971) "Smoke Movement in High-Rise Buildings" *Canadian Building Digest No 133* (Ottawa: National Research Council of Canada)

45. Wilkinson J. (1969) "Automatic Air Flow Control for Escape Route Smoke Movement in Multi-Storey Flats" *Fire* **62** (772) p 269-272.

46. Wilkinson J. (1971) "The Worthing AAC System - Automatic Airflow Control System for Escape Routes in New Multi-Storey Blocks of Flats" in *Symposium No 4 "Movement of Smoke on Escape Routes in Buildings"* (London: HMSO).

47. Leworthy L.R. (1970) "No Fire Without Smoke" *The Architect and Building News,* 19 Feb. 1970, pp 50-54.

48. Hinkley P.L. (1970) "A Preliminary Note on the Movement of Smoke in an Enclosed Shopping Mall" *Fire Research Note No 806* (Boreham Wood: Fire Research Station).

49. Hinkley P.L. (1970) "The Flow of Hot Gases Along an Enclosed Shopping Mall - A Tentative Theory" *Fire Research Note No 807* (Boreham Wood: Fire Research Station).

50. Heselden A.J.M. and Hinkley P.L. (1970) "Smoke Travel in Shopping Malls - Experiments in Cooperation with Glasgow Fire Brigade. Part 1" *Fire Research Note No 832* (Boreham Wood: Fire Research Station).

51. Phillips A.M. (1971) "Smoke Travel in Shopping Malls. Model Studies - Part 1: Rates of Lateral Spread" *Fire Research Note No 864* (Boreham Wood: Fire Research Station).

52. Hinkley P.L. (1971) "Some Notes on the Control of Smoke in Enclosed Shopping Centres" *Fire Research Note No 875* (Boreham Wood: Fire Research Station).

53. Wilson A.G. and Tamura G.T. (1968) "Stack Effect in Buildings" *Canadian Building Digest No 104* (Ottawa: National Research Council of Canada).

54. Wilson A.G. and Tamura G.T. (1968) "Stack Effect and Building Design" *Canadian Building Digest No 107* (Ottawa: National Research Council of Canada)

55. Tamura G.T. and Wilson A.G. (1966) "Pressure Differences for a Nine-Storey Building as a Result of Chimney Effect and Ventilation System Operation" *Trans. ASHRAE* **72** (1) p 180-189.

56. Tamura G.T. and Wilson A.G. (1967) "Pressure Differences Caused by Chimney Effect in Three High Buildings" and "Building Pressures Caused by Chimney Action and Mechanical Ventilation" *Trans ASHRAE* **73** (2).

57. Tamura G.T. and Wilson A.G. (1969) "Pressure Differences Caused by Wind on Two Tall Buildings" *Trans ASHRAE* **74** (2) p 170-181. (also published as Research Paper No 392 of the Division of Building Research, National Research Council of Canada NRC 10628).

58. Butcher E.G., P.J. Rardell and Jackman P.J. (1971) "Prediction of the Behaviour of Smoke in a Building using a Computer" in *Symposium No 4 "Movement of Smoke on Escape Routes in Buildings"* (London: HMSO)

59. Barret R.E. and Locklin D.W. (1971) "A Computer Technique for Predicting Smoke Movement in Tall Buildings" in *Symposium No 4 "Movement of Smoke on Escape Routes in Buildings* (London: HMSO).

60 Tamura G.T. (1969) "Computer Analysis of Smoke Movement in Tall Buildings" *ASHRAE Transactions* **75** (2) p 89.

61. Coggan W.A. (1971) "Present Methods of Smoke Control which Rely on Natural Ventilation" in *Symposium No 4 "Movement of Smoke on Escape Routes in Buildings"* (London: HMSO). .

62. Tryon G.H. (Editor) (1969) *Fire Protection Handbook* - 13th Edition (p 8 - 186) (Boston: National Fire Protection Association)

63. Cottle T.H., Bailey T.A., Butcher, E.G. and Shore C. (1970) "Smoke Tests in the Pressurised Stairs and Lobbies in a 26 Storey Office Building" *Fire Research Note No 850* (Boreham Wood: Fire Research Station).

64. Butcher E.G., Cottle T.H. and Bailey T.A. (1971) "Smoke Tests in the Pressurised Stairs and Lobbies of a 26 Storey Office Building" *The Building Services Engineer,* **39**, December (JIHVE)

65. Silversides R.G. (1967) "Measurement and Control of Smoke in Building Fires" *Symposium on Fire Test Methods -Restraint and Smoke 1966* ASTM SP 422.

66. Malhotra H.L. and Millbank N. (1964) "Movement of Smoke in Escape Routes and effect of Pressurisation - Results of some Tests Performed in a New Departmental Store" *Fire Research Note No 566* (Boreham Wood: Fire Research Station).

67. Cabret A. and Ferrie M. (1971) "Smoke Protection of Escape Routes in Buildings with particular reference to Multistorey Buildings" in Symposium No. 4 *Movement of Smoke on Escape Routes in Buildings* (London: HMSO).

Building Measurement

W.M. Laing, FIOB

INTRODUCTION

If any kind of effective progress is to be made in any construction complex, be it a national concern, a medium or small business, or a mixed group of people brought together to apply their professional, managerial or technical skills to the carrying out of a construction project then procedures are required. By themselves they do not create progress. Progress is measured only to the extent that communication between those concerned has been established. But in turn communication itself is not enough; for in any communication situation there is one person trying to say something and another person trying to understand what is being said and frequently, as the poet said "East is East and West is West and never the twain shall meet".

The point is well illustrated by the story told at the time when the first telephone exchange was established in a crofter's house on one of the remote islands of the Hebrides. Everything connected with the installation was explained to Shamish the Crofter. The inauguration ceremony was duly performed by one of the Under Secretaries of State for Scotland and all concerned settled down to enjoy a convivial evening of whisky and talk. As could be expected the telephone bell rang and Shamish answered it. He mastered the simple processes involved and said "Hello". He then stood for some minutes in concentrated silence and said "Aye", put down the receiver and came back to his drink at the fire, where his wife asked him "Well Shamish and who was that?" Shamish replied "It was a fine woman's voice telling me that it's a long distance from New York!" Someone trying to say something; someone thinking he understands.

The problem then within our construction complex is to establish a network of commonly understood communication. Moreover to give it stability and a chance to be of universal service to all concerned it must rest firmly in the recognised official procedures commonly practised throughout the industry. Further it must be capable of effective development as increasing demands are made on it by the continuing elaboration of work which takes place in the forward progression of a contract.

Reviews and Developments

THE BACKGROUND

Contracts

Contracts of course are the backcloth to any communication system and whilst it is acknowledged that there are many variations as to the form in which a contract may be offered and accepted far and away the most common contractual agreement is that where the contract is based on the use of the three officially accepted documents.

   (i)   The Conditions of Contract

   (ii)   The Standard Mode of Measurement and

   (iii)   The Bill of Quantities.

and it is known as the competitive tendering contract.

The pursuit of the contract in its simplest expression consists of the series of actions and interactions which take place when a client briefs an architect and through him a contractor and has as the end product a building. These interactions between the various people concerned have in the course of time helped to establish what are known as procedures. In fact these procedures are so universally accepted over the whole gamut of functional industry that they offer themselves as the possible binding parameters within which any meaningful system of communication could be established, either for a specific contract, or within the confines of a construction company. Accepting these restraints, and before describing a possible communication system, it would be helpful to look at the three documents upon which it seems contractual procedures are based. These documents, imperfect as they might be, represent in words of instruction and control the evolution of the interplay of action and responsibility which takes place between the various members of the construction team as contract succeeds contract. The words tell how construction men over long periods of time have succeeded in meeting the ever changing economic, social and creative environment which surrounds them.

The Standard Form of Building Contract

Basic to any contract are the conditions under which it has been agreed, even if these are merely in the form of a handshake. However in the construction industry a standard form of building contract has been evolved which demands the observance of almost forty clauses, each with its own train of sub-clauses and implications. As construction, the environment, and economic structures become increasingly compounded this document takes on greater significance and demands more attention than has hitherto been afforded to it.

Unfortunately in recent times, even at the level of a Lord Chief Justice, the seeming deviousness of form in which the conditions are couched has been used to castigate them as being untenable for use in the settlement of cases at law, when in fact the real problem lies in the failure of those involved to establish at the onset a communication system which would make for the understanding of what are or are not the responsibilities of each person involved. This standard form document is excellently dealt with in a recent exposition by Glyn P. Jones*. For a classic, simple, step by step method of communication this book, with the aid of distinctive diagramatic illustration, does exactly what it sets out to do. In the author's own words it "is directed

* A New Approach to the Standard Form of Building Contract by Glyn P. Jones, published by MTP, Lancaster, England.

entirely towards transforming this complex and important document into one that will

(a)   Enable its users to readily review and understand their obligations, rights and remedies, and

(b)   Provide an automatic solution technique for parties in dispute."

But the need, and a desperate need it is, for such a book is in itself an implication that obligations, rights and remedies are transient situations which arise in the course of a contract and are not, as they should be, lawful requirements to be catered for by meaningful and effective communication systems created at the outset of any contract.

The Standard Mode of Measurement   If the standard form of building contract embraces the human interrelationships between the various people concerned in a construction project, then the standard mode of measurement lays down the rules by which the work to be done can be quantified in units of measurement. It came into being in 1922, some thirteen years after it was realised that it was essential that some form of common practice and uniformity of method should be introduced if chaos were to be avoided in the day to day contractual dealings involving the measurement of building works. Since that time the mode has developed only in the sense that additional sections have been added to meet the expanding importance of the trades not included in the first edition. Subsequent editions, including the most recent fifth edition, which metricated the information, show no more signs than the first edition that there is much more to measurement than simply expressing it in bulk form.

Indeed it is an extraordinary fact that at this stage in time, 50 years and more since the concept of rules for measurement was accepted as sound practice, that those who produce the bill of quantities from the standard mode look upon these documents as almost synonymous in role and terminal in themselves, and they fail to perceive that measurement properly presented is the key to founding an effective communication system. How different it could be if it were recognised by surveyors and contractors alike that everything that goes into the physical creation of a construction project can be meaningfully and effectively estimated for, administered, constructed, costed, related to feed-back, and paid for, only if it has been quantified in an ordered and reasonably accurate manner. It could be argued, of course, that the best bills of quantity meet this demand; but fundamentally if communication at this stage in the procedures is to move away from being a non-event then the standard mode itself must be expanded to cope with the incrementation of dimension and quantity, the location of quantity and the creation of identifiable units-of-work; for these are the factors which are vital to the contractor in his deliberations on how much the work will cost, what is involved in the production of it, and in what order it is likely to be accomplished.

In short, little or no development of the standard mode of measurement has taken place since it was introduced in 1922. There are, however, signs that both the RICS and the NFBTE recognise that something should be done. Recently they produced a report from a joint Working Party of measurement conventions which makes most enlightening reading but more significantly reveals that on the part of those who should be concerned there is an alarming apathy to any suggestion that progress is possible. It is however heartening to read in the report such statements as, 'While there is a tendency to think of a standard method of measurement merely as a basis for the preparation of a bill of quantities for competitive tendering, the potential uses of such a convention are much wider' and 'Some waste of effort . . . . can stem from the absence of firm information . . . . but a high proportion is due to lack of recognition, by the original extractors of information, of the needs of subsequent users', and to savour such recommendations as 'That the standard mode of measurement be reconstituted as a related series of sets of rules of measurement accompanied by a code of measurement practice' and 'That such sets of rules should reflect the varying degrees of quantification required at successive stages of the construction process by different interests within the Industry, and that they should accommodate the varying stages of completition of design proposals.'

These extracts do not by any means exhaust the possibilities for change revealed in the report. Indeed so forward looking are the findings and recommendations that one is apprehensive as to the treatment it will receive when it comes before the controlling bodies themselves; for the construction industry has a poor record in the spheres of combined action and the creation of management techniques.

The Bill of Quantities

Whatever the fate or future of the standard mode of measurement is, the bill of quantities will always be the child born out of that mode. This is a modern situation. Historically the use of bills of quantities was an ancient procedure and used long before a standard mode came into being. In fact a reading of the opening chapters of the second book of Chronicles in the Old Testament makes a mockery of all our puny efforts to cope with construction and communication problems; for here is a bill of quantities to out-measure all bills of quantity. The mind boggles at the thought of dealing with the quantities and the procedures involved when 'Solomon resolved to build a house in honour of the name of the Lord' and that to accomplish it 'He engaged seventy thousand hauliers and eighty thousand quarrymen', and most alarming of all 'three thousand six hundred men to superintend it'! One is almost tempted to upbraid the Lord for having withheld the use of the computer from his zealous servant Solomon. However the house was completed and one is left with the impression that not only did the king know what was required but he had the procedures and communications through which to carry it out.

However, as the upholders of the time-space concept would say, to get back to the present. The essential fact to accept in considering the position of the bill of quantities is that the bill is established by the standard form of contract as a definite contractual agent for building procedures. However, in practice it remains a surveyor's document. In format it reflects his method of approach to the construction procedures and what he eventually requires from them in order to give him an economic return. He is not called upon by any of the standard contractual procedures to develop it either information-wide or in format beyond his own interpretation of how to display measurement as ordained by the standard mode.

To say that formats vary in as many different ways as there are surveyors in the land would be to exaggerate the situation, but with exceptions most bills of quantities as they stand create a block in what should be a continuing flow of information from the design stage to the construction and production stages in the procedures. To serve the purposes of the contractor in these stages the bill should provide incremented measurement listed in groups of items of work. These would reflect a possible break-down of the over-all complexities of a contract into manageable units-of-work which would have meaning and could be identified throughout the procedures of estimating, tendering, producing, costing and the hitherto most difficult procedure of all, that of feed-back. At present this kind of approach may seem utopian. But in the aforementioned report there is constant reference to the desirability that changes of such a nature should be made in both the standard mode and the bill of quantities. Indeed one of the conclusions arrived at reads, 'Ideally a bill of quantities should provide a list of items representing, by means of appropriate parameters, sub-divisions of total cost which are pertinent to the construction process, each suitably quantified and guaranteed for accuracy by the employer and each capable of sustaining, for the currency of a contract, a justifiable price.'

Surely a most enlightened conclusion, but one which if acted on would clear the way for just the kind of developments upon which sound communication systems can be founded.

A SYSTEM

The Requirements

These then are the officially accepted supports upon which a communication system must be constructed, by means of which it is hoped understood information will pass from one person to another during the course of a contract, be it within the limits of a construction company itself or in the wider sphere of over-all contract control. The system in fact must be the instrument through which a company or construction project group communicate about and resolve the many problems which have to be faced at every stage of progress in the course of a contract. It must cope *at management and accountancy levels with*

(i) Budgetary balance sheet control
(ii) Cash-flow control
(iii) Measured return against cost control
(iv) Company capacity level control

at estimating and tendering levels with

(i) Performance timing control
(ii) Units-of-work time durations
(iii) Units-of-work material and waste values
(iv) Simple and quick aggragation of information for tendering purposes

at production level with

(i) Work phasing
(ii) Labour resource application
(iii) Effects of variation orders and periods of work delay
(iv) Feed-back information
(v) Real and up to value progress payments
(vi) Labour relations

and at buying level with

(i) Cost against estimate and measured return.

This list of requirements and activities looks sophisticated and only applicable to large concerns, but in fact shows functions of control, which no matter the size of a company, must be given some degree of attention. It must also appear, even to the large concerns, in fact perhaps more so to them, that so diverse are the approaches made to these various functions by the departments having to deal with them, that any attempt to produce an all embracing communication system is doomed to failure. No doubt up and down the country there are many companies using communication systems which deal adequately with the internal isolated workings of any one department, but it is also safe to say that the number of truly integrated systems covering all departments will be few.

The submission here is that, through the systems to be described, such integration is possible, and that the system is remarkably simple to work because it is based on the two fundamental factors of measurement and time. Indeed no department in any construction company can function unless somewhere along the line the work done on site has been measured and timed; for return comes from measurement and cost is registered by time. It must be noticed that cash values have not been mentioned. This is deliberate. Cash-flow, capital available, money, call it what you will, is of course of paramount importance and indeed at the end of the day is what communication is ultimately all about, but money values are essentially token expressions of measurement and time; hence the emphasis here on orientating all departmental thinking into terms of how much (measurement) and how long (time). There is a further observation that must be made concerning the basic thinking or attitudes that should be inculcated upon the minds of the people involved with this communication system. It is that information conveyed by word of mouth or by written display is subject to ambiguity of understanding, while information conveyed by figures may be wrong it is not subject to the ambiguity of acceptance and it can be retrieved unaltered for scrutiny. The system is devised with this concept of communication in mind and is greatly facilitated in this by the introduction of metrication to measurement, decimalisation to money, and the conversion of time recording to the unit of a decimalised hour. An approach which further eliminates a mixture of decimal and fractional thinking, and expedites the use of electronic calculators or micro-computers to give information to a uniform number of decimal points whether dealing with measurement, time or cash.

Components of the System

In diagramatic form the system is simple to follow (Fig. 1). It has three foundation points, all of which are beyond the control of the company. These are, as has been made clear above, The Standard Form of Building Contract, The Standard Mode of Measurement and The Bill of Quantities.

The Standard Form of Building Contract (1): Whatever internal reason they may have for wanting to design a communication system, management must make sure that the system is capable of throwing up visual evidence of production reaction to the demands made upon it by the relevant clauses in the standard form of contract. In normal circumstances this seldom means anything more than documenting the passage of time, and being able to submit requests for interim payments adequately supported by measurement. However when placed in the position of having to make claims for such items as direct loss and/or expense in connection with variation orders or work-delay periods the contractor will be in a very weak position if the evidences supporting the claims are not seen to stem from a reasonable internal communication system. Indeed, the more integrated the system is between the departments of the company the more likely is the company to arrive at the true cost to themselves of the deviations and hence the more likely is the claim to be true and proper.

The Standard Mode of Measurement (2): All that has been written previously about expanding the mode into a medium through which the procedures of estimating, production planning and cost control now becomes relevant. It is at this point in setting-up the system that *the new approach* is introduced. On the diagram, the box following the SMM box is titled *'Performance timing tables'*. These tables are made by taking in each trade section of the standard mode the items involving the handling of materials or the creation of voids and incrementing them into categories of linear, area, volume or enumerated quantities, dimensions, methods and location of fixing and likewise incrementing the labour-only items in categories of complexity. Each item is given a *performance time factor* which is set as the time one man, squad or resource is likely to accomplish one unit of measurement. It is the application of these tables to the items in a bill of quantities that makes it possible to create the full communication system shown on the diagram.

The tables for the Carpenter, Joiner and Ironmonger works showing some 12 000 incremental timing applications have been completed and will be ready for publication in the autumn of this year (1973). Tables in preparation for the other trades in the mode will be published as they are completed over the course of the following twelve months. The putting together of such performance timing tables has only become possible since decimalisation and metrication were introduced. Prior to that, the calculation involved in relating time and incremental imperial measurement and then superimposing an £ s. d. money value on the answers would have made the task impossible, as in fact it has proved to be in previous abortive efforts to do this very thing.

However to get back to the system and the last of the outside agencies which have a direct bearing on the format of the system.

The Bill of Quantities (3): Like the other two key documents involved in setting up this system the bill of quantities comes to the contractor as an outside agency, but, and this is important, it quite literally becomes the corner stone upon which all else is founded. Fortunately today, in general terms, most bills of quantities do show at least a remarkably accurate measurement of the work to be done, and are itemised, if not actually sub headed, in a sequence which follows the possible progress of site work. These bills serve admirably the purposes of the surveyor, the architect and the client but give little or no assistance as they stand to the contractor with his planning and on-site production, and if the truth be known are positively mis-leading on the subject of cost feed-back for forward budgeting.

To help bring meaningful change to this situation it is stated above that to facilitate the creation of a smooth flow of effective communication up and down the path of the construction procedures some production orientated grouping of the items in a bill is necessary. Again one other apposite quotation from the aforementioned official report subscribes to this view when one of its conclusions reads: 'A generalized indication of organisational complexity might be conveyed more effectively by *grouping items of work* with regard to space-use and locational characteristics'. Thus, discarding this cloud of words but accepting the tenet they prescribe as an essential to the structure of this system, the system itself, for the sake of brevity clarity and identification, refers to these groupings simply as units-of-work. The unit-of-work concept is of course 'not new. However the useful development of it as a tool to aid production and to help cost forecasting and control has suffered in the eternal official skirmishing as to who is responsible for producing what and when during the procedure of a contract.

Company Resource Rate (7): Up to this point three outside agencies have been shown to be of prime importance in the setting-up of this communication system but one other prime motivator is required and this time from inside the company. It is the in-company *resource hour rate.* To explain this concept fully would require more space than can be given to it in this article, but in short *a resource* is a craftsman, a squad or a mchine whose work expresses not only his own measureable performance but the latent support of every department in the company; and *a resource hour* is the unit of time in which a measureable quantity of work is done. The resource hour rate itself is the forecasted or established cost of the resource, plus the cost of the latent aids, expressed as a cash rate per order book or capacity hour for the company, the contract, or the unit-of-work. In the actual working of the system it is not too much to claim that this concept of the resource hour rate, plus the use of incremented performance timings opens the flood gates for a plethora of communicable figure-enumerated information to flow freely from management to site and back to management throughout the course of a contract or for that matter over the whole gamut of the company's affairs.

Application of the System

The system then starts with the bill of quantities, and the grouping of the bill items into units-of-work. Further, without waiting for official approbation, the responsibility for this grouping is placed firmly with the contractor, and who better to define the parameters and the sub-divisions, or as this system calls them the units-of-work, than the man who will price, plan and produce them? Accepting this and the bill of quantities in any of the formats it is produced today, it is a comparatively simple matter for the Estimating Department of any construction company to line-off on the pages of the bill numbers of consecutive items into groups which form themselves into acceptable units-of-work within the parameters set by the company to suit their own internal policies. By number coding these units the contractor creates the prime-movers for the system. Round these, because they remain unaltered as controls throughout the course of any contract, all communicative information evolves as it is required by the various departments of a company to satisfy their individually slanted demands as listed above. If for example a group of twenty-three consecutive items in a bill of quantities under the heading *Light framing* have been allocated the number 3 at the estimating stage then no matter in which form the work being done on this framing is being expressed, and this could be in measurement, in planning control, in actual presentation, in wages or in the form of material being ordered, or costed it would be identifiable by that number. Thus is established at the onset the principle that numbers tend to be less ambiguous than words when communication is being made between individuals or departments.

From this point on in the system (Fig. 1 nos. 8 - 32) the whole business of communication by numbers which represent vital information is activated by the application of performance timings to itemised bill quantities or remeasurement quantities. At the first stage viz. estimating, this calculation gives duration time, which by means of the resource hour rate is then converted to a resource (labour) unit rate for the bill item; but more importantly though the same resource hour rate gives the value of the contributions from that unit-of-work which can be expected against the expenditure on the resource. This is all information vital to management for tendering purposes and to the production department for cost and planning control.

In the next stage (viz. production) as the work is being done, the application of the same performance timings and resource hour rate to the remeasured work, or accepted measurement, reveals the actual contribution being made towards the same resources by the same unit-of-work. The new production rate is this contribution divided by the actual resource hours taken; and the real cost rate is the total wages and expenditure on all resources divided by the actual resource hours taken. By these processes comparable ratio rates of production to estimate and to real return are disclosed in unmistakable form for communication and decision making in every department of the company.

From the same sources which set up those production control procedures, especially those established at the estimating stage, a production control master chart may be compiled (figure 2) covering periods of 5 days or multiples thereof. Thereafter throughout the duration of the contract the system is capable of adjusting the resource situation as it is being affected by the production results in each successive 5 day period.

Thus at site level visual evidence in the form of numbered resource hours spent or required to complete, and in the form of resource days gained or lost for any particular unit-of-work, together with the cumulative effect of that on the contract itself, is available. At management or accountancy levels the evidences are no less simply displayed in fact the same figures appear but call for other interpretations and decisions. Fundamentally however the unequivocal figures produced up and down the system keep every person in the company firmly in touch with the gain or loss situation, and surely little more than that could be demanded from any system.

Documentation

Needless to say as with any system of communication clear presentation of the information being given and received is essential. In fact systems will break down unless the documentation of them is standardised, easy to complete and consecutive in use. To illustrate this, in so far as management of production and control of resource costs are concerned in this

Figure No. 1 : Communication System Flowchart

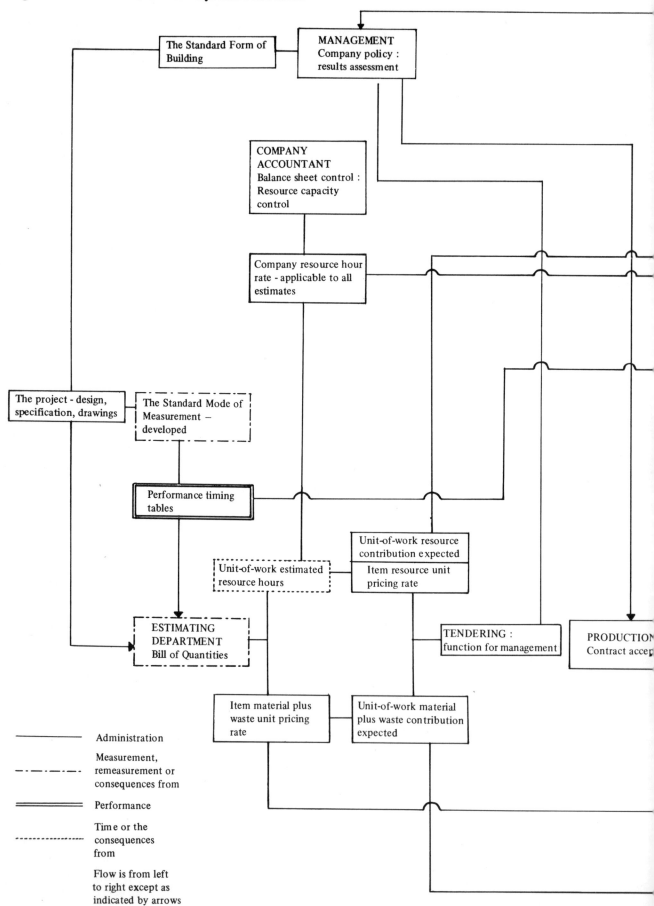

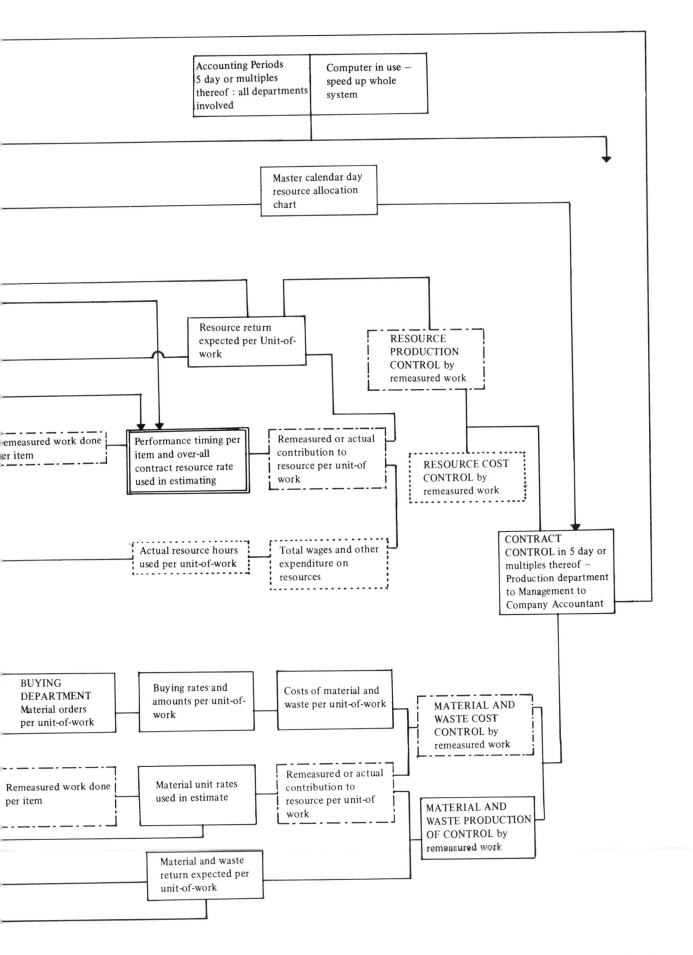

Figure 2. Production control master chart

| Units of Work (operations) | | Period 1 | | | | | | Period 2 | | | | | | Period 3 | | | | | |
Description	Hours*	M	Tu	W	Th	F	Total for period ended 7/7/72	M	Tu	W	Th	F	Total for period ended 14/7/72	M	Tu	W	Th	F	Total for period ended 21/7/72
1. Roofing	448	64	64	64	64	64	320	64	64				128						
2. Heavy framing	112			28	28	28	84	28					28						
3. Light framing	296				37	37	84	37	37	37	37	37	185	37					37
4. Bearer	15							8	7				15						
5. Gutters	175							35	35	35	35	35	175						
6. Roof lights	43								16	16	11		43						
7. Eternit linings	92										23	23	46	23	23				46
8. Facias	112											28	28	28	28	28			84
9. Insulation	22											11	11	11					11
10. Linings	85													17	17	17	17	17	85
Totals	1400	64	64	92	129	129	478	172	159	88	106	134	659	116	68	45	17	17	263

* Estimated number of resource hours required for completion

system the successively accruing information produced from a developing contract is conveyed through the following documents.

1. The Bill of Quantities
2. The Contractors estimating analysis sheet
3. The Contractors tendering analysis sheet
4. The Contract calendar day chart
5. The Contractors unit-of-work bill of quantities
6. The Site unit-of-work and contract production data processing programme
7. Management to site production control reports
8. Site to Management measurement and resource hour used report
9. Resource day chart
10. Updating both calendar and resource day charts.

These documents have been designed to accommodate in rotation the flow of information engendered as a contract proceeds and to pinpoint well defined decision making moments for each department involved.

Some Other Issues

There are two recent far reaching happenings which will come to influence the construction industry procedures more and more. The first is the enactment of the Industrial Relations Act, and the other is the draft Statement of Standard Accounting Practice. Both highlight the necessity for the construction company to have reliable gain and/or loss information in a readily understood fashion. Briefly the Industrial Relations Act Section 56, as the Code of Practice note says, 'will require employers to disclose certain information about their undertakings to representatives of registered trade unions which they recognise for negotiating purposes'; and the Accounting Standards Steering Committee's new proposals state that 'Long-term contract work in progress should be stated in accounts at cost plus attributable profit less anticipated loss'. Both these requirements will most certainly place a premium on construction companies, of whatever size, to establish integrated and easily followed communication systems, whereby reliable controls are set and are seen to be comparable with cost and results.

CONCLUSION

This system set out to create an effective way of helping people, working within a construction company or on a single building project, to understand communications between themselves. If in describing the system the emphasis has been placed on communication within the company itself, it must not be lost sight of that much of the information engendered, and which indeed can be further evolved from the data and processes described, can be readily made available to the surveyor, the architect and the client. It would seem on reflection that should the standard mode be expanded to help in the realms of production planning and control then a system such as the one described could produce a reciprocation of effect in the realms of site-costing and feed-back to architects and clients, and in the realms of making fair and reasonable assessments by the surveyor when dealing with contractor's claims for loss and/or expense in connection with variation orders and work delay periods.

The construction industry is not noted for either integrated planning or for reliable documentation, and this despite the rise of the nationwide contractor of whom it could have been expected would be helping to create a better image of efficiency and to establish a volume of effective feed-back. But always the stumbling block lies in the time lag between any given happening on a site and the decision as to how that change can be met. This generally results in the decision being irrelevant to the situation, which has always changed again, and to a breakdown in effective planning control. The system just described is designed with this problem in mind. As it has been described or as it could be simplified to meet circumstances it can be made to work manually and with effect. However, and again as it stands and certainly as it could be developed, and indeed has been developed it is greatly facilitated by application through a large or micro computer.

Surveying

J.R. Smith, ARICS

Computations

In the last few years there has been a number of significant developments in the land surveying field but none more profound than that in surveying computations. Of course, many calculations are also made in other aspects of Construction but it is the land surveyor who traditionally has been grappling with trigonometric formulae for centuries. In the middle 1960s the first significant breakthrough was achieved with the introduction of the Olivetti Programme 101 desk calculator. However, although this reduced and almost eliminated much of the tedium involved in, say, a traverse computation, it was not the complete answer. It required the use of a large percentage of the programming capacity for the evaluation of each trigonometric function - and goodness knows, the surveyor uses plenty of them.

Even at that time, although various people foresaw the day when such functions would require only the press of a button, even they did not envisage that it would arrive so rapidly and forcibly. By 1970, single key, automatic trig. and log. functions were with us and the death knell of logarithmic and natural tables had been sounded. But at that stage the ultimate had not been reached and even now developments have settled down. Machines such as the Hewlett-Packard 9100B with some 400 program steps and 32 stores turned the traverse computation into a data entry problem. The unadjusted coordinates could be obtained one station at a time, by the successive entry of observed angle and distance. This solution was made the easier by single key operations for converting polar coordinates (bearing and distance) into rectangular coordinates (differences of eastings and northings) and successively accumulating the results. Both Wang and Compucorp machines had similar facilities.

Among the more recent Hewlett-Packard machines is the 9810 with 111 stores and an instruction capacity of 2036 steps; Models 9820 and 9830 are now available with additional facilities. Now all the field data - horizontal angles, slope distances and vertical angles for a 40 leg traverse can be entered into the machine, a rigorous least squares adjustment applied, the adjusted coordinates and bearings and distances between successive points printed out and the station positions plotted automatically - all in less than 20 minutes! Other peripheral equipment that will fit such machines include a cassette extension to the storage and instruction capacity, tabulated typewriter output, digitiser for the calculation of areas, measurement of lengths and similar operations, and punched tape input.

Electronic calculator

1972 was the year of the hand or pocket electronic calculator with around 100 different models on the market. Almost all of these were restricted to the 4 basic arithmetic functions and as such of little advantage to the surveyor but there were one or two exceptions. First among these was the Hewlett-Packard model 35 which is truly pocket size yet has all the trig. and log. functions together with 4 working registers and a store for less than £200. This has now been supplemented with models 45 and 46 with additional automatic function and extra storage. The latest trend is towards making even these programmable and one wonders where it will all end.

Besides being of inestimable use in land surveying the whole range of electronic calculators obviously has great potential in the Construction industry ranging from structural engineering and, in fact, any aspect dealing with figures. The facility of being able to do complicated calculations in the field - when the setting out data needs to be hurriedly checked or changed; or in checking a traverse closure before leaving the field will surely be appreciated by all concerned. Against the rapid change in calculating methods. developments in other aspects of surveying have been less fundamental but nevertheless they are affecting the field procedures, accuracies attainable and overall economics of projects.

Theodolites

The notable change in theodolites is the trend started by Wild in converting to circles graduated in decimal degrees as opposed to degrees, minutes and seconds. This is more readily achieved where a model is also optionally available in grads since a change in magnification and division scale is all that is required. The Wild T1A and T16 theodolites are suitable this way and the decimal version reads directly to 0.01 and by estimation to 0.01 degree. (equivalent to about 4 seconds). The use of decimal degrees is particularly helpful when used in conjunction with any form of electronic calculator that has trig. functions since all of these require the angle to be converted to decimal degrees before taking the function.

Recent articles in the technical press have talked in terms of computerised theodolites on the horizon. No doubt a very few years will see new concepts in combined angle and distance measuring devices but the final equipment could well be even more revolutionary than is being imagined at present. In the past there have been coded tacheometers with film recording of the readings and there are punched tape outputs from some distance measuring equipment but both of these have been very expensive. To be of wide interest to industry any developments along these lines will need to be a combined angle and distance unit with automatic slope reduction, and recording in a permanent form, but all for around £1000. The complete unit, for portability and convenience, to be a little larger than a normal theodolite.

EDM Instruments

In the last three years several new models of short range EDM instruments have appeared on the market, each with its own advantages and disadvantages but in general the range has been up to 3km with an accuracy of ± 10 mm. The Mekometer, forecast in the first edition as being available in 1971, is now expected to appear in mid 1973. It is a sad reflection on British industry that one of the prototypes was on view as long ago as 1965, and that it is now to appear from a Swiss manufacturer. Britain has yet to enter the field of electronic distance measuring equipment manufacture. Such equipment is finding increasing application in the setting out of all forms of construction from motorways to pipelines and large factory complexes. Several such units can now be used in gaseous underground workings. Whilst there are some units giving angles as well as distances they are not as versatile as the existing separate units nor as portable as would be liked. The production of a compact unit consisting of theodolite facilities as well as distance measurement is eagerly awaited.

Lasers

The increasing use of low powered lasers for alignment of excavations, pipe laying, and vertical alignment may soon be augmented with the laser level. Researchers in Canada have developed a laser levelling instrument capable of accuracies comparable with, or even better than, traditional levelling techniques. The staff end of the operation is still being evolved but before long levelling will be a one man operation. In such circumstances the responsibility would lie at the staff end rather than the instrument end.

Photogrammetry and aerial surveys

A further field of surveying where there is increasing development is in the use of terrestrial, or non-topographic photogrammetry. The applications of such techniques now range from the recording and 'contouring' of historic buildings and statues, to the monitoring of soil samples in a centrifuge; the 3 dimensional location of intricate networks of pipes; the periodic movement of landslips; the recording of stock piles; computation of volumes; deformation of buildings, bridges, cranes and the like.

Aerial surveys continue to be widely used in motorway work but can also be of particular advantage in the monitoring of sewer outfalls and the hot and cold water areas around a power station outfall. Other applications include land reclamation, reservoir construction, thematic beach profiles, car parking statistics, and mineral exploration.

Summary

The various rapid advances in such a wide range of aspects of surveying require that those in positions of authority, either from the point of view of purchasing survey equipment or for the writing of specifications, will have great difficulty in keeping up-to-date. As a result they would be well advised to keep a close watch on current survey literature - such as the Survey Review, Chartered Surveyor (land survey supplement), Photogrammetric Record and similar journals, - attend any technical meetings or courses available in their area, and if in any doubt at all, to consult the professional land surveyor. As projects become larger and larger, fundamental errors in site plans or setting out can be extremely expensive, not to say embarrassing or even dangerous in some circumstances.

BIBLIOGRAPHY

Papers from International Federation of Surveyors (FIG) Congress. Wiesbaden. (1971)
Papers from International Conference of Surveyors. Tel Aviv. (1972)
Papers from 15th Congress, Institution of Surveyors. Australia (1972)
British National Report on Photogrammetry (1972)
J.R. Smith (1973) *Desk Calculations* (London: Crosby Lockwood)

Timber

P.R. Harman

Timber Research and Development Association

Timber framed housing

More timber framed houses than ever before are now being built in this country. It is generally accepted that the cost of these is not significantly lower than traditionally built ones of brick or block but it can be claimed that they represent better value for money. The houses are drier and hence may be decorated to full standards by the builder without the usual 12 months wait for reactive salts in wet plaster to gravitate to the surface. They are warmer as a consequence of this but more so because the nature of the framing technique used results in cavities being formed within wall panels convenient for the incorporation of thermal insulation. With such inclusions the resultant "U" values are generally much superior to those of brick built houses of the same cost level. 11in (280mm) cavity brick walls have a "U" value of 0.3 (1.7 W/m^2 ^{o}C) as opposed to a typical one of 0.07 (0.4 W/m^2 ^{o}C) for an insulated timber framed one.

Developments in constructions of timber framed and plasterboard lined party walls has resulted in sound insulation properties much improved upon those provided in traditional houses and what is more this high performance is gained without the restrictive conditions introduced in the Seventh Amendment to the Building Regulations 1965 (and now incorporated in the consolidated Building Regulations 1972). Timber framed houses having comparatively lightweight walls and floors provide sound transmission losses better than the very heavy *deemed to satisfy* brick and block constructions given in the Regulations - contrary to general impressions. A transmission loss of 55 db for a timber framed and 32 mm plasterboard lined party wall compared very favourably with the 50 db average obtained from an 11in brick wall plastered both sides

Compartment floors

Similarly with compartment floors between flats and maisonettes. Development work carried out by British Gypsum Ltd. and TRADA has resulted in a number of timber floor constructions able to provide sound insulation (both airborne and impact) to meet the requirements given for the *deemed to satisfy* floors in the Regulation but at a fraction of the weight per unit area. Sand pugging, at one time thought to be an essential ingredient of compartment floors between flats, has been superceded by additional layers of plasterboard and by the use of resilient means of attachment, British Gypsum's Resilient Bar is one such system.

Solid concrete ground floors are very widely used today but they have their limitations and drawbacks. In connection with intermittent heating systems they are *heat sinks*. That is to say they absorb heat in attempting to attain the building's internal air temperature and, in fact, probably seldom, if ever, attain it. Conversely suspended timber floors of inherently low mass do not absorb nearly so much heat and thus are better suited to intermittent heating systems.

Suspended ground floors

TRADA is encouraging the use of suspended timber ground floors and will shortly have available a detailed account of an investigation into overseas practice of building suspended timber ground floors without the traditional British oversite concrete beneath. Such floors (a variation of the traditional Scottish *deemed to satisfy* one), include either

a) a layer of stout polythene laid over the site area as a ground cover - to prevent rising damp   or

b) a floor system of fully impregnated timbers which is durable without the need for a ground cover.

The latter system is eminently suitable for sloping sites. It eliminates the need for back filling and consolidation beneath a concrete slab and so obviates the risk of slab settlement said by NHBRC to be the biggest single cause of structural failure. Both systems employ deeper joists to cover greater spans and the resultant reduction in sleeper walls aids economy. In an era of continually rising building costs these methods of reducing them should prove of considerable interest to developers.

Clay Products

H.W.H. West, BSc FGS FICeram

Head of the Heavy Clay Division and Officer-in-Charge of the Mellor-Green Laboratories, British Ceramic Research Station

Introduction

The chapter on Clay Products in the last edition of this Handbook covered the years 1965-1970 and this present article brings the record up to April 1973. It thus ends immediately before the Third International Brick Masonry Conference which is to be held in Essen, W. Germany in that month. While the full list of papers to be given is not known, with great interest, world-wide, in brick masonry as an engineering material is exemplified by the major conferences held on this subject. The first international meeting was held in Austin, Texas, in 1968, (1), and the second in England in 1970, (2), thus establishing a three year pattern with the British Ceramic Society Symposia on Load-Bearing Brickwork (3,4,5) interposed between them.

Production

In production on the contrary, although some new products and processes are mentioned below, the accent has been very much on the financial implications of production processes, so that there has been a continuation of the rationalization process begun in the sixties and an increasing interest in productivity, both by mechanization *per se* (6) and by improved understanding of management problems. These problems are partly due to fluctuating demand, which affects the efficiency of production or involves high cost in handling, waste and idle capital when stocking is necessary, and no unique solution can be offered (7). This apart, however, in many countries there is an increasing awareness of the need to justify the heavy capital investment which modern factories demand (8). This leads immediately to consideration of three-shift working (9) but raises social issues and safety issues (10) which are difficult to resolve.

Nevertheless the accent is still on efficient, modern processes to yield a product of clearly defined and more nearly constant properties but great variety of colour and texture, which will satisfy the engineering and aesthetic demands of the construction industry.

LOAD-BEARING BRICKWORK

The increased knowledge of the behaviour of walls and structures has necessitated more frequent revision of the relevant Code of Practice, CP3, *Structural Recommendations for Load-Bearing Walls*. The first version in 1946 was not revised until 1964, that was amended and finally superseded by the Metric version CP3:Part 2:1970, (11) and this was subsequently extensively amended in June 1971. A limit state version is currently being written so that a further edition must follow shortly.

209

Testing

There has been increasing sophistication in the experimentation, so that while in 1964 wall testing was just beginning, now the British Ceramic Research Association (BCRA) and three large brick companies have crushed over 2000 storey-height walls by both axial and eccentric loading. The results have, for example, demonstrated the effect of wall ties on the compressive strength of cavity walls (12), described the performance of modular bricks (13), and compared grouted cavity and solid constructions (14).

Some notable load-bearing brickwork structures have been erected in the UK, the highest being nineteen storeys (15), and an interesting use of the interaction of deep brick panels and reinforced concrete beams has been described (16). The increased height of brick buildings and the use of panels of brickwork in reinforced concrete framed structures leads to higher stresses on damp-proof courses and a number of commonly used materials have been examined in the laboratory (17). An examination of creep in brickwork with and without dpc has been started (18).

Interest has moved from testing walls in compression to testing full scale structures. The Quarry Facility at Edinburgh University which permits structures up to five-storeys high to be tested has provided information on shear resistance (19) which has been subsequently incorporated in a revision of CP3. The requirement under the amended Building Regulations that structures of five storeys and more should remain stable following the removal of a specified length of load-bearing wall has been tested directly in the simple five-storey quarry structure (20) which was shown to be adequate. The 'alternative path' bridging solution was the preferred design method originally put forward (21) and a theoretical analysis of the possibility of progressive collapse in a number of high-rise and low-rise brickwork structures representative of modern building design has been assessed (22).

Gas explosions

Although these new Building Regulations concern the removal of support by an "incident" a gas explosion remains the most likely cause (23). Work has continued at the BCRA Explosion Test Facility at Potters Marston in conjunction with the Gas Council. The results of gas explosions, both natural and town gas, show that brickwork has remarkable competence and that gas explosions achieving pressures of more than 3½ lbf/in² (24.1 kN/m²) are very difficult to generate so that only under the most contrived conditions in the bunkers, and then only with town gas, can 5 lbf/in² (34.5 kN/m²) be achieved. The experiments are continuing and conditions which damage the building have been established (24, 25).

The resistance to pressures either from impact or explosion is provided by the lateral strength of the brickwork under varying degrees of precompression depending upon the head load from the weight of the structure at that point (26). In consequence there has been increasing interest in the lateral load resistance of walls generally measured by using an air-bag to provide the horizontal load while the precompression is applied by a standard wall frame (27). A simple but adequate theory has been proposed for the elementary case of a wall without returns (28) and a more elaborate one for a wall with a return at one or both ends (29).

Windloads

The lateral load resistance of walls is also important in the case of wind loads. A new Code of Practice has been published (30) and the implications in structural design discussed (31). Nevertheless very little information is available concerning walls with little or no precompression to increase the resistance although there are many examples in practice, - free standing walls, walls in framed buildings (especially with clerestorey windows above and fenestration at the sides). In America very thin walls have been used in areas where precipitation is not high (32) usually prefabricated without reinforcement but using mortars of high tensile strength (33). Such mortars are also claimed to give good resistance to rain penetration through the joints, which is where it normally first occurs in brickwork, especially in the perpends, and there are differences in this respect between conventional mortars using different plasticizers (34). Another development in America has been the use of grouted cavity construction which has advantages in very high buildings, especially in seismic areas (35).

The factors of safety in CP3 take account of the possibility of bad workmanship. The 9 in cube test has not been widely used, and a 5-high prism is preferred in America. 4-high prisms are specified in the Australian Code (36), but despite the enthusiasm of the protagonists of these various specimens, it still seems that the best guide to the eventual wall strength remains the strength of the bricks and the composition of the mortar. Attempts can be made to minimize the effects of bad workmanship; the Model Specification has been extensively used and has now been revised in metric form (37).

Labour and mechanisation

Some concern has been expressed over a shortage of bricklayers in times of high demand. While it is difficult to establish the magnitude of this shortage it is undeniable that bricklaying wage rates have risen considerably though load-bearing brick structures can still be remarkably competitive. Nevertheless in most countries there is increasing interest in methods of improving bricklaying productivity or even eliminating the bricklayer completely, though nowhere have prefabricated brick panels been outstandingly successful. The most promising method is essentially a bricklaying aid, a *travelling scaffold* with continuously adjustable height, bricks to hand and mortar piped from a container under pressure so that the bed joint can be laid while travelling across the panel at up to 100 ft per minute (38). The bricks are put in place using a similar technique to the *push* method, a modified method of laying which was evolved as the result of a complete study of bricklaying productivity (39). In South Africa a new machine takes all the craft out of bricklaying by vibrating bricks to the predetermined line and level.

NEW PRODUCTS AND PROCESSES

Metric products

The most important development has been the change to metric dimensions and the availability of bricks in the modular work sizes 290 x 90 x 90 and 190 x 90 x 90 mm together with the architecturally preferred variants 290 x 90 x 65 and 190 x 90 x 65 mm. The metric British Standard brick (40) has a work size of 215 x 102.5 x 65 mm which, with a 10 mm mortar joint, gives a format size of 225 x 112.5 x 75 mm which enables it to course approximately with the Old Imperial brick (9 x 4½ x 3 in format size) for alterations and extensions to existing buildings and also fit the curious modular dimensional framework imposed by the recommended storey-height of 2.6 m. There has been considerable debate on the economic and other advantages of modular bricks but no clear cut quantitative information except for data provided by the Greater London Council (41). However a Draft for Development for modular bricks is now under publication by the British Standards Institution, and a large scale experiment in comparing metric and metric modular bricks is being undertaken by collaboration between the Brick Development Association and the Department of the Environment.

Processing

In processing, the chief interest seems to have been in faster drying and firing to make better use of expensive capital resources. A new development is the shuttle kiln which provides considerable flexibility. It has been particularly successful for the firing of blue bricks by gas to enable reducing conditions to be achieved without the dark smoke inevitably associated with coal firing, but which contravenes the Clean Air Act. Indeed there is a very considerable literature concerned with pollution, both smoke and sulphur dioxide etc., and the greatest single recent process change has been the substitution of natural gas or liquefied petroleum gas for firing heavy clay products. It was first used experimentally on intermittent kilns, rapidly adopted for tunnel kilns but now even continuous Hoffmann and transverse arch kilns have been modified and conversion was the subject of a special symposium (42).

Almost all the processes of brickmaking can be mechanized but the problem of removing fired bricks from tunnel kiln cars automatically has been a source of difficulty because the setting shrinks and moves during the firing process so the accurate location of the 'unsetting' head is not easy. However, now two types of 'de-hacker' are available in America and are a further means of reducing the labour cost of brickmaking while providing the sorted strapped packs that the user has come to demand.

Improvements in the consistency of the product continue to be made in clay pipes. A new standard has been drafted for chemically resistant pipes and for the first time factory-made flexible joints have been standardized (43). Packaging of deliveries has been improved and a system of unloading packs of pipes and conduits from a trailer, by a fork-lift device on the lorry prime mover, has been introduced (44).

Mechanization of the casting of sanitary ware has also taken place with the aim of reducing the number of moulds in use and minimizing the labour required (45). The pressure casting process is a further development in which the same mould may be used immediately after the cast is released (46).

Three years ago it was suggested in this Handbook that the needs of the user would become increasingly important, and nothing has occurred since to change that view. Indeed it has been reinforced by the efforts of the clay building materials industries to maintain their economic advantages in the face of steadily increasing costs from labour, not only within their own plants but also on site both above and below ground.

REFERENCES

1. Johnson, F.B. (ed) (1969) "Designing Engineering and Constructing with Masonry Products" (Houston: Gulf Publishing Co.)
2. West H.W.H. and Speed K.H. (eds) Proc of the Second International Brick Masonry Conference (Stoke-on-Trent: British Ceramic Research Association)

3. *Proc. Brit. Ceram. Soc.,* **11**, (1968).

4. *Proc. Brit. Ceram. Soc.,* **17**, (1970).

5. *Proc. Brit. Ceram. Soc.,* **21**, (1973).

6. West H.W.H. (1970) "Mechanization of the Manufacture of Clay Bricks" *Automation in production, sampling and testing of silicate materials* (London: Soc. Chem. Ind.)

7. Bekker P.C.F. (1972) "Determination of Optimum Production Capacity in the Heavy Clay Industry with Sales Subject to Variation" *Spechsaal* **105**, (1), 3.

8. Hiebel R. (1972) "Reflections on Investment." *Terre Cuite* (53), 2.

9. Enhus H.G. (1971) "A Three-shift Operation in Sweden." *Ziegelindustrie* (**4**), 174.

10. Leitl K. (1971) "Continuous Operation: Technical, Econimic and Psychological Aspects." *Ziegelindustri* (**4**), 166.

11. British Standards Institution (1970) Structural Recommendations for Load-bearing Walls, CP3: Part 2: (London: BSI)

12. Fisher K. " The Effect of Wall Ties on the Compressive Strength of Cavity Walls," Ref 2, p 117.

13. Beech D.G. and West H.W.H. (1973) "The Performance of Modular Bricks in Storey-Height Walls" *Proc. Brit. Ceram. Soc.,* **21**.

14. Beard R. (1973) "The Compressive Strength of Some Grouted Cavity Walls," *Proc Brit. Ceram. Soc.,* **21**.

15. Haseltine B.A. and Au Y.T. "Design and Construction of a Nineteen-Storey Load-Bearing Brick Building." Ref 2, p 282.

16. Buckton G. "Modern Development Utilizing the Interaction of Deep Brick Panels and Reinforced Concrete Beams to Support Multi-storey Construction." Ref 2, p 331.

17. Plowman J.M. and Smith W.F. "The Selection of Damp-Proof-Course Material for Load-Bearing Structures." Ref 2, p 80.

18. Lenczner D. "Creep in Brickwork." Ref 2, P 44.

19. Hendry A.W. and Sinha B.P. (1971) "Shear Tests on Full Scale Single-Storey Brickwork." Structures Subjected to Precompression. *Civil Engineering.* **66**, (12), 1339.

20. Sinha B.P. and Hendry A.W. (1971) "The Stability of a Five-Storey Brickwork Cross-Wall" Structure Following the Removal of a Section of a Main Load-bearing Wall. J. *Inst. Struct. Engrs.* **49**(10), 46.

21. Adams, H.C. "The Design of Brickwork Against Gas Explosions". Ref. 2 p. 273.

22. Morton, J., Davies, S.R. and Hendry, A.W. "The Stability of Load-bearing Brickwork Structures Following Accidental Damage to a Major Bearing Wall or Pier". Ref. 2 p. 276.

23. West, H.W.H. and Haseltine, B.A. (1971) "The Effect of Unusual Hazards on Structures". *10th Ann. Conf. Incorporated Assoc. of Architects and Surveyors,* Southport.

24. Astbury, N.F., West, H.W.H. and Hodgkinson, H.R. "Experiments to Determine the Resistance of Brick Buildings to Gas Explosions". Ref. 2 p. 220.

25. Astbury, N.F., West, H.W.H. and Hodgkinson, H.R. (1973) "Experimental Gas Explosions – Report of Further Tests at Potters Marston". *Proc. Brit. Ceram. Soc.* 21.

26. West. H.W.H. and Hodgkinson, H.R. (1972) "The Resistance of Brick Walls to Lateral Loading". NBS Spec. Pub. 361, Vol. 1 *Performance Concept in Buildings* Philadelphia, Penn.

27. Nilsson, I.H.E. and Losberg, A. "The Strength of Horizontally Loaded Prefabricated Brick Panel Walls. Ref. 2 p. 191.

28. West, H.W.H., Hodgkinson, H.R. and Webb, W.F. (1973) "The Resistance of Brick Walls to Lateral Loading". *Proc. Brit. Ceram. Soc.* 21.

29. Hendry, A.W., Sinha, B.P. and Mauren Brecher, A.H.P. (1973) "Full Scale Tests on the Lateral Strength of Brick Cavity Walls with Precompression". *Proc. Brit. Ceram. Soc.* 21.

30. British Standards Institution (1970) *Wind Loads,* C.P.3, Chapter V, Loading Part 2.

31. Anon (1971) "The New Code of Practice for Wind Loads and its Implications for the Structural Design Codes". *Struct. Engn.* **49**, (2), 98.

32. Anon (1968) "Four-inch Bearing Walls Soar Higher and Higher". *Brick Clay Rec.* **155**, (5), 50.

33. Grenley, D.G. and Terzes, J.G. "University Centre Project, Austin, Texas". Ref. 2, p. 353.

34. Skeen, J.W. (1971) "Experiments on the Rain Penetration of Brickwork". *Trans. and J. Brit. Ceram. Soc.* **70**, (1), 27.

35. Sallada, J.W. and Wakefield, D.A. "Park Lane Towers Complex, Denver, Colorado". Ref. 2 p. 343.

36. Anderson, G.W. "Stack-bonded Small Specimens as Design and Construction Criteria". Ref. 2 p. 38.

37. British Ceramic Research Association (1971) "Model Specification for Load-bearing Clay Brickwork". *B. Ceram. R.A. Spec. Pub. 56 (Revised Edition, Metric).*

38. Svec, J.J. and Jeffers, P.E. (eds) (1952) "Brick Panel Factory Multiplies Masonry Productivity". *Modern Masonry Panel Construction Systems.* (Boston : Cahmers).

39. Mortlock, D.J. and Whitehead, B. (1970) "Productivity in Brick and Block Construction — A Literature Survey". *Bldg. Sci.* **4**, 179.

40. British Standards Institution (1969) "Bricks and Blocks of Fired Brickearth, Clay or Shale. Part 2. Metric Units". *B.S: 3921: Part 2.*

41. Greater London Council (1971) "Work with Imperial, Metric and Modular Bricks- A Cost Comparison". *Development and Materials Bulletin* (50), (2nd Series), Item 1.

42. Beech, D.G. and West, H.W.H., (eds) (1971) *Gas Firing.* (Stoke-on-Trent: BCRA).

43. British Standards Institution (1972) "Clay Drain and Sewer Pipes Including Surface Water Pipes and Fittings. Part 2: Flexible Mechanical Joints". *B.S. 65 and 540: Part 2.*

44. Anon (1972) "Hepworth Iron Introduces Driver-Operated Clay Pipe Transporter". *Claycraft* **45**, (2), 16.

45. Pfuhl, H. (1969) "Rationalization and Mechanization in the Ceramic Sanitary-Ware Industry — Assembly-line Casting of W.C. Basins. *Keram.* **21**, (11), 734.

46. British Ceramic Research Association (1970) *Cast Ceramic Articles.* Brit. Pat. 1,205,952.

Part 2

Properties of
Building Materials

Environmental
Design Data

Information
Sources in the
Construction Industry

The Metric System

The metric system of measurement is now in common use throughout the construction industry. Part 2 of this Handbook is therefore preceded by a brief guide to the system and a set of metric conversion tables.

Background

The first metric system originated in France in the latter part of the eighteenth century. A group of scientists decided that the basic unit of length was to be one ten-millionth of the distance between the Equator and the North Pole on the meridian passing through Paris. This rather crude definition of the *metre* was later defined between two scatches on a bar of platinum kept at a constant temperature at Sevres. But in 1960 the metre was redefined for all time in terms of the wavelength of the radiation emitted due to a specific electronic transition in the krypton-86 atom. Over the years there have been several derivative metric systems, but in 1954 the General Conference of Weights and Measures agreed upon the 'Systeme Internationale d'Unites' *(SI Units)*

The SI System

The SI system is completely decimal. All multiples and sub-multiples (decimal fractions) of units are powers of ten and the names given to the various multiples and sub-multiples are applicable to all units (e.g. 1 kilometre equals 1000 metres and 1 kilowatt equals 1000 watts). The commonly used multiples and sub-multiples are listed below.

Multiples

		Name	Symbol
10^6	= 1 000 000	mega	M
10^3	= 1 000	kilo	k
10^2	= 100	hecto	h
10^1	= 10	deca	da

Sub-multiples

		Name	Symbol
10^{-1}	= 0·1	deci	d
10^{-2}	= 0·01	centi	c
10^{-3}	= 0·001	milli	m
10^{-6}	= 0·000 001	micro	μ

(nb, 10^0 = 1)

The SI system has six basic units. They are as follows:

	Unit	Symbol
1. Length	metre	m
2. Mass	kilogramme	kg
3. Time	second	s
4. Electric current	ampere	A
5. Thermodynamic temperature[1]	degree Kelvin	K
6. Luminous intensity	candela	cd

[1] The practical unit for temperature is the degree Celsius (°C).

Derived Units

Not only is the SI system completely decimal, it is also coherent. This means that the product or quotient of any two units in the system (e.g. mass multiplied by acceleration to give force or distance divided by time to give velocity) is the unit of the resultant quantity. Derived units therefore follow logically from the basic units as the following examples will illustrate.

Velocity. This is the ratio of distance travelled to time taken:

$$\text{velocity} = \frac{\text{distance}}{\text{time}} = \frac{\text{metres}}{\text{seconds}} = \text{m/s}$$

Acceleration. This is the ratio of velocity change to time:

$$\text{acceleration} = \frac{\text{velocity change}}{\text{time}} = \frac{\text{m/s}}{\text{s}} = \text{m/s}^2$$

Force. Newton's second law of motion defines that the absolute value of a force is equal to the acceleration it is able to give to a body multiplied by the mass of the body:

$$\text{force} = \text{mass} \times \text{acceleration}$$
$$= \text{kilogrammes} \times \text{m/s}^2$$
$$= \text{kg m/s}^2$$

This unit of force is defined as one *newton* (symbol N), i.e. $1 \text{ N} = 1 \text{ kg m/s}^2$.

Work. The work done by a force is defined as the force multiplied by the distance through which it operates:

$$\text{work} = \text{force} \times \text{distance} = \text{kg m/s}^2 \times \text{m}$$
$$= \text{kg m}^2/\text{s}^2$$

The work done by a force of one newton in moving through one metre is defined as one *joule* (symbol J), i.e. $1 \text{ J} = 1 \text{ kg m}^2/\text{s}^2$.

SI Conversions

The following tables give the SI equivalents of the commonly encountered non-SI units. An asterisk against a unit indicates that the conversion is exact. In all other cases the quantities have been approximated to a convenient number of decimal places.

1. Length
2. Area
3. Volume
4. Second moment of area
5. Velocity
6. Acceleration
7. Mass
8. Mass per unit length
9. Mass per unit area
10. Volume rate of flow
11. Density
12. Force
13. Force per unit length
14. Moment of force
15. Pressure, stress
16. Viscosity (dynamic)
17. Viscosity (kinematic)
18. Energy
19. Power
20. Heat flow rate
21. Specific energy, calorific value
22. Thermal capacity
23. Intensity of heat flow rate
24. Thermal conductance
25. Thermal conductivity
26. Thermal resistivity
27. Lighting
28. Cost per unit

1. Length

1 in	=	25·4 mm*
1 ft	=	0·304 8 m*
1 yd	=	0·914 4 m*
1 mile	=	1·609 344 km*
1 micron	=	10^{-6} m*
1 Å (angstrom)	=	10^{-10} m*

2. Area

1 in²	=	645·16 mm² *
1 ft²	=	0·092 903 m²
1 yd²	=	0·836 127 m²
1 acre	=	4046·86 m²
1 sq mile	=	2·589 99 km²

3. Volume

1 in³	=	$16·387\ 1 \times 10^3$ mm³
1 ft³	=	0·028 316 8 m³
1 yd³	=	0·764 555 m³
1 fl oz	=	$28·413\ 1 \times 10^3$ mm³
1 pint	=	$0·568\ 261 \times 10^{-3}$ m³
1 UK gal	=	$4·546\ 09 \times 10^{-3}$ m³
1 US gal	=	$3·785\ 41 \times 10^{-3}$ m³
1 litre	=	10^{-3} m³

4. Second moment of area

1 in⁴	=	$0·416\ 231 \times 10^{-6}$ m⁴
1 ft⁴	=	$8·630\ 97 \times 10^{-3}$ m⁴

5. Velocity

1 ft/min	=	5·08 mm/s*	
1 in/s	=	25·4 mm/s*	
1 ft/s	=	0·304 8 m/s	= 1·097 28 km/h*
1 mile/h	=	0·447 04 m/s	= 1·609 344 km/h*

6. Acceleration

1 ft/s²	=	0·304 8 m/s² *
Standard gravity	=	9·806 65 m/s² *

7. Mass

1 oz	=	0·028 349 5 kg
1 lb	=	0·453 592 37 kg*
1 cwt	=	50·802 3 kg
1 ton	=	1016·05 kg = 1·016 05 tonne

8. Mass per unit length

1 lb/in	=	17·858 0 kg/m
1 lb/ft	=	1·488 16 kg/m
1 ton/mile	=	0·631 342 kg/m

9. Mass per unit area

1 lb/in²	=	703·070 kg/m²
1 lb/ft²	=	4·882 43 kg/m²
1 ton/sq mile	=	392·298 kg/km²

10. Volume rate of flow

1 UK gal/h	=	0·004 546 09 m³/h
1 ft³/s	=	0·028 316 m³/s

11. Density

1 lb/in³	=	$27·679\ 9 \times 10^3$ kg/m³
1 lb/ft³	=	16·018 5 kg/m³
1 ton/yd³	=	$1·328\ 94 \times 10^3$ kg/m³
1 lb/gal	=	99·776 3 kg/m³ = 0·099 78 kg/litre
1 g/cm³	=	1000 kg/m³ *

12. Force

1 lbf	=	4·448 22 N
1 tonf	=	9·964 02 kN
1 kgf = 1 kp (kilopond)	=	9·806 65 N*
1 dyn	=	10^{-5} N*

13. Force per unit length

1 lbf/in	=	0·175 127 N/mm
1 lbf/ft	=	14·593 9 N/m
1 tonf/ft	=	32·690 3 kN/m
1 kgf/m	=	9·806 65 N/m*
1 dyn/cm (surface tension)	=	10^{-3} N/m*

14. Moment of force

1 lbf in	=	0·112 985 N m
1 lbf ft	=	1·355 82 N m
1 tonf ft	=	3·037 03 kN m
1 kgf m	=	9·806 65 N m*

15. Pressure, stress

1 lbf/in²	=	6·894 76 kN/m²
1 lbf/ft²	=	47·880 3 N/m²
1 tonf/in²	=	15·444 3 MN/m²
1 tonf/ft²	=	107·252 kN/m²
1 kgf/cm²	=	98·066 5 kN/m² *
1 dyn/cm²	=	10^{-1} N/m² *
1 bar	=	10^5 N/m² *
1 inH₂O	=	249·089 N/m²
1 mmH₂O	=	9·806 65 N/m² *
1 inHg	=	3386·39 N/m²
1 mmHg	=	133·322 N/m²
1 standard atmosphere	=	101·325 kN/m² *

16. Viscosity (dynamic)

1 lbf s/ft²	=	47·880 3 N s/m²
1 kgf s/m²	=	9·806 65 N s/m² *
1 dyn s/cm²	=	100 cP (centipoise) = 0·1 N s/m² *

17. Viscosity (kinematic)

1 ft²/s	=	0·092 903 m²/s
1 cm²/s	=	100 cSt (centistokes) = 10^{-4} m²/s*

18. Energy

1 therm = 10^5 Btu	=	105·506 MJ
1 Btu	$\doteq$	1·055 06 kJ
1 cal (International table calorie)	=	4·186 8 J*
1 ft lbf	=	1·355 82 J
1 kgf m	=	9·806 65 J*
1 erg	=	10^{-7} J*
1 kWh	=	3·6 MJ*

19. Power

1 ft lbf/s	=	1·355 82 W (J/s)
1 kgf m/s	=	9·806 65 W*
1 hp	=	745·700 W

20. Heat flow rate

1 Btu/h	=	0·293 071 W (J/s)
1 cal/s	=	4·186 8 W*

21. Specific energy, calorific value

1 Btu/lb	=	2·326 kJ/kg*
1 cal/g	=	4·186 8 kJ/kg*
1 Btu/gal	=	232·080 kJ/m³
1 Btu/ft³	=	37·258 9 kJ/m³
1 kcal/m³	=	4·186 8 kJ/m³ *

22. Thermal capacity

1 Btu/lb °F	=	4·186 8 kJ/kg °C*
1 Btu/ft³ °F	=	67·066 1 kJ/m³ °C
1 cal/g °C	=	4·186 8 kJ/kg °C*
1 cal/cm³ °C	=	4·186 8 MJ/m³ °C*

23. Intensity of heat flow rate

1 Btu/ft² h	=	3·154 59 W/m² (J/m² s)
1 cal/cm² s	=	41·868 kW/m² (kJ/m² s)*

24. Thermal conductance

1 Btu/ft² h °F	=	5·678 26 W/m² °C (J/m² s °C)
1 cal/cm² s °C	=	41·868 kW/m² °C (kJ/m² s °C)*

25. Thermal conductivity

1 Btu ft/ft² h °F	=	1·730 73 W/m °C (J m/m² s °C)
1 Btu in/ft² h °F	=	0·144 228 W/m °C
1 cal cm/cm² s °C	=	418·68 W/m °C*

26. Thermal resistivity

1 ft² h °F/Btu ft	=	0·577 789 m °C/W (m² s °C/J m)
1 ft² h °F/Btu in	=	6·933 47 m °C/W

27. Lighting

1 lm/ft²	=	10·763 9 lux (lm/m²)
1 cd/ft²	=	10·763 9 cd/m²
1 cd/in²	=	1550·00 cd/m²
1 foot-lambert	=	3·426 26 cd/m²

28. Cost per unit

CU = currency unit

CU/ft	=	3·280 84 CU/m
CU/yd	=	1·093 61 CU/m
CU/mile	=	0·621 371 CU/km
CU/ft²	=	10·763 9 CU/m²
CU/yd²	=	1·195 99 CU/m²
CU/acre	=	247·105 CU/km²

CU/ft³	=	35·314 7 CU/m³
CU/yd³	=	1·307 95 CU/m³
CU/UK gal	=	0·220 0 CU/litre
CU/lb	=	2·204 62 CU/kg
CU/cwt	=	19·684 1 CU/tonne
CU/ton	=	0·984 204 CU/tonne
CU/therm	=	0·034 121 CU/kW h

Properties of Building Materials

Compiled by

H.J. Eldridge, BSc

British member of the CIB Commission on Properties of Building Materials
British member of the CIB Commission on Performance Concepts
Consultant to the Building Research Station
Consultant to the Agrement Board
Formerly Chief Experimental Officer, the Building Research Station.

This listing of the properties of building materials puts into effect the recommendations of the CIB that all building materials properties should be presented in a systematic manner according to an internationally agreed standard method. The result is this uniquely practical section listing the important materials properties in a clear and easily understood manner.

Introduction

The listing of the properties of many building materials was anticipated to be an important feature of the first edition of the Handbook, particularly as it was the first time that this had been done using the system developed by the CIB (Conseil Information du Bâtiment), and this proved to be the case.

The CIB Master List for Materials published in 1964 was a numbered guide to all the possible properties relevant to building materials and general products and provided a systematic basis for the listing of properties of individual materials, being usable also as a check list when compiling data sheets for such materials.

The original List was scheduled for possible revision in 1970. Experience of its use indicated that its scope needed to be widened and, as a result, a major revision was published in 1972 as CIB Report No. 18. The revised scheme consists of five separate Master Lists, one each for Buildings, Building Elements, Components, Materials and Services respectively. The preparation of the Master List for Buildings indicated the desirability of sequencing some of the information on the logical basis that a building should primarily be structurally stable, that it should then be weathertight and comfortably habitable and finally that it should be durable.

This basis has been used throughout, all five lists being structured and numbered similarly, thus making easy any cross-referencing between any of the Lists, e.g. between a building and the materials of which it is constructed. In consequence, there have been a number of changes in the order in which the properties of building materials have been given in the following pages, though little alteration has been required to be made to the information since it was factually correct in the first edition. The opportunity has been taken, however, to unify some of the terms and to make minor corrections.

Obviously only those headings in the Master List relevant to a particular material have been listed for that material. Wherever possible the information has been given in numerical form, though some information has had to be given in the form of minimum values required by the appropriate British Standard. In these latter instances, reference should be made to the individual manufacturer where it is necessary for exact figures to be obtained for, say, specification purposes.

As previously, information has not been provided for paints since the wide range of products makes it very difficult to produce a summary likely to be of any real use.

The information given has been obtained from a number of sources and while every care has been taken to ensure its accuracy, it must be appreciated that materials are often changed in both composition and methods of manufacture and this may result in changes in their properties. The Development Associations representing manufacturers of various groups of building materials are always helpful in providing data on such materials and in giving guidance on their appropriate usage.

H.J. Eldridge.

Although only the special master list for Materials is published in full in this volume, the comments made in the introduction to all the Master Lists by H.J. Eldridge and the other members of the commission are of such importance that they are reproduced here:

Guiding principles

The title of the 1964 edition (which appeared in the first edition of the Construction Industry Handbook) was: A master list of properties for building materials and products. The master list provided a comprehensive set of headings for information on properties and its main use has been in the preparation of product data sheets. The 1964 edition has been adapted for other purposes including preparation of performance specifications.

The title of the 1972 edition is: The CIB MASTER LISTS for structuring documents relating to buildings, building elements, components, materials, and services. For the 1972 edition CIB Commission W 31 decided:

i) To issue five separate Master Lists for buildings, building elements, components, materials, and building services, but not to issue a separate Master List for construction machinery and plant at present.

ii) To structure the five Master Lists on a common Basic List for easy cross-reference.

iii) To use the word 'product' to describe a building as well as the building elements, components, materials, and service which together make up the building.

iv) To provide explanatory notes on the headings used.

v) To take into account the possible use of a Master List for preparing documents other than product data sheets, for example, performance specifications.

Comparison between the main headings of the 1964 list and the 1972 basic list

The 1972 Basic List is given ih an Appendix on page 51. For easy comparison the main headings of the 1964 list and the 1972 Basic List are set out below in parallel columns.

1972 edition	1964 edition
0 Document, Scope and Information for Indexing	
1 Identification	1.1 General Information
2 Description	1.2 Composition, Method of Manufacture
	1.3 Shape, Dimensions, Weight
	1.4 General Appearance
3 Climate, Site and Occupancy Conditions	
4 Characteristics Relating to Behaviour in Use and Working	1.5 Physical, Chemical, and Biological Properties
	1.6 Durability
	1.7 Special Technical Properties
	1.8 Working Characteristics
	1.9 Functional Properties (part)
5 Applications, Design	2 Design Considerations and Details, Suitable Applications (main part)
	4 Economics (part)
6 Sitework	3.1 Working Instructions
	3.2 Site Testing
7 Operation and Maintenance	3.3 Instructions for Cleaning and Maintenance
8 Prices and Conditions of Sale	4 Economics (part)
	6 Sales Organization. Contract Work. Technical Service. (part)
9 Supply	5 Specification of Distribution
10 Technical Services	6 Sales Organization. Contract Work. Technical Service (part)

Attention is drawn to five significant changes:

i) The introduction of a new main heading 0 Document, Scope and information for indexing.

ii) The use of 1 Identification, for headings required in summarising contents of a document and identifying other closely related documents.

iii) The introduction of a new main heading 3 Climate, Site and Occupancy Conditions, to provide a place for information about conditions which could affect the behaviour of a building, or its parts.

iv) The bringing together of 4 Characteristics relating to Behaviour in use and Working, and the introduction of headings which group or collate information required for convenience to be considered together, for example: 4, 12 Side effects.

v) The inclusion in 5 Applications, Design, of information needed when considering economic suitability.

Commentary on the main sections

Matters of general significance only are noted here; more detailed comments will be found in the explanatory notes contained in the five Master Lists. Main headings have been selected to give a common structure to the five Lists, but the importance given to a main heading, and its use, will depend on the purpose of a particular document.

All documents should draw on: 0 Document, Scope and information for indexing, and 1 Identification. Headings under these Sections are meant to ensure that sufficient information is given early in a document to enable a reader to judge with ease its purpose and scope, to check date of publication, validity, authenticity, etc and if need be to file the document for later use.

Sections 2-7 provide headings for information about a product including the conditions in which it is to be, or has been, used. By no means all the headings are relevant to any one product, nor will all the headings be needed in every document. There will be some uses in which very few of the headings will be used. All the headings could have been subdivided in greater detail, but this has not been done to avoid Lists becoming cumbersome. Each heading can be regarded as a 'box' within which all information relevant to an item can be placed. In a data bank using a computer the amount of information stored would be considerable. In a document for practical use it might be limited to a few words.

2 Description, lists headings needed to give 'intrinsic' information about a product either as it is initially erected (eg as a building, building element or service) or as delivered to the site (eg as a component or material). Only when it is necessary to fix a constraint, such as size, weight, or appearance, will headings from this Section be used in performance documents.

3 Climate, Site and Occupancy Conditions, gives headings for documents which are required to include information about factors which may affect behaviour of a product in a specific location or for an identified use. For products which have a wide range of uses general information about use will have been given at 1.03.

4 Characteristics relating to Behaviour in use and Working, includes headings given at 1.5 - 1.9 in the 1964 edition.
These headings are now gruped more logically. They are related in turn to the functional characteristics of a building and its parts, namely strength, stability, safety, habitability, and durability. Headings fall into two groups: a main group, Characteristics relating to Behaviour in use; and Working characteristics. At the end of the first group, Characteristics relating to Behaviour in use, durability* and reliability** have been introduced to draw attention to factors to be considered together when giving information on the performance of a product over a period of time.

Under working characteristics are grouped items which may affect behaviours of a product during handling and working in factory or site, or in maintenance work. Except for materials the information given under this heading may not be great. It has, therefore, not been subdivided to the same degree of detail as Behaviour in use. Information regarding instructions for carrying out work should be given under Section 6, not here. Similarly information regarding instructions relating to maintenance should be given under Section. 7.

Headings under 5 Applications, Design, relate to information needed when considering the suitability of a product. It also provides a starting point for documents which deal with requirements such as performance specifications. Here 1.03 helps also to define the scope of the document, 1.04 to identify related documentation, and Section 3 information about conditions of use.

6 Sitework gives headings for instructions which will mainly be required by the builder. The headings can also be used for instructions relating to subsequent alterations and to demolition work.

7 Operation and Maintenance provides headings for instructions to building owners and others responsible for the operation and maintenance of a completed building and its services.

8 Prices and Conditions of Sale, 9 Supply, and 10 Technical Services, provide headings for use when giving commercial and similar information.

11 References provide headings relating to additional sources of information where required.

The Five Master Lists

Buildings are constructed in many different ways. They may be constructed in situ from materials - bricks, concrete, timber, etc - which can be used in various ways to form buildings meeting quite different requirements. On the other hand a building may be brought to the site fully prefabricated and only requiring to be mounted on prepared foundations and connected to services. It could even be an inflatable structure needing only level ground, an air pump and a source of energy.

---

* Durability. A measure of the resistance of a material to wear and physico-chemical change under specified conditions of use and/or storage.
** Reliability. The ability of an item to perform a required function under stated conditions for a stated period of time.
These definitions are according to EOQC (European Organization for Quality Control, Rotterdam) Glossary 1972

Many buildings are constructed partly of prefabricated elements (designed for a specified function), partly of components (serving a wider range of uses but still having recognisable functions) and partly of materials (having many different uses).

Services may be provided as an integral part of a building, or building element, or may be installed quite separately. A service may be installed as a complete prefabricated unit, or be formed from standard components and materials like pipes and cables manipulated and assembled on site.

The Commission considered the publication of a single Master List covering all products but rejected the idea for two reasons. First, the terms used for properties and characteristics change when considering information at different levels. Second, the detail required varies considerably from level to level, as does the content of the explanatory notes. It decided, as noted earlier, to structure the five Master Lists on a common Basic List and to publish the Lists in one volume.

1 **Buildings:** both for prefabricated buildings and buildings when complete however constructed.

2 **Building Elements:** both for completely prefabricated units like prefabricated walls and floor-ceiling constructions, and elements like external and internal walls, roof structures, etc, however constructed.

3 **Components:** products with one or more expressed purposes, eg a window, a precast concrete inspection chamber, or a water pump.

4 **Materials:** both for materials such as ready mixed concrete and paint which only acquire their final form and characteristics after being moulded or spread, and shaped materials like bricks, tiles, sections, pipes and sheets which are usually cut, fixed or otherwise manipulated on site. A material will often have many uses.

5 **Services:** for systems whose function is to transfer energy, gases, liquids, solids, etc. eg space heating, air handling, waste water disposal, mechanical refuse handling, lifts and elevators.

The product area covered by each Master List, as described above, is broadly that which is commonly recognized in the building industry, though the definitions of building elements and components are slightly different from those of the SfB system of CIB Report No.22.

It was decided not to prepare at present a sixth Master List for construction machinery and plant. Instead the use experimentally of the Master List for services for this group of products is recommended.

There will be occasions when a user may find some difficulty in deciding which is the most appropriate List to use. Because the Lists have been structured on a common Basic List, there is unlikely to be any serious disadvantage in selecting a wrong List. However, it is suggested that List 1 should be used where the three-dimensional 'space enclosing' features of a products are important; List 2 where the product is large and complex, parts of it being designed to satisfy particular functional requirements; and

List 3 where limitations are set on uses of the product by the fact that certain features have been selected to meet an expressed requirement. List 5 will be used for services involving electrical, mechanical or hydraulic equipment.

Application of the Master Lists

The 1972 Master Lists provide headings for a range of documents including:

1   Description of products, including complex products such as a building.

2   Information relating to their manipulation, assembly and erection, including working instructions for builders.

3   Information and instructions on operation and maintenance.

4   Commercial information relating to purchase and delivery; tender documents.

5   Cost information on the construction and maintenance of buildings including services.

6   Statements of requirements of users, owners, designers and authorities, including performance specifications.

7   Descriptions and systematic lists of methods of assessment and test.

8   Assessment and approval documents including documents of a statutory nature.

9   Descriptive surveys and information about the performance in use of buildings, and/or parts of buildings including services; also information about failures.

10   Checklists for different kinds of work relating to design and construction.

Not all the headings will be required in any one document. In some kinds of document none of the headings in a whole Section will be used though some headings in Sections 0 and 1 will always be needed. Choice of headings will depend on the purpose of a document and the nature of the product or work under consideration, and is a matter for the author's judgement. The terms used may differ somewhat between documents or for different products and are often connected with a specific evaluation method. This may sometimes require in practice slight modifications to a heading as given in a particular Master List.

No date is given for a possible revision. The Commission considers that the basic structure should be satisfactory for a considerable time and that only minor amendments might be required. However, in view of developments which could occur in some fields of application the Commission will review the position periodically.

The Secretariat of Commission W 31, or, where appropriate, the national organisation concerned with the Commission's work will give advice on application of the Master Lists. Difficulties met with should be reported to the Secretariat as experience in use will guide future work of the Commission.

The CIB Master List for Materials

Scope:- Formed materials; for example, bricks, blocks, tiles, pipes, sheets, sections.
Formless materials; for example, cement, aggregates, ready mixed concrete, paints, sealants.

© 1972 International Council for Building Research, Studies and Documentation

0 DOCUMENT, SCOPE AND INFORMATION FOR INDEXING

Information given in this Section will normally be placed at the top of the document for ease of reference.

0.01 Scope of document

The scope, form or category of the document should be expressed in the simplest possible terms, eg Product data sheet, but it may be convenient sometimes for it to be linked with the subject of the document, eg ISO Standard for ....

0.02 Classification

This should preferably be according to a system that is of international significance. The system should be identified if any uncertainty could occur.

0.03 Keywords

These should be selected from the national list of words where this has been prepared. If such a list is not available and it is desired to use the principle of keywords, the words used should be simple and unambiguous.

0.04 Organization responsible for the information given

In some documents the organisation responsible for the information will have been included in 0.01, but where this is not so its name should be stated separately.

0.05 Date of publication and period of validity of the document

The period of validity applies particularly to assessment certificates and price lists, but is also often important for product data sheets.

1 IDENTIFICATION

Information given in this Section is to enable the reader of the document to identify the service material, its purpose and use and for the listing of authoritative documents relating to it.

1.01 Generic name

State here the generic name of the material unless it is incorporated in the trade name, in which case it would be given in 1.02.

1.02 Name of material, type, grade, quality, commodity number, manufacturer

When there are several types or grades of quality of the material these should be stated and identified, but the decision as to whether individual documents are required for the different types will depend upon the significance of the differences and the scope and usage of the documents. If the behaviour in use and other items of information are independent of these differences it will often be more convenient to place all the information in the one document. If several documents are produced they should be identified in Section 11 References.

State the commodity number where this is available. Give the name of the manufacturer or producer of the material, with the address if not recorded in Section 9.

1.03 Short description of the material, its purpose and conditions of use, together with any limitations of use

Generally give only a brief description, sufficient for the readers of the document to judge whether the material is likely to be of use to him, the full details being given in subsequent Sections. It may sometimes be helpful or convenient to refer to the more important properties.

1.04 Related documentation

Statutory (legal) documents
Standards: international, national, industry, manufacturer
Quality and Assessment Certificates
Codes of practice; national specifications

Identify under this heading documents of a legal, official or semi-official nature which are concerned with the material, and documents of a similar nature issued by the manufacturer or producer or their industry associations.

The country of origin of the documents should be identified where this is not that of the material itself. The status of the Standards should be given.

There are various forms of certification or assessment for materials and any appropriate Certificate or Approval should be identified. It may be convenient in some documents to state the terms of certification or approval at this part of the document.

Any quality marks which are applicable should be identified.

Identify documents giving guidance to the use of the material. These may be in the form of Codes of Practice, National Specifications or Notes issued by the particular industry or manufacturer.

2 DESCRIPTION

This Section is designed to contain information relating to the description of the material 'as purchased'. Information relating to handling and working characteristics and to its behaviour in subsequent use should be placed in Section 4.

2.01 Constituents, parts, Composition, type of finish

List the principle raw materials used in the manufacture of the material, unless it is more convenient to include the information in 2.02 when describing the method of manufacture.

If the material is supplied in the fully finished form the type of finish or range of finishes should be stated. If not fully finished or if supplied in the raw state the recommended finish or type of finish should be stated.

2.02 Method of manufacture or production

State here, in as much detail as is relevant for the particular document, the method of manufacture or production of the material.

2.03 Accessory materials

List any materials required for use with the product, eg thinners for paints.

2.04 Shape

The shape may be identified by words, drawings, photographs, etc.

It may be convenient to list ranges of shapes, sizes and weights in a single table, particularly if these variations do not affect other data.

2.05 Size; sections; volume

Record here information concerning the size of the material in whatever form is most appropriate, eg sieve analysis for aggregates, together with specified and actual tolerances.

State the system if the material is supplied for a modularly co-ordinated system.

2.06 Weight

Record the weight of the material in appropriate terms. State the condition, eg moisture content, if this affects the weight. If a range of sizes has been given under 2.05, the corresponding weights should be given.

2.07 Appearance, including texture, colour, pattern, opacity, lustre; feel; smell; taste

The information will normally relate to the material 'as purchased', but for some materials will relate to the applied condition, eg paint and paint films.

Describe, with dimensions when relevant, the appearance and character of the visible faces, arrises, edges and corners of the product.

Colour may be given in terms of words, colour classification systems or by reproductions of the colour. Samples may be fixed to the document to replace or amplify the written description.

Describe any characteristics that are sensed by touch, smell, taste or hearing. Such information will generally be in qualitative terms.

3 CLIMATE, SITE AND OCCUPANCY CONDITIONS

This Section is for the recording of detailed information about the climatic, site or occupancy conditions operating in specific situations. It will not normally be used in product data sheets, information about the conditions specific to the use of the material being given at 1.03 unless it is very detailed.

One possible use of the Section is in documents recording the results of surveys of the behaviour of the material in actual use for which the conditions appertaining to its use can be stated. In these circumstances use can be made of the explanatory notes in Section 3 of the Master List for Buildings.

It could also be used for the positioning of information about climatic, site and occupancy conditions in Building Regulations and similar documents.

4 CHARACTERISTICS RELATING TO BEHAVIOUR IN USE AND WORKING

Information given in this Section relates to the characteristics of the material when acted upon by various agents after being fixed in position in the building, except for the last two headings which are for technical characteristics of special interest during construction and maintenance. Each characteristic may need to be evaluated with regard to safety, habitability and durability.

Wherever possible the information should be factual resulting from tests carried out on the material, either in its original form or when, as in the case of Portland cement, it has been mixed with aggregate and water and allowed to set. The test method should be quoted whenever it is a standard method or described if it is non-standard. The methods of test will usually be based on the way in which the various agents act upon the material though some tests may be of an indirect nature in those cases where the direct test is involved and the requisite information can be deduced from a simpler test.

Whenever possible the actual test figures should be quoted rather than making a statement that they satisfy the provisions of the test, giving the pass figures or levels, though this information may sometimes be in a separate document, eg Methods of Assessment.

The conditions under which the material is tested, eg water content, should be stated so that the results can be related to the conditions likely to be operating when the product is in use.

For some materials information may be given about their behaviour when forming part of a component or building element if this helps to give a more complete description of the behaviour of the material, though the functional suitability of the component or building element or building of which it forms a part should be considered at 5.01.

The information in this Section is based on the assumption that the material will be, or has been, used or fixed in position in accordance with recognised good practice.

The extent of the information need only be sufficient for the purposes of the document. In many instances the manufacturer will have additional information covering specialised uses of the material and which can be obtained on request from the manufacturer or from information centres.

4.01 Structural and mechanical; strength and deformations

The information may include data from tests made on the material under both normal and abnormal conditions, and the tests should be appropriate to its probable use.

.01 **Compression**

.02 **Tension**

.03 **Bending**

.04 **Shear**

.05 **Torsion**

.06 **Impact strength**

.07 **Bursting**

.08 **Tearing**

.09 **Splitting**

.10 **Strength related to holding power of nails, screws, etc.**

.11 **Hardness, indentation**

.12 **Wear, abrasion**

.13 **Adhesion**

.14 **Friction**

.15 **Rheological**

.16 **Vibration**

4.02 Fire   The method of recording the behaviour of the material in relation to fire will depend upon the material and the methods of test appropriate to it.

.01 **Fire resistance:** Not applicable to materials as such, though could be if large enough to form an element, eg timber beam.

.02 **Ignitability, combustibility, surface spread of flame, fire propagation**

.03 **Combustion products:** The combustion products are those which may be produced when the product catches fire.

.04 **Explosions:** Record the liability for explosions to occur where there is any such risk.

4.03 Gases   .01 **Gas permeability:** The permeability of a material may be expressed in different ways. It may vary according to pressure, etc. and, when this is to the condition under which the material was tested, it should be stated.

.02 **Gas circulation:** eg rate of passage of gas through pipes.

.03 **Gas quality:** The effects of condensed water vapour should be recorded at 4.04.08.

.04 **Physical and/or chemical changes arising from contact with or absorption of gas:** Include the effect, if any, of gases including polluted air on the material.

4.04 Liquids   The commonest liquid likely to be relevant is water.

.01 **Content:** The water content should be stated where this affects other characteristics of the material. Record the conditions under which the liquid content changes and the extent of the changes.

.02 **Absorption:** The extent of the absorption of liquids may depend upon the finish, the liquid, the temperature and pressure and when this is so the conditions should be given. Any effects of the liquid should be given in 4.04.08.

.03 **Permeability:** The permeability may vary according to the temperature, pressure or physical properties of the liquid and it may be useful to list data for a range of conditions.

.04 **Capillarity:** The movement of liquids by capillarity will be less concerned with individual materials than with narrow gaps between adjacent materials when in position in a building.

.05 **Drying, evaporation:** The rate of drying or evaporation may be important information for some materials, but any effects of the change in liquid content should be given in 4.04.08.

.06 **Solubility:** The extent of the solubility of the material in a liquid, particularly water, may be of importance when considering the use

237

of the product, especially if it affects the durability. Information should be given for liquids likely to come into contact with the material.

.07 Miscibility: Applicable to liquid materials such as thinners for paints.

.08 Physical and/or chemical changes arising from contact with or absorption of the liquid: Record any changes in the size and shape of the material and the character of the surfaces, and any changes that may occur to its composition, eg corrosion. Include any effects arising from liquid absorbed in the form of gas, eg water vapour.

4.05 Solids

Solids are less likely to come into haphazard external contact with materials than gases and liquids; dirt is probably the commonest. Liquids in solution may affect the material so may also any impurities present in the material.

.01 Penetration

.02 Physical and/or chemical changes arising from contact with solids: Physical changes will mainly be confined to changes of appearance by deposition of dirt.

Chemical changes are most likely to take place when the solid is in solution, as for example, the attack of Portland cement products by sulphates.

Electrolytic corrosion is an example of chemical change, though this normally requires the presence of a liquid acting as an electrolyte.

Impurities may cause physical or chemical changes.

4.06 Biological

Various biological agencies may affect the material. The necessary conditions, effects and preventive measures required or taken should be stated.

.01 Mammals, birds and insects.

.02 Fungi, mosses, lichens, moulds, bacteria.

4.07 Thermal

The terms in which statements are made relating to the thermal behaviour of materials will depend partly upon the use to be made of the material and they must be expressed accordingly.

.01 Thermal conductivity.

.02 Thermal capacity.

.03 Surface temperatures.

.04 Thermal absorption; thermal radiation.

.05 Physical and/or chemical changes arising from change of temperature: Include changes in size, colour, composition; also the effects of freezing and thawing.

4.08 Optical   When relevant the amount of information may be considerable in order to take account of the wide range of the quality of light.

    .01   **Daylight** (not used in materials list)

    .02   **Artificial light** (not used in materials list)

    .03   **Combination of daylight and artificial light** (not used in materials list)

    .04   **Transmission of light.**

    .05   **Reflection of light.**

    .06   **Refraction of light.**

    .07   **Physical and/or chemical changes arising from action of light,** including change of colour

4.09 Acoustic   Any effect of sound on the material should be recorded here. Any noise produced as a side-effect should be recorded at 4.12.

    .01   **Effect of noise from internal and external sources** (not used in materials list)

    .02   **Acoustic quality** (not used in materials list)

    .03   **Transmission of sound.**

    .04   **Reflection of sound.**

    .05   **Absorption of sound.**

4.10 Electricity, static electricity, magnetism and radio-activity   The content of the information may be considerable and the terms in which it is given can be very varied, depending very much upon the particular material.

    .01   **Electricity**

    .02   **Static electricity**

    .03   **Magnetism**

    .04   **Radio-activity and nuclear radiation**

4.11 Energy (not used in materials list)

4.12 Side-effects   Most of these will be unwanted effects and include the production of excessive heat, dust, dirt, toxic materials and odours. If none are produced this should be stated.

4.13 Compatibility   In many documents it may be preferable to bring together the information relating to compatibility, given under the preceding headings, although often it will be more convenient to make the statements in terms of incompatibility. The latter may arise when a material is applied to another, eg paints, when mixed together, eg Portland and high alumina cement, or when in juxtaposition, eg copper and aluminium.

4.14 Durability

Statements will be made on the assumption that all the necessary maintenance required to achieve the full durability will be carried out. Any special needs for this purpose will be given under 4.16.

The information on durability will be based either on experience or on the information given under the previous headings, which should be considered in terms of changes to the properties listed in Section 2 produced by the climate, external and internal environmental conditions, including occupancy. These in turn are expressed as agents and the value of the assessment of the durability of the material will depend upon the ability to express the various conditions in terms of agents and to evaluate the effects, both individually and collectively.

The main changes and the more common agents include:

Changes in composition, structure
physical forces
fire
gases, liquids, solids
biological agents
heat and cold
light

Changes in shape, size, weight

Physical forces
gases, liquids, solids
heat and cold

Changes in surface characteristic
including colour
physical forces; wear,
abrasion, impacts
fire
gases, liquids, solids
heat and cold
light

4.15 Working characteristics

This heading is for the collation of technical information concerning the handling and use of the material in the initial constructional process, during subsequent alterations and for final removal or demolition. The instructions for carrying out the work should be placed in Section 6. The items may include the following:

Ease of handling
Consistence. Workability. Working time.
Setting time.
Ease of sawing, cutting, boring, punching,
bending, etc. Work hardening (Include the
effect on the cut by the tool and on the tool)

Capability of being joined to itself or to other
materials by welding, soldering or by the use of

adhesives. Precautions for welding. Suitable
adhesives. Means of fixing the product;
nailability, etc.
Surface treatments including
suitability of the material to receive a surface
treatment
Spreadability. Coverage. Hiding power.
Drying time, etc.

Ability to withstand handling and transport.
Ability to withstand storage; shelf life.
Cleanliness during use.
Side-effects during working, eg production of
toxic materials.

Some products are purchased in a form which is different from their
final form in the building. During this process certain changes may take
place which can be of significance to the constructional work, to the
design considerations and to the durability of the product when in position.
The more important items include:

Heat evolution
Changes in volume due to chemical reactions

Give also any technical information concerning alterations and demolition
especially that which facilitates the work, so that it can be considered at
the design stage.

4.16 Characteristics relating to maintenance

This heading is for the collation of technical information relating to maintenance and repair which in many instances will be more convenient than
having it at the various preceding headings. It is not for the instructions
for carrying out the maintenance which should be placed in Section 7. It
can include information on the amount of wear which can be accepted
before maintenance is required and the methods and materials which should
be used and those which for technical reasons should be avoided.
    The demarcation between this information and that given under instruc-
tions for doing the work may be small and when this is so it will probably
be more convenient to phrase the information so that it can be placed in
Section 7, if the document contains instructions for doing the maintenance
and repair work.

5 APPLICATIONS, DESIGN

This Section is for recording information on the various applications and
uses of the material in a building, building element, component or service,
the design details and the functional and economic factors which need to
be taken into consideration when selecting a material for a particular
purpose.
    It has not been considered advisable to make a detailed list of sub-
headings in the Master List itself, but a suggested sequence of the more
important factors is given below.

5.01 Suitability, functional

The statements made concerning the functional suitability of a material
will be based largely on the information given in Section 4, taking into
consideration that given in Sections 2 and 3 together with the needs of the

user of the building, building element, component or service, of which the material forms a part. The statements should often be read together with the corresponding design details, normally at 5.05, but which for convenience may sometimes be included here.

For many purposes, and especially if the information is comprehensive, there are advantages in listing the functional factors in the following order, since this is in principle the order in which the information is listed in Section 4. If different applications of the material are listed or described, it will generally be preferable to provide the full information for each application in turn.

Shape, size and weight
Appearance
Strength and stability
Fire resistance and other factors
    relating to the effect of fire
Protection against matter
    (gases, liquids and solids)
Effect of biological agents
Protection against heat and cold
Protection against light
Protection against sound
Protection against electrical,
    magnetic and other radiations
Durability
Ease of use during constructional
    work and alteration
Ease of maintenance

Some of the requirements or needs of the user will have been covered by the above factors, but many others may not and they should be included here. They may cover many facets depending upon the material and its possible applications and may need to take into account such aspects as anthropometric and ergonomic.

5.02 Suitability, economic

This heading should be used for information concerning costs of the material, both of the initial construction or installation and the subsequent use, including maintenance, restoration and alteration and possibly demolition. Some of the information required for evaluating the economic suitability, eg purchase price, may be drawn from Section 8. The information could include man-hours for constructional work, cost of plant for such work and for testing.

Information should also be given concerning the costs of ancillary materials required for the constructional work, particularly for protective purposes.

The evaluation of the relation between the functional and economic suitability of the material should also be given here. It may be a formal benefit/cost analysis or it may be informal, using general judgements. Such a judgement may be in terms of its economic life.

5.03 Suitability, statutory

In some documents the statutory aspects will have been included in 5.01, but in others there will be a need to make specific statements concerning the extent to which the material satisfies statutory requirements.

5.04 Resource conservation

Any restrictions on the use of the material should be noted, such as those needed when a material is, or would be, in short supply or required for other purposes. Similar information may be given about labour and plant.

5.05 Design details

Typical design details may be provided as a complement both to the statements on the functional suitability at 5.01 and to the design specification clauses at 5.06.

5.06 Design specification clauses

It is sometimes helpful to provide specimen clauses which can be used in contract or other documents relating to the material.

5.07 Mistakes in use

Place here any statements calling attention to inadvisable or wrong uses of the material and design details that should be avoided.

6 SITEWORK

This section is designed to contain the information relating to the constructional work involved in the use of the material and would normally take the form of instructions for doing the work on the site, though heading 6.03, and sometimes 6.02 and 6.04 refers to work off the site preliminary to work on the site.

The Section can also be used for the instructions for work required in carrying out alterations involving the material and for its removal from the building, either separately or during demolition of the building. The terminology and expressions used in information structured according to this Section may need to be adapted to the needs of the building site.

The headings are considered to be sufficiently explanatory for additional notes not to be necessary.

6.01 Labour, plant and space requirements; special tools

6.02 Work planning

6.03 Work off site

6.04 Transport, handling and storage

6.05 Preparatory site work

6.06 Work on site; erection, site assembly, finishing

6.07 Protective measures

6.08 Cleaning up

6.09 Site quality control; testing

6.10 Labour safety and welfare

6.11 General public safety and welfare

7 OPERATION AND MAINTENANCE

This section is for information relating to the work necessary to ensure that the material continues to operate satisfactorily and that it is maintained so that the anticipated life is obtained.

7.01 Labour, plant, material and space requirements

7.02 Method of operation and control

7.03 Cleaning and maintenance

7.04 Repair and replacement

7.05 Protective measures

7.06 Labour safety and welfare

7.07 General public safety and welfare

8 PRICES AND CONDITIONS OF SALE

Fluctuations in prices will often necessitate publication at more frequent intervals than the remainder of the information and this may be done separately.

8.01 Purchase price

Include to what date, at which place, effect of location of delivery, minimum quantity at stated price, price reductions for quantity and season of delivery, delivery charges, insurance costs, taxes, customs dues.

8.02 Contract conditions; conditions of sale and guarantees

Include liabilities, certifications, quality control and other methods of checking compliance.

8.03 Terms of payment

9 SUPPLY

9.01 Sources of supply and supply capacity, including spares; delivery period

9.02 Packaging, labelling

9.03 Directions for ordering

9.04 Conditions of delivery

10 TECHNICAL SERVICES

10.01 Servicing and maintenance organization and facilities

10.02 Technical advisory services

11 REFERENCES

11.01 Location of examples in use

Examples of the material in use may be illustrated or quoted, with locations or a statement made that such information is obtainable on request.

11.02 Literature

This should include references to related documents issued by the manufacturer as well as references to technical and other literature relating to the material.

Asbestos Cement Sheets

Material	1.01	ASBESTOS CEMENT SHEETS
Use	1.02	Cladding of roofs and walls.
British Standards	1.04	BS 690. Asbestos cement slates, corrugated sheets and semi-compressed flat sheets. BS 1494. Fixing accessories for building purposes.
Composition	2.01	Asbestos fibre and Portland cement.
Method of manufacture	2.02	Raw materials mixed with water and formed into sheets which are then cured.
Accessories	2.03	Cover strips, hooks, bolts and other fixings available.
Shape	2.04	Flat sheets. Corrugated sheets in various profiles.

Dimensions — 2.05

	Length mm	*Width mm*	*Thickness mm*
Flat sheets	1220 to 3050	915, 1220	4.8, 6.4, 9.5, 12.7
Corru. sheets	915-3050	762, 1090	5.6, 6.4

Weight — 2.06

Thickness mm	4.8	6.4	9.5	12.7
Weight kg/m²	8.4	11.2	16.8	22.4

Density	2.06	1520 kg/m³.
Appearance	2.07	Front face has a smooth slightly grained surface, but applied finishes are also available. Reverse face has a textured surface. Grey colour but can be obtained with applied colour finish.

Properties in bending — 4.01.03

Flat sheets — Breaking load, Newtons (BS test).

Thickness mm	*Fibres parallel to bearers*	*Fibres at right angles to bearers*
4.8	218	307
6.4	391	547
9.5	872	1228
12.7	1557	2180

Impact strength	4.01.06	Fairly good when new, but decreases with age.
Combustibility	4.02.02	Non-combustible.
Surface spread of flame	4.02.02	Class O and Grade A.
Change in volume	4.03.04	Shrinks slightly due to carbonation of the cement

Moisture content	4.04.01	10-20 per cent by weight.
Water absorption	4.04.02	28 per cent maximum, completely immersed in water for 24 hours.
Permeability to water	4.04.03	Very low
Solubility in water	4.04.06	Insoluble
Dimensional changes	4.04.08	Dry to fully saturated, 0.25 per cent.
Effect of chemicals	4.04.08	Acids may attack the Portland cement. Alkalies other than ammonia in damp atmosphere have no effect.
Effect of impurities	4.05.02	Any likely to be present will have no harmful effect.
Effect of micro-organisms etc.	4.06	Immune to insect and vermin attack. Does not support mould growth.
Thermal conductivity, k	4.07.01	0.43 W/m ^{0}C
Effect of heat	4.07.05	Withstands heat up to 260^{0}C.
Effect of thermal shock	4.07.05	Liable to shatter if exposed to direct flame or temperatures above 260^{0}C.
Thermal expansion	4.07.05	12×10^{-6} per ^{0}C.
Effect of frost	4.07.05	Unaffected.
Effect of sunlight	4.08.07	Unaffected.
Health hazard	4.12	None in use. Precautions required when material is mechanically cut or worked.
Reaction with other materials	4.13	No reaction with other materials.
Durability	4.14	The normal minimum life is 40 years by which time the material has become brittle.
Ease of cutting, etc.	4.15	Can be cut with an ordinary hand saw. Holes should be drilled and not punched, the size being a little larger than the bolt or hook to be fed through the hole.
Surface treatment	4.15	Paints affected by alkali attack should be applied over an alkali-resistant primer. Sheets should not be painted on one face only as this will restrict carbonation to the other face and cause the sheets to warp.

Asbestos Insulating Board

Material	1.01	ASBESTOS INSULATING BOARD
Use	1.03	Fire protection of structural steelwork, ceilings, walls, partitions, etc
British Standards	1.04	BS 3536:1962. Asbestos insulating boards and wall boards
Chemical analysis	2.01	Hydrated calcium silicate. Slightly alkaline.
Composition	2.01	Asbestos fibre, silica and hydrated lime.
Method of manufacture	2.02	Raw materials, together with any pigments, mixed with water and fed into machines which yield a wet sheet which is then autoclaved.
Shape	2.04	Flat sheets, usually with square edges.

Dimensions	2.05	*Length mm* *Width mm* *Thickness mm* 1220 to 3050 510 and 1220 6.4, 9.5, 12.7

Weight	2.06	*Thickness mm*	6.4	9.5	12.7
		Weight kg/m²	4.6	6.9	9.2

Density	2.06	500-900 kg/m³.
Appearance	2.07	One face fairly smooth, reverse face slightly textured. Normal colour is grey-white. Available in natural and sanded surface finish.
Properties in tension	4.01.02	28 MN/m² across grain 30 per cent loss of strength when 93 MN/m² with grain saturated, recoverable on drying out.
Properties in bending	4.01.03	Modulus of rupture 138 x 10 MN/m² across grain. 93 x 10 MN/m² with grain.
Hardness	4.01.11	Brinell hardness 1.4 to 1.8 mm, 25 kg load, 10 mm ball.
Combustibility	4.02.02	Non-combustible.
Surface spread of flame	4.02.02	Class O and Grade A.
Water vapour diffusivity	4.03.01	0.015 - 0.03 g/MN s.

Moisture content	4.04.01	3 - 5 per cent.
Water absorption	4.04.02	100 per cent by weight.
Dimensional changes due to moisture	4.04.08	0.15 - 0.20 mm per 1000 mm from normal to saturated state.
Effect of chemicals	4.03 and 4.05	Affected by acids, but not necessarily by acidic fumes. Resistant to other materials likely to come into contact with it.
Effect of impurities	4.05.02	None likely.
Effect of micro-organisms, etc.	4.06	Does not nourish mould growth. Immune to insect attack.
Thermal conductivity	4.07.01	0.108 to 0.115 W/m °C.
Thermal expansion	4.07.05	5×10^{-6} per °C up to 200°C. Slight contraction above 200°C.
Light reflection	4.08.05	65 per cent for untreated sanded board.
Sound absorption	4.09.05	Sound absorption varies from 0.05 to 0.08 dependent upon thickness and conditions of usage.
Health hazard	4.12	No effect when in use. Precautions may be required when cut or worked mechanically.
Effect on other materials	4.13	No effect on other materials likely to be in contact with it.
Durability	4.14	Very durable when used internally.
Ease of working	4.15	Can be cut and worked with ordinary wood-working tools.
Surface treatment	4.15	Various decorative materials can be stuck on the boards, using appropriate adhesives.
Painting treatment	4.15	Sealing coat may be required prior to decoration with paints, etc.
Ease of cleaning	4.16	Natural surface is not easily cleaned.

Asphalt

Material	1.01	ASPHALT
Types	1.02	Two main types, one with limestone aggregate and the other with natural rock asphalt aggregate.
Use	1.03	Finish for flat roof construction.
British Standards	1.04	BS 988 Mastic asphalt for roofing (limestone aggregate). BS 1162 Mastic asphalt for roofing (natural rock asphalt aggregate). CP 144 Part 2 - Code of Practice for laying mastic asphalt roofing.
Composition	2.01	Asphalt or bitumen with naturally-containing or added aggregate. Full details of the materials are given in the Standards.
Manufacture	2.02	The natural or derived bitumens may be used separately or blended and the aggregate added and mixed with the hot bitumen. Rock asphalt is commonly used in its natural state.
Sieve analysis	2.05	The BS provides limits for the size and grading of the added aggregates and of the natural rock aggregate.
Density	2.05	2150-2240 kg/m^3.
Colour	2.07	Initially black, but natural mastic asphalt weathers to grey.
Properties in compression	4.01.01	Indents under applied loads.
Impact strength	4.01.06	Liable to fracture under impact, though generally this is unimportant in practice.
Hardness number	4.01.11	Test method BS 598: between 30 and 70 (limestone aggregate). between 40 and 90 (natural rock asphalt aggregate).
Resistance to mechanical wear	4.01.12	Low rate of wear.
Adhesion (bond strength)	4.01.13	Good bond to itself. Poor bond to smooth surfaces. Bond to flat roof surfaces is purposely avoided by the use of underlays.

Rheological properties	4.01.15	Liable to flow under its own weight on sloping or inclined surfaces.
Effect of fire	4.02	Virtually incombustible as laid on roofs. Class I complying with BS 476. Part 1. AA in Schedule 10, Clause E1, Building Regulations 1965.
Permeability to air and gases	4.03.01	Impervious.
Permeability to water	4.04.03	Impervious.
Effect of chemicals	4.04 and 4.05	Liable to attack by oils and fats, though this is not important for roofing unless cars are parked on the material.
Thermal conductivity	4.07.01	1.22 W/m ^{0}C for material having density of 2240 kg/m^3.
Coefficient of linear expansion (thermal)	4.07.05	$30 - 80 \times 10^{-6}$ per ^{0}C.
Melting point	4.07.05	Mastic asphalt is thermoplastic, becoming plastic when heated.
Effect of changes in temperatures	4.07.05	Softens by absorption of solar heat and hardens on cooling.
Effect of sunlight	4.08.07	Absorption of solar heat by dark surfaces may be considerable and white treatments are sometimes applied to reduce the effect. Fine surface crazing may occur.
Acoustic properties	4.09	Non-drumming.
Durability	4.14	Long life without requiring maintenance if correctly laid.
Changes during preparation	4.15	Melts during heating and laying and hardens on cooling.

Bitumen Felt

Material	1.01	BITUMEN FELT
Type	1.02	3 main types according to nature of base. Type 1 - Fibre base, with various finishes. Type 2 - Asbestos base, with various finishes. Type 3 - Glass fibre base, with various finishes.
Use	1.03	Finish for roofs. Material of similar type used for DPC and flashings.
British Standards	1.04	BS 747. CP 144.
Chemical analysis	2.01	Covered in detail in BS 747.
Composition	2.01	Fibre, asbestos or glass fibre impregnated with bitumen.
Manufacture	2.02	The fibre mats are passed through a tank containing bitumen in a hot fluid condition, the excess bitumen being removed by passage between rollers, and appropriate finishes applied.
Dimensions	2.05	Supplied in rolls, length 4.6 and 9.3 m, width 910 mm, thickness up to 3 mm.
Weight (per unit area)	2.06	Type 1 : 0.9-3.6 kg/m² In all cases the heavier grades are those Type 2 : 0.7-3.6 kg/m² with mineral surfaced finishes. Type 3 : 1.8-3.2 kg/m²
Appearance	2.07	Normal finish is blackish in colour, and fairly smooth, but coloured finishes including light colours are produced and these have a rough texture depending upon the surfacing material used.
Strength properties	4.01	Not self-supporting. No tensile strength tests in BS, but tests are given in standards of some other countries. The significance of any figures depends upon the method of use of the material and the temperature changes to which it may be exposed. Pliable, though less so when cold.
Resistance to tearing.	4.01.08	Liable to tear if not handled carefully.
Adhesion	4.01.13	Self-adhesion in the roll prevented by use of a surfacing material or production with a dry surface. CP 144 describes the material to

be used when bonding bitumen felt to concrete and other surfaces and for built-up roofing.

Effect of fire	4.02	The material is inflammable. Types 2 and 3 should be used where fire resistance is important. Softening of the bitumen may cause it to run or drip. The classification for fire resistance depends on a number of factors and reference should be made to the Building Regulations.
Permeability to air and gases	4.03.01	Very low permeability
Water absorption	4.04.02	Very low indeed. No test in BS.
Permeability to water	4.04.03	Very low indeed. No test in BS.
Porosity	4.04.03	Mainly non-porous.
Effect of chemicals	4.03 and 4.05	Not affected by materials normally likely to come in contact with built-up roofing.
Thermal conductivity	4.07.01	Since the material is relatively thin it provides little contribution to the thermal insulation of a roof.
Linear thermal expansion coefficient	4.07.05	Types 1 and 2: 11×10^{-6} per $^{\circ}$C (with machine) 22×10^{-6} per $^{\circ}$C (across machine) Type 3: 26×10^{-6} per $^{\circ}$C (with machine) 33×10^{-6} per $^{\circ}$C (across machine). These values are of US origin. They are of greater significance in cold climates. Actual expansion depends upon method of use.
Effect of high and low temperatures	4.07.05	Solar heat causes softening of the bitumen. Low temperatures result in stiffening and hardening and tendency to become brittle.
Effect of frost	4.07.05	Unaffected apart from contraction.
Effect of sunlight	4.08.07	Sunlight causes changes in constitution of the bitumen contributing to its weathering, but the effects are reduced by site-applied surface dressings to minimise solar heat gain. The surface may craze or blister.
Reaction with other materials	4.13	Direct effects are small, but the hot bonding bitumen may soften expanded polystyrene insulation and some protection may be necessary.
Durability	4.14	Built-up roofing consisting of three layers of bitumen felt laid according to CP 144 should require little maintenance to give a life of upwards of 20 years.
Changes during preparation and use	4.15	Softens on warming. Overheating the bonding bitumen will cause the material to become hard and brittle.

Blocks, Concrete

Material	1.01	BLOCKS, CONCRETE		
Types of concrete	1.02	*Dense*	*Dense*	*Lightweight aggregate*
Types of aggregate	1.02	Gravel	Limestone	Clinker
Use	1.03	Outer leaf of external walls (rendered or other treatment). Inner leaf		
British Standards	1.04	BS 2028:1364:1968	Precast concrete blocks	
		BS 877:1967	Foamed blastfurnace slag for concrete	
		BS 1165:1966	Clinker aggregate for plain and precast	
		CP 121:201:1951	Masonry. Walls ashlared with natural stone or	
		CP 122:1952	Walls and partitions of blocks and slabs.	
Composition	2.01	Portland cement and aggregate in wide range of mix proportions.		
Method of production	2.02			
(a) aggregate		Natural sources	Crushed limestone	Furnace residues
(b) block		Semi-dry concrete mixes are moulded in machines, with tamping,		
Shape	2.04	Rectangular- or square-sectioned blocks, solid or with core holes.		
Dimensions	2.05	Length 448 mm, Height 219 mm, Thickness (mm), 64,76,102,152,		
Weight (kg) 76 mm thick blocks	2.06	14-17	14-17	7-11
Bulk density (kg/m³)	2.06	2000-2400	2000-2400	1050-1520
General appearance	2.07	Plain, textured or riven faced. Natural and limited range of colours.	Plain, textured or riven faced. Natural and limited range of colours	Rough textured as cast. Dark grey.

Lightweight aggregate	*Lightweight aggregate*	*Lightweight aggregate*	*Aerated*
Pulverised fuel ash	Expanded clay	Foamed slag	Finely ground sand, burnt shale or slag.

and partition walls (usually plastered). Internal partition walls, (usually plastered).

aggregate.

concrete.

with cast stone.

			Portland cement or lime and aggregate
Powdered coal ash	Clay heated to bloating temperature	Minimum amount of water on molten slag	Aggregate ground to a fine powder. Wet mix containing aluminium powder cast to produce large blocks which are then cast to size.

vibration and/or pressure, cured naturally or in a steam chamber.

			Rectangular or square sectioned solid blocks.
178, 203 and 209 mm			
7-12.5	5.5-12.5	7-14	2.75-6.75
950-1760	720-1760	950-2000	400-800
As moulded and textured. Grey.	Rough textured (cast). Grey.	Fairly rough textured. Grey.	Relatively fine textured. White or grey.

Properties of Building Materials

		Gravel	Limestone	Clinker
Compressive strength (MN/m²)	4.01.01	13.5-42	13.5-42	2.0-7.0
Resistance to insertion and extraction of nails	4.01.10	Not nailable	Not nailable	Nailable with cut nails
Fire resistance	4.02.01	Concrete is incombustible. Fire resistance of walls up to 6 hours can		
Water absorption	4.04.02	7 per cent by wt. 16 per cent by vol.		Varies according to
Drying shrinkage (per cent)	4.04.08	0.03-0.035	0.02-0.035	0.04-0.08
Effect of chemicals	4.05.02	Normally Portland cement is susceptible to attack by sulphates and unavoidable the blocks should be made with sulphate resistant		
Effect of impurities	4.05.02	None usually present	None usually present	Occasionally contains small pieces of lime which subsequently "blow"
Thermal conductivity (W/m °C)	4.07.01	1.10-1.75	1.10-1.75	0.35-0.60
Thermal expansion coefficient (per °C)	4.07.05	$12\text{-}13 \times 10^{-6}$	$6\text{-}8 \times 10^{-6}$	$8\text{-}10 \times 10^{-6}$
Effect of frost	4.07.05	Frost resistant.		
Acoustic properties	4.09	Transmission of air-borne sound increases with decrease in density.		
Reaction with other materials	4.13	None	None	Liable to corrode iron and steel
Durability	4.14	Excellent		

Pulverised fuel ash	*Expanded clay*	*Foamed slag*	*Aerated*
2.75-55.0	2.0-62.0	2.0-24.0	0.5-5.5 air-cured 2.0-5.0 autoclaved
Nailable with cut nails	Not readily nailable	Nailable with cut nails	Nailable. Nail-holding capacity varies with density. Cut nails preferable to wire nails.

be obtained by using blocks of appropriate chickness, plastered if necessary with gypsum plaster.

density but generally of little importance under normal conditions of use.

0.04-0.07	0.04-0.07	0.03-0.07	0.17-0.45 air-cured 0.06-0.07 autoclaved

concrete blocks should not be used in damp situations where sulphates are present. If this is
Portland cement or high alumina cement.

None usually present	None usually present	None usually present	None usually present
0.20-0.50	0.20-0.60	0.20-0.60	0.85-4.00 air-cured 0.08-0.25 autoclaved
$8\text{-}10 \times 10^{-6}$	$8\text{-}12 \times 10^{-6}$	$10\text{-}12 \times 10^{-6}$	$10\text{-}12 \times 10^{-6}$
None	None	None	None

Bricks, Clay

Material	1.01	BRICKS, CLAY			
Type	1.02	*London Stocks*	*Engineering Bricks*	*Facing Bricks*	*Common Bric*
Use	1.03	Mainly for walls, including foundations. Engineering bricks are used external work where good appearance is required. Common bricks			
British Standards, etc.	1.04	BS 3921:Part 1:1969, Bricks and blocks of brickearth, clay or shale units. CP 121.101 Brickwork			
Composition	2.01	Very variable, depending upon the raw material used, but consist			
Chemical analysis (soluble salts)	2.01	B	A	A or B	B

Because of the variability of the soluble salt content it would be misleading to quote
A. Normally meets the requirements of BS 3921 for *special quality*.
B. Soluble salt content usually moderate, but not normally of special quality.
C. Soluble salt content may be moderate or fairly high but does not normally cause
D. Salt content may be relatively high, especially of gypsum (calcium sulphate) and can

		Brick-earth	————————Wealden clays ————————		
Method of manufacture	2.02	Moulded or pressed wire-cut	Stiff plastic-pressed or wire-cut	Hand-made, machine-moulded or wire-cut	Stiff plastic-pressed or wire-cut
Shape and size	2.04.05	The standard size is 225 x 112.5 x 75 mm with relatively large specials (closers, squints, bullnoses, etc.) are produced for use at			
Weight (dry) kg	2.06	2.0-2.5	3.0-3.3	2.2-3.0	2.5-3.1
Bulk density kg/m³	2.06	1400-1750	2100-2300	1550-2100	1750-2200
Colours	2.07	Yellow with purplish markings	Red or brindled	Red, purple or brown	Reddish brow
Compressive strength MN/m²	4.01.01	5-21	48-110	7-50	34-50
Effect of fire	4.02	The fire resistance of brickwork is high, with no real differences			
Moisture content	4.04.01	Equilibrium moisture content in contact with moist air is generally porosity figures temporarily.			

Flettons	*Facing or Common*	*Engineering Bricks*	*Facing Bricks*	*Common Bricks*

where high strength, low porosity and high resistance to frost are required. Facing bricks are used for
are used where appearance is not important or where they are to be plastered or rendered.

BS 3921:Part 2:1969, specification for bricks and blocks of fired brickearth, clay or shale:Metric

essentially of aluminium silicates

D	D	A	A or B	D

individual figures but the general trend is indicated by letters A, B, C and D.

trouble when the bricks are used in normal conditions.
give rise to troublesome failures if the brickwork remains wet for long periods.

Oxford clay	Keuper marl	————————Carboniferous clays or shales————————		
Semi-dry pressed	Wire-cut	Stiff plastic-pressed or wire-cut	Hand-moulded, stiff plastic-pressed or wire-cut	Stiff plastic-pressed or wire-cut

tolerances in view of method of manufacture. Some non-standard sizes are available. Standard
corners, etc. of walls and are illustrated in BS 3921:Part 1:1965.

2.3-2.6	2.4-3.0	3.0-3.6	3.0-3.3	2.5-3.4
1600-1800	1650-2050	2100-2500	2050-2300	1750-2350
Cream to pink. Other colours available	Cream to red. Other colours available	Red, brown, brindled or blue	Buff, brown or red. Other colours available	Buff, red or blackish
17-36	20-50	45-150	20-110	25-145

between bricks from different sources.

less than 1 per cent. When exposed to rain the moisture content may reach two-thirds of the

259

		London Stocks	Engineering Bricks	Facing Bricks	Common Bric
Porosity per cent by vol.	4.04.02	30-50	8-15	13-42	17-46
Permeability	4.04.03	Not usually of practical importance			
Moisture expansion	4.04.08	Initial moisture expansion of kiln-fresh bricks is variable but may be will have occurred in 1 week, though the remaining 50 per cent will			
Effect of chemicals	4.04 and 4.05	Good resistance to acids and chemicals. The more porous bricks ma contaminated.			
Effect of impurities	4.05.02	Particles of lime, derived from limestone present as an impurity in sulphates may cause surface disintegration or under wet conditions efflorescence on the surface of the bricks but this effect is generally			
Thermal conductivity (W/m °C)	4.07.01	0.45	0.8-1.0	0.5-0.7	0.6-0.8
Linear thermal expansion	4.07.05	$5\text{-}8 \times 10^{-6}$ per °C. Usually of little importance except in long walls			
Effect of frost	4.07.05	Behaviour in frost depends upon conditions of exposure and the into two classes: - Ordinary quality - normally durable in the exposure, e.g. retaining walls. Engineering bricks normally attain Keuper marl.			
Changes in use	4.14	Little foundation for statements that bricks harden on exposure			
Durability	4.14	Very dependent upon the type of brick, degree of firing, soluble salt			

Flettons	*Facing or Common*	*Engineering Bricks*	*Facing Bricks*	*Common Bricks*
30-40	22-42	1-15	2-22	10-38

appreciable, exceeding 0.1 per cent. It decreases rapidly for day-old bricks and approx. 50 per cent of it take a much longer time. Subsequent dimensional changes with changes of moisture content are very small.

be damaged by salt crystallisation either because of original high salt content or becoming

the clay, may cause the overlying brick surface to spall off revealing the lime underneath. Soluble attack mortars containing Portland cement or semi-hydraulic lime. They may also appear as temporary.

| 0.55 | Up to 1.0 | 0.8-1.0 | 0.83 | 0.88 |

built in dense mortar.

water content at the time of freezing, underfired bricks being more susceptible. Bricks are divided external face of a building. Special quality - durable even when used in situations of extreme this quality, facing and common bricks may do so, except those produced from Oxford clay and

except for a limited hardening of bricks of high lime content.

content and conditions of exposure.

Bricks, Concrete

Material	1.01	BRICKS, CONCRETE
Types	1.02	Special purposes. Facings. Internal work.
Use	1.03	General, though mainly for facing work.
British Standards	1.04	BS 1180:1944
Composition	2.01	Portland cement and sand, crushed rock or lightweight aggregates, with addition of pigments for production of coloured bricks.
Manufacture	2.02	Relatively dry mixes of cement and aggregate are pressed or tamped into moulds and generally steam-cured.
Shape	2.04	Normal brick shape.
Size	2.05	As for clay bricks.
Density	2.06	1000-2000 kg/m³ depending upon aggregate and mix.
Appearance	2.07	Texture varies according to aggregate. Facing bricks are usually coloured.
Compressive strength	4.01.01	7-42 MN/m², tested in the wet condition. Dry strength is 30-50 per cent higher than wet strength.
Transverse strength	4.01.02	1.3-3.8 MN/m². Transverse strength is generally of little importance in practice.
Nailability	4.01.10	Bricks especially suitable for nailing are made with lightweight aggregates.
Fire resistance	4.02	Walls built of concrete bricks can attain the required fire resistance.
Water absorption	4.04.02	Mainly between 10-20 per cent, though the value has little practical significance.
Dimensional changes	4.04.08	Initial drying shrinkage 0.020-0.080 per cent depending upon mix and curing. Subsequent reversible movement on wetting and drying 0.010-0.055 per cent.
Effect of chemicals	4.04 and 4.05	Attacked by acids and may be subject to slight surface erosion in industrial atmospheres.

Effect of impurities	4.05.02	No effect from those likely to be present. Can be subject to 'lime-bloom' on the surface.
Thermal conductivity	4.07.01	Varies widely depending upon aggregate. Some guidance can be obtained from concrete blocks data table.
Thermal expansion coefficient	4.07.05	$12\text{-}13 \times 10^{-6}$ per ^{0}C.
Effect of frost	4.07.05	Not affected if properly made and aggregate has adequate frost resistance.
Durability	4.14	Depends upon aggregate and quality of manufacture, but usually adequate.
Properties relative to use	4.15	In order to minimise the effects of dimensional changes with change in water content it is recommended that the strength of the mortar should not be too high. Mixes of $1:3:12$ to $1:1:6$ cement:lime:sand are sufficiently strong for most purposes.
Storage on site	6.04	Bricks should be covered to keep them dry and thus reduce the amount of initial drying shrinkage taking place in the walls.

Bricks, Flint-Lime

Material	1.01	BRICKS, FLINT-LIME
Types	1.02	Coloured facings, No. 1 Engineering, No. 2 Engineering, Semi-engineering.
Use	1.03	Facing bricks for all types of buildings.
British Standards	1.04	BS 187. Calcium silicate (sandlime and flint-lime) bricks.
Chemical analysis	2.01	Hydrated calcium silicate. Alkaline.
Composition	2.01	Crushed flint and lime chemically combined.
Method of manufacture	2.02	The flint and lime, together with pigments, are mixed, pressed and autoclaved.
Shape	2.04	Normal brick shape with one frog, with large range of specials.
Dimensions	2.05	Length 215 ± 3 mm, Width 102.5 ± 1.6 mm, Depth 65 ± 1.6 mm, other depths to order.

Weight	2.06	Facings and semi-engineering	2845 kg per 1000
		Engineering No. 1 and No. 2	3048 kg per 1000

Appearance	2.07	Facing bricks;	16 colours
		Engineering bricks;	off-white
		Semi-engineering;	generally off-white

		Facing	Semi-Engineering	No. 1 Engineering	No. 2 Engineering
Compressive strength MN/m²	4.01.01	31	31	34.5	48.3
Transverse strength MN/m²	4.01.02	4.1	4.1	5.2	6.2
Combustibility	4.02.02	Non-combustible: BS 476.			
Surface spread of flame	4.02.02	Class O and Grade A.			

Water absorption	4.04.02	Facings and semi-engineering	10-20 per cent by weight
		No. 1 Engineering	7 per cent by weight
		No. 2 Engineering	10 per cent by weight

Dimensional changes	4.04.08	Linear drying shrinkage from wet to dry is approx. 0.01 - 0.04 per cent.

Effect of chemicals	4.04 and 4.05	Highly resistant except to mineral acids. Not affected by salts or sulphate-bearing soil.

Effect of impurities	4.05.02	None normally present.

Thermal conductivity	4.07.01	0.5-0.7 W/m °C.

Frost resistance	4.07.05	Very resistant (all grades). May be affected by frost if contaminated with chlorides (sea-water).

Reaction with other materials	4.13	Generally non-reactive.

Durability	4.14	Excellent durability in both atmospheric and sub-soil conditions.

Properties relative to use	4.15	In order to minimize the effects of dimensional changes with change in water content it is recommended that the strength of the mortar should not be too high. Mixes of 1:3:12 to 1:1:6 cement:lime:sand are sufficiently strong for most purposes. Guidance for the mortar mixes is given in Tables 5 and 6 of the BS.

Storage on site	6.04	Bricks should be covered to keep them dry and thus reduce the initial drying shrinkage taking place in the building.

265

Bricks, Sandlime

Material	1.01	BRICKS, SANDLIME
Type	1.02	7 different Classes, designated 1, 2A, 2B, 3A, 3B, 4, 5.
Use	1.03	Load-bearing walls (all classes), facing work (all classes except 1).
British Standards	1.04	187. Calcium silicate (sandlime and flint-lime) bricks.
Composition	2.01	Calcium silicate.
Manufacture	2.02	Intimate mixture of lime (8 per cent) and clean sand or crushed rock (92 per cent) pressed into moulds and autoclaved.
Shape	2.04	Normal brick shape. Special shapes also available.
Dimensions	2.05	Length 215 ± 3 mm, Width 102.5 ± 1.6 mm, Depth 65 ± 1.6 mm.
Weight	2.06	1.2 - 1.4 kg
Appearance	2.07	Uniform appearance, whether smooth or textured, natural or pigmented.
Compressive strength	4.01.01	7-50 MN/m^2.
Water absorption	4.04.02	10-18 per cent by weight
Dimensional changes with changes in water content	4.04.08	Drying shrinkage from wet to dry, approx. 0.01-0.04 per cent of the length.
Effect of chemicals	4.04 and 4.05	Affected by acids. Not affected by sulphates.
Effect of impurities	4.05.02	None normally present.
Algal growth	4.06.02	Not conducive to algal and other growth.
Thermal conductivity	4.07.01	0.5-0.7 W/m ^{0}C.

Thermal expansion	4.07.05	$5\text{-}8 \times 10^{-6}$ per $^{\circ}$C (linear coefficient).
Effect of frost	4.07.05	Unaffected if to BS except for bricks containing chlorides, e.g. from sea water, which may be affected by severe frost.
Light reflection	4.08.05	Appreciable reflection, up to 60 per cent for light coloured bricks.
Effect of sunlight	4.08.07	Unaffected.
Durability	4.14	Excellent.
Properties relative to use	4.15	In order to minimize the effects of dimensional changes with change in water content it is recommended that the strength of the mortar should not be high. Mixes of 1:3:12 to 1:1:6 cement:lime: sand are sufficiently strong for most purposes. Guidance for mortar mixes for the different classes of sand-lime bricks is given in Tables 5 and 6 of the BS.
Storage on site	6.04	Bricks should be covered to keep them dry and thus reduce initial drying shrinkage taking place in the building.

Cement, High Alumina

Material	1.01	CEMENT, HIGH ALUMINA
Use	1.03	Particularly useful where early strength and/or resistance to sulphates is required.
British Standards	1.04	BS 915:1947
Chemical analysis	2.01	Total alumina content must not be less than 32 per cent. Ratio of alumina to lime by weight must not be less than 0.85 nor more than 1.5
Composition	2.01	Mainly calcium aluminates.
Manufacture	2.02	Made by fusing a mixture of bauxite or other high alumina content material with chalk or limestone to a completely molten state and grinding the resulting clinker.
Fineness	2.05	Residue on a No. 170 mesh BS test sieve must not exceed 8 per cent or the specific surface must not exceed 0.2250 Mn/g.
Compressive strength	4.01.01	At 24 hours not less than 41 MN/m² (1:3 cement:sand). At 72 hours an increase on the 24 hours figure and not less than 49 MN/m². At 24 hours average strength of 1:2:4 concrete is 49 MN/m². At 28 days average strength of 1:2:4 concrete is 70 MN/m².
Adhesion	4.01.13	High alumina cement must not be bonded to normal Portland cement until the latter is 7 days old. High alumina cement must be at least 1 day old before Portland cement is bonded to it.
Effect of fire	4.02	Very useful for refractory work when mixes with suitable heat resistant aggregates.
Effect of chemicals	4.04 and 4.05	Very resistant to attack by sulphates. Resistant to weak acids. Not resistant to attack by alkalis. Good resistance to attack by sugar.
Effect of high temperature	4.07.05	Above 30° C the strength of moist concrete is reduced by 50 per cent due to changes in the calcium aluminates. The colour of affected concrete is often brown instead of dark grey.
Reaction with other materials	4.13	Should not be mixed with Portland cement or lime as a flash set will be produced and strength may be reduced. Calcium chloride and integral waterproofers should not be added.

Durability	4.14	Long life except in moist conditions at temperatures above 30°C.
Soundness	4.14	Le Chatelier test not to exceed 1 mm.
Setting time	4.15	Initial - not less than 2 hours nor more than 6 hours. Final - not more than 2 hours after initial set.
Heat evolution	4.15	Rapid evolution of heat which is of use when concreting in frosty weather.

Cement, Portland

		Ordinary and Rapid-hardening	Portland-blast furnace
Material	1.01	CEMENT, PORTLAND	
Type	1.02	*Ordinary and Rapid-hardening.*	*Portland-blast furnace*
Uses	1.03	Can be used neat, but more usually as a binding agent for sand and other aggregates for making mortars and concrete.	As for ordinary Portland cement.
British Standards	1.04	BS 12.	BS 146:1958
Composition	2.01	Mainly calcium silicates and calcium aluminates.	Mixture of Portland cement and granulated blast furnace slag.
Chemical analysis	2.01	Lime saturation factor, min. 0.66, max. 1.02. Insoluble residue, max. 1.5 per cent. Magnesia, max. 4.0 per cent. Sulphuric anhydride (SO_3), max. 3.0 per cent. Loss on ignition, max. 3.0 per cent.	max. 1.5 per cent. max. 7.0 per cent. max. 6.75 per cent. max. 3.0 per cent.
Manufacture	2.02	Produced by burning at high temperature a mixture essentially of chalk or limestone and clay, and grinding to a fine powder with the addition of gypsum to control the rate of set.	Slag may be mixed with PC clinker and ground together or be pre-ground and mixed. Slag content not to exceed 65 per cent.
Specific surface	2.05	Ordinary: Specific surface 0.2250 Mm^2/g. Rapid hardening: 0.3250 Mm^2/g.	0.2250 Mm^2/g
Specific weight	2.05	3.0-3.2	
Colour	2.07	Grey colour normally, but may be pigmented with pigments conforming to BS 1014. White cement also available.	Normally grey.

Low heat	*Low heat Portland BF*	*Sulphate resisting*
As for ordinary Portland cement but particularly useful for mass concrete where evolution of heat may be harmful	As for ordinary Portland cement but particularly useful for mass concrete where evolution of heat may be harmful.	As for ordinary Portland cement but particularly useful where sulphates are likely to be present.
BS 1370:1958.	BS 4246.	BS 4027:1966.
As for ordinary Portland cement	Mixture of Portland cement and granulated blastfurnace slag.	Mainly calcium silicates. Low content of tri-calcium aluminate.
		min. 0.66, max. 1.02.
1.5 per cent. 4 per cent.	max. 1.5 per cent. max. 9.0 per cent.	max. 1.4 per cent. max. 4.0 per cent.
2.75 per cent.	max. 3.0 per cent.	max. 2.5 per cent.
3.0 per cent.		max. 3.0 per cent.
	Sulphur as sulphide 2.0 per cent.	
As for ordinary Portland cement.	As for ordinary Portland blast furnace cement but slag content not less than 50 per cent or more than 90 per cent.	As for ordinary Portland cement.
0.3200 Mm^2/g.	0.2750 Mm^2/g.	0.2500 Mm^2/g.
Grey	Grey	As for ordinary Portland cement.

		Ordinary and Rapid-hardening		*Portland-blast furnace*
Compression strength MN/m² (1:3 cement:sand)	4.01.01	3 days 7 days	15.4 23.9	15.4 23.9
Rate of strength development	4.01.01	Medium (ordinary) High (rapid hardening)		Medium
Resistance to cracking		Medium (ordinary) Low (rapid hardening)		Medium
Effect of fire	4.02	Behaviour largely depends upon the aggregate. The dehydration of		
Permeability to water	4.04.03	Permeability to water and other liquids of mortars and concretes		
Dimensional changes	4.04.08	Mortars and concretes have an initial drying shrinkage 0.3-0.5 per		
Effect of chemicals - weak acids - alkalies -sulphates	4.04 and 4.05	Poor Good Poor		Fair Good Fair
Effect of impurities	4.05.02	Any impurities generally have no effect.		
Thermal expansion coefficient	4.07.05	12-13 x 10⁻⁶ per °C (1:6 gravel concrete).		
Effect of frost	4.07.05	Unset mortars and concrete liable to frost damage. Frost resistance		
Reaction with other materials	4.13	Affects materials susceptible to alkalies, e.g. aluminium. Flash set if		
Durability	4.14	Durability depends upon mix proportions, water/cement ratio and		
Setting time - initial - final	4.15	min. 45 min max. 10 hours		min. 45 min max. 10 hours
Heat of hydration (rate)	4.15	Medium (ordinary) High (rapid hardening)		Medium

Low heat	Low heat Portland BF	Cement, Portland Sulphate resisting
7.7	7.7	15.4
14.1	14.1	23.9
Low	Low	Low to medium
High	High	Medium

the cement is a slow process.

made with PC depends upon proportion of cement:aggregate. Very low for rich mixes.

cent. Subsequent changes in moisture content are accompanied by dimensional changes.

Poor	Fair	Poor
Good	Good	Good
Fair	Fair	V. Good

of hardened material may be very high but depends on mix proportions and water cement ratio.

mixed with high alumina cement.

exposure conditions and is generally excellent.

min. 1 hour	min. 1 hour	min. 45 mins.
max. 15 hours	max. 15 hours	max. 10 hours
Low	Low	Low to medium

Fibre Building Boards

		FIBRE BUILDING BOARDS		
Material	1.01	Hardboards.	Wallboards.	Insulating boards.
Type	1.02	Standard, tempered and medium. Decorative faced.	Homogenous. Laminated. Decorative faced.	Homogenous. Bitumen bonded. Decorative faced.
Use	1.03	Linings for walls and ceilings.	Linings for walls and ceilings.	Linings for walls and ceilings.
British Standards	1.04	BS 1142	BS 1142	BS 1142
Composition	2.01	Wood and other vegetable fibres.		
Manufacture	2.02	Wood fibre pulp with adhesive additives fed on to endless belt or cylinder, excess water sucked out and wet board rolled, dried and cut to size. These boards may be converted into hardboards, but the latter may also be produced by pressing the wet pulp boards at a high temperature.		
Shape	2.04	Rectangular boards.		
Dimensions Width (mm) Length (mm) Thickness (mm)	2.05	915, 1220, 1530 Up to 3660 2-12	610, 915, 1220 1220-3660 6-10	610, 915, 1220 1220-3660 12-25
Density (kg/m³)	2.06	Standard 880 Medium 480-800	Not over 480	Not over 400
Appearance	2.07	Smooth surface on one side. Usually mesh texture on reverse.	Smooth, rough or moulded surfaces. Cream to grey colour.	Smooth, rough or moulded surfaces. Cream to grey colour.
Modulus of rupture (MN/m²)	4.01.02	Standards 35-65 Tempered 50-90		1.8-3.5
Modulus of elasticity (MN/m²)	4.01.01	Standard 3500-5500 Tempered 5500-7000		175-550
Combustibility	4.02.02	Combustible.	Combustible.	Combustible.
Surface spread of flame	4.02.02	Class 3, undecorated. Can be raised to Class 2 with certain	Class 4 undecorated. Can be raised to Class 1 with certain	

		decorative treatments. Can be raised to Class 1 with intumescent paint treatment.	decorative treatments or by impregnation with chemicals.
Permeability to water vapour (g/MNs)	4.03.01	0.001-0.002	0.02-0.060	0.015-0.070

Moisture content	4.04.01	*RH per cent*	*Moisture Content per cent*	*RH per cent*	*Moisture Content per cent*
		40	4-5	40	7-0
		65	5-8	60	10-0
		80	7-11	80	13-0

Water absorption (by weight)	4.04.02	3 mm Standard 10-30 per cent. 6 mm Medium 15-30 per cent. 3 mm Tempered 5-15 per cent.	Maximum 38 per cent.	10-20 per cent.

Moisture expansion per cent increase in thickness	4.04.08	Standard 7-20 Medium 10-20 Tempered 3-11

Effect of chemicals	4.04 and 4.05	Not affected by chemicals normally likely to come into contact with any type of board. Wall-boards and insulating boards suffer loss of strength when wet.

Fungal attack, etc.	4.06.02	Not affected by fungal growth.

Thermal conductivity (W/m°C)	4.07.01	Standard 0.1 Medium 0.07	0.06	0.05

Sound absorption	4.09.05	Sound absorption depends on type and method of use.

Sound transmission dB reduction for single thickness	4.09.03	3 mm 20 6 mm 23 12 mm 27	12 mm 18	12 mm 18

Durability	4.14	Long life under all conditions of usage appropriate to the particular type.

Ease of cutting	4.15	Can be readily cut with fine-toothed saws.

Ease of cleaning	4.16	Depends upon the applied surface finish.

Floor Finishes

Where tiles are given as square, this indicates the commonest shape; obviously for linoleum, etc. they could be circular.

Under dimensions thickness is given last. Other dimensions are given in ranges but for some only the commonest sizes are given.

Unit weights are meant as a broad guide only. In several instances the weight range is very considerable.

Colours where given refer to the commonest ones produced.

In several cases a wide range is given for a property to timber. This is because it varies with species, hardwood or softwood, etc.

Under ease of cleaning any textured surface would be rated Poor so assessments are for smooth surfaces.

Resistance to wear is related to the use categories so should not be compared as if all were used in the same way.

Means of laying or fixing gives where relevant the BS Code of Practice written as CP 201, etc. BRS Digests are given as BRS 33, etc.

Material	1.01	FLOOR FINISHES			
Type	1.02	*Ceramic Tile*	*Composition Block*	*Concrete* *Pre-cast*	*In situ*
Use	1.03	Domestic Commercial Industrial	Domestic Commercial	Industrial	
British Standards	1.04	BS 1286	—	BS 1197	—
Composition	2.01	Ceramic	Portland cement Gypsum Linseed Oil Sawdust	Portland cement Aggregates	
Method of manufacture	2.02	Pressing Extrusion	Pressing	Moulding Pressing	Cast on site
Shape	2.04	Square Tiles	Rectangular Tiles	Square Tiles	Jointless
Dimensions	2.05	75mm x 75mm up to 300mm x 300mm 10mm to 50mm thick	150mm x 50mm 10mm & 15mm thick	300mm x 300mm 15mm to 38mm thick. Terrazzo is obtainable as slabs up to 900mm x 900mm & 50mm thick	15mm thick upwards depending on base and laying methods. Terrazzo is usually 15mm thick
Weight (kg/m²)	2.06	30 (12mm thick)	30 (9mm thick)	55-65 (25mm thick)	

Cork Carpet	*Cork Tile*	*Emulsion Cements*	*Flexible PVC*	*Linoleum*
Domestic	Domestic Commercial	Domestic Commercial Industrial	Domestic Commercial	Domestic Commercial
BS 810	—	—	BS 3261	BS 810
Cork granules Linoleum cement	Cork granules Resin binder	Emulsion of rubber, bitumen, resin, etc. with Cement and Aggregates	Plasticised PVC and fillers	Linseed oil Resins Cork and Wood flour
Calendering	Pressing Heating	Cast on site	Calendering Moulding Coating	Calendering
Sheets	Square Tiles	Jointless	Sheet Tiles	Sheet Tiles
180mm wide Up to 8mm thick	300mm x 300mm 3.2mm, 4.8mm thick	From feather edge up to 25mm thick but commonest thickness 6mm	900mm to 2m wide 2mm and 3mm thick	1800mm wide Up to 4.5mm thick
2.8 (4.5mm thick)	2.8 (7.5mm thick)	Approx. 17 (6mm thick)		5.6 (3.2mm thick)

Properties of Building Materials

		Ceramic Tile	Composition Block	Concrete	
				Pre-cast	In situ
Appearance & colour	2.07	Smooth or textured surface. Red, brown, buff, patterns	Smooth. Various colours	Smooth. Terrazzo is decorative. Various colours and patterns	Smooth
Warmth to touch	2.07	Poor	Fair	Poor	Poor
Bending strength	4.01.03	High	Medium	High	High
Resistance to impact	4.01.06	Very Good to Fair	Fair	Very Good to Good	Very Good
Hardness	4.01.11	High	Medium	High	High
Resistance to wear	4.01.12	Very Good to Good	Good	Very Good	Very Good to Good
Degree of slipperiness	4.01.14	High, wet Low, dry Low when textured	Medium	High, wet Low, dry	
Permeability to water vapour	4.03.01	Medium	Medium	High	High
Water absorption	4.04.02	Low	Low	Low	Low
Permeability to water	4.04.03	Low	Low	Medium	Medium
Moisture expansion	4.04.08	Very Low	Low	Low	Low
Reaction with other materials	4.13	None	None	None	None
Resistance to deterioration through action of water	4.14	Very Good	Very Good	Very Good	Very Good
Acids		Very Good to Good	Good	Good to Poor	Good to Poor

Cork Carpet	*Cork Tile*	*Emulsion Cements*	*Flexible PVC*	*Linoleum*
Textured. Plain colours	Smooth. Various natural shades	Smooth. Colours depend on pigments and emulsions but varied.	Wide range of textures colours and patterns	Smooth. Wide range of colours and patterns
Very Good	Very Good	Poor to Fair	Fair to Good	Fair to Good
Low	Low	Medium	Low	Low
Poor	Poor	Good to Fair	Poor	Poor
Low	Low	Medium	Low	Low
Fair	Fair	Very Good to Fair	Very Good to Poor	Very Good to Poor
High	High	High to Medium	High to Medium	Medium
High	High	Low to Medium	Medium	High
Medium	High	Low to Medium	Low	Medium
Medium	Medium	Low to Medium	Low	Medium
High	High	Low to Medium	Medium	High
None	None	None	Plasticiser migration may affect adhesive	None
Poor	Poor	Very Good to Poor	Good	Poor
Poor	Poor	Good to Poor	Good	Good to Poor

| | | Ceramic Tile | Composition Block | Concrete | |
				Pre-cast	In situ
Alkalies		Very Good to Fair	Good	Very Good	Very Good
Oils and Greases	Vegetable and Animal	Very Good	Good	Good to Fair	Good to Poor
Mineral Oils and Greases		Very Good	Good	Very Good	Very Good
Ease of cleaning	4.16	Good	Fair	Good to Fair	Fair
Means of Laying or Fixing	6.06	CP 202 BRS 79	Set in mortar	CP 202 BRS 47	CP 204 BRS 47

•

Cork Carpet	*Cork Tile*	*Emulsion Cements*	*Flexible PVC*	*Linoleum*
Poor	Poor	Good	Good to Poor	Poor
Poor	Poor	Good to Poor	Good	Good
Poor	Poor	Good to Poor	Good	Good
Poor	Fair	Good to Fair	Good	Good
CP 203	CP 203	CP 204	CP 203 BRS 33	CP 203

Floor Finishes (Continued)

Notes. Domestic means houses, flats, etc. Commercial means offices, shops, schools, etc. Industrial means factories, etc.

Where tiles are given as square, this indicates the commonest shape; obviously for linoleum, etc. they could be circular.

Under dimensions thickness is given last. Other dimensions are given in ranges but for some only the commonest sizes are given.

Unit weights are meant as a broad guide only. In several instances the weight range is very considerable.

Colours where given refer to the commonest ones produced.

In several cases a wide range is given for a property to timber. This is because it varies with species, hardwood or softwood, etc.

Under ease of cleaning any textured surface would be rated Poor so assessments are for smooth surfaces.

Resistance to wear is related to the use categories so should not be compared as if all were used in the same way.

Means of laying or fixing gives where relevant the BS Code of Practice written as CP 201, etc. BRS Digests are given as BRS 33, etc.

Material	1.01	FLOOR FINISHES			
Type	1.02	*Magnesium Oxychloride*	*Mastic Asphalt*	*Pitch Mastic*	*Metal Tiles*
Use	1.03	Domestic Commercial Industrial	Domestic Commercial Industrial	Domestic Commercial Industrial	Industrial
British Standards	1.04	BS 776	BS 1076,1410 1451, Tiles 1325	BS 1450,3672	
Composition	2.01	Magnesium Oxide and Chloride Fillers	Bituminous materials. Aggregates	Pitch Aggregates	Iron, Steel Aluminium
Method of manufacture	2.02	Cast on site	Hot poured on site or in moulds.	Hot poured on site	Casting Pressing
Shape	2.04	Jointless	Jointless or Square Tiles	Jointless	Tiles. Geometric Shapes
Dimensions	2.05	From 15mm thick upwards	From 15mm thick upwards	From 15mm thick upwards	300mm x 300mm. Up to 25mm thick
Weight (kg/m²)	2.06	33-55 (25mm thick)	60 (25mm thick)		180-240 (25mm thick)

Resins	*Rubber*	*Thermoplastic Tile*	*Vinyl Asbestos Tile*	*Wood*
Domestic Commercial Industrial	Domestic Commercial	Domestic	Domestic Commercial	Domestic Commercial Industrial
—	BS 1711	BS 2592	BS 3060	BS 1297,1187
Epoxy or other resin with aggregate or filler	Rubber Fillers	Resins Asbestos Limestone	Plasticised PVC Asbestos Limeston	Wood
Cast on site	Calendering Moulding	Calendering	Calendering	Various
Jointless	Sheet Tiles	Square Tiles	Square Tiles	Blocks Boards, etc.
Usually up to 6mm thick	Sheets 1800mm wide and up to 6mm thick, tiles 150mm x 150mm upwards	300mm square 3mm thick	300mm square 3mm thick	Various
11-12 (6mm thick)	11-12 (6mm thick)	5-6 (3mm thick)	5-6 (3mm thick)	>12 at 22mm thick

Properties of Building Materials

		Magnesium Oxychloride	Mastic Asphalt	Pitch Mastic	Metal Tiles
Appearance & colour	2.07	Smooth. Red, buff and brown	Black	Black	Plain or Textured Grey
Warmth to touch	2.07	Fair	Fair	Fair	Poor
Bending strength	4.01.03	Medium	Low	Low	High
Resistance to impact	4.01.06	Good to Fair	Very Good to Fair	Good to Fair	Very Good
Hardness	4.01.11	High to Medium	Short term: High Long term: Medium to low		High
Resistance to wear	4.01.12	Good to Fair	Very Good to Fair	Good to Fair	Very Good
Degree of slipperiness	4.01.14	Medium	High, wet Low, dry	High, wet Low, dry	High, wet to Low, dry but depends on texture
Permeability to water vapour	4.03.01	Medium	Nil	Nil	Nil
Water absorption	4.04.02	High	Nil	Nil	Nil
Permeability to water	4.04.03	Medium	Nil	Nil	Nil
Moisture expansion	4.04.08	Low to Medium	Nil	Nil	Nil
Reaction with other materials	4.13	Corrodes metals	None	None	None
Resistance to deterioration through action of Water	4.14	Poor	Very Good	Very Good	Very Good
Acids		Poor	Depends on aggregate	Depends on aggregate	Poor

Resins	Rubber	Thermoplastic Tile	Vinyl Asbestos Tile	Wood
Wide range of textures and colours	Smooth or textured. Range of colours	Smooth. Various colours	Smooth or textured. Various colours	Smooth. Various shades
Fair	Fair to Good	Fair	Fair	Good to Very Good
Low to High	Low	Low	Low	High
Very Good to Fair	Fair	Poor	Poor	Very Good to Poor
High	Low	Low	Low	High to Low
Very Good to Poor	Very Good to Poor	Fair	Good	Very Good to Poor
High to Low depending on texture	High, wet Low, dry	High, wet Medium, dry	High, wet Medium, dry	High to Low
Low	Low	Low	Low	Medium to High
Low to Medium	Low	Low	Low	Low to High
Nil to Low	Low	Low	Low	Low to Medium
Very Low	Low	Low	Low	Low to High
None	None	None	None	None
Very Good to Good	Very Good	Good	Good	Good to Fair
Very Good to Poor	Good	Poor	Poor	Good to Poor

Properties of Building Materials

		Magnesium Oxychloride	Mastic Asphalt	Pitch Mastic	Metal Tiles
Alkalies		Fair	Good	Good	Good to Poor
Oils and Greases	Vegetable and Animal	Good	Poor	Fair	Very Good
Mineral Oils and Greases		Good	Poor	Fair	Very Good
Ease of cleaning	4.16	Fair	Good to Fair	Good to Fair	Good to Fair
Means of Laying or Fixing	6.06	CP 204	CP 204	CP 204	Set in mortar, resin or concrete

Resins	*Rubber*	*Thermoplastic Tile*	*Vinyl Asbestos Tile*	*Wood*
Very Good to Fair	Fair	Good	Good	Good to Poor
Very Good to Good	Poor	Poor	Poor	Good
Very Good to Good	Poor	Poor	Poor	Good
Good to Fair	Good	Good to Poor	Good to Poor	Good to Poor
Depends on resin. Some are self-levelling, others are trowelled	CP 203	CP 203 BRS 33	CP 203 BRS 33	CP 201 BRS 18

Glass Sheet

Material	1.01	GLASS SHEET
Types	1.02	Wide range of clear and figured sheets; wire reinforced.
Use	1.03	Glazing of windows, cladding, roof lights (wire reinforced).
British Standards	1.04	BS 952:1964. Classification of glass for glazing and terminology for work on glass. CP 152:1966: Glazing and fixing of glass for buildings.
Composition	2.01	Mainly alkaline silicates and aluminates.
Chemical analysis	2.01	Silica and alumina > 71 per cent, Alkalies < 15 per cent, Lime and magnesia > 10 per cent.
Manufacture	2.02	Sand, soda ash, limestone, alumina, other materials heated in furnaces and drawn or floated into sheets.
Shape	2.04	Usually marketed as rectangular sheets.
Size	2.05	Length, up to 2m Width, up to 1.2m Thickness, up to 6mm.
Weight	2.06	Sheet glass is commonly described in terms of "oz", the normal being 24 oz/sq ft. equal to 3mm thick.
Density	2.06	2500 - 2560 kg/m³.
Appearance	2.07	Clear sheet having smooth surface. Wide range of figured surfaces. Normally almost colourless, but may be tinted (anti-glare, heat absorbing glasses) or coloured by fusion treatment.
Tensile strength	4.01.02	Very wide range up to 175 MN/m².
Modulus of elasticity	4.01.02	70,000 MN/m².
Effect of fire	4.02.02	Non-combustible but cracks and melts in a fire.
Effect of chemicals	4.04 and 4.05	Very resistant, but surface discolouration produced when thin films of water are trapped between sheets of glass.
Effect of impurities	4.05.02	Greenish-tinge produced by iron.

288

Thermal conductivity	4.07.01	1.05 W/m ^{0}C.
Thermal shock	4.07.05	Normal glazing quality cracks when heated.
Thermal expansion coefficient	4.07.05	7-9 x 10^{-6} per ^{0}C.
Melting point	4.07.05	Approx. 1500^{0}C. Depends upon composition.
Light transmission	4.08.04	Up to 90 per cent.
Durability	4.14	Very durable.
Liability to become dirty	4.16	Tends to become dirty readily on external surfaces but readily cleaned.
Safety	5.01	Relative ease of breakage necessitates care in selection of appropriate thickness to reduce liability to breakage. Special glasses are available which do not cause damage when broken.

Limes

Material	1.01	LIMES	
Type	1.02	Quicklime	Hydrated lime.
Use	1.03	Principal uses as constituents of mixes for mortar and plasterwork.	
British Standards	1.04	BS 890:1966.	BS 890:1966.
Composition	2.01	Mainly calcium oxide but semi-hydraulic limes contain smaller amounts of calcium silicates and calcium aluminates.	Mainly calcium hydroxide but with provison as for quicklime.
Chemical analysis (per cent.)	2.01	Lime (CaO) + magnesia (MgO) >85 Magnesia (except for magnesian lines) <5 Carbon dioxide <6 Insoluble material <3	>65 (60 for semihydraulic lime). <4 <6 <1
Manufacture	2.02	By burning limestone or chalk to temp. 1000°C to 1100°C.	By hydration of quicklime with minimal amount of water to yield a dry powder.
Shape	2.04	Generally irregularly shaped lumps.	Fine powder.
Dimensions	2.05	Variable, but unimportant.	Residue on 180 microns sieve <1 per cent. Residue on 90 microns sieve <6 per cent.
Bulk density	2.06	800 - 1000 kg/m^3.	550 - 600 kg/m^3.
Colour	2.07	White to light buff and bluish grey.	White to light buff.
Compressive strength	4.01.01	1:3 lime:sand can attain a compressive strength of up to 7 MN/m^2 in 6 months.	
Transverse strength	4.01.02	Modulus of rupture: 28 days for semi-hydraulic lime only:	Between 0.07 and 0.21 MN/m^2.

Rheological properties BS test for workability	4.01.15	>13 bumps on flow table. Limes produced from high calcium limestone will usually be much higher than this limit.	>13 bumps on flow table.
Effect of chemicals	4.04 and 4.05	Semi-hydraulic limes are attacked by sulphates.	
Effect of impurities	4.08.02	If the quicklime has not been properly slaked and matured before use or the hydrated lime has not been properly manufactured both may contain particles of unslaked lime which will slake and 'blow' after the lime has been incorporated in the building. The BS provides a soundness test for hydrated lime.	
Reaction with other materials	4.13	The presence of lime in mortar or plaster provides an alkaline environment which helps to protect some embedded materials but may adversely affect others, e.g. aluminium, for which additional protection is required.	
Durability	4.14	Mortars made from lime and sand are not very resistant to frost when first used since rate of hardening is slow. Subsequent behaviour is very good except where mortar remains very wet. Plastering mixes made of lime usually require addition of Portland cement or gypsum plaster to provide adequate early strength.	
Changes and behaviour during preparation	4.15	Considerable evolution of heat when water is added.	No evolution of heat when hydrated lime is mixed with water.

Metal, Aluminium Sheet

Material	1.01	METAL, ALUMINIUM SHEET
Type	1.02	Super-purity and commercial grades of aluminium and various alloys, more particularly NS 3.
Use	1.03	Roof coverings, flashings, cladding.
British Standards	1.04	BS 1470:1969. CP 143 Pt. 1 Aluminium corrugated and troughed sheet.
Composition	2.01	Super purity 99.99 per cent aluminium. Commercial grades 99.0 - 99.9 per cent. NS 3 contains 1.25 per cent manganese.
Manufacture	2.02	Electrolytic reduction of bauxite, hot or cold rolled into sheets.
Shape	2.04	Flat sheets and strips. Profiled sheets.
Dimensions	2.05	Length - no limit. Width - up to 1.220mm. Thickness - 0.56 - 1.63mm.
Density	2.06	$2\,700$ kg/m^3.
Appearance	2.07	Natural whitish-grey colour in mill and polished finishes. Limited range of colours for anodized finishes.
Tensile strength	4.01.02	Super purity 50-100 MN/m^2. Commercial grade 50-140 MN/m^2. NS 3 90-180 MN/m^2.
Modulus of elasticity	4.01.02	65 000 - 75 000 MN/m^2.
Hardness	4.01.11	Brinell No. 40 - 100.
Effect of chemicals	4.04.and 4.05	Attacked by alkalies in some mortars and plasters in wet conditions.
Effect of impurities	4.05.02	Impurities, other than copper, have little adverse effect and may be advantageous.
Thermal conductivity	4.07.01	22.7 W/m $^\circ$C.

Thermal expansion	4.07.05	24×10^{-6} per ^{0}C.
Melting point	4.07.05	658^{0}C.
Electrical conductivity	4.10.01	35.4 MS/m.
Reaction with other materials	4.13	Electrolytic corrosion likely when in contact with some metals, particularly copper and copper alloys, and iron and steel. Liable to corrode if in contact with magnesium oxychloride flooring, and wet timber such as western red cedar, Douglas fir and oak, though not affected by most timbers.
Durability	4.14	Very good under all normal conditions.
Ease of working	4.15	Generally good but depends upon the composition. Super purity aluminium is easy to dress to shape.
Liability to become dirty	4.16	Rapid, due to formation of oxide film which is not easy to clean off. Anodized finishes are less liable to become dirty and can be cleaned with water.

Notes. There is a wide range of aluminium alloys which have applications in the building industry ranging from nails to structural members, the properties, including durability, varying considerably according to composition, condition or temper. Sources of information on these include British Standards 1470-1477 and 1490, and the Aluminium Federation.

Metal, Copper Sheet

Material	1.01	METAL, COPPER SHEET
Use	1.03	Covering for roofs. Flashings. Gutters. Tanks and cylinders for water services.
British Standards, etc.	1.04	BS 899:1961. Code of Practice CP 143.
Composition	2.01	Generally not less than 99.0 per cent copper. Contains up to 0.5 per cent arsenic.
Manufacture	2.02	Acid leaching of copper ore, electrically refined, hot or cold rolled into sheets.
Dimensions	2.05	Length 1.2-2.4m for sheets, longer for strips. Width 0.6-1.2m for sheets, various widths for strips. Thickness 0.3-0.6mm.
Density	2.06	8940 kg/m³ .
Appearance	2.07	Smooth-surfaced sheets. Natural copper colour but changes on exposure unless protected by special lacquer.
Tensile strength	4.01.02	215-360 MN/m² depending upon the type and degree of working. Proof stress 0.1 per cent 45-370 MN/m² . Elongation 8-65 per cent dependent upon condition.
Modulus of elasticity	4.01.02	96,500-130,000 MN/m² . Bending or shaping is reasonably easy, but the material tends to harden when cold worked and this should be kept to a minimum.
Hardness	4.01.11	Brinell No. 40-95.
Effect of chemicals	4.03 and 4.05	Resistant to most building materials, soils and corrosive agents likely to come into contact with copper sheet in buildings. A protective skin of green patina slowly forms in certain atmospheric exposure conditions. Some waters are cupro-solvent mainly due to their content of free carbon dioxide.
Effect of impurities	4.05.02	Small amounts of materials such as oxygen, arsenic and silver may be present either as impurities or deliberate additions. These may have an effect on various properties often providing an improvement.

Protection against fungus, etc.	4.06.02	Washings from copper kill vegetable growth such as lichens and algae.
Thermal conductivity	4.07.01	400 W/m $^{\circ}$C.
Linear thermal expansion coefficient	4.07.05	17×10^{-6} per $^{\circ}$C.
Melting point	4.07.05	1083 $^{\circ}$C.
Electrical conductivity	4.10.01	58 MS/m, but varies according to composition and condition.
Taintability	4.12	Drinking water is not affected by the amounts normally taken into solution, even by cupro-solvency, up to 3 p.p.m.
Reaction with other materials	4.13	Copper forms electrolytic cells when in contact with other metals, particularly aluminium, zinc and steel, and direct contact should be avoided. Similar corrosion may occur when water running off copper surfaces comes into contact with these metals. Protective measures are also required where there may be indirect contact via cupro-solvent water. Washings from copper may stain other building materials.
Durability	4.14	Very durable under all normal conditions.

Notes. There is a wide range of copper alloys, including aluminium, manganese and silicon bronzes which are available in various forms and used for a variety of purposes in the building industry. The alloys have, in particular, strength properties which make them suitable for structural purposes. Information concerning the properties of individual alloys is available from the Copper Development Association, though not necessarily in CIB Master List order.

Metal, Lead

Material	1.01	METAL, LEAD
Purpose and Use	1.03	Roofing, flashings, weatherings, cladding, damp-proof courses.
British Standards	1.04	BS 1178.
Composition	2.01	Not less than 99.90 per cent lead.
Manufacture	2.02	By smelting galena and rolling the bars into sheets.
Dimensions	2.05	Width 2.40m. Narrower widths for strips. Length Up to 12m. Thickness 1.25, 1.80, 2.24, 2.50, 3.15 and 3.55mm.
Weight	2.06	1m² sheet 1mm thick weighs 11.34 to 11.37 kg.
Density	2.06	11 340 kg/m³.
Appearance	2.07	Smooth surface. Natural colour.
Tensile strength	4.01.02	15 (rolled), 18 (extruded) MN/m².
Modulus of elasticity	4.01.02	13 800 MN/m².
Hardness	4.01.11	Brinell No. 4
Permeability to air	4.03.01	Impermeable
Permeability to water	4.04.03	Impermeable.
Effect of chemicals	4.03 and 4.05	Highly resistant to most water supplies, to atmospheric pollution and to electrolytic corrosion. Not appreciably affected by lime and cement mortars except fresh mortar in wet conditions. Corrosion can occur when lead is in contact with some timbers, particularly oak and teak.
Effect of impurities	4.05.02	Small quantities of other metals such as silver, copper and tellurium provide improvement in some properties and are not considered as impurities as they may be deliberately incorporated in the lead.

Thermal conductivity	4.07.01	35 W/m $^{\circ}$C
Thermal expansion	4.07.05	1.8 x 10^{-6} per $^{\circ}$C.
Melting point	4.07.05	327.4 $^{\circ}$C.
Acoustic properties	4.09	Because of its high density sheet lead is a very useful material for improving the sound insulation of various forms of construction, the extent of the improvement depending upon the construction.
Electrical conductivity	4.10.01	8 MS/m.
Radiation properties	4.10.04	Excellent, used in various forms including sheet, castings, extrusions, lead shot for radiation protection.
Toxicity	4.12	Soft acid waters may dissolve small quantities of lead (plumbo-solvency).
Reaction with other materials	4.13	Generally inert.
Durability	4.14	Very durable.
Changes during preparation	4.15	Shrinkage on casting table, 2mm/m.
Working characteristics	4.15	Easy to work. Very malleable.

Metal, Stainless Steel

Material	1.01	METAL, STAINLESS STEEL		
Type	1.02	302 S17 304 S16	316 S16	430 S15
Use	1.03	Mainly for components and finishings where a high resistance to corrosion is required.		
British Standards	1.04	BS 1449:1967 Part 4.		
Composition (See also chemical analysis)	2.01	Steel containing appreciable amounts of chromium and nickel and (316 only) molybdenum.		Steel containing appreciable amount of chromium and small amount of nickel.
Chemical analysis (per cent)	2.01			
Chromium		17.5 - 19.0	16.5 - 18.5	16.0 - 18.0
Nickel		8.0 - 11.0	10.0 - 13.0	0.50
Molybdenum		-	2.25 - 3.0	-
Manganese		0.50 - 2.0	0.50 - 2.0	1.00
Silicon		0.20 - 2.0	0.20 - 2.0	0.80
Carbon		0.08 (302 S17) 0.06 (304 S16)	0.07	0.10
		Single figures are minima.		
Manufacture	2.02	By normal steel production methods using appropriate materials. Available in plates, sheets, bars, tubes and other sections.		
Dimensions	2.05	Sheets range in thickness from 0.3 - 2.9mm. Sheets range in width from 100 - 1830mm. Sheets range in length up to 9mm. Tubes for use in building range in nominal tube size from 4.8 - 25mm.		
Density (kg/m³)	2.06	7914	7946	7706
Appearance	2.07	Mill finishes ranging from matt to reflective. Polished finishes up to mirror polished.		
Tensile properties 0.2 per cent proof (MN/m²)	4.01.02	>208.5	>208.5	340

				Metal, Stainless Steel
Tensile strength (MN/m²)		>510	>540	540
Elongation, per cent on 50mm		>40	>40	26
Shear strength (MN/m³)	4.01.04	600	620	-
Young's modulus (MN/m²)		20 000	20 000	23 000
Hardness HV (Vickers test)	4.01.11	<205	<290	<175
Fatigue limit at 10 x 10' cycles (MN/m²)		260	270	310
Resistance to corrosion	4.03.04	High	Very high	Reasonably high
Effect of chemicals	4.03 and 4.05	Chemical resistance high.	Chemical resistance very high.	Attacked by acids and some salts.
Thermal conductivity (W/m°C)	4.07.01	22	15	15
Thermal expansion coefficient (per °C)	4.07.05	16×10^{-6}	16×10^{-6}	10×10^{-6}
Electrical conductivity (MS/m)	4.10.01	1	1	1
Magnetic properties	4.10.03	Non-magnetic	Non-magnetic	Magnetic
Reaction with other materials	4.13	Has no harmful effects.		
Durability	4.14	Very high	Very high	Slightly less than other grades.
Ease of cleaning	4.15	Good	Good	Good

Metal, Steel Sheet

Material	1.01	METAL, STEEL SHEET
Types	1.02	Plain, galvanised, vitreous enamelled, plastic coated and other finishes.
Use	1.03	Wall cladding, roof covering.
British Standards	1.04	BS 1449. Requirements for hot and cold rolled steel plate, sheet and strip. BS 3083. Hot-dipped galvanised corrugated steel sheets for general purposes.
Composition	2.01	Iron containing up to 1.5 per cent carbon.
Manufacture	2.02	Smelting of iron ores, hot or cold rolled into sheets and strips. Surface coatings are usually factory-applied.
Shape	2.04	Flat or corrugated sheets or strips.
Size	2.05	Length, up to 1 830mm. Width, up to 1 320mm. Thickness, up to 5mm.
Density	2.06	7 800 - 7 850 kg/m^3.
Appearance	2.07	Uncoated steel is grey in colour but rusts readily if not protected. Galvanised steel is light grey in colour, dulling on exposure. Vitreous enamelled finishes are obtainable in a wide range of colours. Other finishes are available in a limited range of colours.
Tensile strength	4.01.02	420 - 600 MN/m^2 according to carbon content.
Modulus of elasticity	4.01.02	20 000 MN/m^2.
Hardness	4.01.11	Brinell No. 120 - 140.
Fire resistance	4.02	Depends upon thickness and type of coating.
Effect of chemicals	4.03 and 4.05	Plain steel corrodes readily and requires protection for use in buildings. Galvanised coatings are attacked at a slow rate in polluted atmospheres.

Effect of impurities	4.05.02	The carbon content should not be considered as an impurity. Impurities are kept to a low level in the smelting process and are not harmful.
Thermal conductivity	4.07.01	52 - 62 W/m $^{\circ}$C.
Thermal expansion coefficient	4.07.05	10-12 x 10^{-6} per $^{\circ}$C.
Melting point	4.07.05	1 370°C (plain steel). Coatings melt at lower temperatures.
Durability	4.14	Depends upon the type and thickness of coating.
Liable to become dirty	4.15	Coated sheets do not dirty readily and are easy to clean.

Metal, Zinc Sheet

Material	1.01	METAL, ZINC SHEET
Use	1.03	Roof covering, flashings, cladding.
British Standards	1.04	BS 849. Code of Practice CP 143 Part 5.
Composition	2.01	Minimum purity 98.5 per cent Zn.
Manufacture	2.02	From zinc sulphide by melting or electrolytic process. Sheets or strips produced by rolling.
Dimensions	2.05	Length, up to 2400mm. Width, up to 1mm. Thickness, up to 1mm.
Density	2.06	7 140 kg/m³ (99.9 per cent purity).
Appearance	2.07	Smooth surface. Relatively dull light grey.
Tensile strength	4.01.02	130-140 MN/m² parallel to direction of rolling. 190-220 MN/m² perpendicular to direction of rolling.
Elongation		23-25 per cent parallel to direction of rolling. 10-14 per cent perpendicular to direction of rolling.
Modulus of elasticity		96 500 MN/m² .
Hardness	4.01.11	Brinell No. 45-50.
Resistance to mechanical wear	4.01.12	Not usually walked on. Sufficient for maintenance work to be carried out.
Effect of chemicals	4.03 and 4.05	Slow rate of attack in polluted atmosphere. Liable to attack by soluble salts and gypsum plaster, particularly if damp. Not affected by set lime or Portland cement mortars.
Effect of impurities	4.05.02	Normal impurities are not harmful and may strengthen the zinc sheet.
Thermal conductivity	4.07.01	113 W/m °C.

Thermal expansion coefficient	4.07.05	23×10^{-6} per $^{\circ}$C parallel to direction of rolling. 40×10^{-6} per $^{\circ}$C perpendicular to direction of rolling.
Melting point	4.07.05	419°C.
Electrical conductivity	4.10.01	Approx. 25 per cent of conductivity of copper.
Reaction with other materials	4.13	Liable to electrolytic corrosion in contact with copper or copper-bearing water such as from lightning conductors. Zinc may be attacked by damp timber, especially oak and western red cedar and must be isolated from them.
Durability	4.14	In urban areas a life of 40 years can be expected; longer in rural areas. Longer life on pitched roofs.
Working characteristics	4.15	Resistance to fatigue good.
Liability to become dirty	4.16	Not particularly liable.

Plaster, Gypsum

Material	1.01	PLASTER, GYPSUM
Type	1.02	Neat plasters - Classes A, B, C and D. Pre-mixed - Browning, Metal Lathing, Bonding, Multi-purpose, Finish.
Use	1.03	Internal plastering on bricks, blocks, boards, lathing.
British Standards	1.04	BS 1191. Gypsum building plasters. CP 211. Internal plastering.
Composition	2.01	Class A - hemihydrate gypsum (Plaster of Paris). Class B - retarded hemihydrate gypsum. Class C and D - anhydrous gypsum. Pre-mixed plasters - retarded hemihydrate gypsum with lightweight aggregate. Browning and metal lathing - Perlite. Bonding and multipurpose - Exfoliated vermiculite.
Manufacture	2.02	Calcination of gypsum to 160°C for hemihydrate gypsum plasters and to 500°C for anhydrous gypsum plasters. Retarder of set added to Class B and pre-mixed plasters, accelerator of set added to Classes C and D.
Bulk density (kg/m³)	2.06	Classes A and B 700-950; Classes C and D 800-900; Browning 500-700; Metal lathing and bonding 500-600; Finish 500-600.
Density set plaster	2.06	25 - 30 per cent above bulk density.
Warmth to touch	2.07	Fairly cold for neat plasters, slightly warmer for pre-mixed plasters.
Transverse strength	4.01.02	Unimportant in practice though useful for checking quality. Varies considerably depending upon type of plaster and water/plaster ratio.
Impact strength	4.01.06	Highest for Class D plasters.
Hardness	4.01.11	Depends upon density of set plaster. Plasters containing lightweight aggregates are relatively soft.
Effect of fire	4.02	Gypsum plasters increase the fire resistance of building materials, the extent depending upon thickness of coating.
Permeability to air	4.03.01	Permeable, extent decreasing from Class A to Class D.

Water absorption	4.04.02	High (Class A), decreasing with increasing density.
Solubility in water	4.04.06	Gypsum is slightly soluble, so not used externally, 0.2 per cent at 68° F.
Effect of chemicals	4.03 and 4.05	Not affected by chemicals normally likely to come into contact with plasters, except that water causes softening and loss of strength.
Effect of impurities	4.05.02	Very occasionally unslaked particles of lime may be present which expand in due course and blow off pieces of the surface.
Growth of micro-organisms	4.06.02	Undecorated surfaces do not usually support mould growth.
Thermal conductivity	4.07.01	0.55 - 0.60 W/m °C for neat plasters.
Thermal expansion coefficient	4.07.05	$10\text{-}12 \times 10^{-6}$ per °C.
Effect of high temperatures	4.07.05	Set plaster commences to dehydrate above 105° F.
Reaction with other materials	4.13	May cause corrosion of embedded metals in damp situations.
Durability	4.14	Very durable if kept dry.
Changes and behaviour during use. Setting time	4.15	Setting time varies from 2-5 min for Class A to 3-4 hours for other Classes.
Heat evolution		Appreciable amount of heat evolved, noticeable with Class A.
Change in volume		Gypsum plasters expand when setting.

Plaster Board, Gypsum

Material	1.01	PLASTERBOARD, GYPSUM
Type	1.02	Plain surfaced
Use	1.03	Backgrounds for plastered ceilings. Wall linings, plastered or decorated direct.
British Standard	1.04	BS 1230
Composition	2.01	Gypsum plaster faced on both sides with heavy paper.
Manufacture	2.02	Continuous process, a wet gypsum plaster mix being fed on to a layer of paper with another being fed on top. Plaster sets quickly, board cut into lengths and dried.
Shape	2.04	Rectangular sheets.
Size	2.05	Length, up to 2.4m normally. Width, up to 1.2m. Thickness, up to 15mm.
Weight	2.06	6.5 - 10.0 kg/m² (9.5mm thick).
Modulus of rupture	4.01.02	1.5 - 11 MN/m² in dry condition. Strength reduced appreciably when wet.
Impact strength	4.01.06	Relatively low but improved by being plastered.
Nailability	4.01.10	Readily nailable, relatively large-headed nails preferred.
Fire resistance	4.02.01	Used to improve fire resistance of various forms of construction.
Combustibility	4.02.02	Paper lining is combustible.
Surface spread of flame	4.02.02	Class 1.
Effect of chemicals	4.03 and 4.05	Not affected by chemicals likely to come into contact with it. Softened by water but hardens on drying.
Effect of impurities	4.05.02	None likely to be present.

Effect of micro-organisms, etc.	4.06.02	None, except possibility of mould growth on wet paper surface.
Thermal conductivity	4.07.01	0.16 W/m °C.
Reaction with other materials	4.13	None.
Durability	4.14	Very good, if kept dry.

Notes. The above data applies to plain plasterboard. The material may also be obtained with an aluminium foil backing to improve the thermal insulation of constructions in which it is used and also with decorative plastics facings.

Plastics, Cellular Sheets, Boards and Slabs

PLASTICS, CELLULAR SHEETS, BOARDS and SLABS

Material	1.01	*Expanded polystyrene*	*Expanded polystyrene*	*Expanded PVC*
Type	1.02	Beaded	Extruded	
Use	1.03	Insulation of walls roofs and floors	Insulation of walls, roofs and floors	Insulation of walls, roofs and floors
British Standards	1.04	BS 3837:1965	-	BS 3869:1965
Composition	2.01	Polystyrene	Polystyrene	Polyvinyl chloride
Method of manufacture	2.02	Fusion of expanded beads of polystyrene. Large blocks sliced into sheets.	Extrusion of foamed polystyrene.	Chemical foaming of PVC.
Shape	2.04	Sheets, slabs and special shapes	Sheets and slabs	Sheets and slabs
Internal structure	2.04	Irregular cells	Fairly regular cells	Cells, 1 mm and upwards
Dimensions	2.05			
Width (mm)		610,1220	610,1220	600,1220
Length (mm)		1220,1830,2440	1220,1830,2440	1220,1830,2440
Thickness (mm)		Up to 50	Up to 50	Up to 50
Density (kg/m³)	2.06	16-40	32-40	24-120
Appearance	2.07	White	White or dyed in pale colours	Yellow to brown rigid material
Warmth to touch	2.07	Feels warm	Feels warm	Feels warm
Compression strength (N/m^2)	4.01.01	7×10^4 (d=16) 12×10^4 (d=24)	27×10^4	$27\text{-}90 \times 10^4$

Foamed urea-formaldehyde	*Foamed-phenol formaldehyde*	*Foamed polyurethane* Rigid	*Foamed polyurethane* Flexible	*Expanded ebonite*
In situ cavity fill	Insulation of flat roofs	Insulation of walls, roofs, ceilings, etc.	Insulation of pipes and floors	Underfloor insulation
	BS 3927:1965			
Urea-formaldehyde	Phenol-formaldehyde	Polyurethane	Polyurethane	Ebonite
Formed by foaming an aqueous dispersion of resin	Chemical foaming of liquid components	Chemical reaction between two liquid components causes foaming and setting		Injection of gas into curing rubber
Sheets, but more usually used for in situ filling	Sheets and blocks	Rigid sheets, blocks and sandwich panels. Available for in situ application	Sheets, blocks and special shapes	Sheets and special shapes
	Open cell	Mainly closed cells, irregular	Mainly regular open cells	
Not applicable	Not applicable	600-1200 600-2400 25	Various sizes to fit pipes	300-900 1200
6	32	32-60	40-80	32
White friable material	Pink or deep red, rigid but friable	Colourless to deep brown	White, grey or coloured	Deep brown to black
Feels Warm	Feels warm	Feels warm	Feels warm	Feels warm
Negligible	14×10^4	17×10^4	$2\text{-}8 \times 10^4$	27×10^4

Properties of Building Materials

		Expanded polystyrene	*Expanded polystyrene*	*Expanded PVC*
Resistance to damage by impact	4.01.06	Low	Low	Low
Combustibility	4.02.02	Combustible. Softens and collapses	Combustible. Softens and collapses	Combustible
Spread of flame	4.02.02	Flame-retardant grades available. Increased rate if painted with gloss paints.	Flame-retardant grades available. Increased rate if painted with gloss paints.	Collapses but burns with difficulty.
Water vapour diffusion 25mm board g/m² s bar	4.03.01	0.015 (density 16) 0.0095 (density 24)	0.002 (density 72) 0.0038 (density 40)	
Water absorption (7 days) (Vol. per cent)	4.04.02	Normally low, 2.5-3.0 per cent but can be high if water does not drain away	1.5 per cent but may be higher if water does not drain away	3.0-3.8
Effect of chemicals	4.03 and 4.05	Affected by some organic solvents	Affected by some organic solvents	Very resistant to chemical action
Fungal attack	4.06.02	Resistant	Resistant	Resistant
Thermal conductivity (W/m°C)	4.07.01	0.033-0.035	0.032-0.035	0.035-0.054
Thermal expansion coefficient (per °C)	4.07.05	$5\text{-}7 \times 10^{-5}$ per °C	7×10^{-5} per °C	5×10^{-5} per °C
Softening point (°C)	4.07.05	86-101	86-101	75-165
Max. temperature of use (°C)	4.07.05	80°	80°	65°
Sound transmission (impact)	4.09.03	Appreciable reduction	N.A.	N.A.

Foamed urea-formaldehyde	*Foamed-phenol formaldehyde*	*Foamed polyurethane*	*Foamed polyurethane*	*Expanded ebonite*
Very low	Low	Low	Resilient	Low
Combustible	Combustible	Combustible	Combustible	Combustible
Resistant to ignition	Highly resistant to ignition	Flame-retardant grades available	Flame-retardant grades available	Flame-retardant
0.136	0.140	0.008	>0.1	0.0002
Fairly high	High	2.5	Up to 10, but may be higher if water does not drain away	1.0
Chemically resistant	Chemically resistant	Some are affected by alkali	Chemically resistant	Chemically resistant
Resistant	Resistant	Resistant	Resistant	Resistant
0.038	0.036	0.020-0.025	0.035	0.029
9×10^{-5}	$2\text{-}4 \times 10^{-5}$	$2\text{-}7 \times 10^{-5}$	$5\text{-}7 \times 10^{-5}$	5×10^{-5}
N.A.	N.A.	150-185	150-185	N.A.
100^0	130^0	100^0	100^0	50^0
N.A.	N.A.	Low	May give appreciable reduction	N.A.

Properties of Building Materials

		Expanded polystyrene	*Expanded polystyrene*	*Expanded PVC*
Sound absorption	4.09.05	Low	Low	Low
Durability	4.14	Durable. Full life not known.	Durable. Full life not known.	Durable. Full life not known.
Ease of Cleaning	4.15	Not easy to clean. May be decorated with emulsion paint	Not easy to clean. May be decorated with emulsion paint	Requires surface covering before decoration

Notes. (a) N.A. = non-applicable. (b) Durability assessment is based on proper use of the material.

Foamed urea-formaldehyde	*Foamed-phenol formaldehyde*	*Foamed polyurethane*	*Foamed polyurethane*	*Expanded ebonite*
N.A.	N.A.	Low	High	Low
Durable when properly compounded. Full life not known	Durable. Full life not known	Durable. Full life not known	Durable	Durable. In use for a longer period than other cellular plastics
N.A.	N.A.	Will accept surface treatment	Surface retains dirt	Smooth surface, not good for decoration.

Plastics, Glass Fibre, Reinforced Sheets

Materials	1.01	PLASTICS, GLASS FIBRE REINFORCED, SHEETS
Use	1.03	Roof and wall cladding providing diffused natural lighting but use restricted by fire hazard.
British Standards	1.04	BS 4154:1967. Corrugated plastics translucent sheets.
Composition	2.01	Glass fibre impregnated with polyester resin, with the addition of curing agents. Pigments and fillers may also be added.
Shape	2.04	Flat sheets. Standard and non-standard profiled sheets.
Size	2.05	Lengths from 1060 to 3050 mm, though longer lengths can be supplied. Widths range from 760 to 1 140 mm. Thickness 1.6 mm.
Weight	2.06	Flat sheet 1.4 - 1.6 kg/m^2. The weight per unit area of profiled sheets depends on the profile.
Appearance	2.07	Smooth surface. Limited range of standard colours, though non-standard colours are available.
Tensile strength	4.01.02	130-140 MN/m^2.
Modulus of rupture	4.01.02	260-280 MN/m^2.
Combustibility	4.02.02	Combustible.
Surface spread of flame	4.02.02	Class 3, but may be improved to Class 1 with flame retardant additions.
Permeability to air	4.03.01	Very low
Water absorption	4.04.02	0.5 per cent by weight when fully immersed for 24 hours.
Effect of chemicals	4.03 and 4.05	Unaffected by materials likely to come into contact with the sheets, apart from areas of high industrial pollution.
Effect of impurities	4.05.02	None present

Effect of micro-organisms, algae, etc.	4.06	Immune to insect and vermin attack. Does not nourish mould growth.
Thermal conductivity	4.07.01	0.03-0.04 W/m ^{0}C.
Thermal expansion coefficient	4.07.05	2×10^{-5} per ^{0}C.
Softening point ^{0}C	4.07.05	100-120^{0}C.
Effect of high and low temperatures	4.07.05	Unaffected by temperatures up to 80^{0}C and down to -40^{0}C.
Effect of frost	4.07.05	Becomes brittle in frosty weather.
Light transmission	4.08.04	Up to 85 per cent.
Effect of sunlight	4.08.07	Resistance to sunlight depends upon quality. Colours tend to fade.
Aggressiveness	4.13	Does not affect other materials.
Durability	4.14	Durable, though full length of life not yet known.
Ease of working	4.15	Can be cut with a wood saw or sheet metal saw.
Means of fixing	4.15	Holes must be drilled for fixing purposes. Nails must not be driven into the sheet.

Plastics, PVC Sheet

Material	1.01	PLASTICS, PVC SHEET, RIGID
Use	1.03	To provide natural lighting in roofs; also wall claddings.
British Standards	1.04	BS 4203:1967. Extruded rigid PVC sheeting. BS 2782:1965. Methods of testing plastics.
Composition	2.01	Unplasticised polyvinyl chloride.
Manufacture	2.02	Heated material is extruded through a die and polished by calenders.
Shape	2.04	Flat and corrugated sheets.

			Length mm	*Width mm*	*Thickness mm*
Size	2.05	Flat	1220 to 3050	760	1.6
		Corrugated.	1220 to 3050	1085	1.6

Weight	2.06	2.4 kg/m².
Appearance	2.07	Transparent and practically colourless. Coloured, semi-transparent and opaque.
Tensile strength	4.01.02	50-60 MN/m². Young's Modulus of elasticity 37 000 MN/m².
Impact strength	4.01.06	700-800 N/m².
Combustibility	4.02.02	Combustible.
Surface spread of flame	4.02.02	Difficult to ignite, self-extinguishing.
Permeability to air	4.03.01	Very low
Water absorption	4.04.02	Less than 0.15 per cent.
Effect of chemicals	4.03 and 4.05	Slowly attacked in heavily polluted districts.
Effect of impurities	4.05.02	None present.

Effect of micro-organisms, algae, etc.	4.06	Immune to insect and vermin attack. Does not nourish mould growth.
Thermal conductivity	4.07.01	0.13 W/m ^{0}C. deg
Thermal expansion coefficient	4.07.05	5×10^{-5} per ^{0}C.
Melting point	4.07.05	Softens at 70^0C.
Effect of high and low temperatures	4.07.05	Unaffected between 70^0C. and -40^0C.
Light transmission	4.08.04	Over 85 per cent for transparent grades. No UV light transmission.
Effect of sunlight	4.08.07	Darkens on long exposure.
Reaction with other materials	4.13	No effect.
Durability	4.14	Life depends upon extent of atmospheric pollution, but could be in excess of 20 years.
Ease of working	4.15	Can be sawn with a fine-tooth saw. The material should be drilled and not punched.
Liability to become dirty.	4.16	Tendency to become dirty, but easily cleaned.

Sealants

Material	1.01	SEALANTS		
Type	1.02	*Acrylic*	*Bitumen*	*Bitumen-rubber*
Grade	1.02 .	Gun	Gun (g), knife (k) and preformed strip (ps)	g, k and ps
Use	1.03	Provision of weathertight joints between building materials,		
British Standards	1.04	BS 3712	BS 3712	BS 3712
Colour	2.07	All colours	Black	Black
Tensile properties per cent movement/ joint width	4.01.02	10-15	5 g 5-15 (k, ps)	10
Shear properties per cent movement/ joint width	4.01.04	30-40	15-40	30
Adhesion	4.01.13	Fair to Good	Good. Primer required for g and k grades	Fair
Rheological properties	4.01.15	Elastic/plastic flow	Plastic flow	Plastic flow
Effect of high and low temperatures	4.07.05	Not affected by temperatures experienced in normal use.		
Effect of sunlight	4.08.07	Slight	Moderate	Moderate
Durability expected life (years)	4.14	20	2-10	10-20
Setting time (hours)	4.15	12	Does not skin or set	Does not skin or set

Butyl rubber	*Oleo-resinous*	*Polysulphide*	*Polyurethane*	*Silicone*
g, k and ps	g, k and ps	g and k 1 and 2 part	g 1 and 2 part	g

components and elements, allowing for dimensional changes and other movements.

Butyl rubber	*Oleo-resinous*	*Polysulphide*	*Polyurethane*	*Silicone*
BS 3712	BS 3712	BS 4254 (2-part)	BS 3712	BS 3712
Greyish-aluminium	Various	Various	Black,grey and cream	Various
5-15 g 2-15 k and ps	5-25 g 5-15 k 2 ps	15-25 1-part 20-35 2-part	17-20	8-12
15-50 g 10-50 k 10-30 ps	15-50 g and k 10 ps	40-75 1-part 50-75 2-part	40-60	20-40
Fair to Good	Fairly Good	Primer required on porous surfaces and on glass	Fair	Good
Elastic/plastic flow	Plastic flow	Elastic flow	Elastic flow	Elastic flow
Moderate	Moderate	Slight	Slight	Slight
2-15	2-10	20	15	20
12-24	24-36	24 1-part 6-48 2-part	24	2

Stone, Natural

		Limestone Portland Stone	Limestone Bath Stone	Limestone Others	Sandstone Yorkstones
Material	1.01	STONE, NATURAL			
Type	1.02	*Limestone* Portland Stone	*Limestone* Bath Stone	*Limestone* Others	*Sandstone* Yorkstones
Use	1.03	—————— Walling and Cladding ——————			Paving, walling, cladding and coping.
Composition	2.01	———— Largely calcium carbonate ————			Quartz in all, mica and felspar grains in some. Bonded largely with silica or calcium carbonate
Method of production	2.02	Quarried, cut to size (masoning and sawing), finish as required e.g.			
Density (kg/m³)	2.06	2100-2350	2100-2250	1900-2400	2400-3000
Compressive strength (MN/m²)	4.01.01	15-30	10-14	9-59	42-85
Effect of fire	4.02.02	All non-combustible			
Water absorption (per cent)	4.04.02	6-11	7-8	2.5-11	3-4
Moisture expansion (per cent)	4.04.08	———— About 0.01 ————			Negligible
Effect of chemicals	4.04.08	Attacked by acids	Attacked by acids	Attacked by acids	Resistant to most acids
Resistance to effect of soluble salts	4.05.02	Poor-Very Good	Poor-Good	Poor-Very Good	Good

Sandstones	Granites	Marbles	Slates	Quartzites
Others				
Walling and cladding.	Walling, cladding, plinths, window surrounds and steps.	Window surrounds, cladding, floors and stairs.	Cladding, cills, coping, steps and paving.	Cladding, plinths, paving, floors and stairs.
See Yorkstones	Mainly felspar, quartz and mica.	Mainly calcium carbonate.	Mainly silica, alumina and iron oxides.	Mainly quartz.
patterned, rock faced, fair picked, fine axed, rubbed, eggshell or polished				Finish-Natural riven
1950-2550	2400-2900	2725-2900	2400-2900	about 2600
21-105	90-146	About 60	75-200	About 100
2-8.5	0.1-0.5	0.1-0.5	<0.1	0.1-0.5
0.07	None	Negligible	Negligible	Negligible
Resistant to most acids except calcareous types which are attacked	Resistant to most acids.	Attacked by acids.	Mainly resistant to acids.	Resistant to most acids.
Poor-Good	Poor-Good	Good	Good	Good

		Limestone	Limestone	Limestone	Sandstone
Thermal expansion (coefficient)	4.07.05	———————— About 4 x 10⁻⁶ per °C. ————————			
Thermal conductivity (W/m°C)	4.07.01	————————————— About 1.5 —————————			
Resistance to frost	4.07.05	Poor-Very Good	Poor-Good	Poor-Very Good	Good-Excellent
Durability	4.14	Dependent on 4.07.05, 4.03.04, 4.04.08, 4.05.02 and 4.13			
Ease of working	4.15	Fairly easy	Easy	Easy-Hard	Hard
Liability to become dirty.	4.16	———————Become soiled in urban atmosphere ——			Become soiled in urban atmospheres.
Ease of cleaning	4.16	———————————Fairly easy to clean ————————			Difficult to clean

Sandstones	Granites	Marbles	Slates	Quartzites
About 12×10^{-6}	About 11×10^{-6}	About 4×10^{-6}	About 11×10^{-6}	About 11×10^{-6}
About 1.3	About 3.0	About 2.5	About 1.9	About 3.0
Poor-Excellent	Good-Excellent	Good-Excellent	Good-Excellent	Good-Excellent
Dependent on 4.07.05, 4.03.04, 4.04.08, 4.05.02 and 4.13				
Hard	Hard	Fairly Hard	Hard	Hard
See Yorkstones	Resistant to soiling.	Fairly resistant to soiling.	Resistant to soiling.	Resistant to soiling.
	Difficult to clean.	Difficult to clean.	Difficult to clean.	Difficult to clean.

Tile, Clay Roof

Material	1.01	TILE, CLAY ROOF
Types	1.02	Plain, single lap; Hand made; Machine made.
Uses	1.03	Roofing, but also used for wall cladding.
British Standards	1.04	BS 402
Composition	2.01	Fired clay.
Manufacture	2.02	Suitably prepared clays are cast into moulds either by hand or machine, dried and fired, the temperature depending upon the clay.
Shape	'2.04	Normal shape is rectangular, but various patterns available. Special shapes for ridges, valleys, etc.

Dimensions	2.05	*Plain*	*Single lap*
Length		265 mm	340-400 mm
Width		165 mm	200-340 mm
Thickness		9-15 mm	9-15 mm

Weight	2.06	Plain 60-70 kg/m^2. Single lap 34-40 kg/m^2.
Appearance	2.07	Range of smooth, sand-faced and colour glazed. Natural colours include wide range of browns. Glazed colours include green and blue.
Transverse strength	4.01.02	BS min. plain 790 N breaking load, tested wet. Both plain and single lap tiles have more than adequate strength if properly burnt.
Water vapour permeability	4.03.01	Permeable.
Water absorption	4.04.02	BS Limit is 10.5 per cent.
Drying	4.04.05	Absorbed water dries readily.
Effect of impurities	4.05.02	Small nodules of lime, if present, may cause 'blowing'.
Algae growth	4.06.02	Algae grow on tiles that keep damp. Excessive growth indicates porous tiles. Drippings of rain from copper wires kills algae.

Thermal conductivity	4.07.01	0.8 W/m $^\circ$C.
Effect of frost	4.07.05	Underfired tiles may have low frost resistance. Some machine-made tiles have a life of 25-40 years, while others have a very long life. Well-burnt hand made tiles, though often more permeable, may have a life measured in centuries. Tiles laid on steep pitches are less affected than those laid on shallow pitches.
Durability	4.14	Lightly-fired tiles may have a relatively high content of soluble salts adversely affecting the durability by causing disintegration of the nibs.

Tile, Concrete Roof

Material	1.01	TILE, CONCRETE ROOF
Types	1.02	Plain, single-lap.
Uses	1.03	Roofing primarily, but also wall cladding in the form of tile-hanging.
British Standards	1.04	BS 473,550:1967
Composition	2.01	Portland cement, clean sand or crushed stone and pigments.
Manufacture	2.02	Cement-sand mix cast or extruded, cured sufficiently to handle. Hardening process continues for a long time.
Shape	2.04	Normal shape is rectangular but various patterns available. Specials for ridges, valleys, etc.

Dimensions	2.05	*Plain*	*Others*
Length		270 mm	380 to 460 mm
Width		165 mm	230 to 380 mm
Thickness		Not less than 9 mm	

Weight	2.06	Plain 60-80 kg/m². The weight on a roof depends upon the amount of overlap. Single lap 34-45 kg/m².
Appearance	2.07	Range of fairly smooth and granule faced surfaces. Range of colours
Transverse strength	4.01.02	BS limits min. breaking load 495N (wet), 675N (dry).
Water vapour permeability	4.03.01	Fairly permeable.
Water absorption	4.04.02	Low.
Water permeability	4.04.03	Very low.
Drying	4.04.05	Absorbed water dries readily.
Algae growth	4.06.02	Generally free from algae growth, but may occur on relatively porous tiles.

Thermal conductivity	4.07.01	0.5 W/m °C.
Effect of frost	4.07.05	Tiles unaffected.
Durability	4.14	Excellent.

Timbers, Hardwood

Material	1.01	TIMBER, HARDWOOD			
Type	1.02	*Afrormosia*	*Iroko*	*Mahogany African*	*Meranti light-red*
Use	1.03	High class joinery.	General	Joinery	General, including plywood.
British Standards	1.04	See Softwoods.			
Density (kg/m³)	2.06	630-800	650	520	400-640
Appearance	2.07	Fine texture. Yellow-brown.	Coarse texture. Pale yellowish-brown to dark chocolate brown.	Medium texture. Pinkish brown to deep reddish brown.	Coarse texture Pale pink to mid-red.
Compressive strength (MN/m²)	4.01.01	22	19 (50)	13 (43)	13 (50)
Bending strength (MN/m²)	4.01.03	26	23 (85)	15 (80)	15 (88)
Modulus of elasticity (MN/m²)	4.01.03	12 100	10 300 (10 500)	8500 (9500)	8300 (10 500)
Impact (related to oak)	4.01.06	40 per cent better	30 per cent inferior	30 per cent inferior	20 per cent inferior
Resistance to insertion and extraction of nails and screws.	4.01.10	Marked tendency to split when nailed.	Good nailing and screwing properties.	Good nailing and screwing properties.	Satisfactory nailing and screwing properties.
Hardness (related to oak)	4.01.11	20 per cent harder	40 per cent softer	40 per cent softer	30 per cent softer

Meranti dark-red	*Oak*	*Opepe*	*Sapele*	*Teak*
General, including plywood.	General	General	General	General
580-770	720	730	560-700	640
Coarse texture. Medium to dark red brown.	Coarse texture. Yellowish brown.	Open texture. Yellow or orange-brown.	Fairly fine texture. Dark reddish- or purplish-brown.	Fine texture. Golden brown.
13 (53)	15 (50)	25 (70)	21 (58)	22
15 (92)	21 (92)	31 (110)	23 (110)	26
8000 (11 500)	9500 (10 800)	14 000 (14 200)	11 000 (11 700)	12 000
20 per cent inferior	Standard	10-20 per cent inferior	Similar to oak	10-20 per cent inferior
Good nailing and screwing properties	Holds nails and screws firmly.	Slight tendency to split when nailed but takes screws satisfactorily.	Good nailing and screwing properties.	Fairly good nailing and screwing properties.
30 per cent softer	Standard	20 per cent harder	Similar to oak	10-20 per cent inferior

Properties of Building Materials

		Afrormosia	Iroko	Mahogany African	Meranti light-red
Adhesion when glued	4.01.13	Satisfactory	Satisfactory	Satisfactory	Good
Effect of fire	4.02	All timbers are combustible but production of charred wood reduce:			
Surface spread of flame	4.02.02	Class 3 or 4 when untreated, but Class 1 with suitable surface or			
Moisture content per cent:	4.04.01				
at 90 per cent RH		15	15	20	18.5
at 60 per cent RH		11	11	13.5	12.5
Permeability to preservatives	4.04.03	Extremely resistant	Extremely resistant	Extremely resistant	Resistant to extremely resistant
Dimensional changes per cent 90-60 per cent RH	4.04.08	1.3 T 0.7 R	1.0 T 0.5 R	1.3-1.8 T 0.8-1.3 R	1.6-1.9 T 0.7-0.8 R
Resistance to insect attack	4.06.01	Attacked by ambrosia (pin-hole borer) beetles.	Attacked by ambrosia and powder-post beetle.	As for Iroko	Sap-wood attacked by powder-post beetle.
Effect of fungus	4.06.02	Very durable	Very durable	Mod. durable	Non-durable t‹ moderately durable.
Linear thermal expansion	4.07.05	The coefficient of linear thermal expansion is relatively small, of the			
Thermal conductivity	4.07.01	Thermal conductivity is relatively low, of the order of 0.14 W/m °C.			

Meranti dark-red	*Oak*	*Opepe*	*Sapele*	*Teak*
Good	Satisfactory		Satisfactory	Satisfactory on newly machined surfaces.

rate of combustion and fire resistance of thick sections is relatively good.

impregnation treatments (mainly applicable to plywoods).

Meranti dark-red	*Oak*	*Opepe*	*Sapele*	*Teak*
20 13	20 12	17 12	Not available	15 10
Resistant to extremely resistant	Extremely resistant	Moderately resistant	Resistant	Extremely resistant
2.0 T 1.0 R	2.5 T 1.5 R	1.8 T 0.9 R	1.8 T 1.3 R	1.2 T 0.7 R
Sapwood attacked by powder-post beetle.	Sapwood readily attacked by powder-post beetles. Attacked by common furniture beetle. Sapwood and heartwood attacked by death watch beetle.	Generally good resistance.	Sapwood attacked by powder-post beetle.	Sapwood attacked by powder-post beetle.
Moderately durable to durable.	Durable	Very durable	Moderately durable.	Very durable

order of 4.5 x 10^{-6} per $^{\circ}$C, but individual figures are not available.

		Afrormosia	*Iroko*	*Mahogany African*	*Meranti light-red*
Reaction with other materials	4.13	Becomes stained in contact with ferrous metals and accelerates their corrosion in wet conditions.	No effects	No effects	No effects
Durability	4.14	The durability depends largely upon the resistance to fungal attack			
Ease of working - cutting	4.15	Medium	Medium	Medium (variable).	Medium (variable).
- blunting of tools		Moderate	Fairly severe	Moderate (variable).	Moderate (variable).
- steam bending classification		Moderate	Moderate	Very poor	Very poor

Notes. Single figures are the average of a range which may sometimes be appreciable because of the variation in origin and
4.04.08. T = Tangential. R = Radial.
4.01.01./3. The figures given are for the basic grade (i.e. the best) and refer to the working stresses as classified in CP 112; figures timber.

Meranti dark-red	*Oak*	*Opepe*	*Sapele*	*Teak*
No effects	Tannin content leads to deterioration when in contact with ferrous metals. Accelerates the corrosion of metals when wet. Very corrosive action on lead.	No effects	No effects	No effects

under conditions conducive to such attack. See 4.06.02.

Meranti dark-red	*Oak*	*Opepe*	*Sapele*	*Teak*
Medium (variable). Moderate (occasionally severe).	Medium (variable. Moderate (variable).	Medium Moderate	Medium Moderate	Medium Fairly severe
Poor	Very good	Very poor	Poor	Moderate

condition of the various species. Sapwoods of all species are either perishable or non-durable.

in brackets are the maximum test values. A fuller range of figures is given in P.R.L. Bulletin No. 45. The strength properties of

Timber, Resin-Bonded Wood Chipboard

Material	1.01	TIMBER, RESIN BONDED WOOD CHIPBOARD	
Type	1.02	Standard grades	Flooring grades.
Use	1.03	Partitions, wall and ceiling linings, roof decking.	Flooring and a base for various floor finishes.
British Standards	1.04	BS 2604. Resin bonded wood chipboard. BS 1811. Methods of test for wood chipboard and other particle boards.	
Composition	2.01	Wood chips, asbestos fibres or other materials bonded with resin generally urea formaldehyde.	
Manufacture	2.02	Either by pressing or by extrusion, the latter process providing a slightly rougher surface.	
Dimensions	2.05	Lengths from 1800 mm. to 5200 mm. Widths from 600 mm. to 1700 mm. Thickness from 9 mm to 31 mm.	
Density	2.06	600-650 kg/m³	675-725 kg/m³
Appearance	2.07	Relatively smooth surfaced board, but may be supplied prepared for painting and free from surface blemishes. Available with wood veneer and plastics sheeting finishes. Normal colour of untreated board varies from straw to light yellowish brown.	
Tensile strength	4.01.02	6.5 - 7.5 MN/m²	15 - 20 MN/m²
Modulus of rupture	4.01.02	2.5 - 14 MN/m²	15 - 18 MN/m²
Modulus of elasticity	4.01.02	2050 - 2100 MN/m²	2750 MN/m²
Resistance to splitting	4.01.09	Not liable to split	Not liable to split
Screw holding	4.01.10	Face 620N Edge 355N	Face 710N Edge 530N
Combustibility	4.02.02	Combustible	Combustible
Surface spread of flame	4.02.02	Class III. Proprietory finishes will provide Class I.	Class III. Proprietory finishes will provide Class I.

Permeability to water vapour	4.03.01	40 - 80 MN s/g m	40 - 80 MN s/g m
Moisture content	4.04.01	9 per cent ex-works	9 per cent ex-works
Water absorption	4.04.02	6 per cent	4 per cent
Moisture expansion 60 per cent to 90 per cent RH at 20°C	4.04.05	Length and width 0.2 per cent. Thickness 5 per cent.	Length and width 0.2 per cent. Thickness 5 per cent.
Effect of chemicals	4.04.08	Very slight	Very slight
Insect attack	4.06.01	Not attacked by wood destroying insects but is not immune to termite attack.	
Fungal attack	4.06.02	Liable to fungal attack if moisture content is above 20 per cent.	
Thermal conductivity	4.07.01	0.12 W/m °C.	0.14 W/m °C.
Thermal expansion	4.07.05	Not available	Not available
Sound reduction	4.09.03	Thickness 18 mm. 25-26 dB reduction. Reduction for double skins depends upon construction.	Appropriate construction will provide Grade 1 Impact Sound insulation.
Reaction with other materials	4.13	Virtually none.	
Durability	4.14	Very satisfactory if moisture content is maintained below 20 per cent. May suffer damage if moisture content is higher.	

Timbers, Softwood

		Scots pine or Scotch fir	Baltic redwood
Material	1.01	TIMBER, SOFTWOOD	
Type	1.02	———————— REDWOOD ————————	
Use	1.03	General	General
British Standards	1.04	BS 565:1963. Glossary of terms applicable to timber, plywood and BS 881 and 569:1955. Nomenclature of commercial timbers BS 1186:Part 1:1952. Quality of timber in joinery. Part 2:1955. BS 1297:1952. Softwoods tongued and grooved flooring. BS 1860:Part 1:1959. Structural timber. Measurement of CP 112:1967. The structural use of timber in buildings.	
Density (air dry) kg/m³	2.06	500 (Average figs.)	480
Appearance	2.07	Reddish brown heartwood	Reddish·brown heartwood
Compressive strength parallel to grain (MN/m²)	4.01.01	11.4 (48)	11.4 (45)
perpendicular to grain (MN/m²)		2.1	2.1
Modulus of rupture parallel to grain (MN/m²)	4.01.02	14 (90)	14 (84)
Modulus of elasticity (MN/m²)		8270 (10 150)	8270 (10 150)
Shear strength parallel to grain (MN/m²)	4.01.04	1.5	1.5
Impact strength	4.01.06	Softwoods are readily indented by impact.	

————————————————— WHITEWOOD —————————————————

Baltic whitewood	*Douglas fir*	*Larch*	*Hemlock*	*Western red cedar*
General	Particularly useful for structural work	As for Douglas fir but also for out-side work.	General	Particularly useful for outdoor work.

joinery.
including sources of supply.
Quality of workmanship in joinery.

characteristics affecting strength.

400	500 homegrown 560 imported	560	460	370
Pinkish brown heartwood	Pinkish brown heartwood	Reddish brown heartwood	White or pale brown	Reddish brown
11.4 (36)	13.3 (55)	13.3 (50)	11.4 (48)	8.4 (34)
2.1	2.5	2.5	2.1	1.5
14 (74)	17.5 (96)	17.5 (105)	14 (87)	10 (56)
8270 (10 000)	9660 (13 200)	9660 (10 700)	8270 (10 400)	6890 (7600)
1.5	1.5	1.5	1.5	1.25

Softwoods are readily indented by impact.

		Scots pine or Scotch fir	*Baltic redwood*
Nailability	4.01.10	Good	Good
Effect of fire	4.02	Timber is combustible but the charring action tends to retard	
Spread of flame	4.02.02	Softwoods except western red cedar are Class 3 but the rate can be	
Moisture content	4.04.01	The moisture content of timber as supplied depends on conditons c Varies in use according to humidity of the air and to exposure	
Permeability to preservatives	4.04.03	Moderately resistant	Moderately resistant
Dimensional changes with changes in moisture content (per cent) (90 per cent RH to 60 per cent RH)	4.04.08	2.2 Tangential 1.0 Radial	2.2 Tangential 1.0 Radial
Effect of insects	4.06.01	Softwoods are subject to damage by grubs of the common furniture	
Effect of fungi	4.06.02	Non-durable	Non-durable
Thermal conductivity	4.07.01	Varies according to density and moisture content. Average value	
Linear thermal expansion	4.07.05	$4\text{-}5 \times 10^{-6}$ per $^\circ$C.	
Durability	4.14	The durability of softwoods depends largely upon their moisture	
Ease of working - resistance to cutting	4.15	Low	Low
- blunting effect on tools		Mild	Mild

Notes. 4.01.01 - .04. The figures given are for the basic grade (i.e. the best) and refer to the working stresses as classified in CP 112; Properties of Timber.
4.06.02. Timbers are classified in five grades to denote their durability *under conditions favourable to decay*. The grades are: Very or non-durable.

Baltic whitewood	*Douglas fir*	*Larch*	*Hemlock*	*Western red cedar*
Good	Harder to nail than most softwoods		Good	Good

combustion and large sections last longer in a fire than comparable sized steel sections.

reduced by applying fire-retardant paint or by impregnation with certain chemicals. Class 4.

drying and subsequent storage. Commonly between 10 and 16 per cent.
conditions.

Resistant	Resistant	Resistant	Resistant	Resistant
1.5 T	1.5 T	1.7 T	1.9 T	0.9 T
0.7 R	1.2 R	0.8 R	0.9 R	0.45 R

beetle and in some parts of Surrey by the grubs of the house longhorn beetle.

Non-durable	Non-durable	Mod. durable	Non-durable	Durable

$1.4 - 1.5 \ W/m^{\circ}C$

content being below the limit conducive to fungal attack (See also 4.06.02).				Some grades become dark in colour and deteriorate in 10 years.
Low	Medium	Medium	Low	Low
Mild	Medium	Medium	Mild	Mild

figures in brackets are maximum test values. A complete range of figures is given in P.R.L. Bulletin No. 45. The Strength

durable, Durable, Moderately durable, Non-durable, Perishable. This classification refers to heartwood, sapwood being perishable

Environmental Design Data

Environmental design is a subject of
increasing public concern. In this section
the basic data necessary for designing
buildings with the internal environment
in mind is presented in a co-ordinated
tabular manner under the three broad
headings of **Lighting, Heating** and
Sound Insulation and Acoustics.

Lighting

We would like to thank the Illuminating Engineering Society, York House, Westminster Bridge Road, London S.E.1, for allowing us to reprint the information on pages 342 to 382 from the IES Code, and the Lighting Industry Federation, 25 Bedford Square, London W.C.1, for allowing us to reprint the data in Tables 4 and 5 from their Interior Lighting Design. For further information on lighting reference should be made to both these books.

LAMP DATA

Lamp types

The following types of lamp are commonly used in interior lighting:
incandescent (tungsten filament and tungsten halogen);
[tubular] fluorescent (type MCF);
high pressure mercury with a phosphor coating on the bulb to improve colour rendering (type MBF);
high pressure mercury incorporating a tungsten filament (types MBT, MBTF);
metal halide (types MBI, MBIL, MBIF);
high pressure sodium (type SON).

Low pressure sodium lamps (types SOX and SLI) have very high luminous efficacies but their light is almost monochromatic making them suitable only for outdoor areas where colour rendering is unimportant.

Fluorescent lamps using an indium amalgam in place of mercury can often be used to advantage where the ambient temperature is high. The lamps operate most efficiently at a tube wall temperature of 65°C compared with 40°C for ordinary fluorescent lamps. This last temperature is exceeded in many enclosed luminaires and the use of amalgam lamps in place of ordinary lamps will often increase the light output of the luminaire by about 10 per cent, and by up to 25 per cent if the enclosing diffuser fits closely round the lamps.

In cold rooms and similar interiors where the normal ambient temperature is low, the light output from fluorescent lamps may be considerably less than maximum. Lamps incorporating clear glass jackets may be used to maintain the tube temperature at about the value which gives maximum light output.

**Lamp economics
and luminous
efficacies**

All discharge lamps (including fluorescent lamps) need a stabilizing ballast in circuit; high pressure sodium and mercury halide lamps may also require auxiliary starting equipment. The initial cost of discharge lighting equipment is consequently higher than that of incandescent lamps, but the longer life, the higher luminous efficacy and the availability of discharge lamps in sizes giving very large light outputs will usually more than compensate for the greater initial outlay.

Luminous efficacies vary widely with the lamp type, ranging from 10-15 1m/W for ordinary tungsten filament lamps to above 150 1m/W for some

Table 1 Colour properties of lamps for general lighting

Colour appearance group	Colour rendering group	Lamp type	Lamp designation	Range of luminous efficacy (lighting design lumens/watt)	Approximate correlated colour temperature (K)
Cool	A	Tubular fluorescent	NORTHLIGHT COLOUR MATCHING	35-50	6500
			ARTIFICIAL DAYLIGHT	25-35	6500
Intermediate	B	Tubular fluorescent	^{0}Kolor-rite Trucolor	35-55	4000-4200
	C	Tubular fluorescent	De luxe Natural	30-45	3600
	D	Tubular fluorescent	NATURAL	45-65	4000-4200
	E	Tubular fluorescent	DAYLIGHT	55-80	4300
	F	High pressure discharge	Metal halide fluorescent (MBIF)	65-85	3900
			Metal halide (MBI, MBIL)	60-85	3600-4400
	G	High pressure discharge	Mercury fluorescent (MBF)	35-55	4000
			Mercury-tungsten fluorescent (MBTF)	15-25	3500
Warm	H	Tubular fluorescent	Softone	35-40	2700
	I	Tubular fluorescent	De luxe Warm White De luxe Warm White 32	35-55	3000
	J	Incandescent	Tungsten	8-18	2600-2900
	K	Incandescent	Tungsten halogen	17-22	2800-3100
	L	Tubular fluorescent	WHITE	60-80	3500
			WARM WHITE	60-80	3000
	M	High pressure discharge	High pressure sodium (SON)	75-95	2100
	N	Low pressure discharge	Low pressure sodium (SOX, SLI)	120-175	Not applicable

Notes: ˙The colour characteristics of many types of lamp are subject to change in line with new developments. Manufacturers should be consulted. Names in capitals of tubular fluorescent lamps denote British Standard colours.

General colour rendering effects				Typical applications
Violet and blue	Green	Yellow	Orange and red	
Very bright	Bright	Bright	Fairly bright	Where colour rendering similar to north sky daylight is needed, e.g. industrial colour matching, wall-paper and paint shops. Appears cold at low illuminances
Bright Blues slightly violet	Bright Greens slightly yellow	Bright	Bright	Display lighting, shops, hospitals, museums
Bright Blues slightly violet	Bright Greens slightly yellow	Bright	Very bright	Shops
Bright Blues slightly violet	Bright Greens slightly yellow	Very bright	Fairly bright Reds slightly orange	Offices, departmental stores
Fairly bright	Bright	Very bright	Fairly dull	Factories. Blends well with daylight
Bright	Bright Greens slightly yellow	Very bright Yellows slightly orange	Medium	Industrial and commercial applications, e.g. shops, high-bay and area lighting
Bright Blues appear violet	Fairly bright Greens slightly yellow	Bright Yellows slightly green	Fairly dull	Industrial and commercial applications, e.g. shops, offices, high-bay and area lighting, roadways
Dull	Bright Greens slighly yellow	Bright	Bright	Hotels, restaurants, homes. Blends well with incandescent lamps
Fairly dull Blues appear violet	Bright Greens slightly yellow	Very bright	Bright	Hotels, restaurants, homes
Dull	Bright Greens slighly yellow	Bright Yellows slightly orange	Very bright	Hotels, restaurants, homes
Dull	Bright Greens slightly yellow	Bright Yellows slightly orange	Very bright	Display and area lighting
Fairly dull Blues appear violet	Bright Greens slightly yellow	Very bright	Medium	General purpose, high efficacy
Dull Blues appear violet	Medium Greens slightly yellow	Very bright Yellows slightly orange	Bright Reds slightly yellow	Industrial and commercial applications, e.g. public buildings, high bay and area lighting, roadways
Dark colours appear black, light colours grey	Dark colours appear black, light colours grey	Bright Yellows appear orange	Reds appear brown, light colours grey or yellow	Roadways and industrial area lighting where high efficacy is required and the distortion of most colours is acceptable

low pressure sodium lamps. Efficacies of any given lamp type vary with wattage and details of design. Typical values for lamps used in interior lighting are included in Table 1.

Lamp colour characteristics

The lamps commonly used for interior lighting are classified in respect of their colour appearance as 'cool', 'intermediate' and 'warm' in Table 1.

Within each appearance group the lamps are coded by letters according to their colour rendering properties. The fourteen colour rendering categories (A-N) cover a wide range from lamps specially developed for colour matching work to those giving practically monochromatic light.

The categories A-N are not intended to represent an order of excellence for two reasons: first, because the table includes different lamp types (fluorescent, high pressure discharge and incandescent), and second because the desired colour rendering quality will depend on the colours to be viewed and the requirements of the application. Different degrees of colour rendering fidelity can be obtained in each colour appearance group. The types of lamp thought to give suitable colour rendering for any given application are indicated in the General Schedule, Section 9, by letters from the range A-N. It is not implied that all of the lamps listed against an application are equally suitable. The entries should be regarded rather as a list of possibilities among the chief lamp types and should be used as a guide to final choice.

The list of lamp types given in Table 1 is not exhaustive. Additions and deletions will undoubtedly be made during the life of this edition of the Code. Moreover, the colour rendering properties of certain types may well be modified during that time making them suitable for more applications. Manufacturers' current data should be consulted.

While colour rendering and colour appearance are of great and increasing importance to good lighting, they are not the only factors in the choice of suitable lamps.

Starting of discharge lamps

Some discharge lamps (other than type MCF) take several minutes from switch-on to reach full light output. If the power supply is interrupted the lamps must cool before they can restrike, and this also may take several minutes. This may affect the choice of lamps for applications where any interruption of the lighting for several minutes could have serious consequences.

DAYLIGHTING

Daylighting schedule

This schedule gives recommended daylight factors, the position of measurement and limiting glare indices for interiors where daylight from side windows is the chief source of light during the greater part of the day and for most of the year. These daylight factors do not necessarily apply to the whole area of all interiors; in some circumstances they will apply to part of the area only.

The following notes supplement the Schedule. For a fuller account of daylighting practice IES Technical Report No 4 should be consulted.

A: Where the activity calls for a daylight factor of 4 per cent or more, it is not intended that windows should be designed to give these factors over the whole area of the interior. Work should either be restricted to areas near the windows, or a combined daylighting/electric lighting system should be used to provide the required illuminance at points in the room remote from the window.

Table 2 Recommended daylight factors

	Minimum daylight factor per cent	*Position of measurement*	*Limiting daylight glare index*	*Notes*
Airport buildings and coach stations				
Reception areas	2	Desks	24	
Customs and immigration halls	2	Counters and desks	24	
Circulation areas, lounges	1	Working plane	—	
Assembly and concert halls				
Foyers, auditoria	1	Working plane	—	
Corridors	0.5	Floor	—	
Stairs	1	Treads	—	
Banks				
Counters, typing, accounting, book areas	2	Desks	—	
Public areas	2	Working plane	—	
Churches				
Body of church	1	Working plane	20	Daylight glare index to be calculated for direction of view of congregation
Pulpit and lectern areas, chancel and choir	1.5	On desks	—	
Altar, communion table	3	On table	—	Level depends on emphasis required
Drawing offices				
General	2	On boards	20	
General building areas				
Entrance halls and reception areas	1	Working plane	—	
Hospitals				
Reception and waiting rooms	2	Working plane	—	See DHSS Hospital Building Notes and BS CP3
Wards	1	Innermost bedhead	18	
Pharmacies	3	Working plane	22	
Libraries				
Shelves (stacks)	1	Vertical plane	—	See IES Technical Report No 8. Additional artificial lighting will be required
Reading tables	1	On tables	22	
Museums and art galleries				
General	1	Working plane	20	See IES Technical Report No 14.
Offices				
General offices	2	Desks	22	
Typing, business machines manually operated computers	4	"	22	

Table 2   Recommended daylight factors (continued)

	Minimum daylight factor per cent	Position of measurement	Limiting daylight glare index	Notes
Schools and colleges				
Assembly halls	2	Working plane	20	See DES Building Bulletin No 33
Classrooms	2	Desks	20	and 'Guide lines for environmental
Art rooms	4	Easels	20	design'. DES (1972)
Laboratories	3	Benches	20	
Staffrooms, common rooms	1	Working plane	–	
Sports halls				
General	2	Working plane	–	
Surgeries (medical and dental)				
Waiting rooms	2	Working plane	–	
Surgeries	2	"	20	
Laboratories	3	Benches	22	
Swimming pools				
Pool	2	Pool surface	–	Care should be taken to minimize
Surrounding areas	1	Working plane	–	glare and reflection from water surface
Telephone exchanges (manual)				
General	2	Working plane	20	Avoid specular reflections. Limit daylight on internally lit controls

The recommended daylight factors can be achieved more readily over a greater part of the working space in rooms with windows in two or more walls than in those with windows in one wall only. Alternatively roof lighting may be used.

B: Daylight factors for working interiors with top lighting only should be not less than 5 per cent. However, large rooflights cause excessive heat loss in winter irrespective of their orientation. All rooflights except those facing north may also lead to excessive solar gain in summer unless special precautions are taken.

C: Daylight glare indices can be calculated by the method described in IES Technical Report No 4. At the present time it is recommended that indices calculated in this way should not exceed the values given in the Daylighting Schedule. These values are based on experimental studies and are put forward for guidance and to obtain experience.

These indices are quite different from the IES glare indices for electric lighting systems. They should not be combined in an attempt to derive an index that would give an estimate of the total glare present in an interior which is lit during daytime partly by daylight and partly by electric light.

GENERAL SCHEDULE

This Schedule gives for a large number of interiors and activities the standard service illuminance, the position or plane of measurement, the limiting glare index and the lamp groups having colour appearance and colour rendering characteristics appropriate to the application. Relevant official regulations and any special requirements are indicated.

The following notes explain and supplement aspects of the recommendations.

Standard service illuminance

The standard service illuminance is the illuminance recommended for the activity or interior when none of the modifying factors discussed below are present. The recommended values are neither minima nor optima, but represent good current practice. In multi-use interiors, the highest of the illuminances recommended for the individual activities should be adopted. It is assumed that the lighting system is properly maintained.

The service illuminance is the mean illuminance throughout the life of the lighting system and averaged over the relevant area, which may be the whole area of the interior or the area of the visual task and its immediate surround.

The working plane is that on which the task lies or, where this is not known, a horizontal plane 0.85 m above the floor.

If the location of tasks on vertical planes is not known when a lighting scheme is being designed it may be necessary to plan the scheme so that the average mean cylindrical illuminance is equal to the standard service illuminance.

The recommended standard service illuminance should be increased if
a unusually serious consequences, in terms of cost or danger, could result from mistakes in perception,
b unusually low reflectances or contrasts are present in the task,
c tasks for which the recommended standard service illuminance is less than 500 lux are carried out in windowless interiors.

The Flow Chart (Fig 1) of this Section shows the steps by which the standard service illuminance should be increased when one or more of these conditions applies. The resulting final service illuminance derived from the Flow Chart should then be used as the design value.

The standard service illuminances given in the Schedule have been selected from the following scale which agrees substantially with one of the scales proposed for the forthcoming CIE international guide on interior lighting: 2, 5, 10, 30, 50, 100, 150, 300, 500, 750, 1000, 1500, 3000 lux.

Each step in illuminance represents a significant subjective increase.

Some illuminances not included in this scale have been recommended for a few applications to meet special requirements. Examples are areas in hospitals where it is important to keep the illuminance within certain critical limits.

Scalar illuminance

The scalar (mean spherical) illuminances recommended in the Schedule for some locations where there is no specific visual task are the average values over the whole area of the interior at a height of 1.2 m above the floor.

It may sometimes be convenient to convert the scalar illuminance, E_s,

Figure 1 Flow chart for calculating the standard service illumination

Task group and typical task or interior	Standard service illumin- ance lux	Are reflectances or contrasts unusually low ?	Will errors have serious consequences ?	Is the area window- less ?	Final ser illumina lux
Storage areas and plant rooms with no continuous work	150				150
Rough work Rough machining and assembly	300	no / yes	300 — no / yes	300 — no / yes	300
Routine work Offices, control rooms, medium machining and assembly	500	no / yes	500 — no / yes	500	500
Demanding work Deep-plan, drawing or business machine offices. Inspection of medium machining	750	no / yes	750 — no / yes	750	750
Fine work Colour discrimination, textile processing, fine machining and assembly	1000	no / yes	1000 — no / yes	1000	1000
Very fine work Hand engraving, inspection of fine machining or assembly	1500	no / yes	1500 — no / yes	1500	1500
Minute work Inspection of very fine assembly	3000				3000

Localized lighting, if necessary supplemented by use of optical aids, e.g. binocular loupes, magnifiers, profile projectors, etc.

into the equivalent planar illuminance, E_h, and the conversion can be made using the data in Table 3 provided that the interior has a light ceiling and reasonably light walls.

The limiting glare indices recommended are those calculated for the general lighting of the interior. Where local lighting is used precautions should be taken to avoid glare to the user or other occupants.

Proof luminaire The term 'proof luminaire' indicates that attention must be given to the choice of luminaire to withstand particular hazards of the application. The term is used in a more general sense than in BS 4533 and includes lumin- aires resistant to corrosion.

Table 3: Conversion of scalar illuminance to illuminance on horizontal plane for interior with light ceilings and walls

	Room index		
	1.0-1.6	2.5	4.0
Direct and semi-direct lighting (BZ1-3, 25 per cent upward light)			
Floor reflectance	0.1 0.2 0.3	0.1 0.2 0.3	0.1 0.2 0.3
E_h/E_s	2.6 2.4 2.1	2.6 2.3 2.05	2.5 2.2 2.0
General diffused lighting (BZ4-10, 50 per cent upward light)			
Floor reflectance	0.1 0.2 0.3	0.1 0.2 0.3	0.1 0.2 0.3
E_h/E_s	2.3 2.2 1.9	2.2 2.0 1.8	2.1 1.9 1.7

ALPHABETICAL INDEX TO GENERAL SCHEDULE

The building interiors and tasks or other activities listed in the Schedule are grouped in seven main sections: **general building areas, industrial buildings and processes, offices and shops, public and educational buildings, hospitals, surgeries and consulting rooms, homes and hotels, indoor sports, games and recreational buildings.** *Individual items may be located in the Schedule from the alphabetical index. Items in bold refer to main interiors under which individual processes are grouped in the Schedule.*

Aircraft engine testing	357	**Car parks - indoor**	359
Aircraft factories and maintenance hangars	357	Car parks (outdoor)	356
Airports	376	Car showrooms	373
Apparatus rooms		**Card rooms (games)**	381
(telecommunications)	357	**Carpet factories**	359
Arc and gas welding	371	Cataloguing and sorting (libraries)	375
Art galleries and museums	375	Cellars (hotels)	380
Art rooms	375, 376	Chancels	374
Ash handling plants	361	Changing, locker and cleaner's rooms (staff	
Assembly and concert halls	374	rooms)	357
Assembly shops	358	Changing rooms, showers, locker rooms	
Auditoria	374	(indoor sports)	382
		Chemical works, fine	368
Badminton courts	381	**Chemical works**	359
Bakeries	358	**Chocolate and confectionery factories**	360
Banking halls	372	Choirs	374
Barns, storage	362	**Churches**	374
Bars	380	Church halls	374
Bathrooms	379, 380	Cinema auditoria	374
Battery rooms		Circulation areas (general building, transport	
(electricity generating stations)	361	terminals)	356, 376
Bays, loading	371	Clerical offices	372
Bedrooms	379, 380	Cloakrooms (staff, hotels)	357, 380
Billiard rooms	381	Cloth inspection, upholstery	363
Binding (libraries)	375	**Clothing factories**	360
Boiler houses	358, 361	**Coach and railway stations**	376
Bookbinderies	358	Coal plant	361
Book stacks and shelves		**Collieries (surface buildings)**	360
(libraries)	375	Colour matching (paint works)	367
Booking offices (concert halls, railway		Colour reproduction and printing	369
stations)	374, 376	Composing press	369
Boot and shoe factories	358	Computer room	372
Boxing rings	381	**Concert halls, cinemas and theatres**	374
Brazing	372	Concrete shops	359
Breweries and distilleries	358	**Confectionery factories**	360
Buffing and polishing	368	Conference rooms	372
Building (construction and plant)	359	**Consulting rooms**	356, 379
Business machine offices	372	Control rooms (elect. gen. stns: chemical	
		works)	359 361
Cabinet making	363	Corridors	356
Cafeterias, canteens	357	Cotton mills	370
Canning and preserving factories	359	Covered ways (circulation areas outdoor)	356
Car assembly	367	Cow houses	362

Cricket nets (indoor)	381
Customs and immigration halls	376
Cutting (boot and shoe factories)	358
(carpet factories)	359
(clothing factories)	360
Cutting, upholstery (furniture factories)	363
Dairies	362
Dental laboratories, surgeries	379
Die sinking shops	360
Diesel generator rooms (elect. gen. stns.)	362
Dining rooms, grill rooms, restaurants (hotels)	380
Dining rooms (staff, schools)	357, 376
Distilleries and breweries	368
Drawing offices	373
Dressing rooms (theatres)	374
Dry cleaning works and laundries	366
Dye works	360
Dyehouse laboratories	360
Electrical machine shops	361
Electricity generating stations	361, 362
Engraving shops	362
Enquiry desks	356, 378
Entrance halls	356, 380
Entrances and exits (outdoor)	356
Escalators	356
Executive offices	372
Exterior stairs and ladders (chemical, gas works)	359, 364
Exterior walkways and platforms (chemical, gas works)	359. 364
External aprons (garages)	364
External covered ways	356
Fabrication plant (structural steel)	370
Fan houses (collieries)	360
Farm buildings	362
Fertiliser stores	362
Filing rooms	372
Fine chemical and pharmaceutical works	368
Fire stations	363
First aid and medical centres	356
Fitting and machine shops	367
Flour mills	363
Food factories (see canning and preserving)	359
Food stores	356
Forges	363
Foundries	363
Foyers	374
Further education establishments	374, 375

Garages	364
Gas works	364
Gatehouses	356
Gauge and tool rooms	364
Generating stations, electricity	361, 362
Generator rooms, diesel	362
Glass works and processes	364
Glove factories	365
Graphic reproduction	369
Grass or grain drying	362
Greasing pits (garages)	364
Gymnasia (schools, general)	376, 381
Halls and landings (homes)	379
Hand engraving shops	362
Hand and machine type casting (printing works)	369
Hangars, inspection and repairs	357
Hat factories	365
Homes	379
Homes (old people's)	380
Hosiery and knitwear factories	365
Hospitals	377, 378
Hotels	380
HV substations	362
Hypermarkets	373
Ice hockey and skating rinks	382
Illuminated tables (printing works)	369
Industrialized building plants	359
Inspection,	
aircraft	357
bottles (breweries)	358
(milk bottling plants)	367
cabinet making	363
cloth (furniture factories)	363
clothing	360
colour and registration (printing works)	369
cotton or linen	370
fine chemical manufacture	368
glass	364
gloves	365
hats	365
hosiery and knitwear	365
meat	369
metalwork (sheet)	369
motor vehicles	367
paper mills	368
plate and tinplate	366
printed sheets (printing works)	369
synthetic or silk fabrics	370
woollen fabrics	371
Inspection and testing shops (engineering)	365

Instrument assembly 368
Iron and steel works 366

Jewellery and watchmaking factories 366
Jute mills 371

Kiln rooms (potteries) 368
Kitchens (staff, homes, hotels) 356, 380
Knitwear and hosiery factories 365

Laboratories (general) 366
Laboratories, dental 379
Laboratories, dyehouse 360
Laboratories (**further education estab.**) 375
   (hospitals, general, x-ray) 378
   (schools) 376
Landings and halls 379
Laundries and dry cleaning works 366
Laundries (hotels) 380
Lavatories (staff rooms) 357
Leather dressing, working 367
Lecture theatres (**further education
  estab., schools**) 374, 376
Left luggage and parcels 376
Libraries 375
Lifts (passenger) 356
Linen mills 370
Living rooms 379
Loading bays 371
Lobbies 356
Loose boxes 362
Lounges (hotels) 380

Machine engraving shop (see **die sinking**) 360
Machine and fitting shops 367
Machine and hand type casting 369
Machine shops (electrical) 361
Machinery assembly, heavy 358
Machinery assembly, fine 358
Machining and assembly, wood 363
Maintenance hangars (aircraft) 357
Marshalling and outdoor stock yards
  (iron and steel works) 366
Mattress making 363
Medical and first aid centres 356
Milk bottling plants 367
Milking machine rooms 362
Mills
  Flour 363
  Paper 368
  Textile (cotton or linen) 375
  Textile (jute) 376
  Textile (synthetic or silk) 375
  Textile (woollen) 376

Mortuaries and post-mortem rooms 378
Motor vehicles plants 367
Multi-storey car parks 359
Museums and art galleries 375

Needlework rooms (**schools**) 376
Nuclear reactor plants 361

Office machinery assembly 358
Offices
  business machine 372
  clerical 372
  drawing 373
  dyers 360
  executive 372
  typing 372
Ophthalmic wall and near-vision charts 379
Outdoor construction (**building**) 359
Outdoor storage tanks (**elect. gen. stns.**) 361

Packing and despatch 371
Paint shops and spray booths 367
Paint works 367
Paper mills 368
Parcels and left luggage 376
Parking areas, interior 359
Passageways 356
Petrol pumps 364
Pharmacies (hospitals) 377
**Pharmaceutical and fine chemical
  work** 368
Piggeries 362
Plastics works 368
Plating shops 368
Potteries 368
Poultry houses 362
Precision mechanism assembly 358
Preserving and canning factories 359
Print rooms 373
Printing (**paper mills**) 368
Printing works 369
Projection rooms 374
Proof reading 369
Pump houses (**elect. gen. stns.**) 362
Punch card rooms 373

Racks, storage 371
Radio assembly 358
Railway stations 376
Reading rooms and tables (**libraries**) 375
Reception area (desks)
  Entrances 356
  Transport terminals 376
  Hospitals 378

Reception desks (hotels) 380
Recovery rooms and intensive care units 378
Rehabilitation and training units 378
Relay and telecommunications rooms 362
Repairs and servicing (garages) 364
Repairs and inspection (aircraft) 357
Rest rooms, staff 357
Restaurants, staff 357
Restaurants, dining rooms, grill rooms 380
Rubber processing factories 369

Schools 375, 376
Servicing and repairs (garages) 364
Sewing
Carpet factories 359
Clothing factories 360
upholstery 363
Glove factories 365
Hat factories 365
Homes 379
Sheet metal works 369
Shoe factories 358
Shops 373
Showrooms 373
Slaughter houses 369
Soap factories 370
Soldering and welding shops 371, 372
Special batch mixing (paint works) 367
Spinning
cotton or linen 370
jute 371
synthetic or silk 370
woollens 371
Sports halls, multipurpose 381
Spray booths and paint shops 367
Spray booths (furniture factories) 364
Squash rackets courts 382
Staff restaurants 357
Staff rooms 357
Stairs (general, homes) 356. 379
Steel and iron works 366
Stockyards (farm buildings) 362
Storage barns 362
Storage areas, outdoor (elect. gen. stns.) 361
Storage tanks, indoor and outdoor
(elect. gen. stns.) 362
Storage racks 371
Stores and stockrooms 357
Stores (bulk) 371
Stores, stockyards (outdoor) 356
Stores, farm implements 362
Studies 379
Substations and switchrooms 362
Surgeries 379

Swimming pools 382
Switchboard rooms (telecommunications) 357
Switchrooms (metal clad - cubicle
switchgear) 362

Table tennis 382
Telecommunications 357
Telecommunications and relay rooms 362
Teleprinter rooms 357
Tennis courts (indoor) 382
Textile mills
Cotton or linen 370
Jute 371
Synthetic or silk 370
Woollen 371
Theatre and concert hall auditoria 374
Tobacco factories 371
Tool and gauge rooms 364
Toolrooms 363
Training and rehabilitation units 378
Transformer compounds, outdoor 362
Transport terminal buildings -
airport, coach and railway stations 376
Turbine and boiler houses 361
Type foundries 369
Typing offices 372
Tyre and tube making 369

Underground car parks 359
Unloading areas, outdoor
(elect. gen. stns.) 361
Upholstery (see furniture factories) 363

Vats and baths (plating shops) 368
Vehicle body assembly 367
Veneer sorting and preparation 363

Waiting areas (transport terminals) 376
Waiting rooms (surgeries) 379
Wardrobe, costume racks (theatres) 374
Warehouses and bulk stores 371
Washing and polishing (garages) 364
Washing and sterilising (dairies) 362
Watchmaking and jewellery factories 366
Weaving
cotton or linen 370
jute 371
synthetic or silk 370
wool 371
Weigh cabins (collieries) 360
Welding and soldering shops 371, 372
Windowless rooms (hospitals) 377
Woodworking shops 372
Workshops 372

	Standard service illuminance lux	Position of measurement	Limiting glare index	Colour appearance of light source	Colour rendering group (See Table 1)	Notes

General building areas

Circulation areas

Corridors, passageways	100 scalar	1.2m above floor	22	Intermediate	BDEFGHIJKL	Scalar illuminance to be not less than $\frac{1}{8}$ horizontal planar illuminance in adjacent areas, and not less than 120 lux if there is daylight
Lifts (passenger)	150	Floor	—	"	BDEHIJL	
Stairs	150	Treads	—	"	BDEFGHIJKL	Restrict disability glare
Escalators	150	Treads	—	"	"	Avoid specular reflection
External covered ways	30	Ground	—	"	EFGJKLM	on treads illuminance should be compatible with adjacent lit areas

Entrances

Entrance halls, lobbies, waiting rooms	150 scalar	1.2m above floor	—	Intermediate or warm	BDEFGHIJKL	See Section 9D for equivalent planar illuminance
Enquiry desks	500	Desk	19	"	"	
Gatehouses	300	Desk	16	"	"	Limit luminance to assist view out at night

Kitchens See Sl No 1172: The Food Hygiene (General) Regulations 1970

Food stores	150	Floor	—	Intermediate or warm	BDJL	
General	500	Working surface	22	"	"	Position luminaires relative to working areas. Proof luminaires may be required

Medical and first aid centres

Consulting rooms, treatment areas	500	Desk or bed	—	Intermediate or warm	BDJ	Examination lighting should be provided
Medical stores	100	Vertical on shelves	—	"	BDJL	
Rest rooms	150	Bed	—	"	BDJ	Restrict luminance seen by recumbent patient

Outdoor

Controlled entrance or exit gates	150	Working plane	—	Intermediate or warm	EFGJKLMN	Working plane varies according to requirement
Entrances and exits	30	Ground	—	"	"	
Internal factory roads	See BSCP 1004					
Car parks	"					
Stores, stockyards	30	Working plane	—	"	"	Consider obstructions. Vertical surfaces often important
Industrial covered ways	50	Ground	—	"	"	Illuminance should be compatible with adjacent lit areas

	Standard service illuminance lux	Position of measurement	Limiting glare index	Colour appearance of light source	Colour rendering group (See Table 1)	Notes

GENERAL BUILDING AREAS

Staff restaurants   See Sl No 1172: The Food Hygiene (General) Regulations 1970

Canteens, cafeterias, dining rooms	300	Tables	22	Intermediate or warm	BDHIJKL	

Staff rooms

Changing, locker and cleaners' rooms, cloakrooms, lavatories	150	Floor	–	Intermediate or warm	EJL	
Rest rooms	150	Table height	19	Warm	HIJL	Change in character from general lighting desirable

Stores and stock rooms

	150	Vertical plane	–	Intermediate or warm	EFGJL	

Telecommunications

Cord switchboard rooms	500	Horizontal keyboard	13	Intermediate or warm	DEFGHIJL	Avoid specular reflections on boards
Cordless switchboard rooms	300	Keyboard	16	"	"	Avoid specular reflections on boards. Limit illuminance, including daylight, on internally lit controls.
Apparatus rooms	150	Vertical plane at floor level	25	"	DEL	
Teleprinter rooms	500	Vertical message board	16	"	DEFGHIJL	Avoid specular reflections on machines

Industrial buildings and processes

Aircraft factories and maintenance hangars

Stock parts production	750	Machines	22	Intermediate or warm	EFGJKLM	Portable luminaires required, consider recessed luminaires in floor
Fabrication and inspection	500	Working plane	22	"	"	"
Aircraft engine testing	750	Engine	22	"	"	Portable luminaires required; proof luminaires may be required. See Sl No 1689: The Factories (Testing of Aircraft and Accessories) Special Regulations 1952
Inspection and repairs (hangars)	500	Aircraft, horizontal and vertical	22	Intermediate	BDEFG	

	Standard service illuminance lux	Position of measurements	Limiting glare index	Colour appearance of light source	Colour rendering group (See Table 1)	Notes

INDUSTRIAL BUILDINGS AND PROCESSES

Assembly shops

	Standard service illuminance lux	Position of measurements	Limiting glare index	Colour appearance of light source	Colour rendering group	Notes
Rough work, e.g. frame and heavy machinery assembly	300	Working plane	25	Intermediate or warm	EFGJKLM	
Medium work, e.g. engine assembly vehicle body assembly	500	"	22	"	"	
Fine work, e.g. radio and office machinery assembly	1000	Bench	19	Cool, intermediate or warm	ABDEFGJKLM	Use AB or D if colour r dering critical. Avoid specular reflections. Building illuminance n less than 750 lux.
Very fine work, e.g. instrument and small precision mechanism assembly	1500	Bench	16	"	"	Consider using optical a Use AB or D if colour r dering critical. Building illuminance not less tha 750 lux.

Bakeries
See Sl No 1172: The Food Hygiene (General) Regulations 1970. Enclose luminaires may be required.

	Standard service illuminance lux	Position of measurements	Limiting glare index	Colour appearance of light source	Colour rendering group	Notes
General	300	Working plane	22	Intermediate or warm	BDEFGJL	
Decorating, icing	500	"	22	Cool, intermediate or warm	ABDJ	

Boiler houses

	Standard service illuminance lux	Position of measurements	Limiting glare index	Colour appearance of light source	Colour rendering group	Notes
General	150	Working plane	25	Intermediate or warm	EFGJKLM	Position luminaires rela to major tasks, includin those on vertical planes instrument panels, etc

Bookbinderies

	Standard service illuminance lux	Position of measurements	Limiting glare index	Colour appearance of light source	Colour rendering group	Notes
Folding, pasting, punching, stitching	500	Working plane	22	Intermediate or warm	EFGJLM	
Cutting, assembling, embossing	750	"	22	"	"	

Boot and shoe factories

	Standard service illuminance lux	Position of measurements	Limiting glare index	Colour appearance of light source	Colour rendering group	Notes
Sorting, grading	1500	Working plane	16	Cool or intermediate	ABD	Building illuminance no less than 750 lux in all a
Clicking	1000	"	22	"	"	
Closing						
preparatory operations	1000	"	22	Intermediate or warm	BDEFGJLM	
cutting tables and presses	1500	"	16	"	"	
Bottom stock preparation, lasting, bottoming, finishing, shoe rooms	1000	"	19	"	"	

Breweries and distilleries
See Sl No 1172: The Food Hygiene (General) Regulations 1970. Proof luminaires may be required

	Standard service illuminance lux	Position of measurements	Limiting glare index	Colour appearance of light source	Colour rendering group	Notes
General	500	Working plane	22	Intermediate or warm	EFGJLM	
Bottle inspection.	Special lighting					

	Standard service illuminance lux	*Position of measurement*	*Limiting glare index*	*Colour appearance of light source*	*Colour rendering group (See Table 1)*	*Notes*

INDUSTRIAL BUILDINGS AND PROCESSES

Building

Outdoor construction	See IES Technical Report No 3					
Industrialized building plants	500	Working plane	22	Intermediate or warm	EFGJKL	Vertical surfaces often important
Concrete shops	300	"	25	"	EFGJKLM	

Canning and preserving factories See Sl No 1172: The Food Hygiene (General) Regulations 1970. Enclosed proof luminaires may be required

Preparation	500	Working plane	25	Intermediate or warm	EFGJKLM	
Canned and bottled goods						
retorts	300	"	25	"	"	
high speed conveyor lines	500	"	25	"	"	
Inspection						
raw materials	750	"	22	Cool or intermediate	ABD	Additional special lighting required
finished product	Special lighting					

Car parks - indoor See BSCP 1004 Part 9. Proof luminaires may be required

Underground	30	Floor	22	Intermediate or warm	EFGJLM	Vertical obstructions should be illuminated to higher value than floor, possibly by appropriate positioning of luminaires
Multi-storey						
parking floors	30	Floor	22	"	"	
ramps	50	Vertical sides	19	"	"	

Carpet factories

Winding, beaming	300	Working plane	25	Intermediate or warm	BDEL	
Designing, Jacquard card cutting, setting pattern, tufting, cropping, cutting, hemming, fringing, latexing and latex drying	500	"	22	"	BDEFGL	
Weaving, mending	750	"	22	Cool or intermediate	ABD	

Carpet factories (continued)

Inspection						
general	1000	Inspection surface	19	"	"	
piece dyeing	750	On carpet	–	"	"	Directional local lighting may be required

Chemical works See SR & O No 731: The Chemical Works Regulations 1922. Possible low maintenance factors

Exterior walkways and platforms	50	Walkway level	–	Intermediate or warm	EFGJKLMN	Local lighting on instrumentation, controls and sight glasses required; proof luminaires may be required in all areas
Exterior stairs and ladders	100	Treads	–	"	"	
Exterior pump and valve areas	100	Ground	–	"	"	
Pump and compressor houses	150	Floor	–	"	EFGJLM	
Interior plant areas	300	Working plane	25	"	"	
Control rooms						
desks	300	Desk	16	"	BDEFGJL	Avoid specular reflections in instrument glasses and panels; limit illuminance on internally lit controls
vertical panels	300	On panel	16	"	"	
rear of panels	150	Vertical plane at floor level	–	"	"	

	Standard service illuminance lux	Position of measurement	Limiting glare index	Colour appearance of light source	Colour rendering group (See Table 1)	Notes

INDUSTRIAL BUILDINGS AND PROCESSES

Chocolate and confectionary factories   See Sl No 1172: The Food Hygiene (General) Regulations 1970

	Standard service illuminance lux	Position of measurement	Limiting glare index	Colour appearance of light source	Colour rendering group	Notes
General processes	300	Working plane	25	Intermediate or warm	BDEFGJLM	Proof luminaires may b required
Hand decorating, inspection, wrapping, packing	500	"	22	"	BDEFGJL	"

Clothing factories   (See also Glove factories, Hat factories, Hosiery and knitwear factories)

	Standard service illuminance lux	Position of measurement	Limiting glare index	Colour appearance of light source	Colour rendering group	Notes
Matching-up	750	Working plane	19	Cool	A	
Cutting	750	"	19	Intermediate or warm	BDEJL	
Sewing	1000	"	19	"	"	Additional local lightir should be provided at sewing machines
Pressing	500	"	22	"	"	
Inspection	1500	"	16	Cool	A	Building illuminance n less than 750 lux.
Hand tailoring	1500	"	19	Cool or intermediate	ABD	Local lighting may be Building illuminance n less than 750 lux.

Collieries (surface buildings)   Possible low maintenance factors

	Standard service illuminance lux	Position of measurement	Limiting glare index	Colour appearance of light source	Colour rendering group	Notes
Coal preparation plants						
working areas	300	Working plane	28	Intermediate or warm	EFGJKLM	Proof luminaires may required
other areas	150	"	28	"	"	"
picking belts	500	"	22	"	"	"
Winding houses	150	"	25	"	"	
Lamp rooms						
main areas	150	"	28	"	"	
repair sections	300	"	25	"	"	
Weigh cabins	150	"	28	"	"	
Fan houses	150	"	28	"	"	

Die sinking shops

	Standard service illuminance lux	Position of measurement	Limiting glare index	Colour appearance of light source	Colour rendering group	Notes
General	500	Working plane	22	Intermediate or warm	EFGJKLM	
Fine	1500	"	19	"	"	Building illuminance r less than 750 lux. See Section 2.2.4.1

Dye works   Proof luminaires may be required. Attention should be paid to atmospheric absorpiton

	Standard service illuminance lux	Position of measurement	Limiting glare index	Colour appearance of light source	Colour rendering group	Notes
General areas	300	Working plane	25	Cool or intermediate	ABDEFG	
'Grey' fabric examination (perching)	1000	Inspection surface	19	Cool	A	Local lighting may be
Dyehouses laboratories, dyers' offices	1000	Benches	19	"	"	Accurate colour matc facilities to BS 950 id ical to final examinat required in addition t general lighting

	Standard service illuminance lux	*Position of measurement*	*Limiting glare index*	*Colour appearance of light source*	*Colour rendering group (See Table 1)*	*Notes*

INDUSTRIAL BUILDINGS AND PROCESSES

Dye works (continued)

Final examination (perching)	1500	Inspection surface	16	"	"	Local lighting may be used. Accurate colour matching facilities to BS 950 and identical to above required in addition to general lighting. Building illuminance not less than 750 lux.

Electrical machine shops

Manufacture, winding assembly, testing of large machines	750	Working plane, horizontal or vertical	25	Intermediate or warm	EFGJKLM	In large plant assembly both downlighting and sidelighting may be required

Electricity generating stations

Turbine and boiler houses						
boiler houses, platforms, etc	150	Working plane	–	Intermediate or warm	EFGJKLM	Position luminaires relative to major tasks including those on vertical planes. Additional local lighting for gauge glasses and instrument panels
boiler and turbine house basements (including feed pump bay)	100	"	–	"	"	
turbine and gas turbine houses (operating floor level)	150	Floor	25	"	"	
Plant areas						
ash handling plants, settling pits	100	Ground	–	"	"	
battery rooms, chargers and rectifiers	100	Floor	–	"	'	Proof luminaires required
cable tunnels, cable basement	50	"	–	"	EGJL	
circulating water culverts, screen chambers	50	Working plane	–	"	"	
Coal plant						
conveyors over bunkers	100	"	–	"	EFGJKLM	
conveyor houses, gantries, junction towers and unloading hoppers	100	"	–	"	"	
reclamation hoppers	10	"	–	"	"	
storage areas (outdoor)	5	"	–	"	"	
unloading areas (outdoor)	5	"	–	"	"	
other areas where operators are in attendance	150	"	–	"	"	
Control rooms						
desks	300	Desk	16	"	BDEFGJL	Avoid specular reflections in instrument glasses and panels. Limit illuminance on internally lit controls
vertical panels	300	On panel	16	"	"	
rear of panels	150	Vertical plane at floor level	–	"	"	
Nuclear reactor plants						
gas circulation bays, reactor areas, boilers, platform, reactor charge and discharge faces	150	Floor	25	"	EFGJKLM	

	Standard service illuminance lux	Position of measurement	Limiting glare index	Colour appearance of light source	Colour rendering group (See Table 1)	Notes

INDUSTRIAL BUILDINGS AND PROCESSES

Electricity generating stations (continued)

	Standard service illuminance lux	Position of measurement	Limiting glare index	Colour appearance of light source	Colour rendering group	Notes
Outdoor transformer compounds	30	Ground	–	"	"	Vertical surfaces may important
Precipitator chambers, platforms, etc	100	Working plane	–	"	EFGJLM	
Precipitator dust hopper outlets	50	"	–	"	"	
Pump houses	150	Floor	–	"	"	
Relay and telecommunications rooms	150	Vertical plane at floor level	25	"	DEL	
Storage tanks (indoor), operating areas and filling points of outdoor tanks	50	Operating point	–	"	EFGJKLM	
Sub-stations and switch-rooms						
diesel generator rooms	150	Floor	25	"	EFGJLM	Local lighting over inst mentation and control
HV sub-stations - indoor	100	Vertical on panels	–	Intermediate or warm	EFGJKLM	
HV sub-stations - outdoor	5	Ground	–	"	EFGJKLM	
switch rooms (metal clad and cubicle switchgear)	150	Vertical on switchgear	25	"	"	

Engraving shops

	Standard service illuminance lux	Position of measurement	Limiting glare index	Colour appearance of light source	Colour rendering group	Notes
Hand	1500	Working plane	16	Intermediate or warm	EFGJKLM	Optical aids should no mally be used. Building illuminance not less th 750 lux.
Machine		See Die sinking				

Farm buildings   Enclosed proof luminaires may be required

	Standard service illuminance lux	Position of measurement	Limiting glare index	Colour appearance of light source	Colour rendering group	Notes
Barns						
storage, granary	50	Working plane	–	Intermediate or warm	EGJL	
food preparation	300	"	–	"	"	
Cow houses						
general	150	Vertical plane at floor level	–	"	"	
feeding passages (trough level)	30	Trough level	–	"	"	
Dairies						
milking machine room	300	Working plane	–	"	"	
milk rooms	300	"	25	"	"	
washing, sterilizing	300	"	25	"	"	
Drying, grass or grain						
control points	300	Control position	–	"	"	
general	100	Working plane	–	"	"	
Fertilizer stores	50	Floor	–	"	"	
Implement stores	50	"	–	"	"	
Implement maintenance	300	Work bench or work area	–	"	EFGJLM	
Loose boxes	50	Floor	–	Warm	JL	
Milking parlours		See Cow Houses				
Piggeries						
pig houses	20	Floor	–	"	"	
farrowing pens	100	"	–	"	"	
Poultry houses						
general	50	Floor	–	Warm	JL	Illuminance is maximum
lighting programmes		Special lighting				
Stockyards (general)	30	"	–	Intermediate or warm	EFGJKLM	

	Standard service illuminance lux	Position of measurement	Limiting glare index	Colour appearance of light source	Colour rendering group (See Table 1)	Notes

INDUSTRIAL BUILDINGS AND PROCESSES

Fire stations

Appliance room	300	Floor	22	Intermediate or warm	EFGJL	
External apron	30	Ground	–	"	EFGJKLM	

Flour mills

Roller, purifier, silks and packing floors	300	Working plane	25	Intermediate or warm	EFGJLM	Proof luminaires may be required
Wetting tables	500	"	25	"	"	"

Forges

General	300	Working plane	25	Intermediate or warm	EFGJL	Possible low maintenance factors

Foundries

Charging floors, tumbling, cleaning, pouring, shaking out, rough moulding, rough core making	300	Working plane	28	Intermediate or warm	EFGJKLM	Possible low maintenance factors
Fine moulding, core making, inspection	500	"	25	"	"	

Furniture factories

Raw materials store	100	Floor	28	Intermediate or warm	EFGJLM	
Finished goods store	150	"	25	"	"	
Wood machining and assembly						
rough sawing and cutting	300	Working plane	22	"	"	See SR & O No 1196. Woodworking Machinery Regulations 1922
machining, sanding and assembly of components	500	"	22	"	"	
Cabinet making						
veneer sorting and preparation	1000	"	19	Cool or intermediate	ABD	
veneer pressing	500	"	22	Intermediate or warm	EFGJLM	
components stores	150	Floor	25	"	"	
fitting, final inspection	750	Working plane	22	"	BDEL	
Upholstery						
cloth inspection	1500	"	16	Cool or intermediate	ABD	Special local lighting may be required. Building illuminance not less than 750 lux.
filling, covering	500	"	22	Intermediate or warm	EFGJLM	
slipping	750	"	22	"	"	
cutting, sewing	750	"	22	"	"	
Mattress making						
assembly	500	"	22	"	"	
tape edging	1000	"	22	"	"	Special local lighting may be required
Toolroom						
general	500	"	22	"	"	
benches	750	Bench top	22	"	EFGJL	Special local lighting may be required

	Standard service illuminance lux	Position of measurement	Limiting glare index	Colour appearance of light source	Colour rendering group (See Table 1)	Notes

INDUSTRIAL BUILDINGS AND PROCESSES

Furniture factories (continued)

	Standard service illuminance lux	Position of measurement	Limiting glare index	Colour appearance of light source	Colour rendering group	Notes
Spray booths						
colour finishing	500	Working plane	—	Cool or intermediate	ABD	See SR & O No 990: Cellulose Solution Re-
clear finishing	300	"	—	Intermediate or warm	EFGJL	lations 1934. Refer t\[local authority regula\[Proof luminaires may\[required

Garages

External apron						See Petroleum (Cons\[
general	50	Ground	—	Intermediate or warm	EFGJKLM	dated) Act 1928. Ref\[local authority regula\[
pumps	300	"	—	"	"	Avoid glare for reside\[
Parking areas (interior)	30	"	22	"	"	vicinity and passing t\[
General repair, servicing, greasing pits, washing, polishing	500	Working plane	22	"	"	Proof luminaires are \[tial in pits where petr\[engines are serviced a\[may be necessary else\[Portable luminaires s\[be extra-low voltage

Gas works   Proof luminaires may be required and local lighting on instrumentation and controls. Possible low maintenance factors

Exterior walkways and platforms	50	Walkway	—	Intermediate or warm	EFGJKLMN	
Exterior stairs and ladders	100	Treads	—	Intermediate or warm	EFGJKLMN	
Retort houses, oil gas plants water gas plants, purifiers, indoor coke screening and handling plants	100	Working plane	28	"	EFGJKLM	
Governor, meter, compressor, booster and exhauster houses	150	"	25	"	"	

Gauge and tool rooms

General	1000	Working plane	19	Intermediate or warm	EFGJKLM	Optical aids may be required

Glass works and processes

Furnace rooms, bending, annealing lehrs	150	Working plane	28	Intermediate or warm	EFGJKLM	Liability to specular \[flections at surface o\[
Mixing rooms, forming (blowing, drawing, pressing, rolling), cutting to size, grinding, polishing, toughening	300	"	25	"	EFGJL	glass. Possible low ma\[tenance factors
Finishing (bevelling, decorating, etching, silvering)	500	"	22	"	"	
Brilliant cutting	Special lighting required					
Inspection						
general	500	Working plane	19	Intermediate or warm	EFGJL	
fine	Special lighting required					

	Standard service illuminance lux	Position of measurement	Limiting glare index	Colour appearance of light source	Colour rendering group (See Table 1)	Notes
INDUSTRIAL BUILDINGS AND PROCESSES						
Glove factories						
Pressing, knitting, sorting, cutting	500	Working plane	22	Intermediate or warm	EFGJL	
Sewing	750	"	22	"	"	Additional local lighting should be provided on sewing machines
Inspection	1500	"	16	Cool or intermediate	ABD	Local lighting may be used. Building illuminance not less than 750 lux.
Hat factories						
Stiffening, braiding, refining, forming, sizing, pouncing, ironing	300	Working plane	22	Intermediate or warm	EFGJL	
Cleaning, flanging, finishing	500	"	22	"	"	
Sewing	750	"	22	"	"	Additional local lighting should be provided on sewing machines
Inspection	1500	"	16	Cool or intermediate	ABD	Local lighting may be used. Building illuminance not less than 750 lux.
Hosiery and knitwear factories						
Flat bed knitting machines	500	Needles	22	Intermediate or warm	BDEJL	
Circular knitting machines	750	"	22	"	"	Additional local lighting may be required
Lock stitch and overlocking machines	1000	Working plane	19	"	"	"
Linking or running on	1000	Working plane	19	Intermediate or warm	BDEJL	Additional local lighting may be required
Mending	1500	"	16	"	"	Local lighting may be used.
Examination, hand finishing	1500	"	16	"	ADB	Building illuminance not less than 750 lux.
Inspection and testing shops (engineering)						
Rough work, e.g. counting, rough checking of stock parts	300	Working plane	25	Intermediate or warm	EFGJLM	
Medium work, e.g. 'Go' and 'No-go' gauges, sub-assemblies	500	"	22	"	"	
Fine work, e.g. radio and telecommunication equipment, calibrated scales, precision mechanisms, instruments	1000	"	19	Cool, intermediate or warm	ABDEFGJLM	Use AB or D if colour rendering is important
Very fine work, e.g. gauging and inspection of small intricate parts	1500	"	16	"	"	Use AB or D if colour rendering is important. Local lighting and optical aids may be used. Building illuminance not less than 750 lux.
Minute work, e.g. very small instruments	3000	"	19	–	–	Special lighting and optical aids should be used. Building illuminance not less than 1000 lux.

365

	Standard service illuminance lux	Position of measurement	Limiting glare index	Colour appearance of light source	Colour rendering group (See Table 1)	Notes

INDUSTRIAL BUILDINGS AND PROCESSES

Iron and steel works Possible low maintenance factors

	Standard service illuminance lux	Position of measurement	Limiting glare index	Colour appearance of light source	Colour rendering group	Notes
Marshalling, outdoor stockyards	30	Ground	–	Intermediate or warm	EFGJKLMN	Vertical surfaces often important
Stairs, gangways, basements, quarries, loading docks	150	Floor	–	"	"	
Slab yards, melting shops, ingot stripping, soaking pits, blast furnace working areas, pickling and cleaning lines	150	Working plane	28	"	EFGJKLM	Proof luminaires may required
Mechanical plant, pump houses, mill motor rooms, power and blower houses	150	"	28	"	"	
Mould preparation, rolling and wire mills, slab inspection and conditioning, cold strip mills, sheet and plate finishing, tinning, galvanizing, machine and roll shops	300	"	28	"	"	Proof luminaires may required
Plate inspection	500	Inspection surface	25	"	"	
Tinplate inspection	Special lighting					

Jewellery and watchmaking factories Most processes require directional local lighting

	Standard service illuminance lux	Position of measurement	Limiting glare index	Colour appearance of light source	Colour rendering group	Notes
General lighting	500	Working plane	22	Intermediate or warm	BDEFGJKL	
Fine processes	1000	"	16	"	"	Optical aids should normally be used. Use optical aids and local lighting. Building illuminance less than 1000 lux.
Minute processes	3000	"	19	"	"	
Gem cutting, polishing, setting	1500	"	19	Cool, intermediate or warm	ABDJK	Optical aids should normally be used. Building illuminance not less than 750 lux.

Laboratories (general) For requirements of specialized laboratories see relevant building or process

	Standard service illuminance lux	Position of measurement	Limiting glare index	Colour appearance of light source	Colour rendering group	Notes
General	750	Bench	19	Cool, intermediate or warm	ABDEJL	Position luminaires over benches. Proof luminaires may be required

Laundries and dry cleaning works

	Standard service illuminance lux	Position of measurement	Limiting glare index	Colour appearance of light source	Colour rendering group	Notes
Receiving, sorting, washing, drying, ironing (calendering), despatch, dry cleaning, bulk machine work	300	Working plane	25	Intermediate or warm	BDEFGJL	Proof luminaires may required
Hand ironing, pressing, inspection, mending, spotting	500	"	25	"	"	"

Leather dressing works

	Standard service illuminance lux	Position of measurement	Limiting glare index	Colour appearance of light source	Colour rendering group	Notes
General	300	Working plane	28	Intermediate or warm	BDEFGJL	

	Standard service illuminance lux	Position of measurement	Limiting glare index	Colour appearance of light source	Colour rendering group (See Table 1)	Notes

INDUSTRIAL BUILDINGS AND PROCESSES

Leather working factories

Pressing, glazing	750	Working plane	22	Intermediate or warm	BDEFGJL	
Cutting, scarfing, sewing	1000	"	22	"	"	
Grading, matching	1500	"	16	Cool	A	Building illuminance not less than 750 lux.

Machine and fitting shops

Rough bench and machine work	300	Working plane	25	Intermediate or warm	EFGJKLM	Local lighting on machines may be required. In large shops, both down lighting and side lighting may be required
Medium bench and machine work, ordinary automatic machines, rough grinding, medium buffing, polishing	500	"	22	"	"	
Fine bench and machine work, fine automatic machines, medium grinding, fine buffing and polishing	1000	"	22	"	"	

Milk bottling plants   See Sl No 1172: The Food Hygiene (General) Regulations 1970

General working areas	300	Working plane	25	Intermediate or warm	BDEFGJL	Local lighting required for instrumentation and sight glasses. Proof luminaires may be required
Bottle filling	750	"	25	"	BDEFGJL	Proof luminaires may be required
Bottle inspection	Special lighting					

Motor vehicle plants

General sub-assemblies, chassis assembly, car assembly, body sub-assemblies, body assembly	500	Working plane	22	Intermediate or warm	EFGJLM	Additional lighting should be provided where necessary beneath assembly lines
Upholstery	See Furniture factories					
Final inspection	750	Working plane	19	Cool or intermediate	ABD	Special lighting required
Spray booths	See Paint shops and Spray booths					

Paint works   See SR & O No 990: The Cellulose Solution Regulations 1934

General automatic processes	300	Working plane	25	Intermediate or warm	EFGJLM	Proof luminaires may be required
Special batch mixing	750	"	22	"	"	"
Colour matching	1000	"	19	Cool	A	Local lighting may be used

Paint shops and spray booths   See SR & O No 990: The Cellulose Solution Regulations 1934

Dipping, firing, rough spraying	300	Working plane (may be vertical)	25	Intermediate or warm	EFGJL	Proof luminaires may be required in all areas
Rubbing, ordinary painting, spraying and finishing	500	"	22	Cool or intermediate	ABD	
Fine painting, spraying and finishing	750	"	22	"	ABD	
Retouching and matching	1000	"	22	Cool	A	

	Standard service illuminance lux	Position of measurement	Limiting glare index	Colour appearance of light source	Colour rendering group (See Table 1)	Notes

INDUSTRIAL BUILDINGS AND PROCESSES

Paper mills

Paper and board making - general	300	Working plane	25	Intermediate or warm	EFGJLM	
Pulp mills, preparation plants	300	"	25	"	"	Proof luminaires may required
Inspection, sorting (overhauling)	500	"	19	"	"	
Paper converting processes						
general	300	"	25	"	"	
associated printing	500	"	22	"	"	

Pharmaceutical and fine chemical works   See SR & O No 731: The Chemical Works Regulations 1922

Pharmaceuticals manufacture						
grinding, granulating, mixing and drying, tableting, sterilizing and washing, preparation of solutions and filling, labelling, capping, cartoning, wrapping	500	Working plane	22	Intermediate or warm	EFGJLM	Proof luminaires may required in all areas
inspection	750	"	19	Cool or intermediate	ABD	
Fine chemical manufacture						
plant processing	300	"	25	Intermediate or warm	EFGJLM	"
fine chemical finishing	500	"	25	"	"	
raw materials stores	300	"	25	"	"	
inspection	750	"	19	Cool or intermediate	ABD	

Plastics works   See SR & O No 731: The Chemical Works Regulations 1922

Manufacture of plastics raw materials	See Chemical works					
Plastics processing						
calendering, extrusion, injection, compression and blow moulding, sheet fabrication, shaping, machining, trimming, polishing, cementing	500	Working plane	25	Intermediate or warm	EFGJLM	

Plating shops

Vats and baths	300	Working plane	25	Intermediate or warm	EFGJLM	Proof luminaires may required
Buffing, polishing, burnishing	500	"	22	"	"	
Final buffing and polishing	750	"	22	"	"	Directional lighting may be required

Potteries

Grinding, filter pressing, kiln room, moulding, pressing, cleaning, trimming, glazing, firing	300	Working plane	28	Intermediate or warm	EFGJLM	
Enamelling, colouring, decorating	750	"	16	Cool or intermediate	ABD	

	Standard service illuminance lux	Position of measurement	Limiting glare index	Colour appearance of light source	Colour rendering group (See Table 1)	Notes

INDUSTRIAL BUILDINGS AND PROCESSES

Printing works

Type foundries						
matrix making, dressing type, hand and machine casting	300	Working plane	25	Intermediate or warm	EFGJLM	
font assembly, sorting	750	"	22	"	"	
Composing press						
hand composing, imposition and distribution	750	"	19	"	"	Attention should be paid to direction of lighting
machine composition-keyboard	750	Copy	19	"	"	
machine composition-casting	300	Working plane	22	"	"	
proof presses	500	Bedplate	22	Cool, intermediate or warm	ABDEFGJLM	Use AB or D where colour rendering is important
Proof reading	750	Desk	16	"	"	"
Illuminated tables-general lighting	300	Table top	22	"	ABDEJL	Use AB or D where colour rendering is important. Dimming may be required
Printing machine room						
presses	500	Rollers	22	Intermediate or warm	EFGJLM	
pre make-ready	500	Working plane	22	"	"	
printed sheet inspection	1000	Inspection surface	19	Cool or intermediate	ABD	Use A where required for BS 950
Graphic reproduction						
general	500	Working plane	22	Cool, intermediate or warm	ABDEFGJL	
precision proofing, retouching, etching	1000	"	16	"	"	Local lighting may be used. Use A where required for BS 950
Colour reproduction and printing: inspection-colour and registration	1500	"	16	Cool	A	Colour rendering to BS 950

Rubber processing factories

Fabric preparation creels, dipping, moulding, compounding, calendering	300	Working plane	25	Intermediate or warm	EFGJLM	
Tyre and tube making	500	"	22	"	"	

Sheet metal works

Benchwork, scribing, inspection	750	Working plane	22	Intermediate or warm	EFGJLM	
Pressing, punching, shearing, stamping, spinning, folding	500	"	22	"	"	

Slaughter houses   See SI No 2168: The Slaughterhouse (Hygiene) Regulations 1958

General	500	Working plane	25	Intermediate or warm	BDEFGJL	Proof luminaires may be required
Inspection	750	Working plane (vertical)	19	Cool or intermediate	ABD	"

	Standard service illuminance lux	Position of measurement	Limiting glare index	Colour appearance of light source	Colour rendering group (See Table 1)	Notes

INDUSTRIAL BUILDINGS AND PROCESSES

Soap factories   Proof luminaires may be required

General areas	300	Working plane	25	Intermediate or warm	EFGJLM	
Control panels	300	Panels (may be vertical)	25	"	"	Avoid specular reflect in panels
Machines	300	Machines	25	"	"	
Edible product processing and packing	300	Working plane	25	"	"	See Sl No 1172: The Hygiene (General) Re, tions 1970

Structural steel fabrication plants

General	300	Working plane	28	Intermediate or warm	EFGJKLM	
Marking off	500	"	28	"	"	

Textile mills (cotton or linen)   Proof luminaires may be required in some areas

Bale breaking, blowing, carding, roving, slubbing, spinning (ordinary counts), winding, reeling, combing, hackling, spreading, cabling	300	Working plane (may be vertical)	25	Intermediate or warm	BDEJL	
Beaming, sizing, dressing and dyeing, doubling (fancy), spinning (fine counts)	500	"	25	"	"	
Healding (drawing-in)	1000	Vertical plane	–	"	"	Special local lighting required
Weaving						
plain 'grey' cloth	750	Working plane	19	Cool, intermediate or warm	ABDEL	
patterned cloths, fine counts	1000	"	19	"	"	
Inspection	1500	Inspection surface	16	Cool	A	Special local lighting r be required. Building illuminance not less th 750 lux.

Textile mills (synthetic or silk)

Soaking, fugitive tinting, conditioning or setting of twist	300	Working plane (may be vertical)	25	Intermediate or warm	BDEJL	
Winding, twisting, rewinding, crimping, coning, quilting, sizing, beaming	500	"	25	"	"	
Spinning	500	"	22	"	"	
Flat-bed knitting machines	500	Needles	22	"	"	
Healding (drawing-in)	1000	Vertical plane	–	"	"	Special local lighting
Weaving	1000	Working plane	19	Cool, intermediate or warm	ABDEL	required
Inspection	1500	Inspection surface	16	Cool	A	Special local lighting r be required. Building luminance not less tha 750 lux.

	Standard service illuminance lux	Position of measurement	Limiting glare index	Colour appearance of light source	Colour rendering group (See Table 1)	Notes

INDUSTRIAL BUILDINGS AND PROCESSES

Textile mills (woollen)
Proof luminaires may be required in some areas

Scouring, carbonizing, teasing, preparing, raising, brushing, pressing, back-washing, gilling, crabbing and blowing, blending, carding, combing (white), tentering, drying, cropping	300	Working plane	25	Intermediate or warm	BDEJL	
Spinning, roving, winding, beaming, combing (coloured), twisting	500	Working plane (may be vertical)	22	"	"	
Healding (drawing-in)	1000	Vertical plane	–	'	"	Special local lighting required
Weaving						
heavy woollens	500	Working plane	19	Cool, intermediate or warm	ABDEL	
medium worsteds, fine woollens	750	"	19	"	"	
fine worsteds	1000	"	19	"	"	
Burling	1000	Inspection surface	19	"	"	Directional local lighting may be used
Mending	1500	"	16	"	"	
Inspection (perching)						
'grey'	1000	"	19	Cool or intermediate	ABD	Directional local lighting may be required
final	3000	"	19	Cool	A	Local lighting required. Building illuminance not less than 1000 lux.

Textile mills (jute)

Weaving, spinning flat, Jacquard carpet looms, cop winding, yarn calender	300	Working plane	25	Cool, intermediate or warm	ABDEL	

Tobacco factories

All machine processes	500	Working plane	22	Cool or intermediate	ABD	
All hand processes	750	"	22	" '	"	

Upholstery factories
See Furniture factories

Warehouses and bulk stores

Large material, loading bays	150	Identification labels	25	Cool, intermediate or warm	ABDEFGJKLM	Identification labels may be vertical and/or at floor level. Colour coding may be used. Minimize glare to fork lift truck drivers from high luminance sources
Small material, racks	300	"	25	"	"	
Packing, despatch	300	Bench	25	"	"	
Issue counters	500	"	22	"	"	

Welding and soldering shops

Gas and arc welding, rough spot welding	300	Working plane	28	Intermediate or warm	EFGJLM	

	Standard service illuminance lux	Position of measurement	Limiting glare index	Colour appearance of light source	Colour rendering group (See Table 1)	Notes

INDUSTRIAL BUILDINGS AND PROCESSES

Welding and soldering shops (continued)

	Standard service illuminance lux	Position of measurement	Limiting glare index	Colour appearance of light source	Colour rendering group	Notes
Medium soldering, brazing, spot welding, e.g. domestic hardware	500	"	25	"	"	
Fine soldering, spot welding e.g. instruments	1000	Working plane	19	Intermediate or warm	EFGJL	
Very fine soldering, spot welding, e.g. radio valves	1500	"	16	"	"	Optical aids may be us Building illuminance r less than 750 lux.

Woodworking shops

See also Furniture factories. See SR & O No 1196: The Woodworking Machinery Regulations 1922. Possible low maintenance factors

	Standard service illuminance lux	Position of measurement	Limiting glare index	Colour appearance of light source	Colour rendering group	Notes
Rough sawing, bench work	300	Bench	22	Intermediate or warm	EFGJLM	Unguarded rotating m inery may be in use: l tungsten lighting or ot measures required to a stroboscopic effects. S Section 2.6 Lighting o vertical planes importa at bench
Sizing, planing, rough sanding, medium machine and bench work, glueing, cooperage	500	Working plane	22	"	"	
Fine bench and machine work, fine sanding, finishing	750	"	22	"	"	

Offices and shops

Offices

See Shops, Offices and Railways Premises Act 1963

	Standard service illuminance lux	Position of measurement	Limiting glare index	Colour appearance of light source	Colour rendering group	Notes
General offices with mainly clerical tasks and occasional typing	500	Desk	19	Intermediate or warm	BDEFGHIJLM	Minimize veiling reflec by suitable luminaire l tion
Deep-plan general offices	750	"	19	"	"	
Business machine and typing offices	750	Copy	19	"	"	"
Filing rooms	300	File labels	19	"	"	File labels may be vert and at floor level
Conference rooms	750	Tables	16	"	BDHIJ	Consider variation of il inance to suit different functions, e.g. conferer and lectures. Dimming may be required
Executive offices	500	Desk	16	"	"	Possible need to vary lighting using dimmers
Banking halls,						
working space	500	"	19	"	BDFGJL	
public space	300	Floor	19	"	BDFGJKLM	
Computer rooms	500	Working plane	19	"	BDFGL	Avoid specular reflecti in consoles. Limit illum ance where internally li signals are used

Standard service illuminance lux	*Position of measurement*	*Limiting glare index*	*Colour appearance of light source*	*Colour rendering group (See Table 1)*	*Notes*

OFFICES AND SHOPS

Offices (continued)

Punch card rooms	See Business machines				
Drawing offices					
drawing boards	750	Board	16	Cool, intermediate or warm	ABDEFGJL	Where colour rendering is important use AB or D. Boards may be vertical or inclined
reference tables and general	500	Table	16	"	"	Where colour rendering is important use AB or D
print room	300	"	19	Intermediate or warm	EJL	

Shops   See Shops, Offices and Railway Premises Act 1963. For food shops, see Sl No 1172: The Food Hygiene (General) Regulations 1970

Conventional with counters	500	Counters— horizontal	19	Cool, intermediate or warm	ABCDEFG HIJKL	Type of merchandise will dictate required colour rendering. Localized lighting needed to emphasize particular displays
Conventional with wall displays	500	Display— vertical	19	"	"	
Self-service	500	Vertical on displayed merchandise	19	Intermediate or warm	BCDFGJLK	"
Supermarkets	500	"	22	"	"	"
Hypermarkets	500	"	22	"	BCDFGJKLM	In these very large areas, definition of perimeter walls by higher luminance is desirable
	1000	Horizontal on working plane	22	"	"	
Showrooms					
car	500	Vertical on cars	19	Cool, intermediate or warm	ABDFGJK	
general	500	Merchandise	19	"	ABDFGJKLM	Vertical surfaces may be important. Use AB or D where colour rendering is important

	Standard service illuminance lux	Position of measurement	Limiting glare index	Colour appearance of light source	Colour rendering group (See Table 1)	Notes

Public and educational buildings

Assembly and concert halls, cinemas and theatres

Auditoria

	Standard service illuminance lux	Position of measurement	Limiting glare index	Colour appearance of light source	Colour rendering group	Notes
theatres and concert halls	100	Horizontal at seat level	–	Intermediate or warm	BDHIJK	Dimming facilities requ
cinemas	50	"	–	"	"	"
multi-purpose	500	"	19	"	BDFGHIJKLM	Allow for variation of il luminance to suit funct Dimming facilities usua required
Bars, restaurants, etc	See Hotels					
Booking offices	300	Desk	–	Intermediate or warm	BDHIJ	
Dressing rooms	300	Table	–	Warm	HIJ	Special facial lighting a mirror required, colour rendering group J
Foyers	75 scalar	1.2m above floor	19	Intermediate or warm	BDHIJK	
Platforms and stages	Special lighting					
Projection rooms	150	Working side of projectors	–	Warm	JL	Lighting should not det from view into auditori
Wardrobe, costume racks	100	Vertical on racks	–	Warm	HIJ	

Churches

	Standard service illuminance lux	Position of measurement	Limiting glare index	Colour appearance of light source	Colour rendering group	Notes
Body of church	100	Pews	16	Intermediate or warm	BDFGHIJKLM	
Pulpit, lectern	150	Desk	–	"	"	Additional facial lightin required
Choir	150	Book level	19	"	"	
Chancel, altar, communion table	150	Vertical plane	19	"	"	Lighting should give ap propriate emphasis by colour and direction. Special lighting will be required
Vestries	150	Working plane	22	"	BDFGHIJKL	
Church halls	150	Floor	19	"	"	See also Sports halls an Auditoria, multi-purpos

Further education establishments

Lecture theatres

	Standard service illuminance lux	Position of measurement	Limiting glare index	Colour appearance of light source	Colour rendering group	Notes
general	300	Desk	16	Intermediate or warm	BDFGJL	See IES Technical Repo No 5. Provision for dim ming may be required. Provide suitable lighting lecturer's face and note Low noise level require
chalkboard	500	Vertical plane	–	"	"	Ensure correct offset to give reasonable uniform and avoid reflections or chalkboard surface
demonstration benches	500	Bench	16	"	"	

	Standard service illuminance lux	Position of measurement	Limiting glare index	Colour appearance of light source	Colour rendering group (See Table 1)	Notes

PUBLIC AND EDUCATIONAL BUILDINGS

Further education establishments (continued)

	Standard service illuminance lux	Position of measurement	Limiting glare index	Colour appearance of light source	Colour rendering group	Notes
Examination halls, seminar rooms, teaching spaces	500	Desk	19	"	"	Where the main view is across the space, e.g. to the chalkboard, the LGI should be 16
Art rooms	500	Easel	19	Cool or intermediate	ABD	
Laboratories	500	Bench	19	Cool, intermediate or warm	ABDEFGJL	Type of laboratory may dictate colour rendering group. Local lighting may be used
Workshops	See appropriate industrial process					
Staff rooms, student common rooms, studen hostels, etc	See General building areas					
Gymnasia	See Indoor sports, games and recreational buildings					

Libraries   See IES Technical Report No 8

	Standard service illuminance lux	Position of measurement	Limiting glare index	Colour appearance of light source	Colour rendering group	Notes
Shelves, book stack	150	Vertical at floor level	19	Intermediate or warm	BDEFGH IJKLM	
Reading tables	300	Tables	19	"	"	
Reading rooms						
newspapers and magazines	300	Desk	19	Intermediate or warm	IJKLM	
reference libraries	500	"	19	"	"	
Counters	500	"	19	"	BDEFGHIJLM	
Cataloguing and sorting	500	"	19	"	"	
Binding	500	"	19	"	"	
Closed book store	100	Vertical at floor level	–	"	"	

Museums and art galleries   See IES Technical Report No 14

General	Standard service illuminance lux	Position of measurement	Limiting glare index	Colour appearance of light source	Colour rendering group	Notes
exhibits insensitive to light	300	Display	16	Cool, intermediate or warm	ABDFHIJKL	
light-sensitive exhibits	150	"	16	"	ABDHIJ	Illuminance are maxima
specially light-sensitive exhibits	50	'	16	"	"	"
Ancillary areas - entrances, corridors, staircases, offices, workshops etc	See relevant sections of Schedule. Need to ensure correct adaptation sequences					

Schools   See Sl No 890: The Standards for School Premises Regulations 1959, amended 1970. See also Guide lines for Environmental Design, DES 1972. Where schools are also used for further education the more stringent requirements should be observed

Assembly halls	Standard service illuminance lux	Position of measurement	Limiting glare index	Colour appearance of light source	Colour rendering group	Notes
general	300	Working plane	19	Intermediate or warm	BDFGJKL	Provision for dimming should be included for stage and film use
platform and stage	Special lighting					
Teaching spaces						
general	300	Working plane	19	"	BDFGJL	Illuminance may be reduced to 150 lux in spaces lit by tungsten lamps, e.g. nursery and infant schools. Where

	Standard service illuminance lux	Position of measurement	Limiting glare index	Colour appearance of light source	Colour rendering group (See Table 1)	Notes

PUBLIC AND EDUCATIONAL BUILDINGS

Schools (continued)

	Standard service illuminance lux	Position of measurement	Limiting glare index	Colour appearance of light source	Colour rendering group (See Table 1)	Notes
						the main view is across space, e.g. to the chalk board, the LGI should 16
general where also used for further education	500	"		"	"	
chalkboard	500	Vertical plane	–	"	"	Ensure correct offset t give reasonable uniforr and avoid reflections ir chalkboard surface
Lecture theatres general	300	Desk	16	"	"	See also Lecture theatr Further education esta lishments
chalkboard	500	Vertical plane	–	"	"	Ensure correct offset t give reasonable uniform and avoid reflections ir chalkboard surface
demonstration benches	500	Bench	16	"	"	
Needlework rooms	500	Working plane	19	Intermediate or warm	BDFGJL	Local lighting may be u
Art rooms	500	Easel	19	Cool or intermediate	ABD	
Laboratories	500	Bench	19	Cool, intermediate or warm	ABDEFGJL	Type of laboratory ma dictate colour renderin group. Local lighting m be used
Workshops	300	Working plane	19	Intermediate or warm	EJL	Additional task lighting will be required.
Staff rooms and kitchens	See General building areas					
Dining spaces	150	Table	22	"	BDJL	For multi-purpose use, refer to appropriate recommendations
Gymnasia	300	Floor	–	"	EFGJKLM	Impact resistant lumina required. Wall illumina important
Music practice rooms	300	Music	19	"	BDFGJL	

Transport terminal buildings - airports, coach and railway stations

	Standard service illuminance lux	Position of measurement	Limiting glare index	Colour appearance of light source	Colour rendering group (See Table 1)	Notes
Reception areas (desks), customs and immigration halls	500	Desk or table	22	Intermediate or warm	BDEFGJKLM	
Railway stations						See Shops, Offices & R way Premises Act 1963
booking offices	500	Counter	19	"	EFGJL	Avoid specular reflecti in ticket-issuing machir
parcels and left luggage offices general	300	Floor	22	"	"	
counters	300	Counter	22	"	"	
Circulation areas	150 scalar	1.2m above floor	22	"	BDEFGJKLM	
Waiting areas	300 scalar	1.2m above floor	22	"	"	
Restaurants, bars, kitchens	See Hotels					

	Standard service illuminance lux	Position of measurement	Limiting glare index	Colour appearance of light source	Colour rendering group (See Table 1)	Notes

Hospitals, surgeries and consulting rooms

Hospitals See IES Technical Report No. 12 and DHSS Recommendations for all areas

See IES Technical Report No 12 for glare limitation

	Standard service illuminance lux	Position of measurement	Limiting glare index	Colour appearance of light source	Colour rendering group	Notes
Ward units						
bed heads						
general	30-50	Pillow	–	Intermediate or warm	BJ	
reading	150	Book plane	–	"	"	Book plane may be vertical, horizontal or inclined
night	0.1	Pillow	–	Warm	JL	
night (children)	1	"	–	"	"	
watch	5	"	–	"	"	
circulation space						
evening	150	Bed height	–	Intermediate or warm	BJ	Average illuminance in area between feet of beds throughout depth of bed area
night	0.1 min	"	–	Warm	JL	Pools of light must be restricted to space between feet of beds
nurses' station						
evening	300	Desk	–	Intermediate or warm	BJ	
night	100	"	–	Warm	JL	Restrict luminances visible from beds
Corridors (open to bedbays)						
day	300	Floor	–	Intermediate or warm	B	Avoid visual discomfort to patients on trolleys
evening	200	"	–	"	BJ	"
night	3	"	–	"	"	Restrict luminance visible from beds
Corridors (separate from bedbays)						
day	300	"	–	Intermediate	B	Avoid visual discomfort to patients on trolleys
evening	150	"	–	"	"	"
night	5-10	"	–	Intermediate or warm	BJ	"
Internal rooms without natural lighting, with specific visual tasks						
day	400	Working plane	19	"	"	
evening and night						
general	200	"	19	"	"	
task lighting	400	Work place	–	"	"	
Other internal rooms without natural lighting						
day	300	Working plane	22	"	"	
evening and night	100	"	22	"	"	
Examination, consulting, blood-taking rooms	400	Desk or couch	–	"	"	Examination light required. Restrict luminance of general lighting seen by recumbent patient
Audiometry rooms	150	Vertical plane at bench level	–	"	BDJK	Low noise level required
Pharmacies						
dispensing benches	500	Bench	19	"	BJ	
shelves	150	Vertical plane at lowest shelf	–	"	"	

	Standard service illuminance lux	Position of measurement	Limiting glare index	Colour appearance of light source	Colour rendering group (See Table 1)	Notes

HOSPITALS, SURGERIES AND CONSULTING ROOMS

Hospitals (continued)

	Standard service illuminance lux	Position of measurement	Limiting glare index	Colour appearance of light source	Colour rendering group (See Table 1)	Notes
Physiotherapy departments						
gymnasium	300	Floor	—	Intermediate or warm	BDEJLM	
hydrotherapy	100					
Reception						
general	300	Working plane	19	"	BDEJL	
enquiry desk	500	Desk	19	"	"	
Training and rehabilitation units						
general	300	Working plane	16	"	"	For other uses refer to appropriate recommendations
chalkboards, etc	500	Vertical plane	—	"	"	Ensure adequate offset to give reasonable uniformity and avoid reflections in chalkboard surface
Laboratories	500	Bench	19	Intermediate or warm	BJ	Higher values than recommended in IES Technical Report No 12 may now be justified for critical laboratory work. If colour rendering is critical, source L may used
Mortuaries and post-mortem rooms						
body store	150	Floor	—	"	"	
post-mortem room general	300	"	—	"	"	"
table	Special lighting					
Offices	See Offices and shops					
Operating theatre suites						Explosion hazard from anaesthetic gases in so areas
general	400	Trolley height	—	Intermediate	B	Hose-proof luminaires may be required
operating area	Special lighting					
anaesthetic room	300	Trolley	—	Intermediate or warm	BJ	Local light to BS 354 required. Dimming facilities may be required
Recovery rooms and intensive care units	30-50	Bed head	—	"	"	400 lux to be available bed for supervision on
X-ray departments						
diagnostic departments	See DHSS Hospital Building Note No 6					
radiodiagnostic and fluoroscopy rooms	500	Couch	—	Intermediate or warm	BDJL	Dimming required
radiotherapy rooms	300	"	—	"	"	Decorations and lighting should alleviate claustrophobic effect
laboratories	500	Bench	19	"	BDEJL	

	Standard service illuminance lux	Position of measurement	Limiting glare index	Colour appearance of light source	Colour rendering group (See Table 1)	Notes

HOSPITALS, SURGERIES AND CONSULTING ROOMS

Surgeries

	Standard service illuminance lux	Position of measurement	Limiting glare index	Colour appearance of light source	Colour rendering group	Notes
General	300	Working plane	16	Intermediate or warm	BJ	
Waiting rooms	300	Table level	19	"	BDIJL	
Dental surgeries						
chair	Special lighting					
laboratories	500	Bench	19	Intermediate	B	

Consulting rooms

	Standard service illuminance lux	Position of measurement	Limiting glare index	Colour appearance of light source	Colour rendering group	Notes
General	300	Working plane	16	Intermediate or warm	BJ	
Desk	500	Desk	—	"	BDIJL	Preferably local lighting
Examination couch	500	Couch	—	"	BJ	Preferably localized lighting
Ophthalmic wall and near-vision charts	500	Chart	—	"	BDIJL	Light charts uniformly. Restrict illuminance on internally lit test apparatus

Homes and hotels

Homes

	Standard service illuminance lux	Position of measurement	Limiting glare index	Colour appearance of light source	Colour rendering group	Notes
Living rooms						
general	50	Working plane	—	Intermediate or warm	BDHIJ	In all home areas, attention should be given to the lighting of room surfaces. Luminaires should be selected and positioned to give occupants a compromise between attractive 'sparkle' and unwanted glare. Dimming is useful for changing atmosphere
casual reading	150	Task	—	"	"	
sewing and darning	300	"	—	"	"	
Studies						
desk and prolonged reading	300	"	—	"	"	
Bedrooms						
general	50	Floor	—	"	"	
bedhead	150	Bed	—	"	"	
Kitchens						
working areas	300	Working surface	—	"	"	Additional mirror lighting required in bedrooms
Bathrooms	100	Floor	—	"	"	Additional mirror lighting required. Enclosed luminaires should be used
Halls and landings	150	Floor	—	"	"	High luminance should be screened from view when ascending or descending stairs
Stairs	100	Treads	—	"	"	
Workshops	300	Bench	—	"	BDHIJL	
Garages	50	Floor	—	"	"	

	Standard service illuminance lux	Position of measurement	Limiting glare index	Colour appearance of light source	Colour rendering group (See Table 1)	Notes

HOMES AND HOTELS

Homes (old people's) Illuminances must be increased 50-100 per cent above recommendations for Homes. Particular attention must be paid to avoiding glare and to revealing steps and obstructions. Two-way switches should be installed for through-ways, stairs, etc

Hotels

	Standard service illuminance lux	Position of measurement	Limiting glare index	Colour appearance of light source	Colour rendering group	Notes
Entrance halls						
general	75 scalar	1.2m above floor	19	Intermediate or warm	BDFGHIJ	
reception, cashier	300	Desk	19	"	"	
Public rooms						
bars, coffee bars	150	Table	—	"	BDHIJL	Flexibility of control required to achieve va in lighting
dining rooms, grill rooms, restaurants						
general	100	Table	—	'	BDHIJ	Additional table light may be required
cash desks	300	Desk	—	"	"	
lounges	100 scalar	1.2m above floor	16	"	"	Additional table light may be required
writing rooms	150	Table	19	"	"	
cloakrooms	150	Floor	—	"	BDHIJL	Additional mirror ligh required
Bedrooms and bathrooms	See Homes					
Service areas						
kitchens	See General building areas					
baggage rooms	100	Floor	—	Warm	JL	
laundries	300	Working plane	—	Intermediate or warm	EJL	
cellars	150	Floor	—	"	"	

Standard service illuminance lux	*Position of measurement*	*Limiting glare index*	*Colour appearance of light source*	*Colour rendering group (See Table 1)*	*Notes*

Indoor sports, games and recreational buildings

Sports lighting usually has special requirements. In halls where one sport only is practised every effort should be made to enable the appropriate lighting techniques to be employed, e.g. side lighting, localized and indirect lighting. In multi-purpose halls the lighting system must be a compromise to serve the different sports taking place; some sports are better lit from the sides, others from overhead. Floodlighting techniques can be employed particularly where there are no spectators. Glare requirements for sports are too specialized to be represented by a glare index. Technical Report No 7 must be consulted for methods of glare control. Flicker effects should be minimized. Higher illuminances will be required if events are televised in colour. Sports are classed as 'top', 'club' or 'recreational' depending largely on spectator participation. The following recommendations are a guide. *IES Technical Report No 7 'Lighting for sport' must be consulted.*

Multi-purpose sports halls

Athletics, basketball, bowls, fencing, gymnastics, judo, volley ball	300-700	Floor		Intermediate or warm	DEFGJKLM	For some sports, side lighting or localized lighting (e.g. at the net in badminton) is preferred. Arrange switching to give illuminance appropriate to activity

Badminton courts

	300	Floor		Intermediate or warm	DEJK	Avoid glare from overhead lighting

Billiard rooms

General	100	Floor		Intermediate or warm	DEJKL	
Table		Special lighting				

Boxing rings

Top	1000	Vertical plane		Intermediate or warm	FGJKM	
Club	500	"		"	"	
Recreational	150	"		"	"	

Card rooms

	300	Table		Intermediate or warm	DEHIJKL	

Cricket nets (indoors)

Top	1000	Floor		Intermediate or warm	DEL	
Club	500	"		"	"	
Recreational	300	"		"	"	

Gymnasia general

	500	Floor		Intermediate or warm	DEFGJKLM	Impact resistant luminaires required

Ice hockey and skating rinks

Top	500	Rink level		Intermediate or warm	DEFGJKLM	
Club	300	"		"	"	

	Standard service illuminance lux	Position of measurement	Limiting glare index	Colour appearance of light source	Colour rendering group (See Table 1)	Notes

INDOOR SPORTS, GAMES AND RECREATIONAL BUILDINGS

Ice hockey and skating rinks (continued)
Recreational	150	Rink level		Intermediate or warm	DEFGJKLM	

Rifle ranges
Target	1000	Vertical plane		Intermediate or warm	DEJKL	
Range	100	Floor		"	"	
Firing point	150	"		"	"	

Squash rackets courts
Top	500	Floor		Intermediate or warm	DEL	
Club	300	"		"	"	

Swimming pools
Top						Proof luminaires requi
pool	500	Water level		Intermediate or warm	DEFGJKLM	Access to luminaires fo maintenance must be
spectator areas	150	Seated level		"	"	sidered. Windows and
Club. Recreational	300	Water level		"	"	luminaires must be loc to avoid glare to swim divers and spectators b direct view and by refl tions at water surface

Table tennis
Top						
table	500	Table top		Intermediate or warm	DEJKL	
spectator areas	150	Seat level		"	"	
Club	300	Table top		"	"	
Recreational	200	"		"	"	

Tennis courts (indoor)
Top	500	Floor		Intermediate or warm	DEFGJKLM	Restrict glare from ove head luminaires
Club	300	"		"	"	
Recreational	150	"		"	"	

General
Changing rooms, showers, locker rooms	150	Floor		Intermediate or warm	DEJL	

Table 4   **Utilization Factors**

On the following pages will be found approximate utilization Factors for typical luminaires representative of those widely used for general lighting purposes. All the data have been calculated by the BZ method described in IES Technical Report No. 2. Each group of luminaires, except the last seven, is ascribed a Basic Downward Light Output Ratio* and the data for that group have been calculated for that Basic DLOR. Each fitting in that group is ascribed its own typical DLOR or range of typical DLOR's so that if it is thought necessary a greater accuracy may be obtained by multiplying the utilization factor found from the table by the fraction

$$\frac{\text{DLOR of the actual luminaire}}{\text{Basic DLOR of the group}}$$

e.g. if the Basic DLOR is 60% and the DLOR of the actual luminaire used is known to be 55%, the utilization factor found from the table should be multiplied by 0.916.

In the first column of the table,
(F)   denotes a luminaire for fluorescent lamp(s);
(M)   denotes a luminaire for colour-corrected discharge lamp;
(T)   denotes a luminaire for incandescent (tungsten filament) lamp.

* DLOR   This is the fraction :

$$\frac{\text{Total downward light output from the luminaire}}{\text{Total light output of the lamp(s)}}$$

and can be found from the catalogue or by request from the manufacturer. In the absence of such information, the utilization factor found from the table should be used without any modification.

Table 4   Utilization Factors (continued)

Description of Luminaire, and Typical Downward Light Output Ratio %	Typical Outline	Basic DLOR %	Ceiling / Walls / Room Index	Reflectance % 70			50			30		
			Walls	50	30	10	50	30	10	50	30	
(M) Reflectorized colour-corrected mercury lamp MBFR (80–90)		85	0·6	0·4	0·34	0·3	0·39	0·33	0·29	0·37	0·32	C
			0·8	0·53	0·46	0·41	0·51	0·45	0·4	0·49	0·43	C
			1	0·62	0·55	0·49	0·58	0·52	0·48	0·56	0·51	C
			1·25	0·68	0·6	0·55	0·64	0·58	0·53	0·61	0·56	C
			1·5	0·72	0·65	0·59	0·68	0·62	0·57	0·65	0·59	C
			2	0·81	0·73	0·67	0·75	0·69	0·64	0·69	0·65	0
			2·5	0·85	0·78	0·72	0·79	0·73	0·69	0·73	0·68	0
			3	0·9	0·83	0·78	0·83	0·78	0·75	0·77	0·73	0
			4	0·94	0·89	0·84	0·87	0·83	0·8	0·8	0·77	0
			5	0·97	0·92	0·89	0·9	0·87	0·84	0·83	0·79	0
(F) Open-end enamel trough (75–85)		75	0·6	0·36	0·31	0·28	0·35	0·31	0·28	0·35	0·31	0
			0·8	0·45	0·4	0·37	0·44	0·4	0·37	0·44	0·4	0
			1	0·49	0·45	0·4	0·49	0·44	0·4	0·48	0·43	0
			1·25	0·55	0·49	0·46	0·53	0·49	0·45	0·52	0·48	0
			1·5	0·58	0·54	0·49	0·57	0·53	0·49	0·55	0·52	0
			2	0·64	0·59	0·55	0·61	0·58	0·55	0·6	0·56	0
			2·5	0·68	0·63	0·6	0·65	0·62	0·59	0·64	0·61	0
(F) Closed-end enamel trough (65–83)			3	0·7	0·65	0·62	0·67	0·64	0·61	0·65	0·63	0
			4	0·73	0·7	0·67	0·7	0·67	0·65	0·67	0·66	0
			5	0·75	0·72	0·69	0·73	0·7	0·67	0·7	0·68	0
(T) Standard dispersive industrial reflector (77)												
(M) Aluminium industrial reflector (72–76)		70	0·6	0·39	0·36	0·33	0·39	0·36	0·33	0·39	0·35	0
			0·8	0·48	0·43	0·4	0·46	0·43	0·4	0·46	0·43	0
(T) High-bay reflector, aluminium (72) or enamel (66)			1	0·52	0·49	0·45	0·52	0·48	0·45	0·52	0·48	0
			1·25	0·56	0·53	0·5	0·56	0·53	0·49	0·56	0·52	0
			1·5	0·6	0·57	0·54	0·59	0·57	0·53	0·59	0·55	0
			2	0·65	0·62	0·59	0·63	0·6	0·58	0·63	0·59	0
			2·5	0·67	0·64	0·62	0·65	0·62	0·61	0·65	0·62	0
			3	0·69	0·66	0·64	0·67	0·64	0·63	0·67	0·64	0
			4	0·71	0·68	0·67	0·69	0·67	0·65	0·69	0·66	0
			5	0·72	0·7	0·69	0·71	0·69	0·67	0·71	0·67	0

Table 4 Utilization Factors (continued)

ription of Luminaire, and Typical ward Light Output Ratio %	Typical Outline	Basic DLOR %	Room Index	Reflectance %								
			Ceiling	70			50			30		
			Walls	50	30	10	50	30	10	50	30	10
stic trough, unlouvered (60–70)		70	0·6	0·33	0·28	0·25	0·32	0·28	0·25	0·31	0·27	0·25
			0·8	0·42	0·37	0·33	0·41	0·36	0·33	0·4	0·36	0·33
			1	0·48	0·43	0·38	0·46	0·42	0·38	0·45	0·42	0·38
			1·25	0·52	0·47	0·43	0·5	0·46	0·42	0·49	0·45	0·42
			1·5	0·56	0·51	0·47	0·54	0·5	0·46	0·52	0·48	0·45
			2	0·62	0·56	0·53	0·58	0·55	0·51	0·56	0·52	0·5
			2·5	0·65	0·6	0·57	0·61	0·58	0·55	0·59	0·56	0·53
			3	0·67	0·63	0·6	0·64	0·61	0·58	0·62	0·59	0·56
			4	0·7	0·66	0·64	0·67	0·64	0·61	0·64	0·62	0·59
			5	0·73	0·69	0·67	0·69	0·67	0·64	0·66	0·64	0·62
) uble refractor system. Surface mounted or lly recessed (63)*		65	0·6	0·37	0·34	0·31	0·37	0·34	0·31	0·37	0·34	0·31
			0·8	0·42	0·39	0·36	0·42	0·39	0·36	0·42	0·39	0·36
			1	0·45	0·42	0·39	0·45	0·42	0·39	0·45	0·42	0·39
			1·25	0·49	0·46	0·44	0·49	0·46	0·44	0·49	0·46	0·44
			1·5	0·52	0·49	0·47	0·51	0·48	0·47	0·50	0·47	0·46
			2	0·55	0·53	0·51	0·54	0·52	0·51	0·53	0·51	0·5
			2·5	0·57	0·55	0·53	0·56	0·54	0·53	0·55	0·53	0·52
			3	0·59	0·57	0·55	0·57	0·56	0·55	0·56	0·55	0·54
			4	0·6	0·58	0·56	0·58	0·57	0·56	0·57	0·56	0·55
			5	0·62	0·6	0·58	0·6	0·59	0·58	0·58	0·57	0·56
re lamp on ceiling tten luminaire (60–70)		65	0·6	0·29	0·24	0·19	0·27	0·22	0·19	0·24	0·21	0·19
			0·8	0·37	0·31	0·27	0·35	0·3	0·25	0·31	0·28	0·24
			1	0·44	0·37	0·33	0·4	0·35	0·31	0·35	0·32	0·29
			1·25	0·49	0·42	0·38	0·45	0·4	0·36	0·39	0·36	0·33
			1·5	0·54	0·47	0·42	0·5	0·44	0·4	0·43	0·4	0·37
			2	0·6	0·52	0·49	0·54	0·49	0·45	0·48	0·44	0·41
			2·5	0·64	0·57	0·53	0·57	0·53	0·49	0·52	0·48	0·45
			3	0·67	0·61	0·57	0·6	0·57	0·53	0·56	0·52	0·49
			4	0·71	0·66	0·62	0·64	0·61	0·57	0·59	0·55	0·52
			5	0·74	0·7	0·66	0·68	0·64	0·61	0·62	0·58	0·54
) ection moulded prismatic wrap around closure (55–65)*		55	0·6	0·32	0·28	0·25	0·3	0·27	0·25	0·27	0·24	0·22
			0·8	0·4	0·36	0·32	0·39	0·34	0·31	0·36	0·32	0·3
			1	0·45	0·41	0·38	0·43	0·38	0·36	0·39	0·35	0·33
			1·25	0·5	0·45	0·42	0·47	0·44	0·41	0·43	0·39	0·37
			1·5	0·53	0·48	0·45	0·5	0·46	0·41	0·46	0·43	0·41
			2	0·58	0·53	0·49	0·54	0·5	0·47	0·5	0·47	0·45
			2·5	0·61	0·57	0·53	0·57	0·53	0·51	0·52	0·5	0·47
			3	0·64	0·59	0·56	0·58	0·55	0·53	0·53	0·51	0·49
			4	0·66	0·63	0·6	0·61	0·58	0·55	0·55	0·53	0·51
			5	0·68	0·65	0·62	0·62	0·6	0·58	0·56	0·56	0·54

Table 4   Utilization Factors (continued)

(F) Enclosed plastic diffuser (45–55)

Basic DLOR: 50%

Room Index	70 / 50	70 / 30	70 / 10	50 / 50	50 / 30	50 / 10	30 / 50	30 / 30	30 / 10
0·6	0·27	0·21	0·18	0·24	0·2	0·18	0·22	0·19	0
0·8	0·34	0·29	0·26	0·32	0·28	0·25	0·29	0·26	0
1	0·4	0·35	0·31	0·37	0·33	0·3	0·33	0·3	0
1·25	0·44	0·39	0·35	0·4	0·36	0·33	0·36	0·33	0
1·5	0·47	0·42	0·38	0·43	0·39	0·36	0·38	0·35	0
2	0·52	0·47	0·44	0·47	0·44	0·41	0·41	0·39	0
2·5	0·55	0·51	0·48	0·5	0·47	0·44	0·44	0·42	0
3	0·58	0·54	0·51	0·52	0·49	0·47	0·47	0·45	0
4	0·61	0·57	0·54	0·55	0·52	0·5	0·49	0·47	0
5	0·63	0·59	0·57	0·57	0·55	0·53	0·51	0·49	0

(F) Plastic trough, louvered (45–55)

Basic DLOR: 50%

Room Index	70 / 50	70 / 30	70 / 10	50 / 50	50 / 30	50 / 10	30 / 50	30 / 30	30 / 10
0·6	0·26	0·22	0·19	0·25	0·21	0·19	0·24	0·2	
0·8	0·34	0·29	0·26	0·32	0·28	0·25	0·31	0·27	0
1	0·39	0·34	0·3	0·36	0·32	0·29	0·34	0·31	0
1·25	0·43	0·38	0·34	0·39	0·36	0·33	0·37	0·34	0
1·5	0·46	0·41	0·37	0·42	0·39	0·36	0·39	0·36	0
2	0·5	0·46	0·43	0·43	0·42	0·4	0·43	0·39	0
2·5	0·53	0·49	0·46	0·49	0·46	0·43	0·45	0·42	0
3	0·55	0·51	0·49	0·51	0·48	0·46	0·47	0·45	0
4	0·58	0·54	0·52	0·53	0·51	0·49	0·48	0·47	0
5	0·6	0·57	0·55	0·55	0·53	0·51	0·5	0·48	0

(F) Recessed louvered trough with optically designed reflecting surfaces (50)

Basic DLOR: 50%

Room Index	70 / 50	70 / 30	70 / 10	50 / 50	50 / 30	50 / 10	30 / 50	30 / 30	30 / 10
0·6	0·28	0·25	0·23	0·28	0·25	0·23	0·28	0·25	0
0·8	0·34	0·31	0·28	0·33	0·3	0·28	0·33	0·3	
1	0·37	0·35	0·32	0·37	0·34	0·32	0·37	0·34	0
1·25	0·4	0·38	0·35	0·4	0·37	0·35	0·4	0·37	0
1·5	0·43	0·41	0·38	0·42	0·4	0·38	0·42	0·39	0
2	0·46	0·44	0·42	0·45	0·43	0·41	0·44	0·42	0
2·5	0·48	0·46	0·44	0·47	0·45	0·43	0·46	0·44	0
3	0·49	0·47	0·46	0·48	0·46	0·45	0·47	0·45	0
4	0·5	0·49	0·48	0·49	0·48	0·47	0·48	0·47	0
5	0·51	0·5	0·49	0·5	0·49	0·48	0·49	0·48	0

(F) Suspended louvered metal trough, upward and downward light, optically designed reflecting surfaces (47–54)

Basic DLOR: 50%

Room Index	70 / 50	70 / 30	70 / 10	50 / 50	50 / 30	50 / 10	30 / 50	30 / 30	30 / 10
0·6	0·35	0·32	0·29	0·33	0·31	0·28	0·33	0·3	0
0·8	0·41	0·38	0·35	0·39	0·36	0·34	0·38	0·35	0
1	0·46	0·42	0·4	0·44	0·41	0·39	0·42	0·39	0
1·25	0·49	0·46	0·43	0·47	0·44	0·42	0·45	0·42	0
1·5	0·52	0·49	0·46	0·49	0·47	0·44	0·47	0·44	0
2	0·56	0·53	0·51	0·52	0·5	0·48	0·49	0·47	0
2·5	0·58	0·55	0·53	0·54	0·52	0·5	0·51	0·49	0
3	0·59	0·57	0·55	0·55	0·53	0·52	0·52	0·5	
4	0·61	0·59	0·57	0·57	0·55	0·54	0·53	0·51	0
5	0·63	0·6	0·59	0·58	0·57	0·55	0·54	0·52	0

Table 4   Utilization Factors (continued)

Description of Luminaire, and Typical Downward Light Output Ratio %	Typical Outline	Basic DLOR %	Room Index	Reflectance % Ceiling 70 Walls 50	30	10	Ceiling 50 Walls 50	30	10	Ceiling 30 Walls 50	30	10
amel slotted trough, louvered (45–55)		50	0·6	0·27	0·24	0·22	0·26	0·24	0·22	0·26	0·23	0·22
			0·8	0·32	0·3	0·27	0·32	0·29	0·27	0·31	0·29	0·27
			1	0·35	0·32	0·3	0·35	0·32	0·3	0·34	0·31	0·3
			1·25	0·38	0·35	0·32	0·38	0·35	0·33	0·38	0·34	0·33
			1·5	0·41	0·38	0·36	0·4	0·38	0·35	0·4	0·37	0·35
uvered recessed (module) luminaire (40–50)			2	0·45	0·42	0·4	0·43	0·41	0·39	0·43	0·4	0·39
			2·5	0·47	0·44	0·42	0·45	0·43	0·41	0·45	0·42	0·41
			3	0·48	0·45	0·44	0·46	0·45	0·43	0·46	0·44	0·42
			4	0·49	0·47	0·46	0·48	0·47	0·45	0·47	0·45	0·44
allow ceiling-mounted louver panel (40–50)			5	0·5	0·49	0·48	0·49	0·48	0·47	0·48	0·47	0·46
ecessed (modular) diffuser (43–54)		50	0·6	0·21	0·18	0·16	0·21	0·18	0·16	0·2	0·18	0·16
			0·8	0·28	0·24	0·22	0·27	0·24	0·22	0·26	0·24	0·22
			1	0·32	0·29	0·26	0·31	0·28	0·26	0·3	0·28	0·26
			1·25	0·35	0·32	0·29	0·34	0·31	0·29	0·32	0·3	0·28
			1·5	0·37	0·34	0·31	0·36	0·33	0·31	0·34	0·32	0·3
			2	0·41	0·37	0·35	0·39	0·37	0·34	0·38	0·36	0·34
			2·5	0·43	0·4	0·38	0·42	0·39	0·37	0·4	0·38	0·37
allow ceiling-mounted diffusing panel (40–55)			3	0·45	0·42	0·4	0·44	0·41	0·4	0·42	0·4	0·39
			4	0·47	0·44	0·43	0·46	0·44	0·42	0·44	0·42	0·41
			5	0·49	0·46	0·45	0·47	0·46	0·44	0·46	0·44	0·43
ear-spherical diffuser, open beneath (50)		50	0·6	0·28	0·22	0·18	0·25	0·2	0·17	0·22	0·18	0·16
			0·8	0·39	0·3	0·26	0·33	0·28	0·23	0·27	0·25	0·22
			1	0·43	0·36	0·32	0·38	0·34	0·29	0·31	0·29	0·26
			1·25	0·48	0·41	0·37	0·42	0·38	0·33	0·34	0·32	0·29
			1·5	0·52	0·46	0·41	0·46	0·41	0·37	0·37	0·35	0·32
			2	0·58	0·52	0·47	0·5	0·46	0·43	0·42	0·39	0·36
			2·5	0·62	0·50	0·52	0·54	0·5	0·47	0·45	0·42	0·4
			3	0·65	0·6	0·56	0·57	0·53	0·5	0·48	0·45	0·43
			4	0·68	0·64	0·61	0·6	0·56	0·54	0·51	0·48	0·46
			5	0·71	0·68	0·65	0·62	0·59	0·57	0·53	0·5	0·48

Table 4 Utilization Factors (continued)

Description of Ceiling	Typical Outline	Basic DLOR %	Ceiling	70			50			30		
			Walls	50	30	10	50	30	10	50	30	
			Room Index									
(F) Suspended opaque-sided luminaire, upward and downward light, diffuser, or louver beneath (45–50)		45	0·6	0·28	0·24	0·2	0·26	0·22	0·19	0·24	0·2	0
			0·8	0·36	0·3	0·28	0·33	0·29	0·26	0·31	0·27	0
			1	0·41	0·36	0·32	0·37	0·33	0·3	0·34	0·3	0
			1·25	0·45	0·41	0·36	0·41	0·37	0·34	0·37	0·33	0
			1·5	0·49	0·45	0·4	0·44	0·4	0·37	0·39	0·35	0
			2	0·55	0·5	0·46	0·48	0·45	0·42	0·42	0·39	0
			2·5	0·58	0·53	0·5	0·51	0·48	0·45	0·45	0·42	0
			3	0·6	0·56	0·53	0·53	0·5	0·48	0·47	0·44	0
			4	0·63	0·59	0·57	0·55	0·53	0·51	0·48	0·46	0
			5	0·65	0·62	0·6	0·57	0·55	0·53	0·5	0·48	0
(T) Opal sphere (45) and other enclosed diffusing luminaires of near-spherical shape		45	0·6	0·23	0·18	0·14	0·2	0·16	0·12	0·17	0·14	0
			0·8	0·3	0·24	0·2	0·27	0·22	0·18	0·22	0·19	0
			1	0·36	0·29	0·25	0·31	0·26	0·22	0·26	0·23	0
			1·25	0·41	0·34	0·29	0·35	0·3	0·26	0·29	0·26	0
			1·5	0·45	0·39	0·33	0·39	0·34	0·3	0·31	0·28	0
			2	0·5	0·45	0·4	0·43	0·38	0·34	0·34	0·32	0
			2·5	0·54	0·49	0·44	0·46	0·42	0·38	0·37	0·35	0
			3	0·57	0·52	0·48	0·49	0·45	0·42	0·4	0·38	0
			4	0·6	0·56	0·52	0·52	0·48	0·46	0·43	0·41	0
			5	0·63	0·6	0·56	0·54	0·51	0·49	0·45	0·43	0
(T) Diffuser with open top louvered beneath (30)		30	0·6	0·28	0·23	0·19	0·24	0·2	0·19	0·2	0·18	0
			0·8	0·35	0·3	0·26	0·3	0·26	0·23	0·25	0·23	0
			1	0·4	0·34	0·31	0·34	0·3	0·27	0·27	0·25	0
			1·25	0·45	0·39	0·36	0·38	0·33	0·31	0·3	0·28	0
			1·5	0·49	0·44	0·4	0·41	0·36	0·34	0·32	0·3	0
			2	0·54	0·5	0·46	0·45	0·41	0·39	0·34	0·33	0
			2·5	0·57	0·53	0·5	0·47	0·44	0·42	0·36	0·35	0
			3	0·6	0·56	0·53	0·49	0·46	0·45	0·38	0·37	0
			4	0·63	0·59	0·57	0·51	0·49	0·48	0·4	0·39	0
			5	0·65	0·62	0·6	0·53	0·51	0·5	0·41	0·4	0
(T or F) Totally indirect luminaire. Based on Upward Light Output Ratio 75% (Upper and lower walls the same colour)			0·6	0·1	0·07	0·04	0·07	0·05	0·03			
			0·8	0·13	0·11	0·08	0·11	0·09	0·07			
			1	0·16	0·15	0·12	0·15	0·12	0·1			
			1·25	0·2	0·19	0·16	0·18	0·15	0·13			
			1·5	0·24	0·23	0·2	0·2	0·18	0·16			
			2	0·28	0·27	0·23	0·22	0·2	0·18			
			2·5	0·32	0·31	0·26	0·24	0·22	0·2			
			3	0·36	0·35	0·29	0·25	0·23	0·21			
			4	0·4	0·38	0·31	0·26	0·24	0·22			
			5	0·43	0·4	0·33	0·27	0·25	0·23			

Table 4   Utilization Factors (continued)

Description of Luminaire, and Typical Downward Light Output Ratio %	Typical Outline	Basic DLOR %	Ceiling	70			50			30		
			Walls	50	30	10	50	30	10	50	30	10
			Room Index									
(T or F) As above, but with upper walls the same colour as the ceiling		0·6		0·11	0·08	0·05	0·08	0·06	0·04			
		0·8		0·16	0·13	0·1	0·11	0·09	0·07			
		1		0·21	0·17	0·14	0·13	0·11	0·09			
		1·25		0·25	0·21	0·18	0·15	0·13	0·11			
		1·5		0·29	0·25	0·22	0·17	0·15	0·13			
		2		0·33	0·3	0·27	0·2	0·18	0·16			
		2·5		0·37	0·34	0·32	0·23	0·21	0·19			
		3		0·4	0·38	0·36	0·26	0·24	0·22			
		4		0·43	0·42	0·4	0·28	0·27	0·25			
		5		0·45	0·44	0·42	0·3	0·29	0·27			
(T or F) Indirect cornices, recessed coves and coffers giving all their light above the horizontal. Based on an Upward Light Output Ratio of 40% but details of construction may vary this figure considerably		0·6		0·07	0·05	0·04	0·04	0·03				
		0·8		0·09	0·07	0·06	0·06	0·05				
		1		0·11	0·09	0·08	0·08	0·07				
		1·25		0·13	0·11	0·09	0·09	0·08				
		1·5		0·14	0·12	0·1	0·1	0·09				
		2		0·16	0·14	0·12	0·11	0·1				
		2·5		0·17	0·15	0·14	0·12	0·11				
		3		0·18	0·16	0·15	0·12	0·11				
		4		0·19	0·18	0·16	0·13	0·12				
		5		0·2	0·19	0·17	0·14	0·13				
(F) Complete luminous ceiling composed of translucent corrugated strip or individual pan-shaped elements. Based on ceiling cavity surfaces being white, and cavity width being three times cavity depth		0·6		0·2	0·15	0·12						
		0·8		0·28	0·24	0·2						
		1		0·34	0·31	0·27						
		1·25		0·37	0·34	0·31						
		1·5		0·4	0·36	0·34						
		2		0·45	0·42	0·39						
		2·5		0·47	0·44	0·42						
		3		0·49	0·46	0·44						
		4		0·52	0·49	0·47						
		5		0·54	0·51	0·49						
(F) Complete louvered ceiling composed of half-inch translucent plastic cells. Based on ceiling cavity surfaces being white, and cavity width being three times cavity depth		0·6		0·31	0·28	0·24						
		0·8		0·34	0·31	0·27						
		1		0·37	0·34	0·3						
		1·25		0·39	0·36	0·33						
		1·5		0·41	0·38	0·36						
		2		0·44	0·42	0·39						
		2·5		0·46	0·44	0·41						
		3		0·48	0·46	0·43						
		4		0·5	0·48	0·45						
		5		0·51	0·49	0·47						

Table 4 Utilization Factors (continued)

Description of Luminaire, and Typical Downward Light Output Ratio %	Typical Outline	Basic DLOR %	Ceiling	Reflectance % 70			50			30		
			Walls	50	30	10	50	30	10	50	30	10
			Room Index									
(F) Complete luminous ceiling composed of injection moulded flat prismatic panels.* Based on ceiling cavity surfaces being white, and cavity width being three times cavity depth			0·6	0·37	0·33	0·28						
			0·8	0·47	0·42	0·37						
			1	0·52	0·47	0·43						
			1·25	0·56	0·53	0·48						
			1·5	0·59	0·55	0·51						
			2	0·64	0·59	0·54						
			2·5	0·66	0·62	0·56						
			3	0·68	0·63	0·6						
			4	0·71	0·67	0·63						
			5	0·72	0·7	0·67						
(F) Complete louvered ceiling composed of small metalized plastic parabolic cells. Based on ceiling cavity surfaces being white, and cavity width being three times cavity depth			0·6	0·23	0·21	0·18						
			0·8	0·26	0·23	0·2						
			1	0·28	0·26	0·23						
			1·25	0·29	0·27	0·25						
			1·5	0·31	0·29	0·27						
			2	0·33	0·32	0·29						
			2·5	0·35	0·33	0·31						
			3	0·36	0·35	0·33						
			4	0·38	0·36	0·34						
			5	0·39	0·37	0·35						

* Note: Due to the wide variation in design and arrangement of prisms in optical controllers, the Utilization Factors shown for prismatic materials can only provide a general guide. Reference should be made to the manufacturers concerned for authoritative information.

Table 5   Tabulated Lamp Data

The data in the following tables are correct at the time of going to press, but progress in lamp technology is continuous. It will therefore be advisable to consult the manufacturer concerned to obtain latest data for the lamp(s) being considered for a lighting scheme. See also Bibliography (Electric Lamps).

(a) DISCHARGE LAMPS (*see BS 1270, 1853, 3677, 3767*)

Type and wattage	Bulb shape	Max. Dimensions (mm)		Approx. watts loss in ballast	Lighting design lumens (a)	Cap
		Length	Diameter			
Mercury						
MB 80	Elliptical and Pear	166·5	81	15	3000	ES or 3-pin BC
MB 125	Elliptical and Pear	185·5	91	20	5000	ES or 3-pin BC
MB 250	Tubular	257	52	25	11 000	GES
MB 400	Tubular	292	52	35	19 500	GES
MB 1000	Tubular	382	66	70	49 000	GES
MB 1000	Isothermal	350	167	70	49 000	GES
Metal Halide						
MBI 400	Elliptical	292	122	45	28 000	GES
MBI 1000	Elliptical	410	181	100	80 000	GES
MBI 1000	Tubular	382	66	100	80 000	GES
MBI 2000	Tubular	480	100	80	150 000	GES
MBI 3500	Tubular	480	100	150	260 000	GES
MBIL 750	Linear	256	13	140	60 000	R7S
MBIL 1600	Linear	256	18	290	115 000	R7S
MBIL 10 000	Tubular	743	46		900 000	Special
CSI 400	Tubular	55	20	60	29 000	Special
CSI 1000	Tubular	115	32	200	75 000	Special
Fluorescent Mercury						
MBF 50	Elliptical	130	56	15	1800	ES or 3-pin BC
MBF 80	Elliptical	166·5	81	15	3350	ES or 3-pin BC
MBF 125	Elliptical	185·5	91	20	5500	ES or 3-pin BC orGES
MBF 250	Elliptical	227	91	25	12 400	GES
MBF 400	Elliptical	292	122	35	21 800	GES
MBF 700	Elliptical	368	152	50	37 500	GES
MBF 1000	Elliptical	410	181	70	54 000	GES
MBF 2000	Elliptical	445	187	80	118 000	GES
MBFR 250	Reflector	265	184	25	10 500	GES
MBFR 400	Reflector	306	185	35	18 000	GES
MBFR 700	Reflector	330	210	50	32 500	GES
MBFR 1000	Reflector	384	260	70	47 000	GES
Tungsten Mercury						
MBTF 100	Elliptical	167	81	—	1130	ES or BC
MBTF 160	Elliptical	185	91	—	2560	ES or BC
MBTF 250	Elliptical	227	91	—	4850	GES
MBTF 500	Elliptical	292	122	—	11 500	GES
Low Pressure Sodium						
SOX 35	Tubular	311	51	25	4300	BC
SOX 55	Tubular	424	51	25	7500	BC
SOX 90	Tubular	528	65	40	12 250	BC
SOX 135	Tubular	775	65	40	21 500	BC
SOX 180	Tubular	1120	65	35	30 000	BC
SLI 140	Tubular	902*	39·5	35	20 000	Bi-pin
SLI 200	Tubular	902*	39·5	50	25 000	Bi-pin
SLI 200 HO	Tubular	902*	39·5	50	27 500	Bi-pin
High Pressure Sodium						
SON 250	Elliptical	227	91	40	21 000	GES
SON 310	Elliptical	292	122	40	30 000	GES
SON 360	Elliptical	292	122	40	34 500	GES
SON 400	Elliptical	292	122	50	40 000	GES
SONT 250	Tubular	257	53	40	22 500	GES
SONT 310	Tubular	292	53	40	32 000	GES
SONT 360	Tubular	292	53	40	36 500	GES
SONT 400	Tubular	292	53	50	42 000	GES
SONT 600	Tubular	340	67	60	62 000	GES
SONT 1000	Tubular	410	91	100	110 000	GES
SONR 250	Reflector	260	168	40	17 500	GES

(a) Mean value of manufacturers' published figures.
* Distance from cap face to end of opposite cap pins.

Table 5   Tabulated Lamp Data (continued)

(b) TUBULAR FLUORESCENT LAMPS

Nominal Lamp Watts	Nominal length mm	Nominal tube diameter mm	Approx. total circuit watts*	Lighting design lumens (warm white)	Caps
4	150	15	10	135	Miniature bi-pin
6	225	15	12	245	Miniature bi-pin
8	300	15	15	360	Miniature bi-pin
13	525	15	21	739	Miniature bi-pin
15	450	25	40†	800	Bi-pin
15	450	38	40†	750	Bi-pin
20	600	38	50†	1100	Bi-pin
30	900	25	40	2150	Bi-pin
30	900	38	40	1850	Bi-pin
40	600	38	95†	1700	Bi-pin
40	1200	38	50	2700	Bi-pin
50	1500	25	70	3250	Bi-pin
65	1500	38	80	4650	Bi-pin
80	1500	38	95	5700	Bi-pin or BC
85	1800	38	95	6100	Bi-pin
85	2400	38	100	6700	Bi-pin
125	2400	38	140	8600	Bi-pin or BC or recessed double-contact

CIRCULAR LAMPS

22	210mm dia.	29	31	850	4-pin
32	305mm dia.	32	41	1600	4-pin
40	406mm dia.	32	50	2300	4-pin

* For switch-start circuits.
† For two lamps in series on 200/250V.

Where the supply of electricity is paid for by a fixed quarterly charge based on the installed electrical load, plus a charge per unit consumed, the fixed quarterly charge is seldom if ever calculated by the Electricity Board on the nominal lamp watts.

If the charge is based on *watts* load it is normally the total circuit watts, not the lamp watts alone. In many cases, however, in order to promote the most economic use of the generating plant and distribution network, the fixed charge is based on the volt-amps (VA) drawn from the mains, and this will depend both on the circuit watts and the circuit power factor.

For example, the circuit wattage of a 65W lamp is about 80 watts. It may be assumed that the power factor of the circuit has been improved to a value of 0·85 by the inclusion of the normal power factor capacitor, in which case the volt-amps drawn from the mains are $\frac{80}{0·85} = 94VA$.

Lighting design lumens for lamps other than warm white
The approximate lighting design lumens for lamp colours other than Warm White may be obtained by applying the following multiplier to the relevant figure for Warm White:

White	1
Warm white	1
Daylight	0·95
Natural	0·75
Deluxe warm white	0·65
°Kolor-rite	0·65
Colour matching (Northlight)	0·6
GraphicA 47	0·6
Deluxe natural	0·55
Softone	0·55
Trucolour	0·5
Artificial daylight	0·4

Where a precise figure of lumen output is desired, the manufacturer of the lamp in question should be consulted.

Table 5 Tabulated Lamp Data (continued)

(c) STANDARD INCANDESCENT LAMPS

Pear Shape, Pearl and Clear (see BS 161 and 555)

Watts	Finish	Nominal dimensions		Light centre length, mm	Standard cap	Lighting design lumens		
		Length mm	Diameter mm			At 110V Single coil	At 240V Single coil	At 240V Coiled coil
25	Pearl	105	60	75	BC	225	200	—
40	Pearl	105	60	75	BC	445	325	390
60	Pearl	105	60	75	BC	770	575	665
100	Pearl	105	60	75	BC	1420	1160	1260
150	Pearl	125	68	90	BC	—	—	2040
		126·5	68	91·5	ES	—	—	2040
		160	80	120	BC	2360	1960	—
200	Clear	161·5	80	121·5	ES	3250	2720	—
300	Clear	233	110	178	GES	5050	4300	—
500	Clear	233	110	178	GES	8900	7700	—
750	Clear	300	150	225	GES	—	12 400	—
1000	Clear	300	150	225	GES	—	17 300	—
1500	Clear	335	170	250	GES	—	27 500	—

Inside White lamps are available for the 200/250V range in 40, 60, 100, 150 and 200W rating, having a lumen output approximately 10% less than the corresponding lamps above. Also lamps with pink enamel-glazed bulbs or pink internal coatings in 60, 100 and 150W ratings.

(d) REFLECTOR LAMPS *(see BS 555)*

Watts and type*		Max. dimensions		Cap
		Overall length mm	Diameter mm	
75 and 100	Spotlight	140	96	BC
		141·5	96	ES
150 150	Spotlight Floodlight	182·5	127·5	ES

* A number of other types and sizes of reflector spotlamps and floodlamps are made by individual manufacturers, to whom reference should be made.
Illuminance data is given in Appendix 8.

(e) PRESSED GLASS SPOT AND FLOOD LAMPS

Type and watts		Max. dimensions		Cap
		Overall length mm	Diameter mm	
PAR-38 100		137·5	122	ES
	150	137·5	122	ES

100W PAR-38 Floodlamps also available in Red, Yellow, Blue and Green

Type and watts		Max. dimensions		Cap	
PAR-56 300	Medium Flood	133·4	179	GLX16d	Mogul End Prong
	300 Wide Flood	133·4	179	GLX16d	
	300 Narrow Spot	133·4	179	GLX16d	

Heating

We would like to thank the Institution of Heating and Ventilating Engineers[1] for permission to extract the information contained in the following Tables from the 1970 *IHVE Guide.* The *IHVE Guide* represents the standard source of data on all aspects of heating, ventilating and air conditioning; reference should always be made to it for more detailed or more specialised information. In order to make an accurate assessment of the heat transferred into or out of a building the procedures outlined in section A5 of the *IHVE Guide* should be followed.

The following new approaches in the method of computation of the data should be noted:

(a) Thermal conductivity values for porous structural elements are based upon appropriate moisture contents (protected or exposed).

(b) The three categories of surface resistance 'sheltered', 'normal' and 'severe', express exposure according to geographical location and/or height only, but without reference to orientation.

(c) The temperature difference between the inside and outside of a building is no longer expressed as the air-to-air temperature difference, but is given in terms of difference between the environmental temperatures on either side of the structures.

DEFINITIONS AND SYMBOLS

The following definitions and symbols are used in this Section:

Thermal conductivity	k	The thermal transmission in unit time through unit area of a slab, of a uniform homogeneous material of unit thickness, when unit difference of temperature is established between its surfaces .. .. (W/m °C)
Thermal resistivity	$\frac{1}{k}$	The reciprocal of thermal conductivity .. (m °C/W)
Thermal conductance= $\frac{k}{L}$ ..	C	The thermal transmission in unit time through unit area of a uniform structural component or structure of thickness L, per unit of temperature difference between the hot and cold surfaces .. .. (W/m² °C)
Thermal resistance	R	The reciprocal of thermal conductance .. (m² °C/W)
Thermal transmittance ..	U	The thermal transmission in unit time through unit area of a given structure (e.g. a wall consisting of bricks, thermal insulation, cavities, etc.) divided by the difference between the environmental temperature on either side of the structure .. .. (W/m² °C)

1. Institution of Heating and Ventilating Engineers, 49 Cadogan Square, London SW1 OJB

Standard thermal transmittance (Standard U value) U The value for the thermal transmittance of a building element related to standard conditions . .   . .   . . (W/m² °C)

Design thermal transmittance . . (Design U value) U A value of the thermal transmittance of a building element for the prevailing design conditions   . .   . . (W/m² °C)

Surface conductance   . .   . . h_s
$$h_s = h_c + Eh_r$$
The thermal transmission in unit time to or from unit area of a surface in contact with air or other fluid due to convection and radiation per unit difference between the temperature of the surface and the environmental temperature of the neighbouring air or other fluid . .   . . (W/m² °C)

Surface resistance $= \dfrac{1}{h_s}$ . . R_s The reciprocal of surface conductance   . .   . . (m² °C/W)

Convection conductance   . . h_c Definition as for surface coefficient but refers only to heat transfer by convection   . .   . . (W/m² °C)

Emissivity   . .   . .   . . $\in$ The ratio of the thermal radiation from unit area of a surface to the radiation from unit area of a full emitter ('black body') at the same temperature

Emissivity factor   . .   . . E A factor allowing for the emissivity and geometrical relationship of both emitting and receiving surfaces on the radiant transfer of heat

Environmental temperature (t_{ei}, t_{eo}) t_e The temperature of a hypothetical uniform environment (with surroundings and air at equal temperatures) which would give the same rate of heat transfer through a building element as occurs under the prevailing conditions. Internally, the environmental temperature is t_{ei}, externally it is the sol-air temperature, t_{eo} . .   . . (°C)

Table 1   **Indoor Service Temperatures**

Room or Building	*Temperature* °C
General Spaces Common to Various Types of Building:	
Entrance lobbies, halls, staircases, corridors	16
Cloaks, lavatories	18
Bathrooms	22
Churches and Chapels:	
Main body	18
Vestries	20
Cinemas	18
Exhibition Halls	18

Table 1 (continued)

Room or Building	Temperature °C
Factories:	
Sedentary work	19
Light work	16
Heavy work	13
Flats and Residences:	
Living rooms, bed-sitting rooms	21
Bedrooms	18
Store rooms	10
Service rooms	16
Halls:	
For assembly, lectures, meetings and general purposes	18
Hotels:	
Public rooms, dining rooms, ballrooms	21
Bedrooms	22
Sitting rooms	21
Lavatories	18
Bathrooms	22
Laboratories	20
Libraries:	
Reading rooms	20
Stack rooms	18
Offices:	
General offices	20
Stores	15
Schools and Colleges:	
Classrooms and lecture rooms	18
Assembly halls	18
Gymnasia	16
Laboratories	20
Common rooms and dining rooms	20

Table 2   **Typical Values of Thermal Conductivity for Building Materials**

Material	Moisture content (per cent of dry weight)	Density (kg/m³)	Conductivity (W/m °C)
ASBESTOS:			
Cement sheet	5	1520	0.29 - 0.43
Sprayed		80-240	0.04 - 0.07
ASPHALT:			
Heavy, 20 per cent grit		2250	1.20
Roofing		1600	0.43
		1920	0.58

Table 2 (continued)

BRICK:			
Common, dry	0	1760	0.81
Conditioned at 17.8 °C and 65 per cent RH	6	1870	1.21
Wet	16	2034	1.67

BUILDING BOARD:			
Asbestos insulating	2	720-900	0.11 - 0.21
Fibre board		280-420	0.05 - 0.08
Hardboard, medium		560	0.08
Plasterboard, gypsum		1120	0.16
Woodchip board		350-1360	0.07 - 0.21
Woodwool slab	5	400-800	0.08 - 0.13

CARPETING:			
Wilton type			0.058
Wool felt underlay		160	0.045
Cellular rubber underlay		270	0.065
		400	0.10

CONCRETE:			
Gravel 1 : 2 : 4		2240-2480	1.4
No fines, gravel 1 : 10		1840	0.94
Clinker aggregate	4	1680	0.40
Expanded clay aggregate	5	800-1280	0.29 - 0.48
Pumice aggregate	4.6	770	0.19
Vermiculite aggregate		400-880	0.11 - 0.26
Cellular		320-1600	0.08 - 0.65

CORK:			
Granulated, raw	7	115	0.046
Slab, raw	7	160	0.050
Slab, baked	3-5	130	0.040

FELT:			
Undercarpet felt		120	0.045
Asebstos felt		144	0.078
Roofing felt		960-1120	0.19 - 0.20

GLASS:			
Sheet, window		2500	1.05
Wool, lightweight mat		50	0.033

METALS:			
Aluminium alloy, typical		2800	160
Brass		8400	130
Copper 99.9 per cent		8900	200
Iron, cast		7000	40
Lead		11 340	35
Steel, mild		7850	47
Steel, high alloy		8000	15
Zinc 99.99 per cent		7130	113

PLASTER:			
Gypsum plaster		1120-1280	0.38 - 0.46
Perlite plaster		400-610	0.079 - 0.19
Vermiculite plaster		480-960	0.14 - 0.30
Sand cement		1570	0.53

Table 2 (continued)

PLASTICS, CELLULAR:

Polystyrene, expanded board	15	0.037
Polyurethane foam	30	0.026
Polyvinyl chloride, rigid foam	25-80	0.035 - 0.041
Urea formaldehyde foam	8-30	0.032 - 0.038
P.V.C. floor covering	0.40	2.5

PLASTICS, SOLID SHEET:

Acrylic resin	1440	0.20
Nylon	1100	0.30
Polycarbonate	1150	0.23
Polyethylene, low density	920	0.35
Polyethylene, high density	960	0.50
Polypropylene	915	0.24
Polystyrene	1050	0.17
P.T.F.E.	2200	0.24
P.V.C. rigid	1350	0.16

ROOFING FELT

	960-1120	0.19 - 0.20

SAND:

Building	1500	0.30
Fine silver sand	1600	0.32

STONE:

Granite	2650	2.9
Limestone	2180	1.5
Marble	2700	2.5
Sandstone	2000	1.3
Slate	2700	1.9

TILES:

Burnt clay	1900	0.85
Concrete	2100	1.10
Cork	530	0.085
PVC asbestos	2000	0.85
Rubber	1600-1800	0.30 - 0.50

TIMBER:

Across grain			
Beech	15	700	0.165
Deal	12	610	0.125
Mahogany	10	700	0.155
Oak	14	770	0.160
Pitch pine	15	660	0.140
Spruce	12	420	0.105
Teak	10	700	0.170
Along grain			
Deal	12	610	0.215
Oak	14	770	0.290

VERMICULITE:

Loose granules	100	0.065
Plastering	480-960	0.144 - 0.303

Table 3   **Outside surface resistances (R_{so}) for 'sheltered', 'normal' (standard) and 'severe' exposures.**

Surface resistance for stated exposure
(m^2 $^0C/W$)

Building element	Emissivity of surface (1)	Sheltered (2)	Normal (Standard) (3)	Severe (4)
Wall	High	0.08	0.055	0.03
	Low	0.11	0.067	0.03
Roof	High	0.07	0.045	0.02
	Low	0.09	0.053	0.02

(1) High emissivity factor is taken as 0.9 and low emissivity factor as 0.05.
(2) *Sheltered:*   Up to third floor buildings in city centres.
(3) *Normal:*   Most suburban and country premises: fourth to eighth floors of buildings in city centres.
(4) *Severe:*   Buildings on the coast or exposed on hill sites: floors above the fifth of buildings in suburban or country districts: floors above the ninth of buildings in city centres.

Table 4   **Inside surface resistances. (R_{si})**

Surface resistance
(m^2 $^0C/W$)

Building element	Heat flow	high emissivity surface (E = 0.9)	low emissivity surface (E = 0.05)
Walls	Horizontal	0.123	0.304
Ceilings or roofs, flat or pitched, Floors	Upward	0.106	0.218
Ceilings and floors	Downward	0.150	0.562

Table 5   **Standard thermal resistances of ventilated airspaces.**

Airspace thickness 20.0 mm minimum	*Thermal resistance (m² ⁰C/W)*
Airspace between asbestos cement or black metal cladding with unsealed joints, and high emissivity lining	0.16
Airspace between asbestos cement or black metal cladding with unsealed joints, and low emissivity surface facing airspace	0.30
Loft space between flat ceiling and unsealed asbestos cement sheets or black metal cladding pitched roof	0.14
Loft space between flat ceiling and pitched roof with aluminium cladding instead of black metal or low emissivity upper surface on ceiling	0.25
Loft space between flat ceiling and unsealed tiled roof, pitched roof	0.11
Loft space between flat ceiling and pitched roof lined with felt or building paper, with beam filling	0.18
Airspace between tiles and roofing felt or building paper on pitched roof	0.12
Airspace behind tiles on tile-hung wall	0.12
Airspace in cavity wall construction	0.18

Table 6   **Standard thermal resistance of unventilated airspaces.**

		Thermal resistance (m² ⁰C/W)	
Thickness	*Surface emissivity*	*Heat flow horizontal or upwards*	*Heat flow downwards*
5.0 mm	High	0.11	0.11
	Low	0.18	0.18
20.0 mm or more	High	0.18	0.21
	Low	0.35	1.06
High emissivity planes and corrugated sheets in contact		0.09	0.11
Low emissivity multiple foil insulation with air space on one side		0.62	1.76

Table 7   *U* **values for external walls**

Construction		Sheltered	Normal (Standard)	Severe
			U Value (W/m² °C)	
Brickwork				
Solid wall, unplastered	105 mm	3.0	3.3	3.6
	220 mm	2.2	2.3	2.4
	335 mm	1.6	1.7	1.8
Solid wall, with 16 mm plaster on inside face				
(a) With dense plaster	105 mm	2.8	3.0	3.2
	220 mm	2.0	2.1	2.2
	335 mm	1.6	1.7	1.8
(b) With lightweight plaster	105 mm	2.3	2.5	2.7
	220 mm	1.8	1.9	2.0
	335 mm	1.4	1.5	1.6
Solid wall, with 10 mm plasterboard lining fixed to brickwork with plaster dabs	105 mm	2.6	2.8	3.0
	220 mm	1.9	2.0	2.1
	335 mm	1.5	1.6	1.7
Cavity wall (unventilated) with 105 mm outer and inner leaves with 16 mm plaster on inside face ..	260 mm			
(a) With dense plaster		1.4	1.5	1.6
(b) With lightweight plaster		1.3	1.3	1.3
Lightweight concrete block				
Solid wall, 150 mm aerated concrete block, with tile hanging externally and with 16 mm plaster on inside face		0.95	0.97	1.0
Cavity wall (unventilated) with 75 mm aerated concrete block outer leaf, rendered externally, 100 mm aerated concrete block inner leaf and with 16 mm plaster on inside face 50 mm cavity		0.82	0.84	0.86
Concrete				
Cast	150 mm	3.2	3.5	3.9
	200 mm	2.9	3.1	3.4
Pre-cast panels, 75 mm thick		3.9	4.3	4.8

Table 7 (continued)

	Sheltered	Normal (Standard)	Severe
As above but with 50 mm cavity and sandwich lining panels, composed of 5 mm asbestos-cement sheet, 25 mm expanded polystyrene and 10 mm plasterboard	0.79	0.80	0.82
Pre-cast sandwich panels comprising 75 mm dense concrete, 25 mm expanded polystyrene and 150 mm lightweight concrete	0.71	0.72	0.73

Table 8   *U* **values for roofs.**

		U Value (W/m² °C)	
Flat or Pitched Roofs	*Sheltered*	*Normal (Standard)*	*Severe*
Asphalt 19 mm thick or felt/bitumen layers on solid concrete 150 mm thick (treated as exposed)	3.1	3.4	3.7
As above but with 50 mm lightweight concrete screed and 16 mm plaster ceiling	2.1	2.2	2.3
As above but with screed laid to falls, average 100 mm thick	1.7	1.8	1.9
Asphalt 19 mm thick or felt/bitumen layers on 13 mm cement and sand screed, 50 mm woodwool slabs on timber joists and aluminium foil-backed 10 mm plasterboard ceiling, sealed to prevent moisture penetration	0.88	0.90	0.92
As above but with.25 mm glass-fibre insulation laid between joists	0.59	0.60	0.61
Felt/bitumen layers on 25 mm expanded poly-styrene on metal decking, with vapour barrier	1.1	1.1	1.1
Pitched Roofs (35° slope)			
Tiles on battens, roofing felt and rafters, with roof space and aluminium foil-backed 10 mm plaster-board ceiling on joists	1.4	1.5	1.6
As above but with boarding on rafters ..	1.3	1.3	1.3
As above but with 50 mm glass-fibre insulation between joists	0.49	0.50	0.51

Table 9   *U* **values for typical windows.**

Window type	Fraction of area occupied by frame	U values for stated exposure (W/m² °C)		
		Sheltered	*Normal*	*Severe*
Single glazing:				
Wood frame	30%	3.8	4.3	5.0
Metal frame ..	20%	5.0	5.6	6.7
Double glazing:				
Wood frame	30%	2.3	2.5	2.7
Metal frame with thermal break ..	20%	3.0	3.2	3.5

Note: Where the proportion of frame differes appreciably from the above tabulated values, particularly with wood or plastic, the *U* values should be calculated (metal members have a *U* value similar to glass).

Table 10   *U* **values for solid floors in contact with the earth with four exposed edges.**

Dimensions of floor		U values (W/m² °C of inside/outside temperature difference)
Very long x 30 m broad		0.16*
"	15 m	0.28*
"	1.5 m	0.48*
150 m	x 60 m	0.11
"	30 m	0.18
60 m	x 60 m	0.15
"	30 m	0.21
"	15 m	0.32
30 m	x 30 m	0.26
"	15 m	0.36
"	7.5 m	0.55
15 m	x 15 m	0.45
"	7.5 m	0.62
7.5 m	x 7.5 m	0.76
3 m	x 3 m	1.47

* Applies also for any floor of this breadth and losing heat from two parallel edges. (Breadth here is the distance between the exposed edges.)

Table 11 *U* values for solid floors in contact with the earth having two exposed edges at right angles.

Dimensions of floor		*U values* $(W/m^2 \ ^\circ C$ *of inside/outside temperature difference)*
Very long x 30 m broad		0.09
”	15 m	0.16
”	7.5 m	0.28
150 m	x 60 m	0.06
”	30 m	0.10
60 m	x 60 m	0.08
”	30 m	0.12
”	15 m	0.18
30 m	x 30 m	0.15
”	15 m	0.21
”	7.5 m	0.32
15 m	x 15 m	0.26
”	7.5 m	0.36
7.5 m	x 7.5 m	0.45
3 m	x 3 m	1.07

Table 12 Corrections to Tables 10 and 11 for edge insulated floors.

Dimensions of floor		*Percentage reduction in U for edge insulation extending to a depth (m)*		
		0.25	*0.5*	*1.0*
Very long x 150 m broad		2	6	10
”	60 m	2	6	11
”	30 m	3	7	11
”	15 m	3	8	13
”	6 m	4	9	15
”	2 m	6	15	25
150 m	x 150 m	3	10	15
60 m	x 60 m	4	11	17
30 m	x 30 m	4	12	18
15 m	x 15 m	5	12	20
6 m	x 6 m	6	15	25
2 m	x 2 m	10	20	35

Table 13   *U* values for suspended timber floors directly above ground.

		U values (W/m² °C of inside/outside temperature difference)	
Actual dimensions of floor		*Bare or with linoleum, plastic or rubber tiles**	*With carpet, parquet or cork tiles†*
Very long x 30 m		0.18	0.18
”	15 m	0.33	0.33
”	7.5 m	0.53	0.52
150 m	x 60 m	0.14	0.14
”	30 m	0.21	0.21
60 m	x 60 m	0.16	0.16
”	30 m	0.24	0.23
”	15 m	0.37	0.36
30 m	x 30 m	0.28	0.27
”	15 m	0.39	0.38
”	7.5 m	0.57	0.55
15 m	x 15 m	0.45	0.44
”	7.5 m	0.61	0.59
7.5 m	x 7.5 m	0.68	0.65
3 m	x 3 m	1.05	0.99

* Assuming $R_g = 0.20$.   † Assuming $R_g = 0.26$.

Table 14   *U* values for intermediate floors.

Construction	*U value (W/m² °C)*	
	heat flow downwards	*heat flow upwards*
Wood		
20 mm wood floor on 100 mm x 50 mm joists, 10 mm plasterboard ceiling,	1.5	1.7
allowing for 10% bridging by joists	1.4	1.6
Concrete		
150 mm concrete with 50 mm screed	2.2	2.7
with 20 mm wood flooring	1.7	2.0

Table 14   U values for intermediate floors (continued)

Hollow tile floors
with 50 mm dense concrete over and
between tiles

tile thickness	150 mm	1.7	2.0
	200 mm	1.6	1.9
	250 mm	1.5	1.8

as above with 20 mm wood flooring

tile thickness	150 mm	1.4	1.6
	200 mm	1.3	1.5
	250 mm	1.2	1.4

Sound Insulation and Acoustics

We would like to thank the British Standards Institution[1] for permission to extract the information contained in Tables 1 to 8 from the Tables contained in British Standards Code of Practice CP3: Chapter III, 1960. *Sound Insulation and Noise Reduction.* The conversions into S.I. units were carried out by the editors.

Table 1   **Single and double windows**

Construction	Approximate sound insulation
	dB
Wide-open window	About 5
Slightly open single window	10–15
Closed 'openable' single window	18–20
Sealed single window 0·7–0·9 kg (24–32 oz) glass	23–25
Sealed single window 6·35 mm (¼ in) plate glass	27
Closed 'openable' double window (any weight of glass, with an air-space of 200 mm (8 in) and absorbent-lined reveals)	30–33
Sealed double window 0·91 kg (32 oz) glass with an air-space of 200 mm (8 in) and absorbent-lined reveals)	40

The insulation values given are necessarily approximate since examples of nominally the same construction may show variations of several decibels. All the figures represent expected values in the field, i.e. in ordinary buildings, rather than in the testing laboratory. Many are based directly on field measurements, though others (in the absence of representative field measurements) are assessed from laboratory figures, with suitable allowance for the average conditions of indirect transmission found in normal buildings. Test conditions in the laboratory usually exclude indirect transmission.

1. British Standards Institution (BSI), 2 Park Street, London, W1Y 4AA.

INSULATION VALUES OF WALLS AND FLOORS

Tables 2 to 8 which follow give the sound insulation values of many common types of wall and floor construction. These insulation values are averages for the frequency range 100–3 200 c/s. The slope of the insulation against frequency (i.e. the increase of insulation per octave) is also indicated but only in broad terms, the insulation being classed under three categories of slope, namely:

A (low)   = less than 4 dB per octave.
B (average) = 4 to 6 dB per octave.
C (steep)   = more than 6 dB per octave.

In general slope B is most satisfactory for normal insulation values ranging from 30 dB to 50 dB (average for 100–3 200 c/s); for insulation values below 30 dB slopes A and C may be equally satisfactory; for insulation values above 50 dB slope A is usually an advantage and slope C a disadvantage.

The insulation values given are necessarily approximate since examples of nominally the same construction may show variations of several decibels. All the figures represent expected values in the field, i.e. in ordinary buildings, rather than in the testing laboratory. Many are based directly on field measurements, though others (in the absence of representative field measurements) are assessed from laboratory figures, with suitable allowance for the average conditions of indirect transmission found in normal buildings. Test conditions in the laboratory usually exclude indirect transmission.

Table 2   **Partitions of single sheets or slabs**

Construction	Approx. weight		Average sound reduction (100–3 200	Slope	Remarks
	kg/m^2	(lb/ft^2)	c/s) dB		
25·4 mm (1 in) glass-wool or mineral-wool quilt	2·4	($^1/_2$)	5	A	Porous
12·7 mm ($^1/_2$ in) fibre insulation board	3·7	($^3/_4$)	18	A	Porous
3·2 mm ($^1/_8$ in) hardboard	3·3	($^2/_3$)	20	B	
6·35 mm ($^1/_4$ in) plywood	3·7	($^3/_4$)	21	B	
19 mm ($^3/_4$ in) chipboard	12·2	($2^1/_2$)	26	B	
25·4 mm (1 in) blockboard	14·6	(3)	27	B	
22·2 mm ($^7/_8$ in) t. and g. boarding	12·2	($2^1/_2$)	24	A	Porous at joints
6·35 mm ($^1/_4$ in) asbestos wallboard	7·3	($1^1/_2$)	24	B	
9·5 mm ($^3/_8$ in) plasterboard	9·8	(2)	25	B	
0·68 kg (24 oz) glass	7·3	($1^1/_2$)	23	A	
0·91 kg (32 oz) glass	9·8	(2)	25	A	
9·5 mm ($^3/_8$ in) plate glass	25·6	($5^1/_4$)	30	A	
1·6 mm ($^1/_{16}$ in) aluminium sheet	4·8	(1)	22	B	
3·2 mm ($^1/_8$ in) steel sheet	24·4	(5)	30	B	
12·7 mm ($^1/_2$ in) steel sheet	97·6	(20)	38	B	

Table 3   **Stud-framed partitions**

Construction	Approx. weight* kg/m²	(lb/ft²)	Average sound reduction (100–3 200 c/s) dB	Slope	Remarks
12·7 mm (½ in) fibre insulation board both sides	7·3	(1½)	20–22	A	Porous
3·2 mm (⅛ in) hardboard both sides	6·5	(1⅓)	23	C	
6·35 mm (¼ in) plywood both sides	7·3	(1½)	24	C	
6·35 mm (¼ in) asbestos wallboard both sides	14·6	(3)	28–30	C	
19 mm (¾ in) blockboard both sides	22·0	(4½)	30	C	
9·5 mm (⅜ in) plasterboard both sides	19·5	(4)	30	C	
9·5 mm (⅜ in) plasterboard and 12·7 mm (½ in) plaster both sides	68·3	(14)	35	B	
3-coat plaster on wood or metal lath both sides	78·1	(16)	35–37	B	
12·7 mm (½ in) plaster on 25·4 mm (1 in) wood-wool slab both sides	78·1	(16)	37	B	

*Excludes weight of studding, which does not contribute to insulation.

NOTE. The constructions described above (with the exception of the first which is porous) can be improved for sound insulation by using a double set of studding (or staggered studs), or by inserting a sound absorbent quilt in the cavity or cavities, or (if strong enough and otherwise suitable) by filling the spaces between the studs with sand. The approximate gains in insulation obtainable by these means are as follows:

(a) double studding   2–3 dB
(b) absorbent quilt in cavity   2–3 dB
(c) sand filling   2–3 dB, plus 5 dB for each doubling of weight of the partition by the sand.

If both (a) and (b) are used the gains can be added, giving about 5 dB improvement. It should, however, be noted that the gain due to a cavity, unless it is a wide one (say 200 mm (8 in) or more), is mostly at the higher frequencies, the slope of the insulation curve being steeper than for a solid partition.

Table 4   **Single-leaf walls or partitions**

Construction	Approx. weight kg/m²	(lb/ft²)	Average sound reduction (100–3 200 c/s) dB	Slope	Remarks
57 mm (2¼ in) hollow slab consisting of two sheets of 9·5 mm (⅜ in) plaster-board joined by cardboard eggcrate core	19·5	(4)	26	A	
102 mm (4 in) hollow slab formed with two layers of 15·9 mm (⅝ in) plaster joined by plaster honeycomb core	58·6	(12)	27	A	
51 mm (2 in) wood-wool slab plastered 12·7 mm (½ in) both sides	68·3	(14)	35	A	
19 mm (¾ in) plasterboard with 15·9 mm (⅝ in) thick plaster both sides (total thickness 51 mm (2 in)	63·5	(13)	34	B	Insulation reduced at mid-frequencies
51 mm (2 in) thick solid gypsum plaster (reinforced)	97·7	(20)	35	B	Insulation reduced at mid-frequencies
51 mm (2 in) hollow clay block (unplastered)	44·0	(9)	28	A	Porous at joints
51 mm (2 in) hollow clay block with 12·7 mm (½ in) plaster both sides	83·0	(17)	35	A	

Table 4   Single-leaf walls or partitions (continued)

Construction	Approx. weight kg/m²	(lb/ft²)	Average sound reduction (100–3 200 c/s) dB	Slope	Remarks
102 mm (4 in) hollow clay block with 12·7 mm (¹/₂ in) plaster both sides	122	(25)	37	B	
51 mm (2 in) clinker block with 12·7 mm (¹/₂ in) plaster both sides	107	(22)	37–38	B	
76 mm (3 in) clinker block (unplastered)	98	(20)	23	A	Very porous
76 mm (3 in) clinker block with 12·7 mm (¹/₂ in) plaster both sides	147	(30)	41	B	
102 mm (4 in) clinker block with 12·7 mm (¹/₂ in) plaster both sides	185	(38)	43	B	
204 mm (8 in) hollow clinker block with 12·7 mm (¹/₂ in) plaster both sides	171	(35)	42	B	
204 mm (8 in) hollow dense concrete block with 12·7 mm (¹/₂ in) plaster both sides	244	(50)	45	B	Grade II
114 mm (4¹/₂ in) brick (unplastered)	220	(45)	35–40	A	Porous at joints
114 mm (4¹/₂ in) brick with 12·7 mm (¹/₂ in) plaster both sides	269	(55)	45	B	Grade II
228 mm (9 in) brick with 12·7 mm (¹/₂ in) plaster both sides	488	(100)	50	B	House Party Wall Grade, Grade I
342 mm (13¹/₂ in) brick with 12·7 mm (¹/₂ in) plaster both sides	708	(145)	53	B	,,
456 mm (18 in) brick with 12·7 mm (¹/₂ in) plaster both sides	928	(190)	55	B	,,
178 mm (7 in) dense concrete with 12·7 mm (½ in) plaster both sides	464	(95)	50	B	,,
254 mm (10 in) dense concrete with 12·7 mm (¹/₂ in) plaster both sides	635	(130)	52	B	,,
381 mm (15 in) dense concrete with 12·7 mm (¹/₂ in) plaster both sides	928	(190)	55	B	,,

Table 5   **Double-leaf walls or partitions**

Construction	Approx. weight kg/m²	(lb/ft²)	Average sound reduction (100–3 200 c/s) dB	Slope	Remarks
Double 51 mm (2 in) clinker block with 51 mm (2 in) cavity. Thin wire ties. 12·7 mm (¹/₂ in) plaster both sides	186	(38)	47	C	Grade II
Double 76 mm (3 in) clinker block with 51 mm (2 in) cavity. Thin wire ties. 12·7 mm (¹/₂ in) plaster both sides	244	(50)	49	B	Grade I
Double 102 mm (4 in) clinker block with 51 mm (2 in) cavity. Thin wire ties. 12·7 mm (¹/₂ in) plaster both sides	312	(64)	50	B	House Party Wall Grade, Grade I

Table 5 Double-leaf walls or partitions (continued)

Construction	Approx. weight kg/m²	(lb/ft²)	Average sound reduction (100–3200 c/s) dB	Slope	Remarks
Double 114 mm (4½ in) brick with 51 mm (2 in) cavity. Thin wire ties. 12·7 mm (½ in) plaster both sides.	488	(100)	50–53	B	House Party Wall Grade, Grade I
Double 228 mm (9 in) brick wall with 51 mm (2 in) cavity. No ties. 12·7 mm (½ in) plaster both sides	927	(190)	55	B	House Party Wall Grade, Grade I. (Insulation can be higher if indirect transmission is small)

Table 6 Concrete floors

No.	Construction	Average sound reduction (100–3 200 c/s) dB	Slope	Sound insulation grading in dwellings: Airborne	Impact	Overall
1	Concrete floor (reinforced concrete or hollow pot slab weighing not less than 220 kg/m² (45 lbs/ft²) with hard floor finish	45	B	Grade II	4 dB worse than Grade II	–
2	Concrete floor with floor finish of wood boards or 6·35 mm (¼ in) thick linoleum or cork tiles	45	B	Grade II	Grade II	Grade II
3	Concrete floor with floor finish of thick cork tiles or of rubber on sponge rubber underlay	45	B	Grade II	Probably Grade I	Grade II
4	Concrete floor with floating concrete screed and any surface finish	50	B	Grade I	Grade I	Grade I
5	Concrete floor with floating wood raft	50	B	Grade I	Grade I	Grade I
6	Concrete floor with suspended ceiling and hard floor finish	48	B	Probably Grade I	2 dB worse than Grade II	–
7	Concrete floor with suspended ceiling and wood board floor finish	48	B	Probably Grade I	Grade II	Grade II
8	Concrete floor with suspended ceiling and floor finish of thick cork tiles or rubber on sponge-rubber underlay	48	B	Probably Grade I	Grade I	Probably Grade I
9	Concrete floor with 51 mm (2 in) light-weight concrete screed and hard floor finish	48	B	Probably Grade I	4 dB worse than Grade II	–
10	Concrete floor with 51 mm (2 in) light-weight concrete screed and floor finish of thick cork tiles or of rubber on sponge-rubber underlay	48	B	Probably Grade I	Probably Grade I	Probably Grade I

Table 6   Concrete floors (continued)

No.	Construction	Average sound reduction (100– 3200 c/s) dB	Slope	Sound insulation granding in dwellings		
				Airborne	Impact	Overall
11	Concrete floor weighing not less than 366 kg/m² (75 lb/ft²) (reinforced concrete slab 150–180 mm (6–7 in) thick) with hard floor finish	48	B	Grade I	4 dB worse than Grade II	—
12	Concrete floor weighing not less than 360 kg/m² (75 lb/ft²) with floor finish of thick cork tiles or of rubber on sponge-rubber underlay	48	B	Grade I	Grade I	Grade I

Table 7   **Wood-joist floors**

No.	Construction	Average sound reduction (100–3 200 c/s) dB	Slope	Sound insulation grading in dwellings		
				Airborne	Impact	Overall
1	Plain joist floor with plasterboard and single-coat plaster ceiling (no pugging)					
	THIN WALLS	34	C	8 dB worse than Grade II	8 dB worse than Grade II	—
	THICK WALLS*	36	C	4 dB worse than Grade II	5 dB worse than Grade II	—
2	Plain joist floor with plasterboard and single-coat plaster ceiling and 14·6 kg/m² (3 lb/ft²) pugging on ceiling					
	THIN WALLS	39	C	4 dB worse than Grade II	5 dB worse than Grade II	—
	THICK WALLS*	44	C	Possibly Grade II†	Possibly Grade II	Possibly Grade II†
3	Plain joist floor with 19 mm (³/₄ in) lath-and-plaster ceiling (no pugging)					
	THIN WALLS	40	C	Probably 4 dB worse than Grade II†	Probably 6 dB worse than Grade II†	—
	THICK WALLS*	45	C	Grade II	Grade II	Grade II
4	Plain joist floor with 19 mm (³/₄ in) lath-and-plaster ceiling and 33 kg/m² (17 lb/ft²) pugging on ceiling					
	THIN WALLS	45	B	Grade II	Grade II	Grade II
	THICK WALLS*	48	B	Grade II or possibly Grade I†	Grade II	Grade II

*At least three walls below the floor not less than 440 kg/m² (90 lb/ft²)
†Assumed from other measurements.

Table 7   Wood-joist floors (continued)

No.	Construction	Average sound reduction (100–3 200 c/s) dB	Slope	Sound insulation grading in dwellings		
				Airborne	Impact	Overall
5	Floating floor with plasterboard and single-coat plaster ceiling (no pugging)					
	THIN WALLS	39	C	4 dB worse than Grade II	3 dB worse than Grade II	—
	THICK WALLS*	44	C	Possibly Grade II†	Possibly Grade II†	Possibly Grade II†
6	Floating floor with plasterboard and single-coat plaster ceiling and 14·6 kg/m² (3 lb/ft²) pugging on ceiling					
	THIN WALLS	43	C	2 dB worse than Grade II	2 dB worse than Grade II	—
	THICK WALLS*	48	C	Grade II or possibly Grade I†	Grade II or possibly Grade I†	Grade II or I†
7	Floating floor with 19 mm (³⁄₄ in) lath-and-plaster ceiling (no pugging)					
	THIN WALLS	43	C	2 dB worse than Grade II	Grade II	—
	THICK WALLS*	48	C	Grade II or I‡	Grade I	Grade II or I‡
8	Floating floor with 19 mm (³⁄₄ in) lath-and-plaster ceiling and 14·6 kg/m² (3 lb/ft²) pugging on ceiling					
	THIN WALLS	45	C	Possibly Grade II†	Grade II‡	Possibly Grade II†
	THICK WALLS*	48	C	Grade II or I‡	Grade I	Grade II or I‡
9	Floating floor with 19 mm (³⁄₄ in) lath-and-plaster ceiling and 83 kg/m² (17 lb/ft²) pugging on ceiling					
	THIN WALLS	49	B	Probably Grade I	Probably Grade I	Probably Grade I
	THICK WALLS*	50	B	Grade I	Grade I	Grade I

*At least three walls below the floor not less than 440 kg/m² (90 lb/ft²).
†Assumed from other measurements.
‡May give Grade I with very thick walls.

Table 8   Sound absorption coefficients

	Frequency (c/s)					
	125	*250*	*500*	*1 000*	*2 000*	*4 000*
Asbestos − 25 mm sprayed on solid backing	0·15	0·30	0·65	0·85	0·85	0·80
Audience − per person, seated	1·7	3·8	4·2	4·3	4·7	4·3
Audience − per person in well upholstered seats	2·0	4·3	5·0	5·0	5·4	5·0
Breeze blocks	0·2	0·3	0·6	0·6	0·5	0·5
Brickwork − unpainted	0·02	0·02	0·03	0·04	0·05	0·07
Brickwork − painted	0·01	0·01	0·02	0·02	0·02	0·03
Carpet − thin, over thin felt, concrete floor	0·1	0·15	0·25	0·30	0·30	0·30
Carpet − on wood board floor	0·2	0·25	0·30	0·30	0·30	0·30
Carpet − thick pile over thick felt on concrete floor	0·07	0·25	0·50	0·50	0·60	0·65
Concrete − dense and smooth	0·01	0·01	0·02	0·02	0·02	0·03
Concrete − rough finish	0·01	0·02	0·02	0·04	0·05	0·05
Curtains − hung in folds against solid backing	0·05	0·10	0·15	0·20	0·25	0·30
Curtains − double, dividing two areas	0·03	0·04	0·10	0·15	0·20	0·15
Fibreboard − 12·5 mm on solid backing,						
unpainted	0·05	0·10	0·15	0·25	0·30	0·30
painted	0·05	0·10	0·10	0·10	0·10	0·15
Glass − windows with up to 0·9 kg (32 oz) glass	0·30	−	0·10	−	0·05	−
Glass − 6 mm plate	0·10	−	0·04	−	0·02	−
Glass fibre, resin bonded (25 mm)	0·10	0·25	0·55	0·70	0·80	0·85
Glass wool − uncompressed (25 mm)	0·10	0·25	0·45	0·60	0·70	0·70
Hardboard − on battens with 25 mm air space	0·20	−	0·15	−	0·10	−
Plaster − on solid backing	0·03	0·03	0·02	0·03	0·04	0·05
Plaster − on laths over air space	0·30	0·15	0·10	0·05	0·04	0·05
Plasterboard over 25 mm air space	0·10	0·20	0·40	0·30	0·15	0·20
Polystyrene − expanded, with rigid backing	0·05	0·05	0·10	0·15	0·15	0·20
Polystyrene − expanded, on 50 mm backing	0·05	0·15	0·40	0·35	0·20	0·20
Polyurethane foam − flexible	0·25	0·50	0·85	0·95	0·90	0·90
Stone	0·02	0·02	0·02	0·04	0·05	0·05
Tiles						
Acoustic − solid backed	0·10	0·30	0·60	0·75	0·80	0·80
Cork − solid backed	0·02	0·04	0·05	0·05	0·10	0·05
Fibreboard − 25 mm, on battens over air space	0·15	0·65	0·75	1·00	0·95	0·70
Hard rubber − on concrete floor	0·02	0·04	0·05	0·05	0·10	0·05
Linoleum − on concrete floor	0·02	0·04	0·05	0·05	0·10	0·05
Polystyrene − 12·5 mm over 25 mm air space	0·05	−	0·40	−	0·20	−

Table 8   Sound absorption coefficients (continued)

	Frequency (c/s)					
Wood blocks on solid floor	0·02	0·04	0·05	0·05	0·10	0·05
Wood floor – 25 mm boards on joists	0·15	0·20	0·10	0·10	0·10	0·10
Wood panelling – oak, on 25 mm battens	0·20	0·10	0·05	0·05	0·05	0·05
Wood-wool slabs – 25 mm on solid backing	0·10	–	0·40	–	0·60	–

Information Sources in the Construction Industry

Compiled by

Shirley Crabtree

*Information Officer, Department of Building,
University of Manchester Institute of Science
and Technology.*

This directory has been compiled so as
to provide an informative catalogue of
national and international sources of
information. They range from the small
organisations which serve the interests
of a specialist sector of the industry to
the large institutions catering for the
needs of the major construction professions. The one qualification common
to all those organisations listed is simply
that they are all, either directly or
indirectly, actively involved in providing
for the needs of the construction industry.

ORGANISATIONS IN THE UK

Advisory Service for the Building Industry (BAS)

18 Mansfield Street,
London, W1M 9F6
Phone: 01 580 6244

Established by the N.F.B.T.E. with American financial help. This is a non-profit making organisation providing management consultancy, executive staff recruitment, and training services to the industry. Publications available.

Agrément Board

Lord Alexander House,
Waterhouse St.
Hemel Hempstead, Herts.
Phone: Hemel Hempstead 3701

Established by MOPBW as an official body for the assessment of new building products, for which certificates are issued Scope has since been widened to include traditional construction products which have export potential.

Agricultural Development and Advisory Service (ADAS)

Ministry of Agriculture, Fisheries and Food,
Great Westminster House,
Horseferry Road, London, S.W.1.
Phone: 01 834 8511

Staff of Chartered Surveyors and Architects. Offers an advisory service on matters relating to land ownership, estate management, and capital investment in agricultural buildings and fixed equipment. Publications available.

Regional offices:-

Eastern:	Block C, Government Buildings, Brooklands Av., Cambridge CB2 2DR (0223 58911)
East Midland:	Government Buildings, Chalfont Drive, Western Boulevard, Nottingham NG8 3RH. (0602 292251)
Northern:	Government Buildings, Kenton Bar, Newcastle-on-Tyne, NE1 27A. (0632 869811)
South-Eastern:	Government Buildings, Coley Park, Reading, RG1 6DT. (0734 581222)

South-Western: Government Buildings,
Burghill Road,
Westbury-on-Trym,
Bristol BS10 6NJ.
(0272 622851)

West Midland: "Woodthorne",
Wolverhampton WV6 8TQ.
(0902 754190)

Yorkshire & Lancashire: Government Buildings,
Lawnswood,
Leeds LS16 5PY
(0532 674411)

Wales: Plas Crug,
Aberystwyth SY23 1NG
(0970 3162).

Agricultural Research Council (ARC)

160 Great Portland Street,
London W1N 6DT.
Phone: 01 580 6655

More than 40 research establishments work under the control of ARC. Farm buildings come within the scope of the council's research on agriculture and food, and a large number of handbooks and pamphlets on the design and construction of these buildings may be obtained from HMSO.

Aluminium Federation

Broadway House,
Calthorpe Road,
Five Ways, Birmingham B15 1TN.
Phone: 021 455 0311

Exists to serve the interests of firms and individuals concerned in the preparation and use of aluminium and its alloys. Library and information service available to outside users. Publications available.

Aluminium Window Association (AWA)

26 Store St.
London, WC1E 7EL
Phone: 01 637 3578

Establishes and promotes design, manufacturing, installation, and performance standards for aluminium windows; represents member companies in Government and other organisations, nationally and internationally. Provides advice and information on products and their uses.

Ancient Monuments Society

33 Ladbroke Square,
Condon,
London W11 3NB
Phone: 01 221 6178

Founded for the study and conservation of ancient monuments, historic buildings and examples of fine craftsmanship. Gives advice on repairs and helps with grant applications.

Architectural Association (AA)

34-36 Bedford Square,
London WC1.
Phone: 01 636 0974

Promotes the study of architecture and the built environment. The Association and the AA School of Architecture have close connections. Membership open to laymen. Meetings, lectures and exhibitions organised. Library available to members only. Slide library available also to accredited lecturers. Publications available.

Architectural Granite Association

Audley House,
9 Margaret St.
London W1N 7LF.
Phone: 01 637 7031

Promotes the use of granite in construction work. Provides information and advice on granite cladding. Publications available.

Architects' Registration Council of the United Kingdom   (ARCUK)

73 Hallam St.
London, W1N 6EE.
Phone: 01 580 5861

Established by the Architects (Registration) Act 1931 to maintain a register of persons entitled to practise as Architects, and to deal with matters related thereto, including the recognition of examinations qualifying for registration; the provision of scholarships and maintenance grants for students in architecture; the support and furtherance of education and research in architecture; the dissemination of teaching, or the results of research concerning architecture; the discipline of the profession; and the institution of legal proceedings under the Architects Registration Act, 1938, against persons unlawfully calling themselves architects.

Arts Council of Great Britain

105 Piccadilly,
London W1V OAU
Phone: 01 629 9495

Concerned with improving the accessibility of the arts to the public, the Council makes grants towards the cost of adapting existing buildings or constructing new buildings to house the arts - (e.g. Art Galleries, Theatres).
The Scottish Arts Council, 19 Charlotte Square, Edinburgh, EH2 4DF. tel. 031-226 6051
The Welsh Arts Council, Holst House, Museum Place, Cardiff, CF1 3NX. tel. Cardiff 32722.

Arts Council of Northern Ireland

Bedford House,
Bedford St.
Belfast BT2 7FX.
Northern Ireland.
Phone: 0232 41073

Provides information on the design of buildings for the arts.

Asbestos Information Committee

10 Wardour St.
London W1V 3HG.
Phone: 01 734 7617

Formed by four companies in the industry. Provides technical and general information on all aspects of asbestos. Publications available.

Aslib

3 Belgrave Sq.,
London SW1X 8PL.
Phone: 01 235 5050

A grant-aided research association specialising in problems relating to information collection, retrieval and dissemination. Offers members a comprehensive referral and inquiry service to supply information on any subject and in any depth. An index of translations is maintained, and also a register of specialist translators. Conferences and meetings arranged, publications available. Midlands regional office;- Engineering and Building Centre, Broad St., Birmingham B1 2DB (021 643 1914).

Asphalt and Coated Macadam Association

25 Lower Belgrave St.,
London SW1W OLS.
Phone: 01 730 0761

Founded in 1967 by merging the Asphalt Roads Association and The Federation of Coated Macadam Industries. Provides a technical advisory service. Publications available.

Association of Building Centres

26 Store St.
London, WC1E 7BT.
Phone: 01 637 1022

Represents all building centres in the United Kingdom and Ireland and co-ordinates their services and functions.

Association of Building Technicians (ABT)

9-11 Macaulay Road,
Clapham,
London, SW4 OQR.
Phone: 01 622 2362

A trade union whose objects include the negotiation for its members of fair rates of pay, improved conditions of work and increased status; also the promotion of policies aimed at increasing efficiency in the Construction Industry. Provides employment register, information service, trading facilities and legal advice to members.

Association of Industrialised Building Component Manufacturers Limited (AIBCM)

26 Store St.
London, WC1E 7BT.
Phone: 01-580-9083

Represents those concerned with the manufacture and use of industrialised building components (and materials used in their manufacture). Provides information about members' products. Publications available.

Brick Development Association (BDA)

19 Grafton Street,
London W1X 3LE.
Phone: 01-409-1021

Promotes the use of clay and calcium silicate bricks. Initiates research projects. Structural advisory service available. Publications available.

British Cast Iron Research Assocation (BCIRA)

Alvechurch,
Birmingham B48 7QB.
Phone: Redditch 66414

The BCIRA provides an advisory and consulting service and an information service, and maintains a programme of experimental research covering all aspects of the production of iron castings.
Scottish Laboratories: Blantyre Industrial Estate, Glasgow.

British Ceramic Research Association (BCRA)

Queens Road,
Penkhull,
Stoke-on-Trent, ST4 7LQ.
Phone: 0782 45431

An amalgamation of British Refractories Research Association and British Pottery Research Association. Carries out research on manufacture, properties and uses of all types of ceramics. Some publications available to non-members.

The British Computer Society

29 Portland Place,
London W1.
Phone: 01 637 0471

The professional body for the computing profession, with membership by examination. Publications available.

British Concrete Pumping Association

Sardinia House,
52 Lincoln's Inn Fields,
London WC2.
Phone: 01 405 9292

British Constructional Steelwork Association (BCSA)

Hancock House,
87 Vincent Square,
London, S.W.1.
Phone: 01 834 1713

Represents the interests of the constructional steelwork industry of the United Kingdom both at home and overseas in the technical, commercial and contractual fields. Joint sponsor with CONSTRADO of the Structural Steel Design Awards Scheme for the most outstanding steel structures of the year. Publications available.

British Gas Corporation (H.Q.)

National Westminster House,
326 High Holborn,
London, WC1V 7PT.
Phone: 01 242 0789

The British Gas Corporation came into being on January 1st, 1973, replacing the Gas Council and the 12 Area Gas Boards with a single administrative body. The new structure consists of regions based on the previous Area Boards, with

British Gas Corporation (Continued)

Headquarters Offices in London. Technical information and publications specifically for the construction industry are available from both Regional Offices and British Gas (H.Q.), which also maintains exhibitions and advisory services at the Building Centre, Store St. London and Commercial Gas Centre, Tottenham Court Rd. London.

British Glass Industry Research Association
Northumberland Road,
Sheffield S10 2UA.
Phone: 0742 66201

Formed to carry out research into all aspects of glass manufacture.. Information and consultative services available to members, also library and translation service. Publications mostly available to members only, but annual report is available also to non-members.

British Library Lending Division (BLL)
Boston Spa,
Wetherby,
Yorkshire, LS23 7BQ.
Phone: Boston Spa 843434

The main function of the BLL is to collect, make available and promote the use of the world's scientific, technical, social science and humanities literature. Use of this collection is mainly through postal loan and photocopy services, but any member of the public may consult items from the collection by visiting the reading room during normal office hours.

British Non-Ferrous Metals Research Association (BNFMRA)
Euston Street,
London NW1
Phone: 01 387 6411

Promotes the interests of the industry, and carries out research to this end. Consultancy service available to non-members. Library, technical advice and information for members. Organises conferences. Publications include BNF abstracts - monthly.

British Plastics Federation (BPF)
47 Piccadilly,
London, W1V ODN.
Phone: 01 734 2041

Represents the Plastics industry. Promotes co-operation between manufactures, and sponsors research. Establishes standards for products. Publications available.

British Pre-cast Concrete Federation (BPCF)
60 Charles St.
Leicester LE1 1FB.
Phone: Leicester 28627

Promotes the use of pre-cast concrete, and is concerned with the interests of manufacturers and the makers and suppliers of plant, equipment and materials used in the industry. Conducts research. Publications available.

British Productivity Council (BPC)
Goschen Buildings,
12/13 Henrietta Street,
London, WC2E 8LH.
Phone: 01 836 0723

Aims to improve Britain's economic position by stimulating productivity in all sectors of the National Economy. Constituent Organisations are the CBI, TUC, Association of British Chambers of Commerce and the Nationalised Industries. Basic income is from the sale and hire of films. Since the Department of Employment's grant terminated on 31st March 1973 local Productivity Associations derive their income from Members' Subscriptions and organised activities. Conferences, Seminars, and courses arranged. Publications available.

Information Sources

British Ready Mixed Concrete Association (BRMCA)

19 The Crescent,
Ilford,
Essex.
Phone: 01 554 4133

Promotes and encourages the use of ready mixed concrete. Initiates and conducts research. Publications available.

British Safety Council

National Safety Centre,
Chancellor's Road,
London W6 9RS.
Phone: 01 741 1231

An independent, non-profit making organisation, the largest in the country, concerned with reducing industrial accidents and diseases. Membership restricted to corporate bodies. Training courses provided. Publications available. Safety surveys available on a fee basis.

British Standards Institution (BSI)

2 Park Street,
London W1A 2BS.
Phone: 01 629 9000

The recognised Authority in the U.K. for the preparation of national standards covering specifications for dimensions, preferred sizes, quality, performance, methods of testing, terms, definitions and symbols, and codes of practice. All publications (listed in the British Standards Yearbook) available from B.S.I. Sales Office, Newton House, 101-113 Pentonville Rd. London, N.1.
Regional Offices:

Birmingham:	BSI Sales Office, c/o Birmingham Chamber of Commerce, P.O. Box 360, 75 Harborne Road, Edgbaston, Birmingham 15. (021 454 6171)
Bristol:	BSI Sales Office, c/o The Bristol Incorporated Chamber of Commerce and Shipping Dyrham Lodge, 16 Clifton Park, Bristol BS8 3BY (0272 37081)
Glasgow:	BSI Sales Office, c/o Glasgow Chamber of Commerce, 30 George Square, Glasgow, C2 (041 221 8583)
Liverpool:	BSI Sales Office, c/o Liverpool Chamber of Commerce, 1 Old Hall St., Liverpool L3 9HG (051 227 1234)
Manchester:	115 Portland St., BSI Branch Office, Manchester M1 6EB. (061 236 7227)

British Steel Corporation, Corporate Engineering Labs.

140 Battersea Park Road,
London SW11
Phone: 01 622 5511

British Stone Federation (B St F)

Alderman House,
37 Soho Square,
London W1.
Phone: 01 437 7107

Promotes the use of stone, and is concerned with the interests of those in the stone industry. Information service and publications available.

The British Wood Preserving Association (BWPA)

Evelyn House,
62 Oxford St.
London W1N 9WD.
Phone: 01 580 3185

A professional, scientific and advisory association, supported by Members' Subscriptions, concerned with gathering information on the preservation and fire-proofing of timber. Sponsors research in these fields. Publications available. Offers a free advisory service on all aspects of pre-treatment and remedial treatment of timber. Holds an annual convention and publishes a report on this each year.

British Woodwork Manufacturers' Association (BWMA)

26 Store Street,
London, WC1E 7BT.
Phone: 01 636 9075/6

Exists to promote the interests of joinery and woodwork manufacturers supplying the construction industry. Publications available.

Building Centres

Although differing in the range of facilities provided, all building centres have permanent exhibitions, offer an information service to the construction industry, and have a wide range of trade literature and publications available. Lecture rooms available.

Listed below are the Building Centres and Building Information Centres in Great Britain and Ireland. All are members of the Association of Building Centres.

| Full members are marked | ++ |
| Associate members are marked | + |

The Association of Building Centres is also a member of the International Union of Building Centres (UICB). Members who have retained their individual Full membership of the Union are marked ***. Information about both these organisations can be obtained from The Building Centre, 26 Store Street, London, WC1E 7BT.

LONDON
(a member of The Building Centre Group)

***   **The Building Centre**
++   26 Store Street,
London WC1E 7BT
Phone: 01 637 1022 (Administration)
01 637 4522 (Information)

BELFAST

       The Building Centre of Northern Ireland
++   4 Arthur Place,
Belfast BT1 4HJ
Phone: Belfast (0232) 21601

BIRMINGHAM

       Engineering and Building Centre
++   Broad Street,
Birmingham B1 2DB
Phone: 021 643 1914

425

Building Centres (continued)

BRISTOL   (a member of The Building Centre Group)

The Building Centre, Bristol
++   Colston Avenue,
         The Centre,
         Bristol BS1 4TW
         Phone: (Management) Bristol (0272) 22953
                    (Information) Bristol (0272) 27002

CAMBRIDGE (a member of The Building Centre Group)

The Building Centre, Cambridge
++   15 - 16 Trumpington Street,
         Cambridge CB2 1QD
         Phone: Cambridge (0223) 59625

COVENTRY

Coventry Building Information Centre
+   Council House,
         Earl Street,
         Coventry CV1 5SE
         Phone: Coventry (0203) 25555 (ext. 2512)

DUBLIN

*** The Building Centre of Ireland
++   17 Lower Baggot Street,
         Dublin 2,
         Ireland
         Phone: Dublin 62745

GLASGOW   (a member of The Building Centre Group)

The Building Centre, Scotland
++   6 Newton Terrace,
         Glasgow G3 7PF
         Phone: 041 248 6212

LIVERPOOL

Building and Design Centre, Liverpool
++   Hope Street,
         Liverpool L1 9BR
         Phone: (Management) 051 709 8566
                    (Information) 051 709 8484

MANCHESTER (a member of The Building Centre Group)

The Building Centre, Manchester
++   113 - 115 Portland Street,
         Manchester M1 6FB
         Phone: (Management) 061 236 9802
                    (Information) 061 236 6933

NOTTINGHAM

Midland Design and Building Centre
++   Mansfield Road,
         Nottingham NG1 3FE
         Phone: Nottingham (0602) 45651

Building Centres (continued)

SOUTHAMPTON
(a member of The Building Centre Group)

The Building Centre, Southampton
++   Grosvenor House,
18 - 20 Cumberland Place,
Southampton SO1 2BD
Phone: Southampton (0703) 27350

STOKE ON TRENT

The Building Information Centre
+   College of Building and Commerce,
Stoke Road,
Shelton,
Stoke on Trent ST4 2DG
Phone: Stoke on Trent (0782) 24651

Building Cost Information Service
Royal Institute of Chartered Surveyors,
47 Tothill St.
London, S.W.1.
Phone: 01 839 5600

A service open to anyone of any discipline willing and able to contribute information in accordance with the reciprocal basis of the service. Distributes up-to-date data concerning building economics. The main sections deal with cost indices, cost analyses and cost trends.

Building Research Advisory Service

Advice is available on problems associated with the design construction or performance of buildings. Readily answered queries are dealt with free of charge. For other enquiries a fee is charged, based on the time spent. Site visits may be arranged, testing or laboratory work carried out and reports prepared. Quotations are given before work is put in hand. Advisory centres at:

Garston: Building Research Station,
Garston,
Watford, WD2 7JR.
Phone: Garston 76612

Birmingham: Birmingham Engineering and Building Centre,
Broad Street,
Birmingham B1 2DB
Phone: 021 643 8961

Borehamwood: Fire Research Station,
Borehamwood,
Herts WD6 2BL
Phone: 01 953 6177

Aylesbury: Princes Risborough Laboratory,
Princes Risborough,
Aylesbury,
Bucks HP17 9PX
Phone: Princes Risborough 3101

Scotland: Building Research Establishment
Scottish Laboratory,
Kelvin Road,
East Kilbride,
Glasgow G75 0RZ.
Phone: East Kilbride 33941

427

Building Research Establishment

The scope of the Establishment is broad. It includes work on the design and performance of structures, fire protection and prevention, building materials, including timber, construction techniques and the development of mechanical equipment. It also deals with the efficiency of buildings in respect of heating, lighting, sound insulation, user needs and urban planning - and the organisation, productivity and economics of building work. Some of the results of the work are incorporated in Codes of Practice and British Standards or published in appropriate journals. Some are presented in various free and priced publications lists of which are available.

DEPARTMENTS

Building Research Station,
Garston,
Watford WD2 7JR.
Phone: Garston 76612

Part of the Department of the Environment, this is the major research organisation for the construction industry. Current research is detailed in the 'Research Programme', which is available, together with numerous other free publications, from the publications officer. An advisory service is available (see next entry for details).

Fire Research Station,
Borehamwood,
Hertfordshire.
Phone: 01 953 6177

This section of the Building Research Establishment concentrates specifically on all aspects of fire research. An advisory service is provided and numerous publications are available.

Princes Risborough Laboratory,
Princes Risborough,
Aylesbury,
Bucks, HP17 9PX.
Phone: Princes Risborough 3101

Formerly known as the Forest Products Research Laboratory - or Timberlab - the Princes Risborough Laboratory is concerned with the properties, processing, preservation, durability and uses of timber in all its forms. Research is carried out on the applications of timber generally, but much of the work is of particular relevance to the construction industry. A wide range of publications is available, many through HMSO Technical Library and information service. Courses arranged.

Scottish Laboratory,
Kelvin Road,
East Kilbride,
Glasgow G75 0RZ
Phone: East Kilbride 33941.

Building Research Station

see

Building Research Establishment,
Building Research Station

Cement and Concrete Association (C & CA)

52 Grosvenor Gardens,
London SW1W OAQ.
Phone: 01 235 6661

An independent, non-profit making organisation financed by the manufacturers of Portland Cement in the United Kingdom. The Association provides a service of free technical information and advice for users of cement, mainly in the construction industry, backed up by the Association's Research and Development Station at Wexham Springs in Buckinghamshire. The residential Training Centre at Fulmer Grange in Buckinghamshire provides courses on all aspects of concrete design and construction for the various levels of personnel in the industry. Publications and Films available.

Regional Offices:

Scotland:	2 Rutland Square, Edinburgh 1 (031 229 5085)
North of England and N.Ireland:	18 Appleby House, Town Centre, Thornaby, Stockton-on-Tees, Teesside TS17 9EY (Stockton 65603)
North West:	Crown House, 550 Mauldeth Road West, Chorlton-cum-Hardy, Manchester M21 2SJ (061 881 5394/5)
North Midlands and West Riding:	7 Lindum Terrace, Lincoln (Lincoln 25876)
Midlands:	Engineering and Building Centre, Broad Street, Birmingham B1 2DB (021 643 1914)
East:	109 High Street, Bedford (Bedford 52486)
South West:	67 Park Place, Cardiff CF1 3AS (Cardiff 40840)
South East:	29 High Street, Guildford, Surrey (Guildford 76206)

Centre for Advanced Land Use Studies (CALUS)

College of Estate Management,
University of Reading,
Whiteknights,
Reading RG6 2AW.
Phone: 0734 861101

The Centre for Advanced Land Use Studies is the branch of the College of Estate Management, based at the University of Reading, responsible for the post-qualification education and mid career training of those professionals specialising in the planning, development, construction and management

Centre for Advanced Land Use Studies (Continued)

of land and buildings. The Centre provides a programme of 30-40 conferences and courses each year in London and other principal cities, also residential courses and seminars at the University. The programme includes a number of courses and seminars organised specifically for quantity surveyors and those in allied disciplines.

City & Guilds of London Institute (CGLI)

76 Portland Place,
London W1N 4AA.
Phone: 01 580 3050

An independent body incorporated by Royal Charter. Its Advisory Committees, representing industry and education, develop syllabuses as the basis of courses of further education in technical colleges, colleges of art, and other establishments of further education in Great Britain and Eire, and overseas. The Institute offers examinations on published regulations and syllabuses, and awards certificates, in a wide range of technical subjects at various levels, e.g. operative, craft and technician. It works closely with the Construction Industry Training Board. The Institute and the Regional Examining Bodies have recently announced revised schemes for craft courses in Construction subjects.

Civic Trust

17 Carlton House Terrace,
London SW1Y 5AW.
Phone: 01 930 0914

Financed by voluntary subscriptions and donations, the Trust aims to stimulate public interest in creating and maintaining good appearance of both town and country; initiates improvement schemes, advises local civic and amenity societies; gives annual awards; works closely with four associate trusts:
Civic Trust for the North-East, 34/35 Saddler St. Durham (0385 61182)
Civic Trust for the North-West, 56 Oxford St. Manchester M1 6EU (061 236 7464).
Scottish Civic Trust, 24 George Square, Glasgow G2 1EF. (041 221 1466).
Civic Trust for Wales, 6 Park Place, Cardiff CF1 3DP. (0222 42522 ext. 268).

Committee of Directors of Research Associations (CDRA)

29/30 St. James's St.
London, S.W.1A 1HB.
Phone: 01 930 0820.

Represents the Industrial Research Associations of the U.K. Aims to achieve collaboration between them on matters of common interest and to provide a means of communication for information and ideas from one to another, and with similar organisations in the E.E.C. and elsewhere. Publication available:
Industrial Research and Development (The Report of the Committee of Enquiry into the Research Associations). Price £3.

Computer Services and Bureaux Association (COSBA)

109 Kingsway,
London WC2B 6PU.
Phone: 01 405 2172

COSBA is a trade association for the computer services and computer bureau industries. Its members are computer bureaux, consultancies, software houses, data preparation bureaux and other organisations supplying services associated with data processing. Before election members agree to abide by a code of conduct.

Concrete Society (CS)

Terminal House,
Grosvenor Gardens,
London SW1W OAJ.
Phone: 01 730 8252

A Society with membership open to any individual or group concerned with the use of, and designing in, concrete. Promotes research. Organises conferences, meetings and site visits. Publications available.

Confederation of British Industry (CBI)

21 Tothill Street,
London SW1H 9LP.
Phone: 01 930 6711

Financed by members' subscription the CBI exists to encourage efficiency, to improve the contribution of industry to the national economy and to provide the means of formulating and influencing policies in all fields of industry. Information service and publications available.

Construction Industry Research and Information Association (CIRIA)

6 Storey's Gate,
London, SW1P 3AU.
Phone: 01 839 6881

A non-profit making, grant-aided organisation to promote and manage co-operative research for the benefit of its members. Also provides them with a technical information service. Some reports and publications for members only, others available to non-members.

Construction Industry Training Board (CITB)

Radnor House,
1272 London Rd.
London SW16 4EL.
Phone: 01 764 5060

Established under the Industrial Training Act (1964) CITB has the responsibility of improving training for all levels of staff in the industry, providing facilities for training and spreading the cost by means of levies. A wide range of courses is offered at the Training Centre at Bircham Newton, Near King's Lynn, Norfolk. Many publications are available.

Regional Offices:

Scotland:	3-4 Claremont Terrace, Glasgow, C3 (041 332 3323).
North-West:	Federation House, Hope St., Liverpool L1 9HL. (051 709 8489)
North-East:	Jesmond House, Victoria Avenue, Harrogate, HG1 5QG Yorks. (0423 68322)
Midland:	9 North St., Rugby. (0788 5546)
West & Wales:	18/19 Belmont, Bath, BA1 5DZ. (0225 5695)
Eastern:	56 Park St., Luton, Beds. (0582 27462)
London & S.E.:	Glen House, Stag Place, London, S.W.1. (01 828 7384)

Information Sources

Construction Surveyors' Institute

189/193 Temple Chambers,
Temple Avenue,
London, E.C.4.
Phone: 01 353 6405.

A professional institute whose aims are to improve the status and advance the interests of the construction surveyor. Professional examinations are held annually. Regional activities include both educational and social events. Technical information service and quarterly Journal 'Construction Surveyor', available to members only. Full details available from the Secretary.

Constructional Steel Research and Development Organisation (CONSTRADO)

Albany House,
Petty France,
London, S.W.1.
Phone: 01 222 6984

CONSTRADO works in close collaboration with the various Divisions and Research Departments of the British Steel Corporation. It undertakes research, development and education on all steel products in all types of steel construction, organises courses in collaboration with universities and professional bodies. Technical library, advisory and information services available. Technical literature available.

Contractors' Plant Association (CPA)

28 Eccleston Street,
London, SW1W 9PY.
Phone: 01 730 7117

The Association is concerned with suppliers of contractors' plant and with the plant hire industry. It negotiates hire terms and conditions, takes part in discussions at Government level on matters affecting legislation relating to the industry, promotes the interests of members and encourages high standards of efficiency.

Copper Development Association (CDA)

Orchard House,
Mutton Lane,
Potter's Bar, Herts.
Phone: Potters Bar 50815

Council of Forest Industries of British Columbia

61 The Albany,
Old Hall St.,
Liverpool L3 9EW
Phone: 051 227 2197

Promotes the use of British Columbian Timber, shingles, shakes and Douglas Fir plywood. Carries out research and provides technical advice. Wide range of Technical publications available.

Department of Education and Science (DES)

Elizabeth House,
York Road,
London, S.E.1.
Phone: 01 928 9222

The Department of Education and Science is concerned with schools, universities, establishments for further education and with civil science. Dealing with various aspects of the work are different branches, of which the Architects and Building Branch is one. A wide range of publications is available through H.M.S.O., including the Building Bulletin series on the design and construction of educational buildings.

Department of Employment

12 St. James's Square,
London SW1
Phone: 01 930 6200

Concerned with the distribution of industry and the effective use of manpower on a national level, together with maintaining a high level of employment. Provides advice on all aspects of industrial relations. Organises vocational training and the setting up of training Boards. H.M. factory inspectorate is controlled by this Department, as also are the Radiological Protection Industrial Hygiene Section and the Industrial Health and Safety Centre (see separate entries).

Department of Employment Directorate of Occupational Safety and Health

Baynards House,
1 Chepstow Place,
Westbourne Grove,
London W2 4TF.

The directorate is under the control of the Department of Employment and is divided into two sections :
1:    HM Factory Inspectorate is responsible for the enforcement of the Factories Act and certain sections of the Offices, Shops and Railway Premises Act. Publications are available through HMSO, many regional and district offices.
2:    Employment Medical Advisory Service studies and gives free advice on medical problems related to people's work. It has a staff of more than 100 full and part-time doctors who specialise in occupational medicine.

Department of Employment Industrial Health and Safety Centre (DE-IHSC)

97 Horseferry Road,
London, S.W.1.
Phone: 01 828 9255

A permanent exhibition concerned with all aspects of health and safety of people at work. Offers free advice on these matters and on legal requirements relating to them. Publications available through H.M.S.O.

Department of the Environment (DOE)

2 Marsham St.
London, SW1P 3EB.
Phone: 01 212 3434

The work of the Department is organised in several groups, within each of which are various divisions, branches and inspectorates, together dealing with local Government, development and planning, housing and construction, transport industries, vehicle safety, highways, water supply, sewerage and prevention of pollution. A large number of publications available, mostly through H.M.S.O. Lectures, conferences and exhibitionsarranged. Also within the DOE the Property Services Agency (PSA) manages and provides accomodation for most of the Government's needs.

Department of the Environment and Fire Offices' Committee
Joint Fire Research Organization

Building Research Establishment,
Fire Research Station,
Boreham Wood
Herts.
Phone: 01 953 6177

Supported by the Department of the Environment and the Fire Offices' Committee, the organization undertakes research on the prevention of fires, escape from fires, extinction of fires and on how to keep damage to a minimum. Extensive reference library may be consulted by appointment only. Testing of materials and structures can be arranged. Wide range of publications, some available through HMSO. Large store of fire statistics - every fire attended by UK brigades is the subject of a report which is filed at FRS - more than 200 000 per year.

Department of Health and Social Security (DHSS)

Alexander Fleming House,
Elephant and Castle,
London, SE1 6BY.
Phone: 01 407 5522

In addition to its responsibilies for Health and Welfare Services, the health side of DHSS is concerned with the building and improvement of hospitals and health buildings. Architectural and engineering divisions deal with this aspect of the work, and publish the results of their research. Publications mainly available from H.M.S.O.

Department of Trade and Industry

1 Victoria Street,
London SW1H OET
Phone: 01 222 7877

Responsible for overseas trade and export promotion, and for industry and commerce in the UK. Responsible also for administration of patents and copyright, weights and measures and hire purchase legislation. Operates an EEC/EFTA information centre. Publications available. Many regional offices.

433

Department of Trade and Industry - Export Services Division

Export House,
50 Ludgate Hill,
London EC4M 7HU.
Phone: 01 248 5757

This Division undertakes market research, offers advice and information, and promotes interest in exporting among British firms at home. ESD is also responsible for the Export Sections of the DTI Offices in Scotland, Wales and the 5 Regions outside London, the East and South East. The bulk of day - to - day export promotion business in direct association with individual exporters, trade associations, chambers of commerce and export clubs, and with overseas Posts is also handled by this Division.

Amongst its services the Division provides, and charges for, a computerised Export Intelligence Service to suit firms' particular requirements (a free trial can be arranged).

Design Council

The Design Centre,
28 Haymarket,
London, SW1Y 4SU.
Phone: 01 839 8000

A grant-aided body set up under the Department of Trade and Industry. Aims at improvement in the design standards of British products. Has a permanent, but changing display of products and an illustrated catalogue (Design Index) of approved items. Offers annual awards to manufacturers. Publications available include handbooks on various aspects of domestic design and planning.

Associated Centre: The Scottish Design Centre, 72 St. Vincent St. Glasgow C2 (041 221 6121).

Independent Centre: The Design Centre, Liverpool, Hope St. Liverpool L1 9BR (051 709 8566).

District Heating Association Ltd (DHA)

Derbyshire House,
St. Chad's Street,
London, WC1H 8AE.
Phone: 01 278 1964

Concerned with all aspects of district heating. Organises conferences and meetings. Regional branches. Annual handbook and quarterly journal published.

EEC/EFTA Information Unit

see

Department of Trade and Industry

Economic Development Committees for Building and Civil Engineering (Little Neddies)

National Economic Development Office,
Millbank Tower,
Millbank,
London SW1P 4QX.
Phone: 01 834 3811

Established to examine the economic performance, plans and prospects of the Construction Industry, progress in relation to national objectives, and efficiency; also to supply information to the National Economic Development Council. Forecasts of the industry's output are produced several times a year, and other reports and recommendations as are deemed necessary. Publications available, some through HMSO.

Electrical Contractors Association (ECA)

55 Catherine Place,
London, SW1E 6ET.
Phone: 01 828 2932

Promotes and protects the interests of electrical contractors. To obtain membership, firms must satisfy the Council of the high standard of their work. They must also have been in the electrical contracting business for at least three years. Work of member - firms is guaranteed by the Association against bad workmanship, and all installation work must comply with the IEE (Institution of Electrical Engineers) wiring regulations. Training courses organised - 70 branches throughout the U.K. (Except Scotland). Year book/Desk diary and monthly periodical published.

Electrical Contractors Association of Scotland (ECAS)

23 Heriot Row,
Edinburgh EH3 6EW.
Phone: 031 225 7221

Similar to the Electrical Contractors' Association based in London.

Electrical Research Association (ERA)

Cleeve Rd.
Leatherhead,
Surrey.
Phone: Leatherhead 74151

Conducts sponsored research, development and testing in electrical, electronic and allied technologies. Provides technical and commercial information, computer services and certain design facilities. Publications available.

Electricity Council (Marketing Department)

Trafalgar Buildings,
1 Charing Cross,
London, SW1A 2DS.
Phone: 01 930 6757

Promotes the use of electricity and provides advisory and information services to users. Publications and a film 'A Site Better' are available through Electricity Boards and have been prepared in consultation with building industry representatives.

European Communities Information Office

23 Chesham St.
London, SW1X 8NH.
Phone: 01 235 4904

The official representative in the UK of The Commission of The European Communities (EEC, ECSC, EURATOM). The office supplies a wide range of information on community policies and activities, through publications, films and other means. A reference library is open to the public.

Expanded Polystyrene Product Manufacturers Association

6 St. Alphage House,
Fore Street,
London EC2Y 5DQ.
Phone: 01 628 8431

Establishes standards for expanded polystyrene board materials for insulation and other uses in the construction and refrigeration industries. Advice on usage available from the Technical Information Centre. Publications available.

(Technical Information Centre,
2 Catherine Street,
London WC2.
Phone: 01 836 9571)

Export Group For The Constructional Industries

3 Dean Trench St.
Smith Square,
London, S.W.1.
Phone: 01 799 3732

A non-profit making body whose members, exercising management and control in the U.K., are engaged in construction work abroad. Promotes the interests of its members by collecting and distributing amongst them commercial intelligence and advising on matters of policy, finance, contractual obligations and taxation. Publications available to members only.

Faculty of Architects and Surveyors (FAS)

68 Gloucester Place,
London W1H 3HL.
Phone: 01 935 9966

Promotes the interests of architects and surveyors and provides a forum for the interchange of knowledge and ideas. Library and advisory services available to members only. Regional Branches. Publications: quarterly journal and list of members.

Farm Buildings Centre (FBC)

National Agricultural Centre,
Kenilworth,
Warwicks, CV8 2LG.
Phone: Coventry 22345

Financed by Government, industry, and individuals, the centre deals with technical information on all aspects of farm buildings. The administrative centre for the activities of the farm buildings Association. Permanent, but changing,

435

Farm Buildings Centre (continued)

exhibition on farm buildings and materials. Library for reference only. Farm buildings digest, published quarterly is available on subscription.

Federation of Civil Engineering Contractors (FCEC)

Romney House,
Tufton Street, Westminster,
London, SW1P 3DU.
Phone: 01 222 2544

Promotes and protects the interests of members and maintains a high standard of conduct. Is concerned with labour negotiations and conditions of contract. Training schemes and courses organised. Information service. Publications available, also films and models.

General Section and London S.E. Section:	address and tel. as above
Midland:	507-9 Daimler House, Paradise St., Birmingham 1 (021 643 3839)
N.Eastern:	County Chambers 52 Westgate Rd., Newcastle-on-Tyne (Newcastle 24327)
N.Western:	37 Common Lane, Culcheth, Lancs. (Culcheth 42876)
Scottish:	Empire House, 131 West Nile St., Glasgow C.1 (041 332 5586)
S.Wales and Monmouth:	10 Museum Place, Cardiff (Cardiff 29468)
S.Western:	1 The Crescent, Taunton, Somerset (Taunton 84849)
Yorkshire:	7 South Parade, Leeds 1 (Leeds 21294)

Federation of Epoxy Resin Formulators & Applicators Ltd. (FERFA)

33 Bedford Row,
London, WC1R 4JN
Phone: 01 405 9446

Concerned with providing standards and codes of practice for users of epoxy resin materials. Provides independent advice on technical and general matters, and an information service.

Federation of Master Builders (FMB)

33 John Street,
Holborn,
London WC1N 2BB.
Phone: 01 242 7583

Furthers the interests of the building industry on a national level, and is particularly concerned with the medium and small sized firms. Aims to improve conditions for all levels in the industry and establish fair conditions of contract. Library and information service for members only. Publications available are monthly journal and annual year books.

Federation of Master Builders (continued)

	Regional Offices:	
	London Region:	84 Grays Inn Rd., London WC1X 8AA.
	Eastern Counties:	7 Station Road, Cambridge CB1 2JB
	Midland:	168 Corporation St., Birmingham B4 6TJ
	Northern Counties:	4/5 Hutton Terrace, Newcastle-on-Tyne NE2 1QT
	North-West:	Williams Deacons Bank Chambers, Liverpool Road, Birkdale, Lancs.
	Southern Counties:	71 London Road, Sevenoaks, Kent.
	South-West	1 St. Paul's Road, Bristol BS8 IL2
	South Wales and Monmouthshire:	7 Fitzalan Road, Cardiff CF2 1EB
	Yorkshire:	29-31 Basinghall Buildings, Butt's Court, Leeds, LS1 5HX

Fibre Building Board Development Organisation Limited. (FIDOR)

6-7 Buckingham St.
London, WC2N 6BZ.
Phone: 01 839 1122

Promotes the use of all types of fibre building board. Sample library maintained, and permanent exhibition of correct usage and suggested applications. Lecturers available, also films. Research work commissioned, and training courses organised. A large number of publications is available.

Finnish Plywood Development Association (FPDA)

Broadmead House,
21 Panton St.
London, SW1Y 4DR.
Phone: 01 930 3282

Provides information and advice on the use of Finnish Plywood. Sponsors research and experimental work. Large number of publications available on such subjects as structural applications, flooring, roofing, partitions, formwork, blockboard, laminboard, joints and mechanical fastenings.

Fire Protection Association (FPA)

Aldermary House,
Queen St.
London, EC4N 1TJ.
Phone: 01 248 5222

Financed mainly by insurance companies, the Association provides advice and technical information on all aspects of fire protection. Library and bookshop for all important publications on fire. Films and filmstrips available, also wallcharts, leaflets, data sheets and quarterly periodicals. Residential courses on fire protection organised.

Fire Research Station
> *see*
> Building Research Establishment,
> Fire Research Station

Forestry Commission
> 25 Savile Row,
> London W1X 2AY
> Phone: 01 734 0221

A Government agency concerned with the development of afforestation on a national scale, the maintenance of forests, forestry research and the production and supply of timber for industry. Offers advice and technical information on forestry matters where appropriate and, in certain circumstances, may give financial assistance to help in the work of afforestation by local authorities or private individuals. Publications available through HMSO.

Garage Equipment Association
> 11 Ironmonger Lane,
> London EC2P 2AR
> Phone: 01 606 8943

Promotes the interests of garage equipment manufacturers and distributors who form the membership of the Association. Publishes the Garage Equipment Association Directory, a guide to the specific services provided by members.

Gypsum Products Development Association (GPDA)
> Ferguson House,
> 15-17 Marylebone Road,
> London, NW1 5JE.
> Phone: 01 935 9739

Promotes and encourages the use of gypsum products, and provides information service through member firms (who are manufacturers of gypsum products in the U.K. and abroad). Publications available.

Heating and Ventilating Contractors Association (HVCA)
> Coastal Chambers,
> 172 Buckingham Palace Rd.
> London SW1W 9TD.
> Phone: 01 730 8245

Promotes and protects the interests of firms operating in the heating ventilating and allied trades. Information service for members, but bona fide enquiries from the general public will be dealt with. Publications include guides to good practice specifications, contract documents and year book.

Branches:

Birmingham, West Midlands and East Midlands :	Lancaster King Ridgeway & Co., St. Martin's House, Bull Ring, Birmingham B5 5EN.
Eastern Counties:	Curzon Rix & Co., 6 George St., Colchester.
Lancashire, Cheshire and North Wales :	10-12 James St., Liverpool L2 7PW
London and Home Counties:	Headquarters Address
Northern:	Norham House (4th Floor) New Bridge St., Newcastle-on-Tyne, 1.
Scottish:	MacDonald Jameson & Morris, 124 Vincent St., Glasgow, C2.
Yorkshire:	34 Wellington St., City Square, Leeds 1.

Heating and Ventilating Contractors Association (Continued)

South Wales and West of England:

The Building Centre,
Colston Avenue,
The Centre,
Bristol BS1 4TW.

Heating and Ventilating Research Association (HVRA)

Old Bracknell Lane,
Bracknell,
Berks.
Phone: Bracknell 25071

An industrial research association supported by members and by a grant from the Department of the Environment. Membership is open to companies or other organisations concerned with the design, production, and installation of equipment associated with the built environment. Comprehensive library, technical information and advisory service available. Standard testing facilities available. Contract research undertaken. Wide range of publications.

H.M. Land Registry

Lincoln's Inn Fields,
London, W.C.2.
Phone: 01 405 3488

A Government Agency to establish a state register of land ownership, with precise details of the extent of ownership and the liabilities related to the land. This is open to inspection only on the written authority of the registered owner. Registration is compulsory on sale in greater London and some of the surrounding areas, in some of the larger cities and in many urban areas. It is being extended, in stages, to all parts of the country.

Regional Offices:

Sunley House,
Croydon CR9 3LE

Aykley Heads,
Durham, DH1 5TR

Bruton Way,
Gloucester, GL1 1DQ

Lyon House,
Lyon Road,
Harrow,
Middlesex.
HA1 2EU

East Beach,
Lytham St. Annes,
Lancs
FY8 5AB

Chalfont Drive,
Nottingham NG8 3RN.

Railway Offices,
North Road,
Plymouth,
Devon,
PL4 6AD

Brickdale House,
Danestreet,
Stevenage,
Herts.
SG1 1XG

37 The Kingsway,
Swansea,
Glamorgan,
SA1 5LF

Tunbridge Wells,
Kent.

Her Majesty's Stationery Office (HMSO)

Atlantic House,
Holborn Viaduct,
London EC1P 1BN.
Phone: 01 248 9876

The British Government Publisher and Bookseller. Prints and distributes all official documents, pamphlets, handbooks, and periodicals for Ministries, Departments and many Government organisations and agencies. Also acts as distributor in U.K. for publications of UN, UNESCO, WHO, OECD, EEC, etc.

HMSO (Continued)

HMSO Bookshops: 49 High Holborn,
London WC1V 6HB
(callers only)
01 928 6977

P.O. Box 569,
London SE1 9NH
(trade and mail orders)
01 928 6977

13A Castle Street,
Edinburgh EH2 3AR
031 225 6333

80 Chichester Street,
Belfast BT1 4JY
Belfast 34488

109 St. Mary St.,
Cardiff CF1 1JW
Cardiff 23654

258 Broad Street,
Birmingham, B1 2HE
021 643 3740

50 Fairfax St.,
Bristol BS1 3DE
Bristol 24306

Brazennose St.,
Manchester M60 8AS
061 834 7201

Historic Buildings Councils (HBCs) for England, Scotland, and Wales

Established under the Historic Buildings and Ancient Monuments Act 1953. These Councils advise on the making of grants or loans towards the cost of repair and maintenance of buildings of outstanding historic or architectural importance, the acquisition of such buildings by the Secretary of State and the making of conservation grants under the Town and Country Planning (Amendment) Act 1972.
England - 25 Savile Row, London W1.
Scotland - 21 Hill Street, Edinburgh EH2 3JY.
Wales - Welsh Office, Summit House, Windsor Place, Cardiff.
The annual report for each council (from HMSO) details grants recommended.

House Builders' Federation (HBF)
82 New Cavendish St.,
London W1M 8AD.
Phone: 01 580 4041

Aims to encourage improved standards of design construction and equipment in house-building, and the provision of houses by private enterprise. Monthly periodical and other publications available. Work administered regionally through Branch Offices of the National Federation of Building Trades Employers.

440

House Builders' Federation (Continued)

London :	18-20 Duchess Mews, London W.1.
Southern:	Sterling Buildings, Carfax, Horsham, Sussex.
South Western:	22 Richmond Hill, Clifton, Bristol BS8 1BD.
South Wales and Monmouthshire:	Llys-Tal-y-Bont Road, Maindy, Cardiff.
Midland:	36 Calthorpe Rd., Edgbaston, Birmingham B15 1YA.
Eastern:	95 Tenison Rd., Cambridge CB1 2DL.
North-Western:	2 Conyngham Rd., Victoria Park, Manchester M14 5SH.
Liverpool:	Federation House, Hope St., Liverpool L1 9BS.
Northern Counties:	Green Lane, Durham.
Yorkshire:	Davidson House, Hales Road, Leeds, LS12 4PW.
Scottish:	13 Woodside Crescent, Glasgow, C3.

Housing Centre Trust (HCT)
13 Suffolk St.,
Pall Mall East,
London SW1Y 4HG.
Phone: 01 930 2881

Promotes the improvement of housing conditions, by means of publicity and by acting as a centre for the exchange of ideas and information on all aspects of housing. Library and information service available. Bookshop stocks all British publications on housing, and the Trust also has its own publications. Conferences and study visits organised.

The Housing Corporation
Sloane Square House,
London SW1W 8NT.
Phone: 01 730 9991

Established under the Housing Act 1964 to promote housing societies, assist their development and stimulate the building of new dwellings to let at cost-rents, or for group co-ownership.

Regional Offices:

South Thames:	Prudential House, Wellesley Rd., Croydon, Surrey.
North Thames:	Star House, Potters Bar, Herts, EN6 2QW.

The Housing Corporation (Continued)

Wales:	Caerys House, Windsor Place, Cardiff.
South West:	14 Bedford St., Exeter, Devon.
Midlands:	Provincial House, 37 New Walk, Leicester, LE1 6TE.
North-West:	Elisabeth House, 16 St. Peters Square, Manchester, M2 3DF.
North-East:	Merton House, Albion St., Leeds, LS1 6AG.
Scotland:	9 Manor Place, Edinburgh, EH3 7DH.

The Housing Research Foundation (HRF)

58 Portland Place,
London W1N 4BU.
Phone: 01 387 7201

An independent, non-profit-making body which commissions research through Universities and others into housing needs and customer preferences. It was set up by the National House-Builders Registration Council - see separate entry.

The Illuminating Engineering Society (IES)

York House,
Westminster Bridge Rd.
London, S.E.1.
Phone: 01 928 7110

Established to promote the art, science and technology of lighting. Organises conferences, lectures, meetings and discussions. Reference library for members only. Information service available. Publications available include The I.E.S. Code - recommendations for interior lighting, technical reports and periodicals.

Incorporated Association of Architects and Surveyors (IAAS)

29 Belgrave Square,
London, S.W.1.
Phone. 01 235 3755

Encourages co-operation between architects and surveyors by providing a forum for discussions, and by arranging meetings and working parties to produce occasional reports. 18 branches. Library and information service for members. Periodical published, also practice notes and reports.

The Institute of Advanced Architectural Studies (IAAS)

University of York,
The King's Manor,
York, YO1 2EP.
Phone: York 24919

A graduate Department of the University of York. Carries out research through the York University Design Unit and also operates a smaller, separate Research Unit. Organises short courses on specialised subjects for those in the Architectural and Allied professions. Subjects covered include Architectural History, Design of Buildings, Town Planning, Building Maintenance, Management and Economics.

The Institute of Arbitrators (IArb)

16 Park Crescent,
London, W1N 4BB.
Phone: 01 636 9991

Exists to facilitate the settlement of disputes by arbitration. Maintains panels of arbitrators.

Institute of Building (IoB)

Englemere,
King's Ride,
Ascot, Berks. SL5 8BJ.
Phone: Ascot 23355

The Professional Institute for those engaged in building in a managerial, technical administrative, teaching or commercial capacity. Promotes high standards of conduct and competence. Membership mainly by examination, organises conferences, seminars, lectures and meetings. 52 local groups. Information and library service. Publications available include monthly periodical.

Institute of Clerks of Works of Great Britain (INC). (ICWGB)

6 Highbury Corner,
London, N.5.
Phone: 01 607 5946

Aims to advance the knowledge and status of clerks of works. Membership by examination. Provides an appointments bureau. Organises lectures and meetings in London and in 13 branches. Publishes a monthly journal and an annual year-book.

Institute of Materials Handling (IMH)

St. Ives House,
St. Ives Road,
Maidenhead,
Berks.
Phone: Maidenhead 28011

Established to further the science of materials handling, by education, research and the interchange of knowledge. Organises conferences, courses, meetings, discussions and visits. Library for callers only; information service available Bi-monthly journal and occasional booklets published.

The Institute of Plumbing (IoP)

Scottish Mutual House,
North Street,
Hornchurch, Essex RM11 1RU.
Phone: Hornchurch 51236

Emerged in its new form January 1970 following a merger with the Registered Plumbers Association. An independent, non-profit making body whose main objects are to advance the science and practice of plumbing and domestic central heating, and to raise the status of its members. Advocates a system of statutory registration for plumbers to protect the public from bad workmanship. Technical publications available.

Institute of Quantity Surveyors   (IQS)

98 Gloucester Place,
London W1H 4AT.
Phone: 01 935 1859/4048

Promotes the interests of quantity surveyors and maintains a high standard of conduct. Membership open only to quantity surveyors and to full-time students of quantity surveying. Examinations held. Library and information service for members only. Appointments register maintained. 4 junior sections and 24 Branches, 4 Districts. Publications available.

Institute of Refrigeration (IR)

272 London Rd.,
Wallington,
Surrey.
Phone: 01 647 7033

Promotes the advancement of refrigeration. Reference library available to members and non-members by appointment only. Monthly meetings held. Proceedings published annually.

Institute of Wood Science (IWSc)

62 Oxford St.
London W.1.
Phone: 01 580 3185

The Institute is concerned with advancing the scientific and technical knowledge of wood properties, processing and utilisation. Organises conferences, lectures and meetings. 14 branches. Publications available.

Institute of Work Study Practitioners (IWSP)

9-10 River Front,
Enfield, Middlesex,
EN1 3TE.
Phone: 01 363 7452

The Institute of Work Study Practitioners is a professional body with a membership of 20,000. It operates on a regional basis and through branches and specialist groups. The principal objectives of the Institute are to create professional

443

Institute of Work Study Practitioners (Continued)

standards for the practice of work study and its related fields; to provide a system of qualifying examinations, to encourage research and development in work study and allied spheres, to be a focal point of the practice and wider use of work study and other productivity services, and to collaborate with other bodies in similar fields.

Institution of Civil Engineers (ICE)

Great George Street,
London SW1P 3AA
Phone: 01 839 3611

The senior professional engineering Institution, founded to promote the acquisition of knowledge for the profession of a civil engineer. Organises conferences, meetings and lectures. Publishes technical journals, books and a weekly magazine for the profession and the construction industry. Library of books, films and slides mainly for use of members. 12 branches in the U.K.

Institution of Electrical Engineers (IEE)

Savoy Place,
London WC2R OBL
Phone: 01 240 1871

Promotes the advancement and applications of electrical science and engineering. Provides facilities for the exchange of information relating to the industry. Computer-based information services. Library includes computer programmes. Conferences, courses and meetings organised. 23 branches in the UK. Scholarships awarded. Wide range of publications available.

Institution of Heating and Ventilating Engineers (IHVE)

49 Cadogan Square,
London, SW1X OJB.
Phone: 01 235 7671

Furthers the science and practice of heating, ventilating, air conditioning and related services associated with the environment in buildings. Conducts examinations, by which membership is normally achieved. Library for members only. Information service available. Arranges symposia, lectures and meetings in London and 12 branches in the U.K. Publications available.

Institution of Mechanical Engineers (IMechE)

1 Birdcage Walk,
Westminster,
London SW1
Phone: 01 930 7476

Promotes and encourages invention and research and the general development of mechanical engineering establishes standards of training. Membership normally by examination. Lectures, meetings and discussions organised. Library available to members only. Many publications. It branches in the UK and overseas.

Institution of Municipal Engineers (IMunE)

25 Eccleston Square,
London, SW1V 1NX.
Phone: 01 834 5082.

The senior professional organisation for engineers in local Government service, the Institution promotes the science and practice of engineering as provided by public bodies for the benefit of the community. Organises conferences, meetings and discussions. Library and information service for members of this and other engineering institutions only. Monthly journal published. 15 branches in the U.K.

Institution of Public Health Engineers (IPHE)

32 Eccleston Square,
Westminster,
London, SW1V 1PB.
Phone: 01 834 3017

Formerly the Institution of Sanitary Engineers, the objects of the Institution are the improvement of both the health and the living conditions of the people. Organises meetings for discussion and interchange of ideas, both

Institution of Public Health Engineers (Continued)

in London and in District Centres, on such subjects as, water supply, prevention of pollution, sanitation of buildings, refuse disposal sewage disposal, and a wide range of allied subjects. 'Library and information service available. Journal published six times per year.

Institution of Structural Engineers (IStructE)

11 Upper Belgrave St.
London, SW1X 8BH.
Phone: 01 235 4535

Formed to promote the advancement of the art and science of structural engineering. Membership by examination. Organises, lectures, meetings and discussions. Library and information services for members only. Publications available. Branches in the Provinces and abroad.

Insulation Glazing Association (IGA)

6 Mount Row,
London, W1Y 6DY
Phone: 01 629 8334

Promotes the use of insulation glazing, and is concerned with establishing high standards of manufacture and installation practice. Members are manufacturers of insulation glazing and those engaged in allied trades. Publications available.

International Union of Building Centres (UICB)
see
Building Centres

King's Fund Centre

24 Nutford Place,
London, W1H 6AN.
Phone: 01 262 2641

An independent charitable organisation maintained by King Edward's Hospital Fund for London. The chief aims of the centre are to provide a forum for the discussion of current problems and to help to accelerate the introduction of good ideas and practices in the planning and management of health and social services. Conferences and exhibitions arranged. Library and information service available. Some money available for research and development.

Lead Development Association

34 Berkeley Square,
London W1X 6AJ.
Phone: 01 499 8422

Established to promote the use of lead, the Association is supported by producers of lead in the U.K. and abroad. Technical information service available. Reference and loan library operated jointly with the Zinc Development Association. Publications and films available.

Mastic Asphalt Council and Employers' Federation

24 Grosvenor Gardens,
London, SW1W ODH
Phone: 01 730 7175

Promotes the use of mastic asphalt, and encourages high standards of workmanship in the industry. Provides technical information service. Publishes technical literature on the application of mastic asphalt.

Meteorological Office (Met O)

London Road,
Bracknell,
Berks. RG12 2SZ.
Phone: Bracknell 20242

Provides meteorological services to Government Departments, Local Authorities, the press, radio and television, commerce, industry and the general public. Supplies information on all aspects of climatology. A special service is available for the construction industry, providing forecasts and issuing warnings of adverse weather as required for particular sites, or supplying mean monthly and annual statistics. 37 regional offices.

Modular Society

Alderman House,
37 Soho Square,
London W1V 6AT.
Phone: 01 437 0328.

Promotes the development of modular co-ordination as a means of increasing the effiency of building. Seeks to improve the design of standardised components, both functionally and aesthetically. Organises courses, lectures and visits. Publications available.

National Building Agency (NBA)

NBA House,
Arundel St.
London WC2R 3DZ.
Phone: 01 836 4488

Financed by Government grant and by consultancy fees, managed by Government appointed directors, the agency is an independent advisory organisation which promotes improved management techniques at all stages of the building process. Encourages new building methods, especially industrialised systems, and better financial control. Wide range of publications available from RIBA Publications Limited, 66 Portland Place, London W1N 4AD, or through H.M.S.O.

National Coal Board (NCB)

Hobart House,
Grosvenor Place,
London SW1.
Phone: 01 235 2020

In addition to controlling the coal industry, the National Coal Board provides a technical and advisory service on all aspects of the utilisation of coal. Extensive range of publications available. Regional Offices:

London and Southern:	Coal House, Lyon Road, Harrow, Mddx.
Northern :	Team Valley Trading Estate, Gateshead 11, Co. Durham
North-Western:	Anderton House, Lowton, Warrington, Lancs.
Yorkshire:	Ranmoor Hall, Belgrave Road, Sheffield 10.
Midland:	Eastwood Hall, Eastwood, Nottingham.
South Wales and W. of England:	Coal House, Tyglas Avenue, Llanishen, Cardiff.
Scottish:	Lauriston House, Lauriston Place, Edinburgh, 3.

National Council of Building Material Producers (NCBMP)

18 Chantrey House,
Eccleston Street,
London SW1W 9LN.
Phone: 01 730 9233/4

The Council is consituted to represent the collective interests of its Members to Government, the EEC Commission, the EDC's, CBI, BSI and other bodies including other trade and professional organisations, to promote increased collaboration between building material producers, to nominate representatives on government and other committees and bodies, and to take such action as may be required from

National Council of Building Material Producers (Continued)

time to time for the promotion of home and overseas trade. The Council is supported by an Executive Committee and sub-committees dealing with forecasting, the EEC, legislation, technical matters, contracts and commercial matters.

Publications Available: Annual Report (f.o.c.)

BMP Weekly Information including a fortnightly EEC Supplement and a monthly BSI Publications Supplement - annual subscription £9.90 (Members £8.50).

BMP Monthly Statistical Bulletin - Annual subscription £5.50 (Members £4.50). Various periodic reports and other publications.

National Federation of Building Trades' Employers (NFBTE)

82 New Cavendish St.
London, W1M 8AD.
Phone: 01 637 4771

Founded to improve the effiency of the building industry, mainly by establishing recommended conditions and procedures (such as the code of procedure for selective tendering). Information service available to non-members. Technical advice available to members. Conferences and meetings organised in London and the regions. Wide range of publications.

National Federation of Builders' and Plumbers' Merchants (NFBPM)

High Holborn House,
52-54 High Holborn,
London, WC1V 6SP.
Phone: 01 242 772

Represents the trade, and seeks to improve the speed and efficiency of the distribution of building materials. Organises training courses for members, an annual conference and meetings, through 24 regional offices. Information service for members only.

National Federation of Demolition Contractors (NFDC)

2 Bankart Avenue,
Leicester LE2 2DB.
Phone: 0533 707813

Keeps members informed of all the legal aspects of demolition, and aims to ensure that work is carried out with safety, speed and efficiency. Information service for members, all of whom have been established as demolition contractors for at least five years. List of members published annually. Published nationally negotiated working rule agreement. Meetings held in the regions.

Nat. Fed. of Demolition Contractors
Regional Secretaries:

North & North Eastern: Ingram, Nolan & Co.,
17, Blenheim Terrace,
Leeds, LS2 9HL.   Leeds: 21162

Midland & Welsh: G. Wilson, Esq.,
P.O. Box 1,
63 Temple Row,
Birmingham B2 5ND
021 643 6111

North Western: A.S. Hack, Esq., AACCA,
413/414 Coopers Buildings,
Church Street,
Liverpool, L1 3AG.
051 709 3497

447

National Federation of Demolition Contractors (Continued)

Scotland:	J.E. Hay, Esq., 13 Woodside Crescent, Glasgow G3 7UP. 041 332 0051
London & Southern Counties:	V. Powell-Smith, Esq., LL.M., D.LiTT. 2, Bankart Avenue, Leicester, LE2 2DB. 0533 707813

National Federation of Housing Societies (NFHS)

86 Strand,
London, WC2R OEG.
Phone: 01 836 2741

The Central Organisation for the promotion of housing societies and for advising on their formation and management. Publications available include a quarterly journal.

Scottish Office: Castle Rock Housing Association Ltd.,
26 York Place,
Edinburgh EH1 3EP.

National Heating Centre (NHC)

34 Mortimer St.
London W1N 8AR.
Phone: 01 580 3238

An independent organisation which provides unbiased advice to the trade, the professions and members of the public on all matters relating to domestic heating. Maintains a register of domestic heating engineers who agree to work to approved standards and provide a guarantee on installations. Design and technical services available. Literature available on fuels and equipment. Scale of charges available.

National House-Builders Registration Council (NHBRC)

58 Portland Place,
London W1N 4BU.
Phone: 01 387 7201

An independent, non-profit making body established to protect purchasers of new houses against defects in both materials and construction, and also against the bankruptcy of the builder. Membership is composed of representatives of the various professions and trades concerned with house building, one third of the members being builders - A register is maintained of approved builders, and anyone failing to satisfy the standards required by the council may be removed from the register. Those purchasing new houses from a registered builder qualify for compensation when defects arise within a certain period.

National Joint Consultative Committee (NJCC)

47 Tothill Street,
London SW1H 9LH.
Phone: 01 839 5600

The Committee has five constituent bodies, The Royal Institute of British Architects, The Royal Institution of Chartered Surveyors, National Federation of Building Trades Employers, The Association of Consulting Engineers, & The NFBTE National Group of Subcontractors. It provides a medium whereby matters of national importance in which the Constituent Bodies are mutually interested may be discussed and any appropriate action taken, provided that this does not encroach upon the work of any one of the bodies or any group established between them.

National Joint Council for the Building Industry (NJCBI)

11 Weymouth St.
Portland Place,
London W1N 3FG.
Phone: 01 580 1740

An organisation which determines wages and working conditions for the industry on a national basis, and arranges negotiations between employers and operatives for the settlement of disputes. Operates the National Joint Training Scheme. There are 11 regions, each of which has an Employers' Secretary and an Operatives' Secretary, and certain powers of the Council are delegated to regional, area and local Joint Committees and also to Standing Committees.

National Lending Library (Formerly)

see
British Library Lending Division

National Physical Laboratory (NPL)

Teddington,
Middlesex, TW11 0LW.
Phone: 01 977 3222

The Laboratory, a station of the Department of Trade and Industry, is organized into three groups. The Measurement Group has the responsibility for the establishment of internationally acceptable basic standards of measurement, the development of new techniques of measurement, and the furtherance of their use by Government, Industry and the Universitites. The Materials Group has the responsibility for maintaining the national standards of measurement in chemistry, for providing definitive data on the engineering properties of substances and of materials and for advising on meaningful ways of specification of materials. In support of these functions the Group maintains and develops means of measuring important properties of materials and of examining their structure. Novel methods of material synthesis are investigated when the need arises or when ideas occur which have promise of useful application. The Engineering Sciences Group comprises those Divisions concerned with particular industrial activities and technologies, principally those associated with ships and other marine vehicles, and with computer usage; the Group is also concerned with engineering fluid dynamics and acoustics. The underlying themes are fluid dynamics, information technology and mathematics.

Office for Scientific and Technical Information (OSTI)

Elizabeth House,
39 York Road,
London SE1 7PH
Phone: 01 928 9222. Ext: 3417

OSTI is part of the Department of Education and Science. Its main functions are to promote research and development of new techniques and systems in the field of information science covering natural and social sciences and their related technologies, to stimulate the training of scientists for information work, to help to co-ordinate the information activities of Government and private organisations in this country and to blend them with work being done abroad.

It compiles annually the 3-volume register of research, 'Scientific Research in British Universities and Colleges covering Physical, Biological and Social Sciences', available through HMSO.

Ordnance Survey

Romsey Road,
Maybush,
Southampton SO9 4DH.
Phone: Southampton 75555

The national agency for mapping in the UK. Produces maps in various scales for general or specialist use. Available through OS agents and many booksellers and stationers. Special services provided to order include enlargements, reductions, transparencies, mounting of composite maps, and the supply of advance revision information. 35 mm. negative microfilms also supplied. More detailed information about all or any of these services is available from Ordnance Survey on request.

Plastics Institute (PI)

11 Hobart Place,
London SW1W OHL
Phone: 245 9555

Provides a means for the exchange of ideas and knowledge on all aspects of plastics, and aims to advance education in these fields. Organises lectures, discussions and meetings. Information service available. Libraries maintained at certain Universities and Technical Colleges. Publications available.

Princes Risborough Laboratory

see
Building Research Establishment,
Princes Risborough Laboratory

Research Association of British Paint, Colour and Varnish Manufacturers (RABPM)

Waldegrave Road,
Teddington,
Middlesex.
Phone: Teddington Lock 4427

Aided by a grant from the Department of Trade and Industry, the Association carries out research for the paint and other allied industries. Work covers raw materials, manufacture, application and performance of paints, the painting of different materials, durability and weathering. Most extensive library on paint technology information service mainly for members, but non-members may use these services by special arrangement.

Royal Institute of British Architects (RIBA)

66 Portland Place,
London W1N 4AD
Phone: 01 580 5533

The senior professional body for architects conducts examinations for membership. Appointments register maintained also practices index which contains information on private practices and photographs of their work for reference of the general public. Extensive library, mainly for members, but reference section available to the public. Large collection of British and foreign drawings from 16th century to present day housed separately. Agency for the CI/SfB classification system; classification advisory service available. Wide range of publications.

Royal Institution of Chartered Surveyors (RICS)

12 Great George St.
London SW1P 3AD.
Phone: 01 839 5600

The senior professional body representing surveyors in all branches of the subject. Conducts examinations for membership. Appointments register maintained. Technical information service and Building Maintenance Cost Information Service open to subscribers. Also Building Cost Information Service open to subscribers on a reciprocal basis. Library for use of members only. Conferences and meetings organised through London and regional branches. Wide range of publications available.

The Royal Institution of Chartered Surveyors, Building Maintenance Cost Information Service, (BMCIS)

47 Tothill St.
London SW1H 9LH
Phone: 01 839 5600

Service for all concerned with the design and maintenance of buildings, which operates by distributing up-to-date data to subscribers at regular intervals. Material covers a wide range of subjects, all related to the economic maintenance of buildings and the efficient occupancy of them. Technical, financial, legal, and design/performance aspects are all dealt with. Case studies related to budgetary control, occupancy cost analyses, defective details with suggested remedial work and a bibliography are some of the sections in the (currently) 2 loose-leaf volumes.

The Royal Society of Health

13 Grosvenor Place,
London SW1X 7EN.
Phone: 01 235 9961

The Royal Society for the Prevention of Accidents (RoSPA)

Royal Oak Centre,
Brighton Rd.
Purley, CR2 2UR.
Phone: 01 668 4272

The objective of the Society is to prevent accidents of all kinds, on the road, at the place of work, or in the home. To accomplish this a wide variety of courses and conferences is run, and a large number of publications, periodicals and posters produced, details of which are available on application. In addition, the Industrial Safety Division is able on request to provide a wide variety of services tailored to the individual needs of industrial and commercial organisations.

Rubber and Plastics Research Association of Great Britain (RAPRA)

Shawbury,
Shrewsbury SY4 4NR.
Phone: Shawbury 383.

Carries out research and publishes information on rubber, plastics and allied materials. Undertakes sponsored research Library and information service mainly for members, who are manufacturers, suppliers and users of the materials. Consultancy service available. Meetings and symposia organised. Publications include the weekly 'RAPRA Abstracts'.

Scottish Development Department (SDD)

St. Andrew's House,
Edinburgh EH1 3DD.
Phone: 031 556 8501

Under the jurisdiction of the Secretary of State for Scotland, this is one of the Administrative Departments of the Scottish Office, concerned with local government towmn and country planning, building control, housing, roads, electricity, water supply, environmental pollution and other subjects. Extensive range of publications available through H.M.S.O.
London Office: Dover House, Whitehall, London, S.W.1.

Scottish Education Department (SED)

St. Andrew's House,
Edinburgh EH1 3DB.
Phone: 031 556 8501

One of the Administrative Departments of the Scottish Office and under the jurisdiction of The Secretary of State for Scotland, this Department is responsible for the development of education in Scotland. Publications on courses and educational premises available through H.M.S.O. London, Office, Dover House, Whitehall, London, S.W.1.

Scottish Home and Health Department (SHHD)

St. Andrew's House,
Edinburgh EH1 3DE.
Phone: 031 556 8501

One of the Administrative Departments of the Scottish Office, and under the jurisdiction of the Secretary of State for Scotland. Similar in function to the Home Office and the Department of Health and Social Security in England and Wales. Concerned with law and order, the fire service, legislation affecting public safety, and the administration of the national health and welfare services. Publications available through H.M.S.O.

Scottish Hospital Centre

Crewe Road South,
Edinburgh EH4 2LF.
Phone: 031 332 2335

Promotes and carries out research into the design and operation of hospitals and hospital equipment. Permanent exhibition maintained. Information and library service primarily for those in the Health Service, but available to other bona fide enquirers. Extensive list of publications includes several bibliographies.

Scottish National Housing and Town Planning Council

The Town Clerk's Office,
Municipal Buildings,
Renfrew, Scotland.
Phone: 041 886 2387

Aims to achieve adequate housing for Scotland, of good standards and integrated through town planning schemes. Membership is open to representatives of Local Authorities in Scotland and to those in the construction industry. Organises two annual conferences and publishes papers submitted to these.

The Scottish Office

Dover House,
Whitehall,
London SW1.
Phone: 01 930 6151

The Government Department responsible for Scottish affairs. Controls the four main administrative Departments of the Secretary of State for Scotland - the Department of Agriculture and Fisheries for Scotland, the Scottish Education Department, the Scottish Home and Health Department and the Scottish Development Department - all of which are based in Edinburgh.

Society of Architectural and Associated Technicians (SAAT)

Palladium House,
1-4 Argyll St.
London W1V 1AD.
Phone: 01 437 0976

Promotes the status of the technician as a member of the construction team. Provides a code of conduct and educational facilities. Encourages training towards higher grades and maintains contact with other organisations connected with all aspects of the industry. Organises discussions, visits and meetings. Large number of branches throughout the U.K.

Society for the Protection of Ancient Buildings, (SPAB)

55 Great Ormond Street,
London WC1.
Phone: 01 405 2646

Concerned with all problems relating to old buildings. Provides technical advice on their maintenance and repair and organises courses on these subjects for those in the construction industry and for architects. Arranges lectures, conferences and exhibitions. Maintains an index of buildings threatened with demolition. Publications available.

Special Steels User Advisory Centre, British Steel Corporation

Swinden Laboratories,
Moorgate,
Rotherham, Yorks.
Phone: Rotherham (0709) 73661
(24 hour service)

An advisory centre instituted by BSC, special steels division marketing department to give information on steel selection, properties and performance, fabrication and manipulation, sources of supply, applications and usage. Continues the service formerly provided by the Stainless Steel Development Association.

Steel Window Association (SWA)

26 Store St.
London WC1E 7JR.
Phone: 01 637 3571

Promotes the use of steel windows and represents members interests. Carries out research and development work. Provides technical information and advisory service, and publishes technical news sheets.

The Swedish Timber Council

Sweden House,
14 Trinity Square,
London EC3N 4BN.
Phone: 01 709 9911

An organisation to promote the use of Swedish softwood in the building and construction industry. Operates as a section of the Swedish Trade Commissioner's Office. Technical publications available.

Timber Research and Development Association (TRADA)

Hughenden Valley,
High Wycombe,
Buckinghamshire.
Phone: 0240 24 3091

TRADA maintains an advisory service network with offices in industrial centres throughout the country. Design advice, performance testing and structural consultancy provided. Education and training courses arranged. A comprehensive library is maintained and a wide range of publications is available.

Transport and Road Research Laboratory (TRRL)

Department of the Environment,
Crowthorne,
Berkshire.
Phone: Crowthorne, Berks. 3131.

The laboratory is concerned with research into the design, construction and use of roads and vehicles to achieve greater safety and efficiency. Computerised technical information service and library service available. Wide range of publications, some available through H.M.S.O. Lecture courses organised. Scottish Branch: Craigshill West, Livingston, West Lothian.

Union of Construction Allied Trades and Technicians (UCATT)

9-11 Macaulay Road,
Clapham, London SW4 0Q2.
Phone: 01 622 2362

U.C.A.T.T. has 273,646 members of whom the vast majority are employed within the Construction Industry, making U.C.A.T.T. much the most significant union within the industry. As such, its main aim is a decasualised, safe and properly paid career for building trade workers within the Construction Industry. U.C.A.T.T. has a full time Executive Council and twelve regional organisations, two in Ireland and ten in Great Britain.

Welsh Office

Cathays Park,
Cardiff, CF1 3NQ
Phone: 0222 - 28066 also at -

Gwydyr House,
Whitehall,
London SW1.
Phone: 01 930 3151

Responsible for most matters affecting the physical environment in Wales, including housing and new towns, town and country planning, water and sewerage, roads, national parks, reclamation of derelict land, coast protection, clean air, river pollution and flooding; health service matters and the community health and child-care services; primary and secondary education; local government re-organisation; economic planning; European Economics Communities.

Zinc Development Association

34 Berkeley Square,
London W1X 6AJ.
Phone 01 499 6636

Established to promote the use of zinc, the Association is supported by producers of the material here and abroad. Provides a technical information and advisory service. Reference and loan library operated jointly with Lead Development Assocation. Publications available.

INTERNATIONAL ORGANISATIONS

The following short list has been selected from an immense number of international organisations. Attention is drawn to the London-based secretariat of the International Union of Building Centres, which provides a convenient source of information. For those requiring further details of organisations throughout the world a useful publication is the "Directory of Building Research, Information and Development Organisations", published by the International Council for Building Research, Studies and Documentation. Because of its particular relevance to the construction industry, this section is preceded by a more detailed account of the work of the CIB.

International Council for Building Research, Studies and Documentation (CIB)

704 Weena,
P.O. Box 20704,
Rotterdam,
The Netherlands.
Phone: 11 61 81 - Telex 22530

Financed from membership fees. The primary purpose of CIB is to encourage, facilitate and develop international co-operation in building research, studies and documentation covering not only the technical but also the economic and social aspects of building. International working commissions deal with a variety of topics within this field of interests, and are composed of representatives of member institutions together with other co-opted experts. International congresses are held every three years, and the proceedings published. Other publications include a directory of building research, information and development organisations, and a bi-monthly journal: Building Research & Practice.

Council of Europe
55 Av. Kleber
Paris 16e
France

European Cement Association (CEMBUREAU)
(Associate Member of CIB)
2 rue Saint-Charles
Paris 15e
France

European Committee for Concrete (CEB)
>Permanent Secretariat:
>9 rue la Perouse
>75 Paris 16e
>France

European Convention for Constructional Steelwork Associations
(Associate Member of CIB)

Technical Secretariat:	Administrative Secretariat:
20 rue Jean-Jaures	Weena 700
92-Puteaux	Rotterdam-3
France	The Netherlands

International Association for Bridge and Structural Engineering
>Swiss Federal Institute of Technology,
>8006 Zurich
>Switzerland

International Commission on Illumination (CIE)
>Central Bureau
>25 rue de la Pepiniere
>75 Paris 8e
>France

International Council for Scientific Management (CIOS)
>Centre International
>1 rue de Varembe
>1211 Geneve 20

>Switzerland

International Federation of Building and Woodworkers (IFBWW)
>27 - 29 rue de la Coulouvreniere
>1204 Geneva
>Switzerland

International Federation of Consulting Engineers (FIDIC)
>Secretariat:
>Javastraat 44,
>The Hague
>The Netherlands

International Federation for Documentation (FID)
>7 Hofweg
>The Hague
>The Netherlands

International Federation of European Contractors of Building and Public Works
9 rue la Perouse **(FIEEBTP)**
Paris 16e
France

International Federation for Housing and Planning (IFHP)
43 Wassenaarseweg
The Hague
The Netherlands

International Federation of Pre-stressing (FIP)
Terminal House
Grosvenor Gardens
London SW1W 0AU

International Federation of Surveyors (FIG)
Kiedricher Strasse 6
62 Wiesbaden
Federal Republic of Germany

International Labour Organisation (ILO)
Branch Office: or   Geneva
Sackville House   Switzerland
40 Piccadilly
London W1

International Organization for Standardization (ISO)
1 rue de Varembe
1211 Geneva 20
Switzerland

International Society of Biometeorology (ISB)
Permanent Secretariat:
Hofbrouckerlaan 54
Oegstgeest
Leiden
The Netherlands

International Society for Soil Mechanics and Foundation Engineering
The Instution of Civil Engineers
Great George Street
London SW1P 3AA
England

International Union of Architects (UIA)
4 Impasse D'Antin
Paris 8e
France

International Union of Building Centres (UICB)
Secretariat:
The Building Centre
26 Store Street
London WC1
England

International Union of Testing and Research Laboratories for Materials and Structures (RILEM)
12 rue Brancion
Paris 15e
France

United Nations - Economic Commission for Europe (ECE)
Palais des Nations
1211 Geneva 10
Switzerland

United Nations - Educational, Scientific and Cultural Organization (UNESCO)
Unesco House
9 Place de Fontenoy
75 Paris 7e
France

United Nations Industrial Development Organization (UNIDO)
Rathausplatz 2
P.O. Box 707
1010 Vienna
Austria

United Nations - Office of Technical Co-operation (OTC)
United Nations
New York
N.Y.
U.S.A.

World Health Organization (WHO)
1121 Geneva 27
Switzerland

Index

Accidents, Royal Society for the Prevention of, 451
Accounts, construction company, 64, 81
    balance sheets, 82, 90, 117, 136, 193
    capitalisation, 144
    cash flow, 89, 128, 193
    debtors and creditors, 85
    depreciation, 88
    financial gearing, 95, 139
    financial ratios, 94, 135
    fixed assets, 94, 131
    investments, 87
    liabilities, 82
    liquidity, 89
    liquidity schedule, 129
    loan interest and other income, 89
    loans, 82
    net current assets, 142
    overdrafts, 82
    pre-interest margins, 142
    productivity performance, 95, 142
    profit and loss, 87, 92, 123, 138
    shareholders, 82
    sources of finance, 91
    stock and work-in-progress, 86
    taxation, 94, 133
    working capital, 86
Acoustics, 407
    also see Sound insulation
Advance Land Use Studies, Centre for, 429
Advanced Architectural Studies, Institute of, 442
Advisory Service for the Building Industry, 419
Aerial surveys, 205
Agrement Board, 419
Agricultural Development and Advisory Service, 419
Agricultural Research Council, 420
Aluminium Federation, 420
Aluminium sheet, properties, 292
Aluminium Window Association, 420
Analysis, network, 156
Ancient Buildings, Society for the Protection of, 452
Ancient Monument Society, 420
Arbitrators, Institute of, 442

Architects
    in Belgium, 8
    in France, 19
    in W. Germany, 28
    in Italy, 37
    in Netherlands, 47
Architects, International Union of, 457
Architects Registration Council of the
    United Kingdom, 421
Architects, Royal Institute of British, 450
Architects and Surveyors, Faculty of, 435
    – Incorporated Association of, 442
Architectural Association, 420
Architectural and Associated Technicians,
    Society for, 452
Architectural Granite Association, 420
Arts Council of Great Britain, 421
Arts Council of Northern Ireland, 421
Asbestos
    cement sheets, properties, 246
    insulating board, properties, 248
Asbestos Information Committee, 421
Aslib, 421
Asphalt, 250
Asphalt and Coated Macadam Association, 421
Association of Building Centres, 421, 425
Association of Building Technicians, 422
Association of Industrialised Building Component
    Manufacturers, 422
Automatic airflow control, 178

Belgium
    building approval, 7
    building laws and regulations, 6
    contract procedure, 8
    finance, 7
    government finance, 6
    housing, 7
    investment, 7
    land tenure and development, 7
    political structure, 5
Bill of quantities, 192, 195, 200

Biometeorology, International Society of, 456
Bitumen felt, properties, 252
Blocks, concrete, properties, 254
Board
    asbestos insulating, properties, 248
    fibre, building, properties, 274
Brick Development Association, 422
Brick Masonry Conference, International, 209
Bricks
    clay, properties, 258
    concrete, properties, 262
    flint-lime, properties, 264
    sand-lime, properties, 266
Brickwork
    gas explosions in, 210
    load-bearing, 209
    wind loads, 210
Bridge and Structural Engineering,
    International Association for, 455
British Cast Iron Research Association, 422
British Ceramic Research Association, 422
British Computer Society, 422
British Concrete Pumping Association, 422
British Constructional Steelwork Association, 422
British Gas Corporation, 422
British Glass Industry Research Association, 423
British Library Lending Division, 423
British Non-Ferrous Metals Research Association, 423
British Plastics Federation, 423
British Pre-Cast Concrete Federation, 423
British Productivity Council, 423
British Ready-mixed Concrete Association, 424
British Safety Council, 424
British Standards Institution, 424
British Steel Corporation,
    Corporate Engineering Laboratories, 424
    Special Steels Users Advisory Centre, 452
British Stone Federation, 425
British Wood Preserving Association, 425
British Woodwork Manufacturer's Association, 425
Builders' and Plumbers' Merchants,
    National Federation of, 447
Building Centres, 425
    Association of, 421, 425
    International Union of, 425
Building contracts, 190
    Standard Form of, 190, 194
Building control, 154
Building Cost Information Service, 427
Building in the EEC, 1
    in Belgium, 5
    in France, 15
    in W. Germany, 25
    in Italy, 34
    in Netherlands, 44
Building Industry
    Advisory Service for, 419

development of, 149
    future developments, 158
    organisation and control, 154
    see also Construction Industry
Building, Institute of, 443
Building Material Producers,
    National Federation of, 446
Building materials
    properties of, 223
    smoke production of, 163
    thermal conductivity of 396
Building measurement, 189
    Standard Method of, 191, 195
Building organisation, 157
Building Research Advisory Service, 427
Building Research Establishment, 153, 428
Building Research Station, 428
Building Technicians, Association of, 422
Building Trades' Employers,
    National Federation of, 447
Building and Woodworkers,
    International Federation of, 455
Buildings, smoke control in, 161
Bureau d'Etude, 20

CIB Master List for Materials, 233
    application, 231
    commentary, 228
    comparison, 227
    guiding principles, 226
Cast Iron Research Association, British, 422
Calculation, electronic, 204
Cement and Concrete Association, 429
Cement
    high alumina, properties, 268
    Portland, properties, 270
    sheets, asbestos, properties, 246
Cement Association, European, 454
Centre for Advanced Land Use Studies, 429
Ceramic Research Association, British, 422
Chipboard
    properties, 334
    smoke production, 163
City and Guilds of London Institute, 430
Civic Trust, 430
Civil Engineers, Institution of, 444
Civil Engineering Contractors, Federation of, 436
Clay bricks, properties, 258
Clay products, 209
    labour and mechanisation, 211
    new products and processes, 211
    production, 209
    testing, 210
Clay roof tiles, properties, 324
Clerks of Works of Great Britain, Institute of, 443

Combustion
    gaseous products of, 161, 165, 175
      — ammonia, 168
      — carbon dioxide, 165, 168
      — carbon monoxide, 162, 166, 167, 168
      — carbohaemoglobin, 166, 167, 168
      — hydrochloric acid gas, 168, 169
      — hydrogen cyanide, 168
      — hydrogen sulphide, 168, 169
      — nitrogen dioxide, 169
      — oxygen, 162, 165, 166, 168, 175
      — polyisobutylene, 170
      — polypropylene, 170
      — sulphur dioxide, 169
Committee of Directors of Research Association, 430
Companies, construction
    accounts (see acounts, construction company)
    by trade, 105
    by turnover, 112
    classifiable to construction, 107
    selected for analysis, 116
Computer Service and Bureaux Associations, 430
Computer Society, British, 422
Concrete
    Association, Cement and, 429
    blocks, properties of, 254
    bricks, properties of, 262
    European Committee for, 455
    mixing and placing, 154
    Pumping Society, British, 422
    roof tiles, properties, 326
    Society, 431
Confederation of British Industry, 431
Construction and Building Materials Review, 97
Construction Industry
    activity within
    — private sector, 74
    — public sector, 72
    analysis of, 61
    Belgium, 5
    changes in, 64
    development of, 149
    employment in, 71, 79
    France, 15
    W. Germany, 25
    Italy, 34
    Netherlands, 44
    output, 69, 70, 78
    performance trends, 67
    profile of, 66
    profit measures, 97
    quoted companies, 77
    — accounts, 94
    — employment, 79
    — numbers, 77
    — output, 78
    — structure, 77
    — turnover, 79

    review of structure, 77
    Standard Industrial Classification, 63
    structure of, 66
    turnover, 78
Construction Industry Research and Information
    Association, 431
Construction Industry Training Board, 431
Construction Steel Research and
    Development Organisation, 432
Construction Steelwork Association, British, 422
Construction Surveyors Institute, 432
Constructional Steelwork Association,
    European Convention for, 455
Consulting Engineers
    in Belgium, 8
    in France, 20
    in W. Germany, 29
    in Italy, 37
    in Netherlands, 47
Consulting Engineers, International Federation of, 455
Contractors
    in Belgium, 11
    in France, 21
    in W. Germany, 30
    in Italy, 39
    in Netherlands, 48
Contractors' Plant Association, 432
Conversions, metric, 218
Copper Development Association, 432
Copper sheet, properties, 294
Council of Europe, 454
Council of Forest Industries
    of British Columbia, 432
Cranes
    portal, 154
    tower, 153
Cultural Affairs, Ministry of, 19

Daily Statistics (Card) Service, 98
Daylighting factors, 346
Daylighting schedule, 346
Demolition Contractors, National Federation of, 447
Department of Education and Science, 432
Department of Employment, 432
    — Industrial Health and Safety Centre, 433
Department of the Environment, 433
    — Joint Fire Research Organisation, 433
Department of Health and Social Security, 433
Department of Trade and Industry, 433
    — Export Services Division, 434
Design Council, 434
Developers
    in Belgium, 10
    in W. Germany, 30
    in Italy, 38
Developments in the industry, 147
Development of the industry, 149

Directorate of Occupational Safety and Health, 433
District Heating Association Ltd, 434
Documentation, 197
Documentation, International Federation for, 455

EEC, Building in, 1
    effects on building industry, 52
EEC/EFTA Information Unit, 433
Economic Development Committees for
    Building and Civil Engineering, 434
Education and Science, Department of, 432
Electrical Contractors Association, 434
Electrical Contractors Association of Scotland, 435
Electrical Engineers, Institution of, 444
Electrical Research Association, 435
Electricity Council (Marketing Department), 435

Electronic distance measuring instruments, 204
Employment, Department of, 432
Environment, Department of, 433
Environmental Design Data, 341
    heating, 394
    lighting, 393
    sound insulation and acoustics, 407
Epoxy Resin Formulators and
    Applicators Ltd., Federation of, 436
Escape routes, 170
    design, 170
    openings, 172
    rate of movement on, 173
European Cement Association, 454
European Committee for Concrete, 455
European Communities Information Office, 435
European Convention for Constructional
    Steelwork Associations, 455
European Economic Community, 1
Expanded Polystyrene Products
    Manufacturers Association, 435
Export Group for the Construction Industries, 435
Extel Cards, 98

Faculty of Architects and Surveyors, 435
Farm Buildings Centre, 435
Federation du Batiment, 21
Federation of Civil Engineering Contractors, 436
Federation of Epoxy Resin Formulators and
    Applicators Ltd, 436
Federation of Master Builders, 436
Felt, bitumen, properties, 252
Fibre building boards, properties, 274
Fibre Building Board Development
    Organisations Ltd, 437
Field test unit, 152
Finance, studies in company, 97
Financial Times, 97
Finnish Plywood Development Association, 437

Fire
    combustion products (see Combustion)
    escape design, 170
    human tolerance in, 162
    smoke control, 161
    venting, 176
Fire Protection Association, 437
Fire Research Station, 428
Flint-lime bricks, properties, 264
Floors
    compartment, 207
    concrete, 211
    finishes, 276
    ground, suspended, 208
    sound insulation, 408 ff
    U values, 403 ff

Forest Industry of British Columbia,
    Council of, 432
Forestry Commission, 438
France
    building approval, 17
    building laws and regulations, 17
    contract procedure, 19
    finance, 18
    government finance, 16
    housing, 18
    investment, 18
    land tenure and development, 18
    political structure, 15

Gantt bar charts, 155
Garage Equipment Association, 438
Gas Corporation, British, 422
Germany (West)
    building approval, 26
    building laws and regulations, 26
    contract procedure, 27
    finance, 27
    government finance, 26
    housing, 26
    investment, 26
    land tenure and development, 26
    political structure, 25
Glass fibre, reinforced sheets, properties, 314
Glass Industry Research Association, British, 423
Glass Sheet, properties, 288
Guide to Key British Enterprises, 98
Gypsum
    plaster, properties, 304
    plaster board, properties, 306
    Products Development Association, 438

Hardboard, smoke production of, 163
Hardwoods, properties, 328
Health, Royal Society of, 457
Health and Social Security, Department of, 433

Heating
    definitions and symbols, 395
    indoor service temperature, 395
    surface resistances, 399
    thermal conductivity, 396
    thermal resistance, 400
    U values, 401
Heating and Ventilating Contractors Association, 438
Heating and Ventilating Engineers, Institution of, 444
Heating and Ventilating Research Association, 439
Her Majesty's Land Registry, 439
Her Majesty's Stationary Office, 439
Historic Buildings Councils for England,
    Scotland and Wales, 440
House Builders Federation, 440
House Builders Registration Council, National, 448
Housing, 150
    Belgium, 7
    France, 18
    W. Germany, 26
    Italy, 35
    Netherlands, 45
Housing Centre Trust, 441
Housing Corporation, 441
Housing and Planning,
    International Federation of, 456
Housing Research Foundation, 442
Housing Societies, National Federation of, 448

Illuminating Engineering Society, 442
Illumination, International Commission on, 455
Incorporated Association of Architects and
    Surveyors, 442
Industrial Relations Act, 200
Industrialised building, 152
Industrialised Building Component
    Manufacturers, Association of, 422
Institute of Advanced Architectural Studies, 442
Institute of Arbitrators, 442
Institute of Building, 443
Institute of Clerks of Works of Great Britain, 443
Institute of Materials Handling, 443
Institute of Plumbing, 443
Institute of Quantity Surveyors, 443
Insitute of Refrigeration, 443
Institute of Wood Science, 443
Institute of Work Study Practitioners, 443
Institution of Civil Engineers, 444
Institution of Electrical Engineers, 444
Institution of Heating and Ventilating Engineers, 444
Institution of Mechanical Engineers, 444
Institution of Municipal Engineers, 444
Institution of Public Health Engineers, 444
Institution of Structural Engineers, 445
Insulating board, asbestos, properties, 248
Insulation Glazing Association, 445

International Association for Bridge and
    Structural Engineering, 455
International Brick Masonry Conference, 209
International Council for Buildings Research,
    Studies and Documentation, 454
International Council for Scientific Management, 455
International Federation of Building and
    Woodworkers, 455
International Federation of Consulting Engineers, 455
International Federation for Documentation, 455
International Federation of European Contractors
    of Building and Public Works, 456
International Federation for Housing and Planning, 456
International Federation of Pre-stressing, 456
International Federation of Surveyors, 456
International Labour Organisation, 456
International Organisation for Standardization, 456
International Society of Biometeorology, 456
International Society for Soil Mechanics and
    Foundation Engineering, 456
International Union of Architects, 457
International Union of Building Centres, 425, 457
International Union of Testing and Research
    Laboratories for Materials and Structures, 457
Italy
    building approval, 35
    building laws and regulations, 35
    contract procedure, 36
    finance, 36
    government finance, 35
    housing, 35
    investment, 36
    land tenure and development 35
    political structure, 34

Key British Enterprises, Guide to, 98
King's Fund Centre, 445

Lamps (see lighting)
Lasers, 205
Lead, properties, 296
Lead Development Association, 445
Lighting
    daylighting, 346
    – recommended factors, 346
    – schedule, 346
    general schedule, 349
    – general building areas, 356
    – homes and hotels, 379
    – hospitals, surgeries and consulting rooms, 377
    – index, 352
    – indoor sports, games and recreational halls, 381
    – industrialised building, 357
    – office and shops, 372
    – public and educational, 374
    lamp data, 343

lamps
 – circular, 392
 – colour characteristics, 346
 – colour properties, 344
 – data, tabulated, 391
 – discharge, 391
 – discharge, starting of, 346
 – economics, 343
 – flood, 393
 – pressed glass, 393
 – reflector, 393
 – standard incandescent, 393
 – types, 343
 – tubular fluorescent, 393
 – utilisation factors, 383
 Proof Luminaire, 351
 scalar illuminance, 349
 standard service illuminance, 349
Limes, properties, 290
Line of balance method, 155
Luminous efficacies, 343

Master Builders, Federation of, 436
Mastic Asphalt Council and Employers'
 Federation, 445
Materials Handling, Institute of, 443
Materials, properties, 223
 asbestos cement sheets, 246
 asbestos insulating board, 248
 asphalt, 250
 bitumen felt, 252
 blocks, concrete, 254
 bricks, clay, 258
 bricks, concrete, 262
 bricks, flint-lime, 264
 bricks, sandlime, 266
 cement, high alumina, 268
 cement, portland, 270
 fibre building boards, 274
 floor finishes, 276
 glass sheet, 288
 limes, 290
 metal, aluminium sheet, 292
 metal, copper sheet, 294
 metal, lead, 296
 metal, stainless steel, 298
 metal, steel sheet, 300
 metal, zinc sheet, 302
 plaster, gypsum, 304
 plasterboard, gypsum, 306
 plastics, cellular sheets, boards and slabs, 308
 plastics, glass fibre reinforced sheets, 314
 plastics, PVC sheets, 316
 sealants, 318
 stone, natural, 320
 tile, clay roof, 324
 tile, concrete roof, 326
 timbers, hardwood, 328
 timber, resin-bonded wood chipboard, 334
 timbers, softwood, 336
Mechanical Engineers, Institute of, 444
Mechanisation, 152
Metal
 aluminium sheet, properties, 292
 copper sheet, properties, 294
 lead, properties, 296
 stainless steel, properties, 298
 steel sheet, properties, 300
 zinc sheet, properties, 302
Meteorological Office, 445
Metric system, 217
Ministry of Cultural Affairs, 19
Modular Society, 446
Moodies Cards, 98
Municipal Engineers, Insitution of, 444

National Building Agency, 446
National Coal Board, 446
National Council of Building Material
 Proudcers, 446
National Federation of Building
 Trades' Employers, 447
National Federation of Builders' and
 Plumbers' Merchants, 447
National Federation of Demolition
 Contractors, 447
National Federation of Housing Societies, 448
National Heating Centre, 448
National House-Builders Registration Council, 448
National Joint Consultative Committee, 448
National Joint Council for the Building
 Industry, 449
National Physical Laboratory, 449
Netherlands
 building approval, 45
 building laws and regulations, 45
 contract procedure, 46
 finance, 46
 government finance, 45
 housing, 45
 investment, 45
 land tenure and development, 45
 political structure, 44
Network analysis, 155
Non-Ferrous Metal Research Association, British, 423
Norwich Experiment, 153

Occupational Safety and Health, Directorate of, 433
Office for Scientific and Technical Information, 449
Ordnance Survey, 450

PVC sheet, properties, 316
Partitions
 double leaf, 410

single leaf, 409
single sheets and slabs, 408
stud-framed, 409
Photogrammetry, 205
Plant
mechanical, 152
programming and use, 155
Plaster, gypsum, properties, 304
Plaster board
properties, 306
smoke production, 103
Plastics
cellular sheets, boards and slabs, properties, 308
glass fibre reinforced sheets, properties, 314
PVC sheets, properties, 316
Plastics Federation, British, 423
Plastics Institute, 450
Plumbing, Insitute of, 443
Plywood, smoke production of, 163
Polyurethene, smoke production of, 163
Pre-Cast Concrete Federation, British, 423
Prefabrication, 150
alternative methods, 151
industrialised building, 152
temporary prefabs, 151
traditional, 151
Pre-stressing, International Federation of, 456
Princes Risborough Laboratories, 428
Productivity Council, British, 423
Programming, 155
Proof Luminaire, 351
Properties of Building Materials, 223
Public Health Engineers, Institution of, 444

Quantity Surveyors, Insitue of, 443

Ready-mixed Concrete Association, British, 424
Refrigeration, Institute of, 443
Research, 158
Research Association of British Paint,
Colour and Varnish Manufacturers, 450
Resin bonded wood chipboard, properties, 334
Royal Institute of British Architects, 450
Royal Institution of Chartered Surveyors, 450
– Building Maintenance Cost Information
Service, 451
Royal Society of Health, 451
Royal Society for the Prevention of Accidents, 451
Rubber and Plastics Research Association of
Great Britain, 451

S.I. Conversions, 218
Safety Council, British, 424
Sand-lime bricks, properties, 266
Savory Milln's Building Book, 98
Schedule, liquidity, 129
Scottish Development Department, 451
Scottish Education Department, 451

Scottish Laboratories (BRE), 428
Scottish Home and Health Department, 452
Scottish Hospital Centre, 452
Scottish National Housing and Town Planning
Council, 452
Scottish Office, 452
Sealants, properties, 318
Scientific Management, International Council
for, 455
Simon Report, 150
Smoke
control in buildings, 161
– buildings, tall, 182
– buildings, vertically divided, 183
– corridors, 178
– long vertical spaces, 181
– partially enclosed spaces, 177
– shopping malls, 180
– single rooms, 175
– single-storey buildings, 176
– stairways, 182
control systems
– mechanical, 179
– natural, 178
flow, 175
load, 161
production, 163, 168
– in different building boards, 163, 164
– in terms of visibility, 164
Society of Architectural and Associated
Technicians, 452
Society for the Protection of Ancient
Buildings, 452
Softwoods, properties, 336
Soil Mechanics and Foundation Engineering,
International Society for, 456
Sound
absorption coefficients, 414
insulation and acoustics, 407
– floors, compartment, 207
– floors, concrete, 411
– floors, woodjoist, 412
– partitions, double leaf, 410
– partitions, single leaf, 409
– partitions, single sheets or slabs, 408
– partitions, stud framed, 409
– timber-framed houses, 207
– walls, double leaf, 409
– walls, single leaf, 409
– walls and floors, insulation value, 408
– windows, single and double, 407
Special Steels Users Advisory Centre,
British Steel Corporation, 452
Stack effect, 181
Stainless steel sheet, properties, 298
Stairways, movement along during fire, 182
Standard Form of Building Contract, 190, 194
Standard Industrial Classification, 63

Standard Method of Building Measurement, 189, 195
Standard Service Illuminance, 349
Standards Institution, British, 424
Statistics
    annual bulletin of, 97
    Daily (Card) Service, 98
    Extel cards, 98
    monthly bulletin of, 97
    monthly digest of, 97
Steel Corporation, British, 424, 452
Steel sheet, properties, 300
Steel Window Association, 453
Stock Exchange Year Book, 98
Stone Federation, British, 425
Stone, natural, properties, 320
Structural Engineers, Institution of, 445
Supervision, 156
Surface resistances
    inside, 399
    outside, 399
Surveying, 203
    aerial surveys, 205
    computations, 203
    EDM instruments, 204
    lasers, 205
    theodolites, 204
Surveyors, Royal Institution of Chartered,
    450, 451
Surveyors, quanity
    in Belgium, 9
    in France, 21
    in W. Germany, 29
    in Italy, 38
    in Netherlands, 47
Swedish Timber Council, 453

Temperature
    toleration, 162
    indoor service, 395
Testing and Research Laboratories for
    Materials and Structures, International
    Union of, 457
Theodolites, 204
Thermal resistance
    in unventilated air spaces, 400
    in ventilated air spaces, 400
Tile
    clay roof, properties, 324
    concrete roof, properties, 326
Timber
    compartment floors, 207
    developments in, 207
    framed houses, 207
    hardwoods, properties, 328
    resin bonded wood chipboard, properties, 334
    softwoods, properties, 326
    suspended ground floors, 208

Timber Research and Development Association, 453
Trade and Industry, Department of, 433
Trade and Industry Export Services Division,
    Department of, 434
Training
    management, 157
    supervisors, 156
Transport and Road Research Laboratory, 453

U-values
    floors
    – edge insulated, 404
    – intermediate, 405
    – solid 403, 404
    – suspended timber, 405
    roofs, 402
    timber framed houses, 207
    walls, external, 401
    windows, 403
Union of Construction and Allied Trades and
    Technicians, 453
United Nations - Economic Commission for
    Europe, 457
United Nations Educational, Scientific and
    Cultural Organisation, 457
United Nations Industrial Development
    Organisation, 457
United Nations Office of Technical Co-operation, 457
Utilization factors, 383

VAT
    Belgium, 6, 8
    France, 16
    W. Germany, 26
    Italy, 35
    Netherlands, 45
Ventilation
    airspaces, 400
    fire, 176

Walls
    double leaf, 410
    external, U values, 401
    insulation value, 408
    load bearing, 209
    single leaf, 409
Welsh Office, 453
Westminster Chamber of Commerce, 3
Windows
    single and double, 407
    U-values, 403
Winter building, 157
Wood Preserving Association, British, 425
Wood Science, Institue of, 443
Woodwork Manufacturers' Association,
    British, 425

World Health Organisation, 457
Work study, 156
Work Study Practitioners, Insitute of, 443

Zinc Development Association, 453
Zinc sheet, properties, 302